D1593442

Achievement
and Achievement
Motives

A Series of Books in Psychology

Editors: Richard C. Atkinson
Gardner Lindzey
Richard F. Thompson

Achievement and Achievement Motives

Psychological and Sociological Approaches

Edited by
Janet T. Spence
University of Texas at Austin

W. H. Freeman and Company
San Francisco

Project Editor: Pearl C. Vapnek
Designer: Nancy Benedict
Production Coordinator: William Murdock
Illustration Coordinator: Richard Quiñones
Artist: Eric Hieber
Compositor: Graphic Typesetting Service
Printer and Binder: The Maple-Vail Book Manufacturing Group

Library of Congress Cataloging in Publication Data

Main entry under title:

Achievement and achievement motives.

(A Series of books in psychology)
Bibliography: p.
Includes index.
Contents: Achievement-related motives and behaviors /
Janet T. Spence and Robert L. Helmreich — Expectancies,
values, and academic behaviors / Jacquelynne Eccles
(Parsons) — Achieving styles / Jean Lipman-Blumen, Alice
Handley-Isaksen, and Harold J. Leavitt — [etc.]
1. Personality and academic achievement—Addresses,
essays, lectures.   2. Achievement motivation—Addresses,
essays, lectures.   I. Spence, Janet Taylor.   II. Series.
BF698.9.A3A25   1983   370.15'3   82-18389
ISBN 0-7167-1396-9
ISBN 0-7167-1397-7 (pbk.)

Copyright © 1983 by W. H. Freeman and Company

Printed in the United States of America

1 2 3 4 5 6 7 8 9 0   MP   1 0 8 9 8 7 6 5 4 3

Contents

Preface

T he contributors to this volume, psychologists and sociologists, address themselves to some aspect of the broad area of achievement: the properties of individuals and their families and of social institutions that influence individuals' accomplishments.

Plans for the present volume grew out of discussions among several of the authors who were Fellows at the Center for Advanced Studies in the Behavioral Sciences during the 1978–1979 academic year and who shared an interest in achievement-related phenomena. Two other active investigators were also invited to contribute chapters.

Achievement has been a perennial topic of investigation among American social scientists. The study of the factors contributing to successful attainment, particularly in academic and vocational spheres, has taken on renewed vigor in recent years with the development of new social-psychological approaches and the extension of investigations into new areas. Earlier research, for example, tended to focus on the achievement of majority-group males. Demographic and ideological changes have led current investigators to have a special concern with the factors inhibiting or facilitating the accomplishments of women and members of ethnic minorities. The chapters in this volume, which summarize the findings of the authors' ongoing research or their theoretical integration of certain portions of the research literature, reflect these trends.

Although the intended audience of the volume includes the authors' research colleagues, the various chapters provide enough background information and explanation of technical detail to make the book useful to graduate students, advanced undergraduates, and investigators from other disciplines.

The permission of the American Psychological Association to reproduce certain materials is gratefully acknowledged. Special thanks go to Dr. Gardner Lindzey, Director of the Center for Advanced Studies in the Behavioral Sciences, and to members of the Center staff who were of assistance to the editor and several of the contributors during the germination phase of their chapters.

December 1982   Janet T. Spence

Contributors

A. Wade Boykin
Professor of Psychology
Howard University
Washington, DC 20059

Kathleen A. Camara
Assistant Professor
Eliot–Pearson Department
of Child Study
Tufts University
Medford, MA 02155

Nancy E. Dunton
Demographer
New York State Council
on Children and Families
Albany, NY 12223

David L. Featherman
Professor of Sociology
and Director of Institute
on Aging
University of Wisconsin
Madison, WI 53706

Alice Handley-Isaksen
Consultant in Psychology
Mountain View, CA 94041

Robert L. Helmreich
Professor of Psychology
University of Texas at Austin
Austin, TX 78712

E. Mavis Hetherington
Professor of Psychology
University of Virginia
Charlottesville, VA 22901

Harold J. Leavitt
Professor of Organizational
Behavior
Graduate School of Business
Stanford University
Stanford, CA 94305

Jean Lipman-Blumen
Vice President
Center for Organizational
and Policy Research
Bethesda, MD 20817

Jacquelynne Eccles (Parsons)
Associate Professor
of Psychology
University of Michigan
Ann Arbor, MI 48109

Janet T. Spence
Professor of Psychology
University of Texas at Austin
Austin, TX 78712

Introduction

Janet T. Spence

University of Texas at Austin

[T]he old saying that, in the United States, "Any boy can grow up to be President" is characteristically American. It reflects, most directly, faith in the democratic ideal and the optimistic belief that the humbleness of a man's origins is no barrier to his success in life. In the style of Horatio Alger, with perseverance, pluck, and hard work, anyone can make of himself what he will. Similarly, many Americans have preferred to interpret literally the philosophical principle, enunciated in the Declaration of Independence, that "all men are created equal." If people appear to differ in talent and ability, deficiencies in their life experiences—which we are ingenious enough to be able to remedy—are to blame.

The expression is also significant in revealing the value that this society has traditionally placed on individual achievement and the attainment of worldly success. This stress on achievement arose from a confluence of secular, theological, and philosophical sources that, together, formed a world view that has been dominant in this country throughout much of its history. Central to this belief system has been the perception of the world of nature as a set of impersonal forces that human beings, by application of their intelligence, are challenged to understand, master, and exploit for their own benefit. With the emergence of industrialization, material affluence and the accumulation of capital became synonymous with progress.

The belief in individual rights, including the right to private property and to the fruits of one's labor, has also been paramount. The individual, however, has duties as well as rights. Work, according to the old Puritan ethic, is good for its own sake, and idleness is the handmaiden of the devil. Other virtues have also traditionally been treasured: sobriety, thrift, and responsibility. In this climate, ambition and making something of oneself came close to being moral obligations, and the degree to which men prospered became a yardstick against which their virtue could be assessed.

With the increase in urbanization, the depletion of natural resources, and the integration of waves of immigrants from different countries and cultures into the economic and social mainstream, some of these beliefs and ideals have become diluted or have encountered internal contradictions. Our economic system, for example, is a stratified one, with built-in inequities in status and material rewards. On the one hand, individuals, whatever their origins, are encouraged to get a good education, to develop their talents, and to become occupationally successful, that is, to obtain well-paying, prestigious positions. On the other hand, the economic health of the country depends on having a large number of workers at the lower occupational levels who are simultaneously well trained, productive, and content with their lesser status. Nonetheless, most Americans continue to aspire to material prosperity for themselves and their children and to admire and reward achievement in others. They also value education highly, less for its own sake, than as a route to vocational success.

The boast that it is any boy, rather than any child, who can become President is no accident. A century ago, women were typically regarded as inherently inferior to men in intellect and temperamentally suited only to assume their divinely ordained duties as caretakers of the home and children. Women had limited civil rights, in comparison to men, and were denied equal access to higher education and to business and the professions. Over the decades, the status of women has changed radically. They have gained increasing parity with men before the law and, through the college level, have come to equal or surpass men's educational attainments. After World War II, there was a dramatic increase in women's participation in the labor force, particularly among middle-class women with minor children, and today almost 60% of all women have paid employment. Commensurately, beliefs about differences between men and women in intellect and personality have become considerably muted and are more likely to be attributed to their life experiences than to genetic inheritance.

Public attitudes toward women's vocational and educational achievements, both signaled and stimulated by the emergence of the feminist movement, began to change in the late 1960s and early 1970s. Although the majority of women worked, most were found in female-dominated occupations, which are typically low in pay and prestige, or, if they worked in the same positions as men, were often paid less and limited in their advancement. Backed by federal legislation banning sex discrimination in hiring, salary, and promotion, and by the institution of affirmative-action programs, attempts have been made, with partial success, to remove the internal and external barriers that discourage women from entering traditionally masculine occupations, particularly those of higher status. The emphasis changed from hostility or indifference toward women's vocational and educational achievements to an active effort to promote them.

Women are not the only group that has historically been regarded as innately inferior and thus not worthy of equality of treatment and opportunity. In the century following the abolition of slavery, Black Americans, along with members of a number of other racial and ethnic minorities, were particularly subject to discrimination, often with the active connivance of prohibitive legislation. Their limited access to schools, jobs, housing, and public facilities has had the inevitable result of suppressing their educational and vocational attainments. Black Americans and other minorities have had the additional challenge of trying to reconcile their own cultural traditions and values with those of the dominant White society. Stirred by the civil-rights movement, the tide of public opinion about the status of minorities began to turn, as reflected in the civil-rights legislation of the 1960s and 1970s and in the implementation of affirmative-action programs (from which women were also to benefit). As a consequence, the identification and remediation of the factors contributing to the failure of Black Americans and a number of other ethnic and racial minorities to achieve academically and vocationally on a par with the majority became one of the nation's priorities. Although a general shift toward political conservatism has recently slowed these impulses, women, Blacks, and other minorities have become increasingly active in their own behalf, seeking to consolidate their gains and to continue their upward progress.

The values of the larger society are frequently mirrored in the research of social and behavioral scientists. It is thus understandable that for some years the factors associated with academic and vocational attainment have been prominent subjects of investigation in psychology, sociology, and related disciplines. The chapters in this volume, reporting the authors' research or theoretical integration of the empirical literature, attest to the continued vitality of these inquiries.

Early research on late adolescents and adults concentrated disproportionately on the behaviors and characteristics of White males. Over the past decade, however, social scientists have become responsive to societal efforts to encourage the achievement of women and members of racial minorities. The chapters in this volume are illustrative of this development, each showing sensitivity to gender or race, if not directly addressed to these topics.

The research traditions represented by the chapters are diverse. Within psychology, one of the most influential approaches to achievement and achievement motivation has been the expectancy–value theory of John Atkinson and his colleagues. This theory (summarized in Chapter 1) postulates three major types of constructs. Two of these have come to be regarded as primarily cognitive in nature: the subjective probability or expectancy of task success or failure, and the incentive value of success or failure. The third component consists of stable dispositional tendencies to approach success or to avoid failure—constructs that are ordinarily considered to involve motivational rather than cognitive processes. In recent years, psychologists have tended to focus their empirical investigations and theoretical analyses on one or the other of these two sets of variables. In Chapter 1, Spence and Helmreich continue the search for individual

differences in intrinsic and extrinsic achievement motives that influence a broad range of real-life achievement behaviors. In Chapter 3,
Lipman-Blumen, Handley-Isaksen, and Leavitt carry this approach
one step further, presenting a theoretical model of achieving styles—
the means that individuals prefer to employ in striving toward their
achievement goals, primarily in the vocational arena.

In Chapter 2, Parsons and her associates pursue the cognitive
trail, testing a model of academic achievement that traces its lineage
to Atkinson's expectancy–value constructs and to more recently
developed cognitive notions, such as causal attributions for success
and failure.

The central focus of these three chapters is on properties of the
individual that determine achievement-related behaviors. The
emphasis shifts in the following two chapters to the family and the
school. In Chapter 4, Hetherington, Camara, and Featherman present
an integrative review of research on academic achievement in children from one-parent homes—typically headed by a divorced woman.
These data are viewed from the perspective of a social-psychological
model that places the child within the context both of a family unit
that must reconstitute itself following divorce or a parent's death and
of a school that can assist or hinder the child during this life transition. In Chapter 5, sociologists Dunton and Featherman examine the
place men and women occupy in the hierarchy of social positions
that determine the material rewards and prestige they are accorded
and the mobility of men and women within this stratification system
throughout the socioeconomic life cycle. Vocational achievement is
viewed as a lifelong, intergenerational process in which men's and
women's attainments over the course of their work careers are related
to their educational and vocational accomplishments in childhood
and youth (and the accomplishments of their spouse). These early
attainments are, in turn, related to their parents' place in the stratification system.

In the final chapter, Boykin considers the failure of Black children to achieve academically at the same level as their White peers.
One of the major dilemmas faced by these children, Boykin contends,
is how to reconcile the beliefs and behavioral styles of the Afro-
American culture and the belief systems and expectations of the dominant White society with which they are confronted in school. Boykin's analysis of mainstream versus Afro-American society gains added
importance by calling attention to the cultural context in which social
scientists conduct their research and the values that influence the
nature of their inquiries.

1

Achievement-Related Motives and Behaviors

Janet T. Spence
Robert L. Helmreich

University of Texas at Austin

EDITOR'S OVERVIEW

The study of achievement by behavioral scientists is ordinarily confined to activities relevant to academic and vocational attainments. In this chapter, Spence and Helmreich adopt a broader definition of achievement that admits any type of performance that may be evaluated by the individual or by others according to its excellence and that may occur in a wide variety of settings. Proceeding from this perspective, the authors examine certain achievement-related motives and goals and their implications for real-life behaviors. Particular attention is given to individual differences in these motives and to a comparison of the motivational systems of women and men.

The authors first present a conceptual analysis of intrinsic versus extrinsic motives and incentives, noting that little is known about the interactions of these two types of motives in determining achievement-related behaviors. They review two very different research literatures with indirect relevance to this question: one concerned with the nature of on-the-job worker motivation, and the other with the experimental study of the influence of external rewards on intrinsic motives, as observed in laboratory and other time-limited settings. The authors conclude that intrinsic and extrinsic motives and goals are not necessarily additive or mutually facilitative in their effects on achievement-oriented behavior.

The bulk of the chapter is addressed to intrinsic achievement motives which, following the personality theorist Henry Murray, the authors define as a striving toward performance excellence and which they regard as stable personality characteristics whose strength varies from one individual to the next. After describing the highly influential expectancy–value theory of John Atkinson and his colleagues, which incorporates Murray's conceptions, the authors present their multidimensional conception of achievement motivation. By means of their objective self-report instrument, the Work and Family Orientation Questionnaire (WOFO), they identify three relatively independent motives: mastery (the preference for challenging tasks and for meeting internal standards of excellence), work (the desire to work hard), and competitiveness (the enjoyment of interpersonal competition).

Contrary to the implications of theories suggesting that the genders differ in the nature of their achievement motives, the authors' data with the WOFO suggest that the structure of men's and women's achievement motives is similar. However, they report that, in unselected groups, sex differences in motive strength emerge, women tending to be somewhat higher than men in work, and men tending to be somewhat higher in mastery and substantially higher in competitiveness. A series of studies relating these achievement motives to measures of quality of academic performance in college students and of vocational performance in several occupational groups shows that, in both sexes, individuals high in work and mastery achieve more than those whose motive strengths are relatively low. Contrary to the belief that interpersonal competitiveness facilitates successful attainment, the authors' data indicate that, in the groups studied, highly competitive individuals do less well, especially if they are also high in work and mastery. The authors caution, however, that the processes by which competitiveness results in deleterious effects are not known and that competitiveness may not have negative consequences in all individuals or types of endeavors.

The authors' conceptions of achievement and achievement motives suggest that these motives can find expression not merely in academic and vocational pursuits but in a variety of everyday activities in which individuals elect to participate. They report data from several studies that give credence to these hypotheses.

$\boxed{A}$ mbition and the drive to achieve excellence are widely recognized as crucial ingredients in successful attainment. Education, ability, social background, and opportunity—being at the right place at the right time—make important contributions to success; but even among individuals who are similar in all these respects, wide differences in accomplishments may still be observed. If we are to understand what makes some people more successful than others, we must also take into account the intensity and the nature of their achievement-related motives.

This chapter is devoted to an examination of certain of these achievement-related motives and their implications for real-life achievement behaviors. Our principal concern is with *intrinsic* achievement motives—the enjoyment of achievement-related activities and of striving toward performance excellence. However, we also consider *extrinsic* motives and goals—the desire for the tangible or intangible rewards that are often obtained as a consequence of successful performance—and their possible interactions with intrinsic motives in determining achievement behavior.

Individual differences in intrinsic achievement motives have been the subject of extensive theorizing and empirical investigation by psychologists and other behavioral scientists. Perhaps the best-known and most highly influential of these theories has been developed by Murray (1938) and by Atkinson and McClelland and their colleagues (Atkinson, 1958; Atkinson and Raynor, 1974; McClelland, Atkinson, Clark, and Lowell, 1953). Our conception of intrinsic achievement motivation as a striving toward excellence is in the classical tradition of these investigators, although we view achievement motivation as a cluster of interacting factors rather than as a single, unitary dimension. In the course of this chapter, we describe our operationalization of these constructs and present some of our empirical studies showing the relationship between our measures and naturally occurring achievement behaviors. We also attempt to place intrinsic achievement motivation in a broad conceptual framework as a guide to future theoretical analysis and empirical research. The task we have set

Support for the research reported here was provided by NSF Grant BNS 78–08911 and NIMH Grant 32066 (Janet T. Spence and Robert L. Helmreich, Principal Investigators). The chapter was initiated while the first author was a Fellow at the Center for Advanced Studies in the Behavioral Sciences, Stanford, California, with support from the Spencer Foundation, NIMH Grant 5T32 MH14581–03, and the University of Texas Research Institute.

ourselves here is not to present a comprehensive theory of achievement behavior or even a preliminary sketch for such a theory. Instead, we have chosen to focus on several types of achievement-related motives and to explore in a preliminary way some of their implications for real-life achievement-oriented activities. In the absence of systematic empirical data, much of this exploration is perforce descriptive and speculative.

A recurring theme in our discussion is the relationship between achievement motivation and gender. Until quite recently, research on achievement-related motives in late adolescents and adults has concentrated primarily on males. This male-dominated approach is rapidly being remedied. Economic, political, and social forces that have propelled or lured an increasing proportion of women into the labor force, combined (not entirely coincidentally) with the rise of the feminist movement and a shift in societal attitudes toward a more egalitarian view of men's and women's roles, have belatedly forced recognition that many women not only may be motivated to achieve but also may desire to express these motives in the same kinds of activities as men engage in.

Women, however, have yet to achieve as much as men vocationally. Those who enter the labor force in full-time jobs tend to congregate in positions that are simultaneously low in prestige and female-dominated; further, within a given type of position, men as a group typically rise higher than their female colleagues (Schrank and Riley, 1976; see also Chapter 5, this volume). The identification of the internal and external social-psychological factors that act to suppress, facilitate, or channel women's achievement-oriented activities is thus a topic of growing concern to social scientists.

The implicit or explicit aim of most inquiries into achievement-related motives has been to predict or to bring theoretical understanding to very limited types of real-world behaviors, namely, those occurring in academic and vocational settings. Other forms of attainment in which achievement strivings could theoretically find expression have received scant attention, particularly as they occur in women. Women—or at least those women who elect not to pursue careers—have often been viewed as lacking in the same intrinsic achievement motives as men have or as being able to satisfy their achievement needs vicariously through their husband's accomplishments. This dismissal appears to denigrate as genuine accomplishments women's contributions to the home and family and to organizations to which they give unpaid labor and at the same time to disallow the capacity of these activities to satisfy achievement needs. However, women high in achievement motivation may find an outlet for these motives in tasks associated with their traditional role responsibilities, such as child care, housekeeping, and other domestic activities, whether or not they also have paid employment (Veroff and Feld, 1970). We have therefore adopted the position, which we share with such writers as Stein and Bailey (1973), that nontraditional activities may provide significant avenues of expression for intrinsic achievement motives, particularly in noncareer women perhaps, but also in men. We will therefore attempt to consider achievement motives and their implications for behavior from a broad perspective that goes beyond work and school.

ACHIEVEMENT NOMINALLY DEFINED

Guiding our discussion is the following nominal definition of achievement (modified from Smith, 1969): *Achievement is task-oriented behavior that allows the individual's performance to be evaluated according to some internally or externally imposed criterion, that involves the individual in competing with others, or that otherwise involves some standard of excellence.*

Our definition of achievement admits two types of behaviors. The first is composed of activities occurring in settings in which there are generally agreed-upon standards by which to judge the quality of performance and in which evaluation of the performer routinely occurs. Performance on the job, in school, or in other formal training programs provides the major examples of this type of behavior. In light of the social significance of these activities, it is understandable that formal investigations of the effect of achievement motives on behavior have almost exclusively been limited to school and work performance or to performance on laboratory tasks relevant to these settings. Our definition also encompasses, however, achievement-oriented behavior occurring in avocational and extracurricular contexts. Common examples are hobbies or amateur sports; participation in civic, religious, or professional groups on a volunteer, nonpaying basis; and domestic activities, such as gardening, home maintenance and decoration, sewing and cooking, and childrearing.

Our definition also permits either the participating individual or an outside agency to specify whether the individual's performance is being evaluated according to some standard of excellence as well as to designate what that standard is. In conventional areas such as the workplace, society and its organized institutions define the situation as being achievement-related, expecting the participants to do their best on their assigned tasks or to meet some minimal standard of performance, and devise systems of tangible and intangible rewards for successful attainment that simultaneously provide the participants with evaluative feedback about the quality of their performance. The participants, although typically aware that they are expected to perform well, do not necessarily share these aspirations, usually because they are low in achievement motivation or because their achievement motives are not aroused by the particular activities being demanded of them.

Although achievement-oriented individuals often express their achievement motives in conventional job- and school-related activities, they may also find an outlet for their achievement strivings in other activities in which they voluntarily engage. As the Guiness book of records amusingly attests, human beings can turn performance in almost any situation into a challenge—a task to be mastered, a record to be established, a skill to be perfected, a race to be won. Often these activities engage the individual's interest over substantial periods of time, provide deep personal satisfaction, and have considerable social value. Although some writers have intimated that individuals are unlikely to express their intrinsic achievement motives in nontraditional ways because of the relative absence of recognized standards of performance excellence and the unavailability of clear performance feedback from external sources, it seems more likely that most people have the capacity to establish their own performance standards and to evaluate the quality of their own behaviors. We have therefore made our definition of achievement broad enough to include activities that the *individual* specifies as the target of his or her own achievement strivings and may thus provide outlets for achievement motives that are personally gratifying.

TYPES OF ACHIEVEMENT-RELATED MOTIVES AND REWARDS

In the following sections, we discuss intrinsic and extrinsic motives and rewards and consider the relationship that may exist between them.

Intrinsic Versus Extrinsic Motives and Goals

Behavior is ordinarily described as intrinsically motivated if it is pleasurable in its own right and is not being undertaken merely to obtain some external reward; the reward for performing is inherent in the performance itself. When the individual's goal is more specifically to meet some standard of performance excellence and part of the reward for indulging in the activity is striving toward and reaching this goal, we refer to intrinsic achievement motivation.

Successful achievement often brings about consequences that are gratifying to their recipients, such as a pay raise and social recognition. Achievement-oriented behaviors whose *goal* is to obtain these external or extrinsic rewards can be described as extrinsically motivated. It is possible, of course, for a single set of behaviors to be driven simultaneously by both intrinsic and extrinsic motives.

Extrinsic Motives and Goals

In American society, worldly success has always been widely admired, and ambition (at least in males) is considered praiseworthy. This emphasis on success can be seen in the reward systems operating in recognized areas of achievement. Our society has set up countless prizes, titles, elite societies, and honorific awards whose primary function is to call attention to academically and vocationally successful individuals and their accomplishments. Success in the vocational sphere typically brings higher salary, status, privileges, and prestige, and access to still more advantageous positions in which the extrinsic rewards are even greater.

The existence of these formal mechanisms for honoring accomplishment mirrors the value our society places on individual achievement and the expectation that it be recognized and encouraged. We tend to be ambivalent, however, toward achievement that is obviously extrinsically motivated. On the one hand, we seem to view the individual who is driven by intrinsic motives and whose goals are fundamentally unselfish as more deserving of reward than is the individual whose goals are crassly materialistic or self-aggrandizing. On the other hand, we tend to regard individuals who are indifferent to the worldly consequences of their achievement as deviant—as amusing eccentrics, otherworldly saints, or even as dangerous radicals—and to be uncertain about whether much useful work would be accomplished in the absence of external incentives. We expect people to want and be pleased by extrinsic rewards but not to work too conspicuously with no other goal but to obtain them.

Although individual differences in the strength of intrinsic achievement motives have been extensively investigated, surprisingly few formal attempts have been made to measure individual differences in the strength of extrinsic motives and to determine their effects on achievement-related behaviors. It seems undeniable, however, that people vary in the degree to which they value for their own sake the various kinds of tangible and intangible consequences of successful accomplishment and hence the degree to which these outcomes are inherently rewarding. Some individuals are relatively unconcerned with financial rewards, desiring only enough income to maintain a modest standard of living; whereas others are greedy for money, prizing it for what it can buy or for the security it offers. Some are indifferent to high status and position, and some hunger after them. People also vary in the degree to which their behaviors are shaped and stimulated by their strivings after these external rewards, that is, the degree to which their achievement-oriented behavior is extrinsically *motivated*. While the value that individuals place on receiving these various kinds of rewards and the intensity of their motivation to achieve them are undoubtedly correlated, the *reward* value and the *motivational* value of things not only are conceptually separate but very probably also have a substantial degree of independence.

In the extreme case in which an individual's behavior is motivated only by the expectation of extrinsic rewards, his or her achievement-oriented activities have nothing but instrumental significance. That is, the behaviors are undertaken solely to gain these rewards, the individual finding no inherent pleasure in engaging in these behaviors but only in anticipating their consequences. The person engages in activities that eventuate in extrinsic rewards only because the rewards are not otherwise available. The pure case is probably rare, most individuals wanting, if nothing else, to assure themselves and others that they personally deserve the fruits of success because those fruits were obtained through their own efforts. It is also unlikely that anyone would work hard and successfully over long periods of time at tasks of any consequence for purely extrinsic reasons.

Whether those with strong extrinsic motives in performing some task are any more or less likely than others simultaneously to have strong intrinsic achievement motives is unknown. Observation suggests, however, that it is possible for individuals with substantial intrinsic motivation to place considerable value on the tangible or intangible benefits of successful attainment at the same time and to be highly motivated to obtain them. Those who are jointly motivated by intrinsic and extrinsic motives may choose their jobs or plan their whole educational and vocational careers to maximize the probability that they will obtain not only intrinsic satisfactions but also the monetary rewards or the kinds of recognition and prestige to which they aspire. One may choose to become a physician, for example, rather than a Ph.D. biologist, because M.D.'s ("real" doctors) tend to be more highly regarded by many segments of society and to have higher incomes than "mere" doctors of philosophy, particularly if the latter are employed in academic institutions.

Activities and occupations that are equally demanding vary in the probability of various kinds of "payoffs," and individuals who allow extrinsic considerations to guide their choices of career or career activity are likely to improve their chances of obtaining the rewards they desire. However, if only individuals who are engaged in a specific endeavor are considered, those who have strongly extrinsic motivations do not necessarily have a greater probability of success than those whose behaviors are more exclusively motivated by intrinsic considerations. In fact, several sources of evidence, which are reviewed in later sections, indirectly suggest that the contrary may often be the case.

It should again be emphasized that those whose achievement-related activities are primarily motivated by intrinsic factors are not necessarily indifferent to the extrinsic rewards their accomplishments may bring them. Reflecting our society's stress on the value of individual accomplishment, many whose achievement behaviors are driven and shaped primarily by intrinsic considerations may nonetheless expect and highly prize recognition of their accomplishments. Having weighed their accomplishments and found them worthy in their own eyes, they may demand that their achievements be acknowledged by others in the form of tangible or intangible rewards. In many instances, the actual value of the reward may be less important than the recognition it signifies. The salary a person is paid often has this symbolic function; beyond a certain level, the absolute amount is less important than the amount relative to that earned by members of the person's reference group. Often, of course, there are discrepancies between people's evaluation of their performance and the recognition they believe is therefore owed them and the rewards they actually receive. These disparities may have the effect of decreasing individuals' intrinsic interest in their job responsibilities (Adams, 1965).

Extrinsic rewards may also be useful in allowing individuals to evaluate their own efforts. Excellence in performance is sometimes obvious, but often the yardstick by which quality can be measured is not clear-cut. In the face of ambiguity, people may compare themselves with others or seek the judgments of others to verify or to correct uncertain self-evaluations (Festinger, 1954; Smith, 1968). The consequences of successful achievement—good grades in school, salary raises, promotions, honorific awards, the respect of others, and the like—are sources of information that may be used in this process. For those who simultaneously hold a high but uncertain opinion of themselves, the need for constant reassurance and recognition may be almost insatiable.

To summarize these distinctions, individuals differ in the inherent value they place on extrinsic factors such as money, prestige, and status, and in the degree to which their achievement-related behaviors are actively motivated and shaped by their desires for these external rewards. The achievement-oriented behaviors of those whose intrinsic motives are weak and who are trapped in situations that do not provide satisfactory outlets for their achievement needs may be driven only by external incentives; the work involved is sheer drudgery and to be avoided if their extrinsic needs can be satisfied in other ways. For persons with some degree of intrinsic motivation, these extrinsic outcomes may also have additional functions, providing information about the quality of their performance and personal competence and serving as ego-gratifying recognition of their accomplishments.

In actuality, most people's achievement efforts are probably spurred by a number of interacting motives that vary in strength and saliency across individuals, and within individuals, across situations. Similarly, the consequences of successful performance may have multiple meanings and values to their recipients. Although these various aspects of motives and rewards may in practice be difficult to disentangle and measure separately, it is imperative that distinctions be maintained since they may have different implications for achievement behaviors.

Peripheral Motives and Goals

We have been discussing the external benefits that are direct consequences of achievement behavior and their functions in motivating and rewarding behavior. Other aspects of particular achievement settings that are only incidental or peripherally related to the execution of assigned responsibilities may be satisfying to other kinds of motives. The fulfillment of affiliative and other similar needs is a major example, some achievement-related situations permitting the individual to interact with others, to develop friendships, or to be helpful to others.

Affiliative needs, although found in both sexes, are most frequently mentioned in discussions of the motives underlying girls' and women's achievement-oriented behaviors. Some theorists (e.g., Hoffman, 1974) have proposed that, in general, females tend to be deficient in intrinsic achievement motivation in comparison with males but simultaneously to have stronger needs than males to affiliate with others. Correlatively, females are also described as being more motivated than males by the need for social approval. Thus, the motivations underlying the achievement-related behaviors of males and females in school or on the job may not be identical.

In this context, the implication seems to be that females more often than males seek the favor of teachers, employers, or others of higher status for being dutiful and doing what is expected of them in order to please—much as a child seeks to please the parent by being "good." Another kind of need for social approval, however, may be more likely to affect men in their occupational lives. In this society, men are expected to work, and a good deal of significance is attached to their abilities to support themselves and their families adequately. Men who live up to this masculine role expectation receive society's approval and bolster their own self-esteem. They may thus gain considerable satisfaction from their work roles even in the absence of intrinsic gratifications provided by their actual job responsibilities (Lawler and Hall, 1970; Veroff and Feld, 1970).

NATURE OF WORK MOTIVATION

Although the significance of both intrinsic and extrinsic factors for achievement has been widely recognized by social scientists, we noted earlier that little is known not only about individual differences in the intensity of extrinsic motivation within each sex but also about the interactions between intrinsic and extrinsic motives and rewards in determining real-life achievement behaviors. We will review briefly two areas of research that have some indirect relevance to these issues. The first has to do with the nature of work motivation, based on the reactions of individuals to their jobs. The second, discussed in the following section, is more theoretically and experimentally oriented and considers the influence of extrinsic rewards on intrinsic motivation, as observed in time-limited, contrived settings.

Most men—and an increasing proportion of women—must have paid employment in order to support themselves and their dependents. Work is not an option, freely undertaken, but a necessity, and jobs are typically structured and defined by persons and organizations rather than the workers themselves. As the same time, the economic and political health of an industrialized society is dependent on having a productive, effective work force. Enlightened self-interest suggests that conditions should be arranged to promote worker motivation and satisfaction and, ultimately, worker production. As a result, extensive theoretical and empirical attention has been paid to the contribution of intrinsic and extrinsic factors to work behavior both by social theorists and by those interested in organizational effectiveness.

McGregor (1960) has contrasted two extreme views about work motivation, which he calls Theory X and Theory Y, that have very different implications for managerial strategies. According to Theory X, which has guided managerial policy until relatively recently, people work primarily because they must; most have little ambition and prefer to avoid responsibility. This theory implies that the way to increase work motivation and hence productivity is to improve pay, working conditions, and other benefits external to the job itself. Theory Y, which has roots in the sociological theories of Karl Marx and Max Weber and is related to the Protestant ethic, holds that work is inherently good and self-fulfilling. As Marx wrote, work is the "existential activity of man, his free conscious activity—not as a means of maintaining his life but for developing his universal nature" (1844).

More contemporary versions of this latter theory stress the significance of work in bolstering self-esteem and in fulfilling needs for self-realization and self-actualization (e.g., Argyris, 1964; Maslow, 1954). In an analysis of the concepts of job alienation and involvement, Kanungo (1979) has noted that theories postulating the inherently self-fulfilling properties of work imply that, ideally, work should be voluntary, noninstrumental in fulfilling basic physical needs, and designed to permit individuals to develop and express their fullest potential. This type of theoretical approach suggests that the failure of workers to be satisfied and productive fundamentally lies within the system. Jobs that permit the worker no autonomy or sense of personal achievement are stultifying and destroy motivation; this state of affairs cannot be remedied by increasing material incentives or improving the quality of the work environment. The key to maintaining adequate levels of motivation and productivity is to restructure jobs to permit self-direction and self-actualization.

Empirical attempts to identify sources of job satisfaction have left unsettled the question of the relative importance of factors quite directly pertinent to the nature of the job and the individual's performance in it, versus factors more external to job performance. Based largely on the results of a study by Herzberg, Mausner, and Snyderman (1959), in which employees were asked to describe a positive and a negative situation in their job, Herzberg (1966) has proposed a highly influential theory that distinguishes between two categories of events, identified as satisfiers and dissatisfiers. Self-actualizing factors associated with the work itself, such as recognition, advancement, and achievement, serve as satisfiers and motivators. In contrast, work conditions, pay, and other factors external to the job (which Herzberg has identified as needs to avoid discomfort) do not provide positive gratification or act as motivators. If they are perceived as inadequate, however, they lead to worker dissatisfaction.

A number of studies involving blue-collar as well as white-collar and professional workers have confirmed that individuals holding jobs in which they can use their abilities, have more autonomy in structuring their work, and gain feedback about their accomplishments tend to be more satisfied not only with their work but also with their lives in general (e.g., Hackman and Lawler, 1971; Korn-hauser, 1965). However, the validity of the categorical system of satis-fiers versus dissatisfiers has been questioned on both empirical and methodological grounds, as has the assumption of a linkage among satisfaction, motivation, and job performance (e.g., Dunnette, Camp-bell, and Hakel, 1967; House and Wigdor, 1967; Vroom, 1964). More specifically, later studies have provided little support for the hypoth-esis that external factors can serve only as dissatisfiers, and not as possible sources of gratification or motivation. After reviewing the evidence, Lawler (1973), for example, has concluded that pay and factors related to the job context rank higher as sources of satisfaction than suggested by Herzberg (1966), especially when jobs are not structured to provide intrinsic satisfactions.

Responding to theoretical analyses stressing the importance of intrinsic factors in motivating job performance, a number of com-panies have introduced job innovations designed to reduce monotony and to permit workers greater autonomy and flexibility in executing their job responsibilities or in planning their schedules. The effec-tiveness of these job-enrichment programs has not been uniform, the outcome being related to the nature of the jobs and those who hold them (e.g., Hackman and Lawler, 1971; Hulin and Blood, 1968; Old-ham, Hackman, and Pearce, 1976). Lawler (1973) has concluded that individuals vary in the nature of their motives and needs, so that no single method of promoting work motivation and effectiveness is equally successful with all workers. For individuals who are low in intrinsic motives, who are trapped in jobs that do not allow the expression of intrinsic motives, or who are unsuccessful in their jobs, the only real incentive to work may be the necessity of earning a living, and extrinsic factors may be the only source of job satisfaction. For those who find their jobs challenging and their efforts recognized, salary and characteristics of the work setting may be perceived as less important sources of satisfaction, becoming salient only if they fall below an acceptable level.

This conclusion is congruent with the stance implicitly taken in our earlier discussion. However, some of the consequences or accom-paniments of achievement-related behavior that we have labeled extrinsic rewards are often considered intrinsic in the work-motiva-tion literature. Factors such as advancement to positions of greater responsibility, status, and recognition by others are directly job-related and, in the sense of being performance-contingent, are "intrinsic" to the job. But, unlike undertaking an activity because of the pleasure inherent in the activity itself or in doing it successfully, advancement and other forms of recognition are *consequences* of performance. In this sense, they constitute *extrinsic rewards* for achievement. According to our theoretical schema, if individuals are motivated to perform in order to earn the coinage of status and recognition, they are extrinsically motivated in the same way as when they perform in order to earn money.

The finer distinctions we have imposed may be unessential or impractical in making managerial decisions about how to restructure or enrich jobs or about how to improve the work setting in order to maximize worker motivation, morale, and productivity. Conclusions on this point cannot be drawn confidently until more is known about the interaction between intrinsic and extrinsic motives and rewards (as we have defined them).

Sex Differences

The increasing numbers of women who not only have full-time employment but also are entering positions and occupations traditionally almost exclusively occupied by men have prompted the investigation of possible sex differences in work-related motives and goals. Comparisons of male and female employees and job applicants on these variables have been complicated by their interaction with such variables as type of occupation, organizational level, and the individual's age and educational background. The results of investigations in which these variables are held constant or controlled indicate that sex differences are small, some studies finding no significant differences at all (e.g., Brief and Oliver, 1976; Brief, Rose, and Aldag, 1977). However, studies in which discrepancies between men and women have been found report similar findings. Men tend to place higher value than do women on factors related to career advancement and recognition, such as opportunity for promotion, high pay, and increasing responsibilities; whereas women tend to place a higher value than do men on characteristics of the work environment, such as pleasant working conditions and congenial co-workers (Bartol, 1976; Bartol and Manhardt, 1979; Jurgensen, 1978; Manhardt, 1972; Schuler, 1975). However, these same studies also indicate that factors related to intrinsic job satisfaction, such as intellectual challenge, the opportunity to be creative, and the chance to feel a sense of accomplishment, do not discriminate between men and women.

Manhardt (1972), one of the investigators finding the sex differences just described, has suggested that many women in his sample did not have a long-term investment in their jobs, expecting to work only a short time or regarding their work as less important than other aspects of their lives. The differences between men and women that emerged in his study, Manhardt speculated, may have been brought about solely by this subset of women with little or no long-term career involvement. Data reported by Bartol and Manhardt (1979) indicate that women's overall commitment to their careers may be on the rise, at least at some occupational levels. From 1966 to 1974, these investigators questioned new employees of a large insurance company, all college graduates, about their preferences in job outcomes. Women who were hired in the 1970s rated interpersonal factors and working conditions lower and career goals higher than women who joined the company in the 1960s. Men's ratings on these variables did not change over the eight-year period. Thus, the discrepancy between male and female employees systematically decreased with year of employment.

On the whole, these investigations suggest that, within a given type of occupation, only minor sex differences in work-related motives and goals are likely to be found and that, with changes in sex-role attitudes, even these differences may be on the wane. It would be premature to conclude from this evidence alone that men and women are essentially the same in the nature of their motives. There continue to be striking differences in the occupations that the sexes enter, proportionately more women being found in types of jobs that are relatively unchallenging, ill-paying, nonprestigious, and often filled almost exclusively by women. It could be argued that one of the factors responsible for this discrepancy is the lower intrinsic motivation and, even more particularly, the lower achievement motivation displayed by women in general in comparison with men. Thus, while women who aspire to demanding professional and managerial careers may be motivationally similar to their male counterparts, it may still be true that relatively few women "have what it takes" and, if they enter the job market, gravitate in larger numbers than do men to lower-level positions. Evidence relevant to this general issue will be presented in a later section.

EFFECTS OF EXTRINSIC REWARDS ON MOTIVATION AND PERFORMANCE

While motivational theorists differ in the exact role they assign to salary and other external factors, most appear to agree that intrinsic and extrinsic motivational systems essentially operate in parallel and that, if extrinsic rewards do not necessarily facilitate work performance, they at least do not detract from it. Other psychological theorists have explicitly postulated that extrinsic rewards facilitate performance and that intrinsic and extrinsic motives are essentially additive in their effects (e.g., Atkinson, 1974).

Although the powerful influence of rewarding outcomes on performance is beyond dispute, serious questions have arisen about whether their effects are uniformly benign, particularly in circumstances in which individuals are performing a task that they find intrinsically motivating, i.e., activities that they find enjoyable and will perform without expectation of reward. Data demonstrating that positive reinforcers do not always have beneficial effects come primarily from experimental investigations of reactions to specific tasks, often studied within the laboratory. We examine some of these data here, with an eye toward their possible implications for real-life achievement behaviors.

Effects on Intrinsic Motives

One extensive group of studies has been addressed to the proposition that, under some circumstances, the introduction of extrinsic rewards may actually reduce the individual's intrinsic motivation. (For reviews of these studies and the theories developed to explain their results, see Deci, 1980; Lepper and Greene, 1978). These investigations have employed tasks presumed to be enjoyable or challenging to the participants and, as such, intrinsically motivating. The measure of intrinsic motivation to perform the task has typically been participants' ratings of its interest value or the amount of time they voluntarily devote to it in the absence of any external incentives.

In the first of these studies, Deci (1971) had college students (most of them male) work on a series of puzzles under one of three conditions. Subjects in the first condition received a monetary reward for each puzzle they completed. Subjects in the second condition received praise. In the third, control condition, subjects received neither monetary reward nor verbal feedback. Unobtrusive observation of each subject immediately after the experimental session indicated that those who had been praised for their performance spontaneously played with the puzzles more than did those in the other experimental conditions, whereas subjects given monetary reward played with them least. From these results, it was concluded that the introduction of extrinsic, material rewards for performance reduced intrinsic motivation. In another prototypic study, Lepper, Greene, and Nisbett (1973) found that nursery-school children who were promised an award for playing with drawing materials less frequently chose those materials during a later free play period in the classroom than did children in a nonrewarded control group.

The phenomenon demonstrated in these studies has been shown to be dependent on the initial interest value of the tasks (Calder and

Staw, 1975; Loveland and Olley, 1979; McLoyd, 1979). Individuals given tangible rewards for performing interesting tasks subsequently showed a drop in indices of intrinsic motivation in comparison with nonrewarded individuals. However, the reverse was found in groups given tasks that had low interest value. Loveland and Olley (1979), who employed preschool children as subjects, found these changes in intrinsic motivation one week after the children performed the task. By seven weeks, however, the influence of rewards had dissipated, indicating that the reward effects, while persistent, are not permanent.

In explaining their results, Lepper and his colleagues (e.g., Lepper and Greene, 1978; Lepper, Greene, and Nisbett, 1973) have appealed to self-attributional processes, as outlined by Bem (1967) and Kelley (1967). Basically, attribution theory proposes that individuals seek reasons to explain or justify the activities in which they engage and that these attributions guide their future behaviors. Under conditions in which external pressures to perform are weak and are thus perceived as insufficient to explain or justify their behavior, people are likely to attribute their behaviors to causes within themselves, such as their interests and desires. On the other hand, under conditions in which marked external pressure to perform is perceived, people are likely to ascribe their behaviors to this external cause. The deleterious effects of introducing a tangible reward into a situation in which intrinsic motivation would otherwise be sufficient to guarantee performance is hypothesized to be due to this attributional process. According to this hypothesis, the anticipation of reward leads people to reevaluate their reasons for performing an initially interesting task and to attribute their behaviors to the controlling influence of the reward—a phenomenon that has been called the *overjustification effect*. Behavior comes to be perceived as an instrumental means to an end rather than as an end in itself (Kruglanski, 1975), which, in the hands of attribution theorists, is tantamount to saying that behavior becomes extrinsically rather than intrinsically motivated.

Deci (1975, 1980; Deci and Porac, 1978) has proposed a theory of cognitive evaluation that is not incompatible with the attributional analysis just described but is cast in a broader conceptual framework. A central tenet of cognitive-evaluation theory is that human beings have an innate need to be competent, effective, and self-determining (deCharms, 1968; White, 1959). These strivings form the psychological basis for intrinsic motivation, which in turn "underlies an ongoing cyclical pattern in which people *seek out and conquer challenges that are optimal for their capacities*" (Deci and Porac, 1978, p. 151; emphasis in original). This hypothesis, which closely resembles the hypothesis, discussed earlier, that work motivation is inborn, implies that neither a striving toward competence nor the motivation to master challenges (achievement motivation) needs to be acquired but that life experiences may weaken or destroy these motives.

While extrinsic rewards may decrease the intrinsic motivation to perform a particular task, cognitive-evaluation theory implies that this is not an inevitable effect. Rewards, according to Deci, have two properties or aspects: the *control* of behavior, and the communication of *information about competence*. Individuals who receive material rewards for performance may begin to perceive them as the cause of their behaviors and their behaviors as controlled by reward. However, rewards may also convey information about the individual's competence. In instances in which the reinforcers enhance feelings of competence, intrinsic motivation may actually be increased rather than decreased by their use.

According to cognitive-evaluation theory, the relative salience of the controlling versus the informational properties of rewards in any given situation determines their influence on intrinsic motivation. Praise and other similar events used to signal that the person has done well are likely to enhance intrinsic motivation. Tangible rewards, such as money, food, and prizes, are more likely to be perceived as controlling events and to decrease intrinsic motivation. However, if their receipt is made contingent not merely on performing but on performing *well*, the informational aspect of these tangible rewards may become strengthened so that it minimizes or overrides the controlling aspect. The net result may be that intrinsic motivation is left relatively intact or even enhanced. Some studies investigating this aspect of cognitive-evaluation theory have confirmed these predictions (e.g., Boggiano and Ruble, 1979; Enzel and Ross, 1978), but others (e.g., Harackiewicz, 1979) have not. In explaining her negative results, Harackiewicz has suggested that the informational properties of tangible rewards may become salient only when the task involves skills that individuals value and thus arouses their competency concerns, as opposed to tasks that they regard as merely entertaining.

A series of studies by Deci and his colleagues (1971, 1972; Deci, Cascio, and Krusell, 1975) has suggested that, in predicting the influence of extrinsic rewards on intrinsic motivation, individual differences in the value and the meaning of the feedback events should also be taken into account. The first of these studies (Deci, 1971) was described earlier: college students, most of them male, who were praised for performance on interesting puzzles subsequently showed greater spontaneous interest in the puzzles than did tangibly rewarded or nonreinforced students. In later studies in which substantial numbers of both sexes were tested, males showed this increase in intrinsic motivation following praise, but females who were praised showed the opposite effect, exhibiting less spontaneous interest in the task than did women who received no reinforcement. Deci and his colleagues interpreted these results within the context of theories about personality differences between the sexes, suggesting that females have stronger needs for social approval and weaker achievement motives than do males. For males, praise may have been interpreted as signaling their personal competency and, as such, it enhanced their feelings of self-efficacy and the strength of their intrinsic motivation. For many of the women, on the other hand, praise may have signaled the experimenter's approval and aroused their needs to please and to gain the experimenter's continued approbation. As this aspect of the reinforcer became salient, the reattributional process may have occurred, the women coming to perceive their behaviors as being caused or controlled by the praise they received. Recalling Harackiewicz's (1979) suggestion, it also seems possible that the use of puzzles rather than more ego-involving tasks that elicit competency concerns may have made the women more sensitive to the experimenter and to receiving the latter's approval.

It is theoretically important, in our view, to distinguish even more sharply than is implied in these attributional accounts between the meaning an individual gives to extrinsic rewards and the degree to which their receipt is gratifying versus the capacity of these events to act as *motivators* of behavior in anticipation of their receipt. It is also important to identify the several components of the motivational complex. In accord with classical theories of motivation, we suggest first that motivators serve to activate behavior and have hedonic accompaniments. Other crucial properties of the motivational complex determine the direction of behavior; these include *expectancies* about the outcomes of performance (i.e., response-reinforcer contingencies) and *behavioral intentions* (the purposes and goals that the behavior is meant to fulfill).

Attributional analyses of intrinsic motivation have tended to limit themselves to the expectancy and intentional aspects of the motivational complex and to posit that reinforcer salience determines behavioral intentions. Thus, in the case in which an attractive tangible reward is given for performing an otherwise interesting task, it has been proposed that individuals not only develop *expectancies* about receiving rewards after the required performance but also change their perceptions of their *intentions* in performing the task. Task activity comes to be seen as a means to an end, as behavior whose purpose is to obtain the external reward. As a consequence, the task itself is perceived as less inherently interesting than it had been and is less likely to be performed when reinforcers are withdrawn.

This attributional formulation also implies a close reciprocal linkage between the strength of intrinsic motives and that of extrinsic motives: as one goes up, the other goes down, and behavior is governed primarily by one or the other. However, it seems likely that there is often considerable independence between the intensities of the two types of motives and that they may influence behavior simultaneously. Attributional theories also appear to exaggerate the inevitability of an association between expectations about the reward consequences of behavior and behavioral intentions. Even when tangible extrinsic rewards for performance are anticipated and their receipt is valued for their own sake, these events do not *necessarily* lead to a shift in behavioral intentions.

The conditions under which the introduction of extrinsic reinforcers simultaneously reduce intrinsic motivation and increase extrinsic motivation are not well understood. However, the context of the experimental situations that have been used to investigate changes in intrinsic motivation seems particularly favorable for demonstrating this phenomenon. Generally speaking, tangible rewards may be particularly likely to weaken intrinsic motivation and to encourage the development of extrinsic motives in instances in which intrinsic interest in an activity is shallow or in the process of developing. Intrinsic motivation implies that performance is self-initiated, self-sustaining, and self-rewarding; whereas extrinsic motivation implies that performance is externally driven and is likely to be extinguished or diminished in the absence of reward (e.g., Kazdin and Bootzin, 1972). At least in some settings, the maintenance of behavior that is purely extrinsically motivated requires quite constant surveillance and monitoring by an external reinforcing agent—a condition that is often difficult to meet practically and that may itself have adverse effects (e.g., Lepper and Greene, 1976). For these reasons, parents and teachers would be well advised to encourage the development in their charges of intrinsic motivation for performing desirable behaviors and to use extrinsic rewards judiciously.

Noting the findings of the types of experiments we have reviewed above, some investigators interested in industrial and organizational problems (e.g., Notz, 1975) have suggested that extrinsic rewards may undermine intrinsic interest in job performance in adults. Although this possibility cannot be discounted, it is unlikely. Once stable motivational systems and interest patterns have become established, it seems improbable that individuals' intrinsic interests would be easily corrupted by the introduction of or increases in extrinsic rewards. Even if tangible extrinsic reinforcers come to be expected and their receipt is gratifying, the behavior itself may continue to be intrinsically motivated and have as its immediate goal successful performance. In the vocabulary used earlier, expectancy of reward is not inexorably linked to behavioral intention. During the performance sequence, intrinsic and extrinsic reinforcers may change in salience—intrinsic motives and goals being in the ascendancy during task performance, and expectancies of extrinsic rewards becoming important at task completion.

An important addendum to attribution theory that supports these suggestions has been proposed and given some experimental confirmation by Kruglanski (1975) and by Staw, Calder, and Hess (1974). These investigators have proposed that, under conditions in which rewards are ordinarily associated with task performance, standards of rewards have been established, and rewards are appropriate in the context of these standards, the introduction of rewards is unlikely to result in reattribution, i.e., in a shift from intrinsically to extrinsically motivated behavior. Performance in vocational settings and, at least in older children and adults, in academic situations seems particularly likely to fulfill these conditions.

Effects on Performance

In addition to studies of the effects of tangible rewards such as money or prizes on intrinsic motivation, investigations have been conducted to determine the effects of rewards on actual task performance. Typically, these tasks require mastery, e.g., memorizing words, solving problems. In some of these studies, experimental subjects (children or adults) were given a tangible reward for each correct response, which also served to inform them they were correct; whereas control subjects were given symbolic feedback that served the same informational function but had no inherent value. In other studies, the experimental subjects were promised tangible rewards for completing the task, and the control subjects were given no such incentive. In many of these investigations, subjects given tangible rewards did not perform as well as control subjects (e.g., Loveland and Olley, 1979; McGraw and McCullers, 1976; Miller and Estes, 1961; Spence, 1970). After reviewing the evidence, McGraw (1978) and Condrey and Chambers (1978) concluded that the use of material reinforcers leads to performance decrement when the task holds some intrinsic interest for the individual (and would thus be performed without the reward) and mastery of the task requires the acquisition of a novel response or method of solution rather than the application of previously learned, well-perfected strategies. In the absence of one or both of these conditions, performance may be facilitated or unaffected by the use of tangible rewards.

The results of the studies of intrinsic motivation reviewed earlier suggest that, with the introduction of extrinsic rewards, subjects' motives in these laboratory experiments may have shifted from being primarily intrinsic to being primarily extrinsic. Few studies have included measures of both intrinsic motivation and task performance. The evidence presently available suggests that tangible reinforcers may produce performance decrement even when intrinsic interest is not damaged (McCullers, 1978) and, conversely, that a drop in intrinsic interest accompanying the introduction of reinforcers may not produce a decrement in performance (Harackiewicz, 1979). Thus, the performance inferiority of individuals given or promised tangible rewards cannot be attributed simply to a decrease in the intensity of their overall motivation to perform.

It has been suggested that, on tasks requiring new solutions, extrinsically rewarded individuals may be distracted from central features of the task in a way that hinders their performance (McGraw and McCullers, 1976; Reiss and Sushinsky, 1975; Spence, 1971) or may shift to performance strategies that are aimed at earning tangible rewards but that turn out to be less effective than those used by individuals who are unrewarded and thus perform for more intrinsic reasons (Condry and Chambers, 1978). Evidence showing that the introduction of material incentives leads subjects to adopt different approaches to the task at hand has been provided by Condry and Chambers (1978), Garbarino (1975), and Loveland and Olley (1979).

It is a large leap from the laboratory study of performance on contrived tasks to the naturalistic study of long-term achievement behaviors. We are nonetheless stimulated by the results of these studies to suggest, by analogy, that individuals whose aspirations have a heavy dose of extrinsic motivation may not only tend to use different "career strategies" than do those who are more purely intrinsically motivated but may also sometimes use strategies that produce less adequate performance than is found in their more intrinsically motivated peers.

Perhaps the most valuable contribution to date of these experimental studies of extrinsic reinforcers is the demonstration that intrinsic and extrinsic motives and goals are not necessarily additive or mutually facilitative in their effects on performance. Thus, those interested in intrinsic achievement motivation can no longer safely ignore the role of extrinsic incentives in determining naturally occurring achievement behavior. However, our current understanding of the development of individual differences in these motives and goals and in the interaction between intrinsic and extrinsic factors in determining achievement-related behavior can most charitably be described as limited.

INTRINSIC ACHIEVEMENT MOTIVES
AND EXPECTANCY–VALUE THEORY

We turn now to a more detailed consideration of intrinsic achievement motives, which we have defined as striving toward performance
excellence and which we regard as stable personality characteristics
whose strengths differ from one individual to the next. This general
conception of achievement motivation, which owes much to the seminal work of the personality theorist Henry Murray, is at the heart of
the highly influential theories of achievement proposed by John
Atkinson, David McClelland, and their colleagues that are the most
immediate precursors of our own work on achievement motivation.

Achievement Motivation and the Thematic Apperception Test

Murray conceived of personality as a series of needs, described as an
"organic potentiality or readiness to respond in a certain way under
given conditions" (1938, p. 60). Among these needs is the need to
achieve, which Murray described as "the desire or tendency to do
things as rapidly and/or as well as possible . . . to accomplish something difficult. To master, manipulate and organize physical objects,
human beings, or ideas . . . . To overcome obstacles and attain a high
standard. To excel one's self. To rival and surpass others" (1938, p.
164).

Influenced by psychoanalytic thought, Murray postulated that
needs are largely unconscious; accordingly, he devised a projective
instrument, the Thematic Apperception Test (TAT), to assess them.
The TAT consists of a series of ambiguous pictures of one or more
people about whom test respondents are asked to tell a story. The
fantasy material is then coded for the presence of imagery relating to
various needs.

McClelland and Atkinson adopted the TAT technique to measure
the need (or motive) to achieve, selecting pictures having the capacity
to elicit achievement imagery. The TAT scoring system specifies 10
subcategories of achievement-related themes, representing various
components of the motive to achieve as specified in Murray's definition. However, neither they nor other investigators using the TAT
have attempted to determine the relationships of these separate themes
to one another or to achievement behavior. Instead, a single score is
obtained for each individual by summing the number of achievement
themes occurring in all subcategories.

In adopting the TAT as their measure of the motive to achieve,
McClelland and Atkinson accepted Murray's view that motives are

acquired dispositional tendencies that are general in nature and not tightly linked to specific situations and that they tend to be stable over time. They further conceived of motives as having both activating and affective properties and directive or goal-oriented properties. As Atkinson put it, describing both motives in general and the motive to achieve in particular:

> A motive is conceived as a disposition to strive for a certain kind of satisfaction, as a capacity for satisfaction in the attainment of a certain class of incentives. The names given motives—such as achievement— are really names of classes of incentives which produce essentially the same kind of experience of satisfaction [for example, in the case of the achievement motive]: pride in accomplishment . . . . The general aim of one class of motives, usually referred to as appetites or approach tendencies, is to maximize satisfaction of some kind. The achievement motivation is considered a disposition to approach success (1966, p. 13).

Like other motives, the motive to achieve remains latent until aroused by appropriate internal or environmental cues.

In early work done in the 1950s, environmental conditions under which the TAT was administered were manipulated to determine whether responses varied in a manner consistent with the assumption that what was being measured by the TAT was a motive. The specifics of these studies need not concern us here. We note only that the results from males generally conformed to prediction, thus upholding the construct validity of the TAT as a motivational measure, but that the data from females were inconsistent and difficult to interpret. As a consequence of these findings, the suspicion was voiced that achievement motivation, as it operated in men, might not have an exact counterpart in most women. McClelland went further: "Clearly we need a differential psychology of motivation for men and women" (1966, p. 481). However, the attempt to understand men came first and, for some years, experimental studies of achievement motivation in the Atkinson–McClelland tradition employed male subjects almost exclusively.

Expectancy–Value Theory

The concept of achievement motive, defined as a stable personality characteristic, was incorporated into a larger theory of achievement motivation proposed by Atkinson (1957). This theory, which has come to be known as expectancy–value theory, specifies that the strength of the achievement motive (or, as it is alternately labeled, the tendency to achieve) actually aroused in any achievement-oriented situation is determined by the sum of two tendencies with opposing signs:

1. The *tendency* to approach *success* (T_S), which is manifested by engaging in achievement-oriented activities.

2. The *tendency* to avoid *failure* (T_{AF}), which is manifested by not engaging in these activities.

The strength of each of these opposing tendencies is determined by three components:

1. The *motive* to approach *success* (M_S) or the *motive* to avoid *failure* (M_{AF}).

2. The *expectancy* (*probability*) that an achievement-oriented act will result in *success* (P_S) or the *probability* that it will result in *failure* (P_F).

3. The *incentive* value of *success* (I_S) or the *incentive* value of *failure* (I_F).

It is the latter two variables that give Atkinson's theory its expectancy–value label.

The motive to approach success (M_S) is an individual-difference variable, typically measured by the TAT. The motive to avoid failure (M_{AF}), also called fear of failure, is proposed as a separate dispositional tendency that, like the motive to approach success, is a stable personality characteristic that has been acquired as a result of past experience. Individual differences in the motive to avoid failure have usually been measured by objective self-report instruments, most often the Mandler–Sarason Test Anxiety Questionnaire (Mandler and Sarason, 1952) or the Alpert–Haber Debilitating Anxiety Scale (Alpert and Haber, 1960). Heckhausen (1963) has attempted to bring more symmetry into the measurement of the two motivational constructs by extending the TAT projective technique to include a measure of the motive to avoid failure, but the measure has not been widely adopted.

The second component determining the tendency to approach success or the tendency to avoid failure is expectancy, defined as the probability that engaging in an achievement-oriented activity will result in success (P_S) or in failure (P_F). Since success and failure exhaust all possibilities, their probabilities add up to unity ($P_S + P_F = 1$). The probability of failure, P_F, can therefore be expressed as ($1 - P_S$). In experimental situations designed to test the implications of expectancy–value theory, the expectancy variable either has been subjectively defined by having subjects give their estimate, prior to undertaking the task, of the probability that they will succeed or has been experimentally manipulated by such methods as supplying subjects with performance norms from which the task's level of difficulty can be inferred or first giving them similar tasks on which they succeed or fail.

The third component, incentive value of success or failure, has been described by Atkinson as the degree of anticipated satisfaction or pride in succeeding at a task or the degree of anticipated shame in failing. In practice, Atkinson's operationalization of the incentive factor has usually been reduced to a property of probability of success. Based on the contention of Lewin, Dembo, Festinger, and Sears (1944) that the attractiveness or incentive value of success increases with task difficulty, the incentive value of success (I_S) and the incentive value of failure (I_F) are $(1 - P_{FA})$ or $[1 - (1 - P_S)]$.

The three components associated with the tendency to approach success (T_S) and with the tendency to avoid failure (T_F)—motive, expectancy, and incentive—are assumed to combine multiplicatively to determine the strength of each of these tendencies. These two tendencies (given opposite signs), in turn, sum algebraically to determine the strength of the resultant achievement motivation, or the tendency to achieve ($T_A = T_S - T_{AF}$). When the complete set of assumptions about each component is considered and the formula is algebraically simplified, the tendency to achieve is defined as

$$T_A = (M_S - M_{AF}) [(P_S \times (1 - P_S)]$$

Most of the tests of the implications of the theory have been brief experimental studies that were conducted in the laboratory and that involved the manipulation of such variables as task success and failure. (Reviews of these studies may be found in such sources as Atkinson and Raynor, 1974.) Relatively few attempts have been made to explore the implications of the theory for task performance per se (e.g., number of tasks mastered, speed of mastery, quality of performance). More thoroughly investigated have been the predictions of the theory for such measures as level of aspiration, task persistence, and risk taking in choice of task difficulty.

Perhaps the most intriguing aspect of the theory involves predictions about individuals' preferred level of task difficulty. The equation for determining the tendency to achieve (T_A) implies that, for individuals in whom the motive to approach success is stronger than the motive to avoid failure ($M_S > M_{AF}$), the tendency to achieve is strongest in situations in which the probability of success is ½. These success-oriented individuals are therefore more likely to choose tasks of intermediate difficulty and to persist at them longer than at tasks that are either higher or lower in difficulty. The mathematics of the theory also implies that those in whom the motive to avoid failure dominates $(M_S < M_{AF})$ are least likely to choose or to persist at tasks of intermediate difficulty. For these failure-avoidant individuals, the tendency to achieve is predicted to be highest when task difficulty is either high or low. The bulk of the evidence suggests, however, that individuals tend to prefer tasks of intermediate difficulty, whatever the strength of their motive to achieve (Weiner, 1972). Other theoretical accounts of task choice have also been developed and have received empirical support (e.g., Buckert, Meyer, and Schmalt, 1979; Trope, 1975).

Although the empirical studies conducted to test the theory's implications have mostly been short-term laboratory experiments, some have involved achievement-related behaviors occurring in real-world settings. Crockett (1962), for example, has shown that, among men whose fathers' occupations are relatively low in prestige, those who score high in achievement motivation, as measured by the TAT, exhibit greater upward occupational mobility than do lower-scoring men. In a study by Malone (1960), vocational aspirations among male college students have also been related to motivational factors. In Malone's study, the difference was found between each student's motive to achieve and motive to avoid failure (defined, as usual, by scores on the TAT and an anxiety measure). Evaluation was made of the realism of the students' vocational choices, as reflected in such measures as the discrepancy between the individual's ability and the ability required by the specified vocation. In correspondence with the theory's prediction about achievement-oriented individuals preferring tasks of intermediate difficulty, men in whom the motive to achieve predominated tended to make more realistic choices than did those in whom the motive to avoid failure was stronger. The latter were more likely either to underaspire or to overaspire.

Elaborations of the Theory   Following the initial formulation of expectancy–value theory, Atkinson and others working within this framework have proposed a number of revisions, qualifications, and additions in order to improve and extend the theory's predictive utility. Several of these elaborations are important for us to consider here.

The theory as originally stated implied that individuals in whom the tendency to avoid failure was greater than the tendency to approach success would avoid all achievement-related activity. Since the many individuals who are failure-avoidant (as defined by the theory) obviously *do* engage in achievement-oriented behaviors—in school, on the job, and even in the laboratory—this aspect of the theory was in conspicuous need of repair. To remedy this deficiency, Atkinson (1974) added another construct to the theory: the *tendency to seek extrinsic rewards* (T_E). This tendency combines additively with the tendencies to approach success (T_S) and avoid failure (T_{AF}), so that $T_A = T_S - T_{AF} + T_E$. The evidence we reviewed in the preceding section, however, suggests that intrinsic and extrinsic motives may be related in a complex manner and do not necessarily add together in any simple way to form a resultant motivational state. It does seem reasonable to assume, however, that extrinsic motives may buoy up achievement-oriented efforts in those whose intrinsic achievement motivation (or the tendency to approach success) is weak and/or in those whose fear of failure is strong.

A second addition to expectancy–value theory is the concept of future orientation proposed by Raynor (1969, 1970). As noted by Vroom (1964) and others, success on a task is often instrumental in allowing the individual to proceed to the next in a sequence of tasks that ultimately lead to a future goal. Building on this observation, Raynor has suggested that each step in the sequence arouses a *component tendency*, each consisting of the by-now-familiar triad: the motives to approach success and avoid failure (the stable personality factors), the subjective probability that the activity will lead to success or failure, and the incentive value of each of these outcomes. Also following Vroom (1964), Raynor assumed that the component tendencies for all steps in the path to the future goal sum together to determine the strength of the tendency to achieve that is operative in a given task in the sequence. The tendency to achieve is thus a result of both immediate and more distant expectancies and their associated incentive values.

In a test of the implications of these hypotheses for achievement behavior, Raynor (1970) attempted to predict the course grades of students enrolled in introductory psychology. He reasoned that, among success-dominated individuals $(M_S > M_{AF})$, higher course grades would be earned by those who believed that doing well was important to the fulfillment of their career aspirations than by those who perceived grades as unimportant to their future plans. Raynor derived a very different prediction for individuals in whom $M_{AF} > M_S$. Among these failure-avoidant individuals, the perceived instrumentality of grades was expected to act as an inhibitory factor, depressing course performance. However, Raynor qualified this prediction by noting that extrinsic incentives might overcome this negative effect to some degree. In the first of a pair of studies (Raynor, 1970), these hypotheses were confirmed: success-motivated students who rated their course grade as important to future career success earned a significantly better grade than those who rated the course as unimportant; failure-avoidant students showed a trend in the opposite direction. Significant differences in grades between success-oriented and failure-avoidant students thus appeared only among those who perceived the course as being instrumental to their future success. For those who rated it as unimportant, course grades of the two motivational groups were similar.

In Raynor's (1970) second study, introductory psychology students were asked to specify the relative importance of all their courses for their future plans. Those who ranked the psychology course high in this list earned a higher grade than those who ranked it low. However, no significant effects were found for the motivational measures—a result Raynor attributed to the offsetting effects of extrinsic motives.

The best-known addition to expectancy–value theory is Horner's (1968) *motive to avoid success*. This motive (also commonly identified as fear of success) is described as a stable dispositional tendency, acquired relatively early in life, to become anxious about achieving success. Like fear of failure, fear of success is postulated to reduce resultant achievement motivation (or the tendency to achieve) and hence to inhibit achievement-related behavior.

The addition of this third personality variable to expectancy–value theory represented an attempt to reconcile the puzzling findings that had been obtained from females with the tenets of expectancy–value theory by expanding the theory so that it would be applicable to both sexes. Women are particularly likely to develop fear of success, Horner contended, their sex-role socialization leading them to believe that achievement strivings are incompatible with femininity and that women incur a number of social penalties if they violate role expectations by attempting to become successful.

To measure fear of success, Horner (1968) developed a TAT-like method that utilizes a verbal rather than a pictorial cue and depicts an individual of the same sex as the respondent who is successful in a competitive situation: "At the end of the first term, (Anne) (John) finds (herself) (himself) at the top of (her) (his) medical school class." Using a simple present–absent method of scoring, Horner found that the stories of female college students contained fear-of-success imagery far more often than those of their male peers.

Horner's hypotheses quickly commanded both popular and scientific attention and led to an outpouring of empirical studies. As reviews of this literature have indicated (Condry and Dyer, 1976; Tresemer, 1977; Zuckerman and Wheeler, 1975), subsequent studies have produced conflicting outcomes. Whereas some investigators have reported significantly more fear of success in women than in men, although not in the lopsided proportions that occurred in Horner's original 1968 study, many others have reported either the reverse or no differences between the sexes. Contradictory results have also been found in studies investigating the effects of fear of success on behavior in competitive situations with same- versus opposite-sex partners, while expected relationships between fear of success and measures of achievement motivation, vocational aspirations, and other indices of achievement strivings have turned out to be minimal.

The consensus is that the inconsistency in the data can be partially attributed to the lack of reliability and validity in the method used to measure fear of success (e.g., Condry and Dyer, 1976; Zuckerman and Wheeler, 1975). The amount and kind of negative imagery have also been shown to vary in a predictable manner with changes in cue content, such as from medical to nursing school (e.g., Alper, 1974; Spence, 1974). These data have led several investigators (e.g., Condry and Dyer, 1976; Monahan, Kuhn, and Shaver, 1974; Spence, 1974; Zuckerman and Wheeler, 1975) to conclude that the fantasy material elicited from women by the story-telling technique has relatively little relationship to a gender-differentiating personality characteristic but instead largely reflects the respondents' perceptions of society's current sex-role attitudes and their expectations about the consequences of role conformity or violation under the particular circumstances described in the verbal cue. With greater societal acceptance of women's educational and vocational aspirations, sex differences in fear-of-success studies appear to be evaporating.

A number of objective self-report instruments have been devised in an effort to overcome some of the psychometric difficulties associated with the projective method of measuring fear of success. A factor-analytic study of several of these instruments by Sadd, Lenauer, Shaver, and Dunivant (1978) has yielded two factors. The first has to do with insecurity, self-doubt, and inhibition of assertiveness; the investigators noted that these characteristics seemed to touch on the conception of the neurotic success-fearing personality described by Canavan-Gumpert, Garner, and Gumpert (1978). The second factor has to do with concerns about the negative consequences of success and appears to be closer to Horner's original theoretical conception of fear of success. Investigations of the relationships of objective measures of the fear of the consequences of success to measures of achievement motivation and to achievement behavior are just beginning to be undertaken.

Current Status of the Theory   Especially during the 10–15 years following its initial presentation, expectancy–value theory stimulated a large volume of research aimed at verifying its predictions. Although some of the theory's detailed predictions have received only equivocal support, the usefulness of the general theory has been well established.

The theory has also served as a springboard for still further theoretical developments. Many of these formulations have focused on the expectancy–value components of the theory, stressing the importance of cognitive factors and attributional processes in determining achievement-related behaviors (e.g., Weiner, 1972) and downplaying the role of motivational factors, as represented by Murray's original conceptualization of the need to achieve. Increasing attention has also been given to these cognitive variables as they operate naturalistically in real-life settings. A major example of this type of theory may be found in Chapter 2, this volume, in which Parsons presents a theoretical model of achievement-related behavior that stresses subjective expectancies, task values, and causal attributions and the application of this model to the study of achievement in courses in mathematics.

Other investigators, such as the present authors, have chosen to focus on individual differences in achievement motivation but have attempted to develop more satisfactory measures of this concept than the TAT. Investigators have been especially critical of the TAT's low reliability, noting that respondents' stories are overly responsive both to the particular pictorial material used to elicit them and to the situational conditions under which the test is taken, and that scores derived from respondents' stories are not stable from one testing occasion to another. Atkinson (1981; Atkinson and Raynor, 1974) has countered this criticism by arguing that, since the achievement themes appearing in individuals' stories vary predictably with variations in conditions expected to arouse or engage their achievement motivation, the responsiveness of the TAT technique to transient factors constitutes evidence for the validity of the achievement-motive construct. While this contention is reasonable, the sensitivity of the instrument to testing conditions and the resulting instability of scores reduce its usefulness as a measure of the strength of an underlying disposition that is postulated to be enduring over time and is to be used to predict individual differences in real-life achievement that occurs at other times and places. Use of projective devices such as the TAT also has a practical drawback. The amount of time required to administer such measures and, even more critically, the time required of judges to read and properly score the respondents' stories are often prohibitive and may make large-scale research impossible.

Another aspect of the TAT measure is perhaps more theoretically critical. As mentioned earlier, the scoring manual lists a number of achievement themes, but in practice a single score is derived from respondents' stories to reflect the intensity of their achievement motivation. This scoring method presupposes that achievement motivation is unifactorial; i.e., it is assumed that, underlying the several kinds of achievement-oriented themes, there is a single, broad disposition that influences a variety of behaviors in achievement-related situations. However, several factor-analytic studies (e.g., Jackson, Ahmed, and Heapy, 1976; Veroff, McClelland, and Ruhland, 1975; Weinstein, 1969), each employing a number of projective and/or objective measures of achievement motivation, have revealed the presence of a number of more or less independent factors. Some of the factors identified in these studies go beyond the conception of achievement motivation as a striving toward excellence into other types of achievement-related motives and attitudes, some of which appear to be more related to extrinsic motives, e.g., the need to achieve status. Other factors, however, do appear to be related to Murray's original conception of the need to achieve. These findings suggest that it may be more useful to try to identify and measure components of intrinsic achievement motivation than to postulate a single, unitary dimension.

A number of objective self-report measures of achievement motivation have been developed that overcome some of the practical limitations of the TAT. Illustrative of these efforts are the scales developed by Mehrabian (1968), which incorporate items tapping both the motive to approach success (M_S) and the motive to avoid failure (M_{AF}) and thus were designed to yield a measure of resultant achievement motivation. In apparent support of the contention that the sexes are not identical in the nature of their achievement motivation, Mehrabian found it useful to develop different scales for males and females. While some items are common to both scales, others are unique.

Objective measures, such as Mehrabian's, have tended to be substituted for the TAT in recent research and have been shown to have some modest degree of predictive validity in both laboratory and field studies (e.g., Covington and Omelich, 1979). However, the correlations of these objective instruments with one another and with projective devices are generally found to be low (e.g., Weinstein, 1969).

RECONCEPTUALIZATION OF INTRINSIC ACHIEVEMENT MOTIVATION

Several years ago, the present authors became interested in the topic of achievement motivation as an outgrowth of a program of research investigating certain core dimensions of personality said to differentiate the sexes (masculine instrumentality and feminine expressiveness) and the implications of these clusters of characteristics for other attributes and behaviors. Central among the latter have been achievement motivation and achievement-related behaviors.

As has been discussed earlier, we conceived of intrinsic achievement motivation in the classical sense as a striving toward excellence in performance for its own sake. However, like many other investigators, we were dissatisfied with the limitations of the TAT and sought an objective measure that was both reliable (and thus more likely to reflect stable individual differences) and simple to administer and score. Examination of the evidence also suggested to us that intrinsic achievement motivation was not necessarily a unitary phenomenon. Building on the work of others (e.g., Mehrabian, 1968), we set out to devise an objective measure, being particularly alert to the possibility of multidimensionality in its content. It was also our hope that an instrument could be perfected that would be valid for both males and females. Success in achieving this goal was contingent on the two sexes having similar motivational structures, differing (if at all) only quantitatively rather than qualitatively, as some theorists (e.g., McClelland, 1966) would have it.

Work and Family Orientation Questionnaire

The ultimate outcome of our psychometric efforts is an objective self-report instrument called the Work and Family Orientation Questionnaire (WOFO) (Helmreich and Spence, 1978). The WOFO consists of two parts, the second of which is used primarily with student groups and contains items that gave the instrument its name. These items are mixed in content, inquiring about the respondents' educational aspirations, the relative importance of work versus marriage as anticipated sources of life satisfaction, and extrinsic goals such as the desire for pay, prestige, or job advancement for oneself and one's spouse. These latter items were initially included because of our interest in vicarious achievement aspirations in females, but they have also permitted some preliminary exploration of the relationship between intrinsic and extrinsic achievement motives.

The first part of the WOFO contains items dealing with attitudes toward achievement-related activities. Factor analyses of these motivational items, conducted on the responses of male and female college students, revealed three major oblique factors[1] (i.e., factors that are modestly correlated but still show substantial independence) that are similar in each sex (Helmreich and Spence, 1978). This latter finding is of considerable theoretical significance in and of itself,

---

[1]Factor analyses revealed a fourth factor in each sex that is conceptually similar to Horner's fear-of-success concept, containing items expressing concern about others' negative reactions to the individual's success. These items have been assigned to a scale labeled Personal Unconcern. Comparisons of men's and women's scores on this scale have rarely yielded sex differences and, within each sex, few relationships of scores with other variables have been uncovered. For this reason, we do not discuss this scale further.

suggesting that, at least with respect to the particular components of achievement motivation tapped by this pool of items, the structures of men's and women's motivational systems are not qualitatively different. The factor analyses also confirmed the suspicion, voiced earlier, that achievement motivation is a multidimensional phenomenon.

Based on the results of the factor analyses, items have been assigned to one of three scales, designated as work orientation, mastery, and competitiveness. (The items and the scale to which each belongs are shown in Table 1-1.) The work factor represents an effort dimension, the desire to work hard and to do a good job of what one does. The mastery factor reflects a preference for difficult, challenging tasks and for meeting internally prescribed standards of performance excellence. The competitiveness factor describes the enjoyment of interpersonal competition and the desire to win and be better than others. Unlike mastery, which involves a task-oriented standard of excellence, competitiveness involves pitting oneself against other individuals. In the scoring of these scales, items are keyed so that high scores reflect a high degree of work, mastery, or competitiveness.

Like the TAT, the WOFO scales of intrinsic achievement motive are intended to measure *general personality traits*. That is, the WOFO items are relatively free of references to specific situational contexts, and individuals' responses to the items are assumed to reflect dispositional tendencies that may influence behavior in a variety of settings. It is further assumed that, once established, these tendencies are relatively stable over time, rarely showing sudden changes or developmental discontinuities. This kind of measure of achievement motivation is to be contrasted with measures that are situationally constrained, attempting only to measure intensity of achievement striving in very particular contexts (e.g., Crandall, 1969).

Traits Versus Behavior

It does not follow from a general-trait approach that individuals are necessarily expected to show a high degree of behavioral consistency over all situations in which a trait could be overtly manifested. In the instance of achievement, we noted earlier that almost any situation can be turned into an achievement-oriented challenge by anyone sufficiently ingenious or interested in doing so. Common-sense observation indicates that even highly motivated individuals do not bring the same degree of achievement striving to every situation they encounter, even within conventional types of activities in which performance standards have been clearly established and high levels of achievement are encouraged and rewarded. Achievement motives, to

Table 1-1
Items on work, mastery, and competitiveness scales of Work and Family
Orientation Questionnaire

Work

1. It is important for me to do my work as well as I can even if it isn't popular with my co-workers.
2. I find satisfaction in working as well as I can.
3. There is satisfaction in a job well done.
4. I find satisfaction in exceeding my previous performance even if I don't outperform others.
5. I like to work hard.
6. Part of my enjoyment in doing things is improving my past performance.

Mastery

1. I would rather do something at which I feel confident and relaxed than something which is challenging and difficult.
2. When a group I belong to plans an activity, I would rather direct it myself than just help out and have someone else organize it.
3. I would rather learn easy fun games than difficult thought games.
4. If I am not good at something, I would rather keep struggling to master it than move on to something I may be good at.
5. Once I undertake a task, I persist.
6. I prefer to work in situations that require a high level of skill.
7. I more often attempt tasks that I am not sure I can do than tasks that I believe I can do.
8. I like to be busy all the time.

Competitiveness

1. I enjoy working in situations involving competition with others.
2. It is important to me to perform better than others on a task.
3. I feel that winning is important in both work and games.
4. It annoys me when other people perform better than I do.
5. I try harder when I'm in competition with other people.

Note: Each item is accompanied by a 5-point rating scale ranging from "Strongly agree" to "Strongly disagree."

affect behavior, must be aroused or engaged. Such interlocking variables as individuals' interests, abilities, educational levels, expectations of success, and long-term goals determine the achievement-related tasks or roles in which the individual elects to participate (e.g., vocational choice or the kind or amount of education sought) or the degree to which particular activities in which the individual takes part elicit behaviors designed to satisfy achievement needs as opposed to other kinds of needs, such as gregariousness.

Role expectations also channel the overt expression of achievement needs. For example, paid employment is both literally and figuratively obligatory for men in this society; a major outlet for achievement motives in most men is their jobs. For many adult women, achievement needs are more likely to be expressed in other directions, such as volunteer work and activities associated with the care of home and family. Men may also be achievement-oriented in their leisure activities, but their specific interests often differ from women's. The effects of sex-role expectations on academic choices have also been demonstrated (see Chapter 3, this volume).

In both sexes, individuals vary in the number of activities that engage their achievement motives. Some focus on doing well in one type of task or role. "Workaholics," who voluntarily devote most of their waking hours to their jobs or professions, are an extreme example. Others attempt to become expert or to develop their capacities in many areas.

Since we have conceded that, as a result of choice as well as circumstance, individuals of both sexes vary in the specific activities that engage their achievement motives, it is reasonable to ask whether it is either theoretically meaningful or empirically useful to conceive of achievement motives as general dispositional tendencies or response styles rather than as a series of more or less independent tendencies or response styles that are situation-specific. Although our answer to both questions is affirmative, we should point out that, if an investigator's intent is to predict only one type of achievement behavior, it is probably more parsimonious to tailor devices assessing achievement motivation and other relevant person variables to the behavior being scrutinized and the situation in which it occurs. One might measure, for example, academic achievement motivation or, even more narrowly, motivation with respect to a specific subject-matter area, such as mathematics. Although an individual's motivation to do well in, for example, mathematics may theoretically be represented as the result of more general achievement motives interacting with constellations of other factors such as interest, self-concepts of ability, and prior success in the subject, it may be more useful to act as if there were a highly specific "mathematics achievement motive."

One implication of our conceptualization of achievement motives as general tendencies is that changes in such internal factors as interests or in such external factors as job opportunities may occur relatively independently of variations in achievement motives. Individuals may make a radical career shift, for example, not because of changes in the intensity of their achievement motives but because they have for the first time a chance at a desired job, have developed new interests, or have exhausted the challenges in their previous position, to name but a few possibilities. As a still further example, relatively sudden shifts in academically oriented behaviors are quite frequently observed in adolescents (particularly males) who, as the time for applying to college approaches, become motivated to do well in school rather than expending most of their energies in sports or other extracurricular activities. It is also not unusual to find, in the biographies of eminent scholars, that academically oriented intellectual interests developed relatively late in their undergraduate careers, their prior academic histories having been mediocre if not disgraceful; nonetheless, they showed early signs of strong achievement striving but expressed it in nonacademic directions.

To restate the basic assumptions of our theoretical model: achievement motivation is conceived as a series of more or less independent motives, each reflecting general dispositional tendencies or traits that are relatively enduring over time and that remain latent until engaged or aroused by particular tasks or situations. Since individuals differ not only in the strengths of their motives but also in the tasks or roles that elicit them, achievement behavior cannot necessarily be predicted either cross-sectionally or longitudinally, only from information about individuals' motives. To test the implications of this conception, it is necessary both to assess the strength of general achievement motives and to have some information about the individuals' specific interests and aspirations or the activities in which they voluntarily engage. Over groups of individuals at various levels of achievement motivation, we would nonetheless expect some cross-situational consistency, as, for example, in their work and their leisure-time activities.

RESULTS WITH THE WORK AND FAMILY ORIENTATION QUESTIONNAIRE

Sex Differences in Unselected Groups

Psychological theorists, we have mentioned, have often proposed that personality differences between men and women contribute to women's lesser worldly success. Women are said to be more expressive and interpersonally sensitive than men and, simultaneously, to be lower in instrumental qualities reflecting self-assertiveness and independence. This constellation of characteristics allegedly leads women to be less self-confident and to develop weaker intrinsic achievement motives than men and to be more motivated in their achievement-related activities by their needs for affiliation and social approval than by intrinsic motives.

Data relevant to these speculations were obtained in our research from the achievement-motivation scales of the WOFO and from a second self-report measure, the Personal Attributes Questionnaire (PAQ) (Spence and Helmreich, 1978). The PAQ contains two major scales: one consisting of socially desirable instrumental traits (e.g., independence, decisiveness) that are stereotypically more characteristic of males than females (M scale), and the other consisting of socially desirable expressive traits (e.g., tactfulness, awareness of others' feelings) that are stereotypically more characteristic of females (F scale).

Self-report data from unselected groups of individuals varying widely in age and socioeconomic level have uniformly revealed significant sex differences in the predicted direction on both the M and the F scale (Spence and Helmreich, 1978, 1979). However, the differences are of degree: men are somewhat less expressive than women (rather than being nonexpressive), and women are somewhat less instrumental than men, with the distributions of the sexes showing considerable overlap. Further, the common belief that instrumental and expressive characteristics tend to be mutually incompatible (Foushee, Helmreich, and Spence, 1979) has been found to be erroneous. In each sex, correlations between individuals' scores on the two scales are close to zero, indicating that "masculine" instrumentality and "feminine" expressiveness are essentially independent dimensions and that many individuals of both sexes are relatively high in both trait clusters (and others relatively low on both clusters).

The theoretical explanations of sex differences in achievement that stress the relationship between these personality dimensions and intrinsic achievement motivation imply that men, as a group, should be higher in motive strength than women and that, within each sex, instrumentality should be positively correlated with achievement motives. The predictions of these theories about the relationships between expressiveness and achievement motivation are more ambiguous, but, presumably, any correlation that occurs should be negative.

Data obtained from the PAQ and the WOFO provide some support for these expectations. Illustrative data are shown in Tables 1-2 and 1-3. Table 1-2 reports the correlations between the WOFO and PAQ scales within each sex. Reported in Table 1-3 are the means for the three WOFO scales obtained from large groups of male and female college students. Examining first the pattern of means, we note that men were significantly higher than women on the mastery scale and on the competitiveness scale. However, they were significantly *lower* than women on the work scale. Within each sex, the anticipated pos-

Table 1-2

Correlations of PAQ masculinity (instrumentality) and femininity (expressiveness) scales with WOFO achievement scales for male and female introductory psychology students

	PAQ	
WOFO	Masculinity (Instrumentality)	Femininity (Expressiveness)
Males		
Work	.27	.20
Mastery	.48	.16
Competitiveness	.36	−.03
Females		
Work	.24	.20
Mastery	.49	.09
Competitiveness	.31	−.14

Note: N per sex > 600. For $N = 600$, $r_{.05} = .08$ (2-tailed); $r_{.01} = .11$ (2-tailed).
Source: Data from Helmreich and Spence, 1978.

itive correlations were found between instrumentality and each of the three achievement scales. Relationships with expressiveness were both weaker and inconsistent in direction: expressivity was positively correlated with work and with mastery, and negatively correlated with competitiveness.

Statistical analyses indicated that, when scores on the two PAQ scales were held constant, men and women no longer differed on work and mastery; i.e., sex differences on these two achievement scales could be attributed to sex differences in instrumentality and expressiveness. However, men remained significantly more competitive than women, even when instrumentality and expressiveness were taken into account. This result may reflect the emphasis that many American parents place on competitiveness in rearing their sons (e.g., Block, 1973, 1979) in the belief that this characteristics is needed for future career success.

These results are not unique to college students. We have obtained similar data from high school students, having a wide range of socio-economic backgrounds (Spence and Helmreich, 1978), and from middle-class married couples. This pattern of sex differences appears to be established early, having been found in fifth- and sixth-grade children given a simplified version of the WOFO (Helmreich, Spence, and Hill, in preparation). These findings all suggest that, in general,

Table 1-3
Mean scores on WOFO work, mastery, and competitiveness scales for
college students, male varsity athletes, businesspersons, and academic
psychologists

	Work		Mastery		Competitiveness	
	Males	Females	Males	Females	Males	Females
College students	19.8	20.3	19.3	18.0	13.6	12.2
Varsity athletes	21.2	21.9	20.4	20.9	15.7	14.3
Businesspersons	21.1	20.7	22.3	22.1	14.6	13.8
Academic psychologists	21.1	21.9	21.5	22.4	11.7	11.1

males tend to have an edge in mastery and competitive motives and
in related instrumental personality characteristics. However, sex differences are not marked (the distribution of scores show a high degree
of overlap) and do not uniformly favor males (women are higher in
work orientation).

Theories attributing women's lesser vocational achievement in
part to their relative deficiency in instrumental qualities and in
achievement motivation thus received only weak support. These theories also appear to imply that affiliative needs, which are presumed
to be stronger in women than in men, are incompatible with achievement motivation. Our data give little support for this assumption,
only competitiveness showing a (small) negative correlation with
expressiveness.

Achievement Motives in Selected Groups

Some achievement-related activities are more demanding than others,
their successful accomplishment requiring talent and training as well
as a high degree of achievement motivation. Achievement motivation
is a multidimensional phenomenon, however, and different profiles
of motives may characterize achieving individuals, depending on the
particular arena in which the individuals express them.

To explore these possibilities, we administered the WOFO to several groups of specially selected individuals. Data obtained from three
such groups are shown in Table 1-3. These groups consisted of male
varsity athletes (many of them football players) and female varsity
athletes (representing a variety of sports) from a large state university

whose teams were nationally ranked; male and female businesspersons, all graduates of a master's program in business administration who had been out of school ten years or less; and groups of male and female Ph.D. psychologists with academic appointments. For purposes of comparison, the data from the sample of male and female college students, described earlier, are also included in the table.

Looking first at the work factor, we see that the mean scores of athletes, businesspersons, and academic psychologists are all higher than the means of same-sex individuals in the unselected sample of college students. The same is true of the mastery factor. On mastery, athletes of both sexes scored lower than businesspeople and academic psychologists—a fact that may reflect the bias of the questions on this scale toward the mastery of intellectual challenges. Within-group comparisons of the sexes indicate that, with two exceptions (businesswomen on work and women psychologists on mastery), females continued to score somewhat higher on work and lower on mastery than did their male counterparts.

In all the groups, males reported themselves to be more competitive than females. Within each sex, athletes scored highest on competitiveness, followed by businesspeople, unselected students, and, lowest of all, academic psychologists. The low degree of competitiveness reported by this sample of psychologists is not unique to this academic discipline; similar results have been obtained from a group of academics drawn from a broad spectrum of the behavioral and physical sciences (Helmreich, Beane, Lucker, and Spence, 1978). These group differences are hardly surprising. In athletics—particularly in varsity athletics of this caliber—winning is the name of the game. The value of competition between business organizations is heavily stressed in our capitalistic system—an attitude that appears to filter down to the level of the individual businessperson. At the other extreme, the academic and scholarly enterprise is not aimed at head-to-head contests. Obviously, some academicians are competitive individuals, even in their professional roles. However, striving to "beat" someone else is not encouraged by the scholarly value system, which honors instead the ideal of the dispassionate pursuit of knowledge.

Contribution of Motives to Attainment

It seems likely that the differences in work, mastery, and competitiveness reported in Table 1-3 between unselected students and members of highly achieving groups reflect the role of achievement motives in promoting successful attainment. We would thus expect that, even within groups having relatively similar abilities and interests, achievement motives are related to level of real-life attainment.

Academic Achievement in College Students   In collaboration with
our students and colleagues, we conducted several studies to determine the relationship between patterns of achievement motives and
actual achievement behavior. In one of these, scores on the work,
mastery, and competitiveness scales were used to predict college students' grades. The WOFO was administered to over 1300 students
enrolled in introductory psychology courses, most of whom were
first- or second-semester freshmen. Two semesters after the one in
which the testing took place, data were obtained about the students'
cumulative grade-point averages (GPA's). This procedure was followed because it seemed likely that a measure of academic performance based on three or more semesters of course work would be
more stable than a measure based on performance in a single course
or during a single semester, particularly one that occurred early in
the students' academic careers. One important consequence of using
this measure is that most of the courses that entered into the students'
GPA's were taken *after* the WOFO was administered; the achievement-
motive scores were thus largely being used to predict *future* academic
performance.

The nature of the relationship between GPA and the WOFO scales
turned out to be interactive. As a device for illustrating the nature of
this interaction, the students of each sex were divided into four groups
on the following basis. Since work and mastery scores were similarly
related to GPA, they were combined to form a single work–mastery
score for each individual. Students of each sex were then divided into
two groups: those scoring above the median composite (those scoring
in the upper 50% of the total group), and those scoring below the
median composite. Each of these groups was then broken down into
those scoring above and below the median (for the total sample) on
competitiveness. Four groups of each sex thus resulted: those above
the median on both work–mastery and competitiveness, those above
on work–mastery and below on competitiveness, those below on work–
mastery and above on competitiveness, and those below on both.
The mean GPA's for the four groups of male and female students are
plotted in Figure 1-1.

In both sexes, relatively low grades were earned by those who
were low (below the median) in both work–mastery and competitiveness—a not-surprising outcome. What was unexpected was the
pattern exhibited by the motive group with the highest GPA's. In both
sexes, these were students high in work–mastery but low in competitiveness. Those high not only in work–mastery but also in competitiveness did not do as well academically; in fact, of the males,
these individuals were the poorest of the four groups.

One of the factors that determines how well an individual does
academically is scholastic ability. It might be claimed that, because

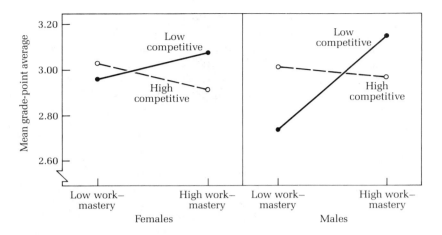

Figure 1-1
Mean grade-point average in the four achievement-motive groups of male and female undergraduates.

able students tend to do better than their less-talented peers, their positive attitudes about working hard and attempting to master challenging materials are reinforced and they have less need to try to prove themselves by competing with others. Motivational differences between students of different degrees of academic success may thus be merely a *consequence* of attainment; the basic *cause* of the obtained performance differences may be ability level or self-concept of ability. In an attempt to evaluate this possibility, we obtained male and female students' scores on the Scholastic Aptitude Test (SAT) and correlated these scores with both GPA's and scores on our achievement scales. As typically occurs, significant correlations of moderate magnitude (r's > .30) were found between GPA and SAT score. However, the correlations between SAT score and our achievement-motives scales were around zero, suggesting that there is very little relationship between achievement motives (as we have defined them) and scholastic aptitude. Second, the relationships we uncovered between constellations of achievement motives and GPA's remained even when analyses were performed in which SAT scores were taken into account. Related evidence was reported by Covington and Omelich (1979). These investigators found that, whereas a measure of achievement motivation was significantly related to students' grades in a particular course, the degree to which the students attributed their examination performance to ability factors was unrelated to grades. Without exhausting alternate possibilities, we cannot conclusively state that differences in students' achievement motives directly bring about differences in academic performance. However, the data we have just presented argue persuasively against the possibility that our findings occurred as an incidental byproduct of a correlation between motivation and academic ability.

It will be recalled that, in addition to the motivational scales, the WOFO contains a number of items describing vocational and educational aspirations. Three of these items relate to what might be considered extrinsic goals: the importance to future satisfaction of having a job or career that pays well, that brings prestige and recognition from others, or that has opportunities for promotion and advancement. Correlations between these items and the achievement-motive scales revealed that, in both sexes, students' work and mastery scores have significant but modest correlations (r's ranging from .15 to .26) with scores on the promotion-and-advancement item. Even lower correlations were found between work–mastery and the rated importance of prestige and recognition, while correlations close to zero appeared between these motive scores and the importance of pay. These results suggest that intensity of work and mastery motivation has little or no relationship with the value students place on the rewards of successful attainment. Even the modest correlations with importance of promotion and advancement may have been brought about more by the desire for jobs with increasing challenge than by the desire for extrinsic rewards. In contrast, highly significant relationships appeared in both sexes between all three of these items and competitiveness. (The r's ranged from .28 to .38 for females and from .41 to .45 for males.)

These latter data raise the question of whether the negative association between competitiveness and academic performance might be mediated by extrinsic factors. Students with strong desires for the tangible rewards that often accompany vocational success might have less intrinsic interest in their course work or approach their undergraduate experience differently from students with less concern about these aspects of their future lives. This possibility was given some credence by the finding that, in both sexes, there was a negative correlation (r's > .20) between GPA and the importance of a well-paying job—the item that most unambiguously tapped an extrinsic goal. However, a regression analysis for males indicated that both the desire for pay and the constellation of achievement motives made independent contributions to GPA, with the effects of the other partialed out. In other words, the interaction between competitiveness and work–mastery in determining grades was not simply a byproduct of the relationship between competitiveness and the pay variable.

For women, on the other hand, the regression analysis indicated that the effects of the motive variable were no longer significant when the pay variable was taken into account. The meaning of this apparent sex difference is at present unclear. Further complicating the interpretation of this general set of findings is the fact that the deleterious effects of competitiveness, particularly when combined with high work–mastery needs, are not confined to the academic situation (as will be seen shortly). Although these data raise more questions than they answer, they do suggest that the implications for performance of strength of extrinsic motives and goals and the interactions of these extrinsic variables with intrinsic achievement motives deserve further exploration.

Academic Achievement in Elementary School Students   The relationship between academic motivation and academic attainment was also explored in the previously mentioned samples of fifth- and sixthgraders (Helmreich, Spence, and Hill, in preparation). Work and mastery were positively related, and competition negatively related, to the children's scores on standardized achievement tests. These relationships could not be explained by IQ. That is, mastery and competitiveness were orthogonal to scores on standardized IQ tests, as was work motivation in the older sample. In the younger sample, however, a significant *negative* relationship was found between IQ score and work. The etiology of the latter relationship in younger children is unknown at present; it is possible that these bright youngsters were insufficiently challenged by their school work to develop strong needs to work hard. Whether this motivational deficit among the bright is transient or permanent poses an important and challenging research question.

Salary in Businessmen   The studies just described indicate that, whereas a high level of mastery and work motives is associated with high academic achievement, interpersonal competitiveness tends to be negatively related to academic attainment. To explore the possibility that the negative impact of competitiveness is not restricted to students' scholastic performance, a very different type of group was studied by one of our students, Deborah Sanders (1978). These were the businessmen whose achievement data are reported in Table 1-3. The sample included too few women to permit further analysis of their data—a fact that reflected the small number of women who had obtained M.B.A.'s from the university whose graduates were surveyed. As we pointed out in commenting on Table 1-3, this sample of businessmen (and businesswomen, for that matter) scored relatively high on the competitiveness scale, seeming to verify the widely held belief that, in order to get ahead in the business world, one must have a strong streak of competitiveness. Perhaps in this group, com-

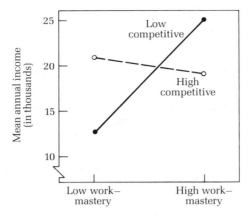

Figure 1-2
Income in the four achievement-motive
groups of businessmen corrected for
years of experience [*Source*: Data from
Sanders, 1978.]

petitiveness as well as work and mastery would contribute positively
to performance.

The measure of attainment was the men's annual salaries, corrected for number of years of postgraduate experience. The salary
data, shown in Figure 1-2, dramatically refute the contention that
competitiveness is vital to a successful business career. While competitiveness was associated with a higher salary in those who were
relatively weak in work–mastery, the high work–mastery groups told
a different story. Among the men who scored high in work–mastery,
those who scored low in competitiveness earned more than their
competitive peers and were the best-paid of all the four groups.

Citations in Academic Scientists   The motive–performance relationship has also been investigated in a group of behavioral and physical scientists, all with Ph.D.'s and holding academic appointments
at a major research university where scholarly publications by faculty
members are both expected and rewarded (Helmreich, Beane, Lucker,
and Spence, 1978). In this instance, the measure of attainment was
number of citations to each individual's published works by other
scientists over a specified period of years, the citation count being
obtained from the Scientific Citation Index. Citations have been widely
used as an objective measure of an individual's scientific influence
and visibility and, inferentially, of the quality of the individual's work

(e.g., Clark, 1967; Cole and Cole, 1973; Garfield, 1977). As a method of showing the interaction between patterns of motives and citations, the scientists were classified into four motive groups on the basis of work–mastery and competitiveness scores, using the same procedures described above in the study of students. The results of this analysis are shown in Figure 1-3. Because of the small number of women in the sample, only the data from male scientists are presented. It will be observed that the results are similar to those obtained with students and businessmen, the highest citations being found in the scientists who were high in work–mastery but low in competitiveness. Particularly when combined with a high degree of work and mastery motivation, competitiveness appeared to deter rather than enhance scientific eminence.

It would be premature to conclude that, in all areas of endeavor, the pattern of achievement motives most likely to be associated with successful performance is a relatively low level of competitiveness combined with a high level of work and mastery strivings. For example, the influence of competitiveness on the performance of professional athletes or world-class amateur athletes, particularly participants in individual sports, cries out for exploration.

Further, the mechanisms by which competitiveness has its deleterious effects are not yet known, and we can only speculate about what they might be. To mention a few possibilities, highly competi-

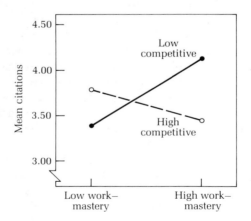

Figure 1-3
Citations to published research in the four achievement-motive groups of male academic scientists. [Source: Data from Helmreich, Beane, Lucker, and Spence, 1978.]

tive individuals may alienate and threaten others who are in a position to assist and support them in their activities. Competitive individuals who are not successful in besting others in a valued activity
may stop trying and turn their energies to other areas (a special kind
of fear of failure). Or they may become so preoccupied with winning
over their rivals—which may take the form of competing with others
for the extrinsic badges of success—that they become distracted from
the task at hand. It is also unknown whether competitiveness has
adverse effects on most individuals or only on a subset of them. Quite
possibly, the competitiveness effect is brought about by different factors in different individuals and settings.

In a second investigation (Helmreich, Spence, Beane, Lucker, and
Matthews, 1980) of scientists, we studied the relationships between
their published work and a number of personality and demographic
variables in addition to achievement motivation. The participants
were male and female psychologists, whose motivational data are
reported in Table 1-3. All had had their doctorates for at least five
years, currently held academic appointments, and specialized in personality–social psychology.

Several types of information were collected about these psychologists. In addition to achievement motivation as measured by the
WOFO, data were collected on instrumentality and expressiveness,
as measured by the Personal Attributes Questionnaire. Information
was also obtained about such demographic variables as marital status, number of children, the reputation of the graduate department
in which the individuals earned their doctorates, and the reputation
of the department in which they currently taught.

Previous investigations have shown that there are differences in
achievement between men and women within various scientific disciplines, including psychology. Of those who enter graduate school,
women are less likely than men to complete their degree requirements (Hirschberg and Itkin, 1978). Among those who are awarded
their doctorates, women are less likely than men to be employed by
prestigious departments and they tend both to publish and to have
their work cited by others less often than men (Cole, 1979; Cole and
Cole, 1973). Many internal and external barriers have been suggested
as inhibiting women's academic achievement. (For a review of these
factors and a summary of the relevant empirical evidence, see O'Connell, Alpert, Richardson, Rotter, Ruble, and Unger, 1978.)[2] One of our

---

[2]One factor that does not appear to be responsible for sex differences in the achievements of Ph.D. scientists is ability. Women admitted to graduate departments have
been shown to have undergraduate grade-point averages similar to men's and to score
at least as well as men on standardized aptitude tests such as the Graduate Record
Examination.

major interests was to determine whether gender differences in productivity and citations would be found even in this relatively homogeneous group of male and female academic psychologists and, if they did occur, to determine whether they could be attributed to several variables that have frequently been mentioned as deterring women's scholarly contributions.

A comparison of the sexes revealed the usual differences in favor of men in both productivity (number of publications) and citations by others—differences that were both highly significant statistically and substantial in size.

Although men and women differed in productivity and in citations, the associations between these measures and other variables were parallel within each sex. The two measures of attainment were substantially correlated, but the relationships between these measures and other variables were not identical, indicating that the citation measure is not a mere byproduct of rate of publication.

As in our previous study of scientists (Figure 1-3), the greatest number of citations in both sexes was found for those high in work–mastery and low in competitiveness. At all but the very low levels of work–mastery, competitiveness suppressed the citation measure, its negative effects becoming more marked as work–mastery increased. Competitiveness had a very different relationship, however, with number of publications. As competitiveness (as well as work–mastery) increased, so did publications. This outcome is a particularly convincing demonstration that the productivity and citiation measures do not tap the same facets of attainment.

A causal model of the factors leading to scientific visibility, as reflected in citations by others, was developed and evaluated by path analysis. Six variables were entered into the model: a composite of the achievement measures, reputation of graduate department, reputation of current department, sex, number of publications, and number of citations.[3] The theoretical model and the obtained path coefficients, indicating the magnitude of the relationships, are shown in Figure 1-4. The figure shows direct paths between all five predictors and the citation measure, i.e., achievement motives (represented by the work–mastery × competitiveness interaction); the reputation

---

[3] The demonstration of a correlation between two variables, we are taught in elementary statistics, gives no indication of whether A "causes" B, whether B "causes" A, or whether both are "caused" by a third factor. One can, however, develop a theoretical model of "what leads to what" and then, by applying the path-analytic technique to a matrix of correlations, test the model and trace the series of causal links or paths among variables and their strengths. The theoretical assumptions underlying the model presented in Figure 1-4 may be found in Helmreich, Spence, Beane, Lucker, and Matthews (1980). The numbers in the figure represent significant standardized path coefficients. Two nonsignificant paths have been omitted.

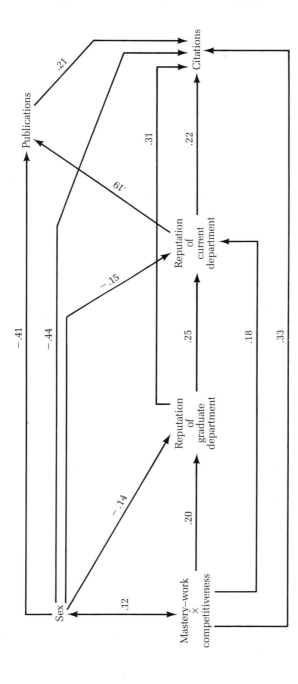

Figure 1-4

A path model of attainment in academic psychologists. Numbers are standardized path coefficients. [Source: Data from Helmreich, Spence, Beane, Lucker, and Matthews, 1980. Copyright © 1980 by the American Psychological Association.]

measures, number of publications, and sex all make independent contributions to number of citations. The only direct links to publications, however, are sex and reputation of current department.

The relationships revealed by the model are not trivial. The R^2 for citations is .62; i.e., 62% of the variability among individuals in citations has been accounted for by the five predictors. (Even when sex is partialed out, R^2 remains high, .50.) In contrast, the R^2 for publications is only .22.

The sources of sex differences in the criterion measures remain elusive. The citation difference could not be accounted for solely by number of publications; when productivity was controlled, women continued to be cited less often than men. We were singularly unsuccessful in identifying the factors that accounted for these differences. Mean scores on the WOFO achievement scales, seen in Table 1-3, revealed slight sex differences that were all in favor of females, including their somewhat lower scores on the competitiveness factor. Similarly, these men and women did not differ on our PAQ measure of instrumental and expressive personality characteristics.

The greater domestic burdens and child-care reponsibilities that married women professionals assume in comparison with their male peers have also been cited as suppressing their scholarly attainments. However, we found no relationships in either sex between marital status and our criterion measures, and only a weak suggestion that number of children influenced a woman's scholarly performance. Finally, the mean reputation rating of the graduate department that awarded the women their degrees was only slightly lower than the mean for men. A larger and highly significant difference in favor of males was found for the ratings of current department, indicating that women were less likely to be employed in prestigious institutions where research is likely to be encouraged and rewarded. However, these differences were traceable largely to the older individuals in the sample. Reflecting changes in societal attitudes and the impact of affirmative-action programs, men and women under the age of 40 were similar in the quality of both their doctoral departments and the departments in which they were employed. However, men's superiority in productivity and visibility could not be attributed solely to these departmental factors. Analyses controlling for differences in the reputation ratings of the doctoral and employing departments continued to show men's greater productivity and number of citations.

Many possible explanations of these sex differences remain to be explored. These range from past and present discrimination against women that may take either overt or subtle forms, to internal factors that differentiate the sexes. For example, as a result of their socialization training, men's feelings of identity and self-worth are often strongly tied to their work roles. Even when young girls are encouraged by their parents or other influential adults to develop career aspirations, they are simultaneously trained to aspire to the "career" of wife and mother. As a result, women may be less single-minded than men about their careers and less likely to make their work the central focus of their lives.

Data relevant to these speculations are found in a study of work, leisure, and achievement motivation conducted by one of our doctoral students, Thomas Runge (1980). A sample of married male and female university faculty and staff completed a questionnaire that included items on overall life satisfaction and satisfaction with work, leisure activities, and close personal relationships (spouse and other family members). Within both groups of men, satisfaction with work was the highest correlate of life satisfaction. The next highest correlate of life satisfaction in both groups was leisure activities, whereas close personal relationships came in a poor third. These data suggest the greater value that men place on their work than on their other roles. For both faculty and staff women, on the other hand, life satisfaction was most highly correlated with satisfaction with personal relationships (r's > .50). For faculty but not staff women, the relationship between life and work satisfaction was a fairly close second. These results suggest that women in demanding careers tend to have heavy investments in both their work and their personal, family relationships; whereas for men, their careers are of singular importance. While the outcome of men's more exclusive dedication to their work may be greater attainment, there may be attendant costs for themselves and their intimates. Whether men's greater single-mindedness is regarded as a virtue or a limitation is, ultimately, a value judgment.

Other Factors Affecting Academic Achievement

Fear of Failure   In the Atkinson expectancy–value model, it will be recalled, resultant achievement motivation or the tendency to approach success is a function of two individual-difference components with opposite signs: the motive to achieve success, which is conceptually parallel to the WOFO achievement-motive factors; and the motive to avoid failure (fear of failure).

One of our students, Peter Gollwitzer, developed an objective measure of fear of failure whose items more closely capture the kinds of themes Heckhausen (1963) specified in his TAT measure of fear of failure and thus might more adequately measure the fear-of-failure concept than do the test-anxiety scales typically used. (Sample items:

"Even when I work my hardest, I worry about being unsuccessful"
and "When I work on a problem, I am often distracted by thoughts
of failure.") Introductory psychology students were given this fear-of-
failure scale, along with three frequently used anxiety scales. Correlations of these measures in each sex with the fear-of-failure scale
ranged from .47 to .74, indicating that the new scale was measuring
similar but not identical properties.

Correlations were next obtained between each of these measures
and the WOFO achievement scales. For the fear-of-failure measure,
small but significantly negative relationships were found in both sexes
with all achievement-motive scores except for competitiveness in
males. This same pattern of results was also found in two additional
samples of students. Even smaller relationships were found between
the WOFO scales and the other anxiety measures, most of the correlations being nonsignificant.

Expectancy–value theory states that the motive to approach success and the motive to avoid failure have opposite effects on the
tendency to approach success ($T_S = M_S - M_{AF}$). This proposition
prompted Gollwitzer to determine whether prediction of students'
grades would be improved if fear-of-failure scores as well as WOFO
scores were taken into account. He therefore obtained the GPA's of
students enrolled in an upper-division course in psychology who
had been given the several personality measures. Our previous findings of an interactive relationship with the WOFO achievement measures were replicated, the highest GPA's being found in those high in
work–mastery but low in competitiveness. Expectancy–value theory
implies that a negative relationship should be found between fear-of-
failure score and GPA. A negative correlation was indeed found, but
it was small and nonsignificant. Finally, a regression analysis was
performed to determine the joint contribution of the WOFO and fear-
of-failure scores to GPA. This analysis, which included terms for the
achievement scores (work–mastery × competitiveness), fear-of-failure scores, and the interaction between the achievement and fear-of-
failure measures, indicated a significant effect only for the WOFO
achievement scales. In short, including fear-of-failure scores did not
improve prediction.

These results do not imply that individual differences in fear of
failure or evaluation anxiety have no effects on performance. They
do cast doubt, however, on the specific proposition that fear of failure
acts to lower the individual's overall level of achievement motivation,
as specified by Atkinson's original theory.

It is possible, of course, that fear of failure could have the simple
subtractive role assigned to it by expectancy–value theory if other
types of behavioral measures were employed, such as choice of task

difficulty. It is difficult to evaluate this aspect of expectancy–value theory even on its own terms, since investigators working within this tradition have not usually examined the independent effects of the two personality measures. Typically, predictions from the theory have been tested by obtaining a difference score for each individual and relating only these difference scores to the criterion variable.

Future Orientation   In addition to the individual difference variables, M_S and M_{AF}, expectancy–value theory specifies two other major variables as determinants of resultant achievement motivation: probability of success (P_S), and incentive value of success (I_S). According to our theoretical perspective, one of the factors that determine the incentive value of success is the inherent interest that an achievement-related activity has for an individual. Tasks that an individual finds attractive or challenging activate achievement-oriented behavior by engaging the individual's achievement motives, and successful performance on such tasks is likely to be particularly satisfying.

As suggested by Raynor (1970), the incentive value of success may also be determined by the degree to which successful accomplishment in a particular setting is perceived as instrumental in reaching future goals. It might be noted parenthetically that instrumental activities often have many features in common with the activities associated with the future goal, so that perceived instrumentality and the inherent interest value of a current activity may be related.

Following Raynor's lead, we have recently begun to explore the contribution of perceived instrumentality to college students' academic performance. An indirect measure of instrumentality can be found in an item on the second part of the WOFO (which inqures about various vocational, educational, and marital aspirations), namely, the minimum amount of education that would satisfy the respondent: some college, completion of college degree, or postgraduate study. It seems reasonable to assume that doing well academically would be perceived as more instrumentally important by those who plan to graduate from college and, even more, by those who aspire to go on to graduate or professional school than by students who would be content not to complete their undergraduate degrees.

Responses to this item by the more than 1300 introductory psychology students whose achievement-motivation and GPA data were reported earlier revealed that, in both sexes, students' educational aspirations were unrelated to their Scholastic Aptitude Test scores (which students submitted as part of their admissions applications). However, even in the absence of measurable differences in scholastic aptitude, students of both sexes who aspired to postgraduate training earned significantly ($p > .001$) higher grades than did those with lower aspirations, thus confirming the general implications of Raynor's (1970) hypothesis about the role of instrumentality. Educational aspirations also showed small but significant positive correlations with the achievement-motive measures, the largest being with mastery (r's of .24 and .25 for males and females, respectively).

A regression analysis of student grades (GPA) was also performed for each sex that took educational aspirations, WOFO achievement motive scores, and SAT scores into account. Inclusion of the educational-aspiration measure significantly increased R^2 (variance accounted for) from .28 to .32. However, the constellation of achievement motives (mastery–work × competitiveness) was more predictive of GPA than was educational aspiration.

Finally, it will be recalled that Raynor (1970) found some support for his hypothesis that perceived instrumentality of grades would lead to poorer performance in those with a low motive to achieve. Our regression analyses, however, did not confirm this aspect of Raynor's theory. That is, achievement motives were positively related to GPA at all levels of educational aspiration and, conversely, educational aspirations were positively related to GPA at all levels of achievement motives.

We will mention only briefly the results of a study (Carsrud, Dodd, Helmreich, and Spence, 1982) in which (among other things)[4] introductory psychology students were asked to rate the importance of grades to their future goals—a measure of instrumentality similar to Raynor's. This measure turned out to be unrelated to course performance—an outcome that can be attributed to the extreme skewness in the instrumentality measure. Perhaps in response to the greater concern of contemporary college-age youths with their economic futures than of students tested a decade ago, those in the Carsrud et al. study overwhelmingly rated grades as very important.

ACHIEVEMENT MOTIVES IN NONSCHOOL AND NONJOB ACTIVITIES

In our introductory remarks, we noted that research on intrinsic achievement motives has been directed almost exclusively toward increasing our understanding of performance in academic and voca-

---

[4] A major purpose of the Carsrud et al. study was to determine the effects of causal attributions (to ability, effort, and so forth) of prior course performance on subsequent course performance. Analyses indicated that, when only attributions were considered, attributions were significantly related to later examination grades (r = .21). However, in regression analyses that also included SAT scores, achievement-motive scores, and prior performance, attributions were not significant predictors of subsequent performance, although each of the other measures was.

tional settings. With few exceptions (e.g., Veroff and Feld, 1970), the implications of achievement motivation for other kinds of activities have gone unexplored. This neglect can in large part be attributed to the value that our society places on vocational success and on education as a stepping-stone to it. However, the tacit presumption of some investigators appears to be that achievement motives rarely find expression outside of school and job. This assumption is particularly likely to appear in discussions of women's achievement. Women with strong achievement motives, it is implied, have the option of expressing them directly through their own vocational activities or of satisfying them vicariously through the accomplishments of their husbands or children.

Our conception of achievement motives as general dispositional tendencies implies, on the contrary, that they have broad implications for behavior and are not narrowly constrained to specific outlets. Further, as our definition of achievement behavior (see page 12) makes clear, we hypothesize that people are capable of setting their own performance standards and that they can transform any activity into the object of self-induced achievement strivings.

Indirect evidence in support of these contentions can be found in a study by Bonjean, Moore, and Macken (1977) of members of a national women's organization. Although the purpose of the organization is to provide community service through its local chapters, membership is also considered to be highly prestigious socially. Statistical analyses of members' reasons for participating in the organization revealed several independent clusters. Two of these—the desire to have an impact in solving community problems, and the opportunity to obtain training and experience in leadership skills and related kinds of self-development—quite clearly reflect the need for accomplishment. A third cluster concerns opportunities to be sociable and to develop friendships—the classic pattern of "feminine" motivation, according to the popular stereotype. A fourth cluster refers to extrinsic motives: gaining social prestige, associating with people who can help their husbands' careers, and the like. For the group as a whole, sociability and friendship received the highest importance ratings. However, these motives did not preclude the desire for community impact and the development and exercise of leadership skills. Absolutely, these latter motives were also rated as important by the group as a whole. Further, in a group of women who were part of the organization's governing councils, motives related to self-development had the highest ratings.

More direct evidence that achievement motives are general qualities that may be manifested in various activities is provided by two recent studies employing the WOFO. In the first of these (Nyquist,

Slivkin, Spence, and Helmreich, submitted for publication), married couples (all parents of at least one first- or second-grade child) were asked about the relative responsibility of husband and wife for a number of domestic decisions and routine household tasks. Scores were also available for the husbands and wives on the WOFO achievement-motive scales and the PAQ measure of instrumental and expressive personality traits. For the group as a whole, there was a conventional division of labor, even working wives assuming most of the responsibility for "feminine" tasks and duties, with husbands assuming most of the responsibility for "masculine" tasks. However, the two individual-difference measures accounted for a significant proportion of the variability among couples in a number of areas. Mastery motives, for example, were related to several kinds of decision making and management of the family's financial affairs. When both husband and wife were high in mastery, these responsibilities were likely to be shared equally; but when scores were discrepant, responsibility tended to grativate toward the spouse with the higher mastery orientation.

Additional evidence is found in the investigation by Runge (1980) in which the relationships among leisure, work, and achievement motivation were explored. As part of his survey of male and female faculty members and staff members at several universities, Runge asked respondents about their preferences in leisure-time activities and to indicate their sources of satisfaction in these activities. In all four groups, significant correlations were found between a composite of work and mastery scores and the respondents' participation in leisure activities that demanded demonstration of skill, in the number of additional activities in which they would have liked to develop expertise if they had time, in their preference for leisure activities that demanded hard work, and in their desire to keep busy. Parallel results were found in all four groups for competitiveness. Thus, competitiveness scores were significantly related to number of leisure activities inherently involving interpersonal competition, number of competitive activities in which they would have liked to take part if they had time, and the degree to which respondents indicated that the competitive aspects of these activities provided a source of satisfaction (as opposed to being incidental to them).

Other findings in the Runge study are also worthy of note. When asked about their preferred work environments, respondents who were high in mastery and work motives preferred to be challenged and kept busy in their jobs; whereas those high in competitiveness enjoyed aspects of their jobs that allowed them to compete with others and liked to look on their work as a contest with others. Some relationship was found between the work and leisure measures, but they were weaker than those with achievement motives. Further, statistical analyses demonstrated that significant correlations between motive scores and leisure preferences remained even when work preferences were held constant and, conversely, between motive scores and work performance when leisure preferences were held constant.

These latter findings have several implications. A number of theories of work suggest that, for men, vocational activities are central to their lives. The nature of men's job-related motives and the degree to which their work satisfies these motives affect other aspects of their lives, such as their choice of leisure-time activities.

The Runge findings suggest that, at least with respect to the WOFO measures, achievement motives independently drive both work and leisure-time preferences. The data further indicate that, although the concepts of general achievement motives have considerable scientific utility, men and women do not necessarily manifest these motives in every activity in which they take part. The specific activities that individuals elect or the activities in which they find it possible to express their achievement motives are dictated by additional external and internal factors that must be independently assessed.

SUMMARY AND DISCUSSION

A multiplicity of historical and contemporaneous factors, some external and some internal to the individual, determine both the particular achievement-oriented activities in which people engage and, in any given activity, the nature of their performance. The primary focus of this chapter is on two types of determinants: intrinsic achievement motives, and extrinsic motives and goals.

The concept of achievement motivation, as formulated by Murray (1938), posits a stable dispositional tendency to strive toward performance excellence—a tendency whose strength varies from one individual to another. As exemplified by the expectancy–value theory of Atkinson and his co-workers, the motive to achieve has traditionally been conceptualized as a unitary dimension. The authors' model traces its lineage to the seminal work of Murray, Atkinson, McClelland, and their colleagues, but conceives of achievement motivation as multifaceted rather than unidimensional. By means of an objective self-report instrument, the Work and Family Orientation Questionnaire (WOFO), we have identified three relatively independent factors: mastery (the preference for challenging tasks and for meeting internal standards of performance), work (the desire to work hard and do a good job), and competitiveness (the enjoyment of interpersonal competition and the desire to do better than others).

Contrary to the implications of early data from the TAT measure of achievement motivation that the concept had utility primarily for men, analyses of data from the WOFO achievement scales suggest that the structure of achievement motives is similar for both sexes. However, in unselected groups, sex differences in the strength of these motives appear, women tending to score higher on work and men higher on mastery and competitiveness. Differences also occur between unselected groups and members of highly achieving groups (e.g., Ph.D. scientists and businesspersons), achieving individuals of both sexes scoring higher on mastery and work than do their same-sex peers. Achieving groups differ, however, in their levels of inter-personal competitiveness.

The implications of individual differences in achievement moti-vation, as measured by the WOFO scales, for scholastic and voca-tional success have been demonstrated in a series of studies involving measures of academic performance in elementary school children and college students, of salary in businesspersons, and of number of citations to published work in scientists. These investigations have revealed an interactive relationship between achievement motives and performance: whereas strength of mastery and work motives is positively associated with quality of performance, competitiveness tends to detract from it, particularly when combined with a high degree of work and mastery.

The universality of this interactive effect of achievement motives— whether it holds for all types of achievement-related behavior or only for some—has yet to be established, and the mechanisms by which interpersonal competitiveness interferes with effective performance have yet to be determined. However, the available data unambigu-ously demonstrate the utility of a multidimensional conception of achievement motivation, as well as the significant contribution of achievement motives to real-life behaviors.

Historically, achievement-motivation research has largely been concerned with predicting behaviors that directly or indirectly have implications for performance in academic and vocational settings. However, the conception of achievement motives as general response tendencies implies that these motives can also be manifested through other activities, many of them of a constructive, socially significant nature. Initial investigations show considerable support for this con-tention.

The second major topic to which this chapter is addressed con-cerns extrinsic motives and goals. The value that our society places on achievement, particularly vocational achievement, is reflected in the system of tangible and intangible rewards that has been designed to recognize successful attainment. In turn, the successful individual is assumed to want and expect these rewards, for both the material benefits and the ego gratification they provide. The degree to which the anticipation of these extrinsic rewards serves to motivate job performance is a matter of continuing debate. Two extreme theories can be identified. One specifies that, for most individuals and jobs, work is drudgery, motivated primarily by the necessity of earning a living and the desire for extrinsic rewards. The other specifies that, when jobs are structured to permit worker autonomy and to encourage a sense of self-worth, work is intrinsically motivated and inherently satisfying, and extrinsic rewards are motivationally ineffective. Most contemporary investigators take an intermediate position between these extremes, proposing that sources of motivation and satisfaction vary according to the characteristics of the individual worker and individual job. Despite this recognition that individuals differ in the degree to which they value extrinsic rewards or are motivated in their job performance by extrinsic considerations, few attempts have been made to measure individual differences in these factors and to determine their significance for vocational choice, worker productivity, job satisfaction, and so forth. In this sense, research on extrinsic motives and goals lags far behind research on intrinsic achievement motivation, which has traditionally been treated as an individual-difference variable.

Psychologists interested in achievement motivation, on the other hand, have failed to consider how extrinsic motives and goals interact with intrinsic motives. Extrinsic rewards are known to have powerful effects on behavior, positively reinforced acts typically increasing in frequency of occurrence. Apparently influenced by such findings, investigators have at least tacitly assumed that extrinsic motives and rewards act in parallel with intrinsic motives; i.e., their relationship is assumed to be essentially additive so that, in order to understand the latter, it is not necessary to take the former into account.

Recent evidence, however, has indicated that the introduction of rewards for performing inherently interesting tasks may undermine intrinsic motivation and/or may lead to poorer rather than better performance. The studies demonstrating these effects have been short-term investigations, most of them conducted in the laboratory. The conditions under which tangible rewards will or will not have deleterious effects, even in these restricted settings, are not yet established. Nonetheless, the available data, as well as common-sense observation, argue compellingly that the interaction between extrinsic motives and intrinsic achievement motivation cannot safely be ignored in future research.

REFERENCES

Adams, J. S. 1965. Inequality in social exchange. In L. Berkowitz (ed.), *Advances in experimental social psychology*. Vol. 2. New York: Academic.

Alper, T. G. 1974. Achievement motivation in college women: A now-you-see-it-now-you-don't phenomenon. *American Psychologist, 29,* 194–203.

Alpert, R., and R. N. Haber. 1960. Anxiety in academic achievement situations. *Journal of Abnormal and Social Psychology, 61,* 207–215.

Argyris, C. 1964. *Integrating the individual and the organization.* New York: Wiley.

Atkinson, J. W. 1957. Motivational determinants of risk-taking behavior. *Psychological Review, 64,* 359–372.

Atkinson, J. W. (ed.). 1958. *Motives in fantasy, action, and society.* Princeton, NJ: Van Nostrand.

Atkinson, J. W. 1966. Motivational determinants of risk-taking behavior. In J. W. Atkinson and N. T. Feather (eds.), *A theory of achievement motivation.* New York: Wiley.

Atkinson, J. W. 1974. The mainspring of achievement oriented activity. In J. W. Atkinson and J. O. Raynor (eds.), *Motivation and achievement.* Washington, DC: Winston.

Atkinson, J. W. 1981. Studying personality in the context of an advanced motivational psychology. *American Psychologist, 36,* 117–128.

Atkinson, J. W., and J. O. Raynor (eds.). 1974. *Motivation and achievement.* Washington, DC: Winston.

Bartol, K. M. 1976. Relationship of sex and professional training area to job orientation. *Journal of Applied Psychology, 61,* 368–370.

Bartol, K. M., and P. J. Manhardt. 1979. Sex differences in job outcome preferences: Trends among newly hired college graduates. *Journal of Applied Psychology, 64,* 477–482.

Bem, D. J. 1967. Self-perception: An alternative interpretation of cognitive dissonance phenomena. *Psychological Review, 74,* 183–200.

Block, J. H. 1973. Conceptions of sex roles: Some cross-cultural and longitudinal perspectives. *American Psychologist, 28,* 512–526.

Block, J. H. 1979. Socialization influences on personality development in males and females. *The master lecture series on psychology,* Tape 15/11. Washington, DC: American Psychological Association.

Boggiano, A. K., and D. N. Ruble. 1979. Competence and the overjustification effect: A developmental study. *Journal of Personality and Social Psychology, 37,* 1462–1468.

Bonjean, C. L., B. M. Moore, and P. O. Macken. 1977. The Association of Junior Leagues: A profile of member attitudes and orientations. Unpublished manuscript.

Brief, A. P., and R. L. Oliver. 1976. Male–female differences in work attitudes among retail sales managers. *Journal of Applied Psychology, 61*, 526–528.

Brief, A. P., G. L. Rose, and R. J. Aldag. 1977. Sex differences in preferences for job attitudes revisited. *Journal of Applied Psychology, 62*, 645–646.

Buckert, U., W. U. Meyer, and H. D. Schmalt. 1979. Effects of difficulty and diagnosticity on choice among tasks in relation to achievement motivation and perceived ability. *Journal of Personality and Social Psychology, 37*, 1172–1178.

Calder, B. J., and B. M. Staw. 1975. Self-perception of intrinsic and extrinsic motivation. *Journal of Personality and Social Psychology, 31*, 599–605.

Canavan-Gumpert, D., K. Garner, and P. Gumpert. 1978. *The success-fearing personality.* Lexington, MA: Heath.

Carsrud, A. L., B. G. Dodd, R. L. Helmreich, and J. T. Spence. 1982. Predicting performance: Effects of scholastic aptitude, achievement motivation, past performance, and attributions. Paper presented at meeting of American Psychological Association, Washington, DC.

Clark, K. E. 1967. *America's psychologists: A survey of a growing profession.* Washington, DC: American Psychological Association.

Cole, J. R. 1979. *Fair science: Women in the scientific community.* New York: Free Press.

Cole, J. R., and S. Cole. 1973. *Social stratification in science.* Chicago: University of Chicago Press.

Condry, J. G., and J. Chambers. 1978. Intrinsic motivation and the process of learning. In M. R. Lepper and D. Greene (eds.), *The hidden costs of rewards: New perspectives on the psychology of human motivation.* Hillsdale, NJ: Lawrence Erlbaum.

Condry, J., and S. Dyer. 1976. Fear of success: Attribution of cause to the victim. *Journal of Social Issues, 33*, 63–83.

Covington, M. O., and C. L. Omelich. 1979. Are causal attributions causal? A path analysis of the cognitive model of achievement motivation. *Journal of Personality and Social Psychology, 37*, 1487–1504.

Crandall, V. C. 1969. Sex differences in expectancy of intellectual and academic reinforcement. In C. P. Smith (ed.), *Achievement-related motives in children.* New York: Russell Sage.

Crockett, H. J., Jr. 1962. The achievement motive and differential occupational mobility in the United States. *American Sociological Review, 27*, 191–204.

deCharms, R. 1968. *Personal casuation: The internal affective determinants of behavior.* New York: Academic.

Deci, E. L. 1971. Effects of externally mediated rewards on intrinsic motivation. *Journal of Personality and Social Psychology, 18*, 105–115.

Deci, E. L. 1972. Intrinsic motivation, extrinsic motivation, and inequity. *Journal of Personality and Social Psychology, 22*, 113–120.

Deci, E. L. 1975. *Intrinsic motivation*. New York: Plenum.

Deci, E. L. 1980. *The psychology of self-determination*. Lexington, MA: Lexington Books.

Deci, E. L., W. Cascio, and J. Krusell. 1975. Cognitive evaluation theory and some comments on the Calder and Staw critique. *Journal of Personality and Social Psychology, 31*, 81–85.

Deci, E. L., and J. Porac. 1978. Cognitive evaluation theory and the study of human motivation. In M. R. Lepper and D. Greene (eds.), *The hidden costs of rewards: New perspectives on the psychology of human motivation*. Hillsdale, NJ: Lawrence Erlbaum.

Dunnette, M. D., J. P. Campbell, and M. D. Hakel. 1967. Factors contributing to job satisfaction and job dissatisfaction in six occupational groups. *Organizational Behavior and Human Performance, 2*, 143–174.

Enzel, M. E., and J. Ross. 1978. Increasing and decreasing intrinsic interest with contingent rewards: A test of cognitive evaluation theory. *Journal of Experimental Social Psychology, 14*, 588–597.

Festinger, L. 1954. A theory of social comparison processes. *Human Relations, 7*, 117–140.

Foushee, H. C., R. Helmreich, and J. T. Spence. 1979. Implicit theories of masculinity and femininity: Dualistic or bipolar? *Psychology of Women Quarterly, 3*, 259–269.

Garbarino, J. 1975. The impact of anticipated rewards on cross-age tutoring. *Journal of Personality and Social Psychology, 32*, 421–428.

Garfield, E. 1977. The 250 most cited primary authors, 1961–1975. Part II: The correlation between citedness, Nobel prizes and academy memberships. *Current Contents, 9*, 5–15.

Hackman, J. R., and E. E. Lawler, III. 1971. Employee reactions to job characteristics. *Journal of Applied Psychology, 55*, 259–286.

Harackiewicz, J. M. 1979. The effects of reward contingency and performance feedback on intrinsic motivation. *Journal of Personality and Social Psychology, 37*, 1352–1363.

Heckhausen, H. 1963. *Hoffnung und Furcht in der Leistungsmotivation*. Meisenheim I Glon: Horn.

Helmreich, R. L., W. E. Beane, G. W. Lucker, and J. T. Spence. 1978. Achievement motivation and scientific attainment. *Personality and Social Psychology Bulletin, 4*, 222–226.

Helmreich, R. L., and J. T. Spence. 1978. The Work and Family Orientation Questionnaire: An objective instrument to assess components of achievement motivation and attitudes toward family and career. *JSAS Catalog of Selected Documents in Psychology, 8*, 35.

Helmreich, R. L., J. T. Spence, W. E. Beane, G. W. Lucker, and K. A. Matthews. 1980. Making it in academic psychology: Demographic and personality correlates of attainment. *Journal of Personality and Social Psychology, 39*, 896–908.

Helmreich, R. L., J. T. Spence, and C. Hill. In preparation. Children's achievement motives: Relationships with measures of academic achievement.

Herzberg, F. 1966. *Work and the nature of man*. Cleveland: World.

Herzberg, F., B. Mausner, and B. B. Snyderman. 1959. *The motivation to work*, 2nd ed. New York: Wiley.

Hirschberg, N., and S. Itkin. 1978. Graduate student success in psychology. *American Psychologist, 33*, 1083–1093.

Hoffman, L. W. 1974. Fear of success in males and females: 1965 and 1972. *Journal of Consulting and Clinical Psychology, 42*, 353–358.

Horner, M. 1968. Sex differences in achievement motivation and performance in competitive and non-competitive situations. Unpublished doctoral dissertation, University of Michigan.

House, R. J., and L. A. Wigdor. 1967. Herzberg's dual-factor theory of job satisfaction and motivation: A review of the evidence and a criticism. *Personnel Psychology, 20*, 369–389.

Hulin, C. L., and M. R. Blood. 1968. Job enlargement, individual differences, and worker responses. *Psychological Bulletin, 69*, 41–45.

Jackson, D. N., S. A. Ahmed, and N. A. Heapy. 1976. Is achievement motivation a unitary construct? *Journal of Research in Personality, 10*, 1–21.

Jurgensen, C. E. 1978. Job preference (What makes a job good or bad?). *Journal of Applied Psychology, 63*, 267–276.

Kanungo, R. N. 1979. The concepts of alienation and involvement revisited. *Psychological Bulletin, 86*, 119–138.

Kazdin, A. E., and R. R. Bootzin. 1972. The token economy: An evaluative review. *Journal of Applied Behavior Analysis, 5*, 343–372.

Kelley, H. H. 1967. Attribution theory in social psychology. In D. Levine (ed.), *Nebraska symposium on motivation*. Vol. 15. Lincoln: University of Nebraska Press.

Kornhauser, A. 1965. *Mental health of the industrial worker: A Detroit study*. New York: Wiley.

Kruglanski, A. W. 1975. The endogenous–exogenous partition in attribution theory. *Psychological Review, 82*, 387–406.

Lawler, E. E., III. 1973. *Motivation in work organizations*. Belmont, CA: Wadsworth.

Lawler, E. E., III, and D. T. Hall. 1970. Relationship of job characteristics to job involvement, satisfaction, and intrinsic motivation. *Journal of Applied Psychology, 54*, 305–312.

Lepper, M. R., and D. Greene. 1976. On understanding "overjustification": A reply to Reiss and Sushinsky. *Journal of Personality and Social Psychology, 33*, 25–35.

Lepper, M. R., and D. Greene. 1978. Overjustification research and beyond: Towards a means–ends analysis of intrinsic and extrinsic motivation. In M. R. Lepper and D. Greene (eds.), *The hidden costs of rewards: New perspectives on the psychology of human motivation.* Hillsdale, NJ: Lawrence Erlbaum.

Lepper, M. R., D. Greene, and R. E. Nisbett. 1973. Undermining children's intrinsic interest with extrinsic rewards: A test of the "overjustification" hypothesis. *Journal of Personality and Social Psychology, 28,* 129–137.

Lewin, K., T. Dembo, L. Festinger, and P. S. Sears. 1944. Level of aspiration. In J. McV. Hunt (ed.), *Personality and the behavior disorders.* Vol. 1. New York: Ronald.

Loveland, K. K., and J. G. Olley. 1979. The effect of external reward on interest and quality of task performance in children of high and low intrinsic motivation. *Child Development, 50,* 1207–1210.

McClelland, D. C. 1966. Longitudinal trends in the relation of thought to action. *Journal of Consulting Psychology, 30,* 479–483.

McClelland, D. C., J. W. Atkinson, R. A. Clark, and E. L. Lowell. 1953. *The achievement motive.* New York: Appleton-Century-Crofts.

McCullers, J. C. 1978. Issues in learning and motivation. In M. R. Lepper and D. Greene (eds.), *The hidden costs of rewards: New perspectives on the psychology of human motivation.* Hillsdale, NJ: Lawrence Erlbaum.

McGraw, K. O. 1978. The detrimental effects of reward on performance: A literature review and a prediction model. In M. R. Lepper and D. Greene (eds.), *The hidden costs of rewards: New perspectives on the psychology of human motivation.* Hillsdale, NJ: Lawrence Erlbaum.

McGraw, K. O., and J. C. McCullers. 1976. Monetary reward and water-jar task performance: Evidence of a detrimental effect of reward on problem solving. Paper presented at meeting of Southeastern Psychological Association, New Orleans.

McGregor, D. 1960. *The human side of enterprise.* New York: McGraw-Hill.

McLoyd, V. C. 1979. The effects of extrinsic rewards of differential value on high and low intrinsic interest. *Child Development, 50,* 1010–1019.

Malone, C. H. 1960. Fear of failure and unrealistic vocational aspiration. *Journal of Abnormal and Social Psychology, 60,* 253–261.

Mandler, G., and S. B. Sarason. 1952. A study of anxiety and learning. *Journal of Abnormal and Social Psychology, 47,* 166–173.

Manhardt, R. J. 1972. Job orientation of male and female college graduates in business. *Personnel Psychology, 25,* 361–368.

Marx, K. 1844. Economic and philosophical manuscripts. In *Marx–Engels Gesantausgabe.* Vol. 3. Berlin: Marx–Engels Institute, 1932.

Maslow, A. H. 1954. *Motivation and personality.* New York: Harper.

Mehrabian, A. 1968. Male and female scales of tendency to achieve. *Educational and Psychological Measurement, 28,* 493–502.

Miller, L. B., and B. W. Estes. 1961. Monetary reward and motivation in discrimination learning. *Journal of Experimental Psychology, 61,* 501–504.

Monahan, L., M. Kuhn, and P. Shaver. 1974. Intrapsychic versus cultural explanations of the "fear of success" motive. *Journal of Personality and Social Psychology, 29,* 60–64.

Murray, H. A. 1938. *Explorations in personality.* New York: Oxford University Press.

Notz, W. B. 1975. Work motivation and the negative effects of extrinsic rewards: A review with implications for theory and practice. *American Psychologist, 30,* 884–891.

Nyquist, L., K. Slivkin, J. T. Spence, and R. L. Helmreich. Submitted for publication. Division of household tasks as related to the personality characteristics of husbands and wives.

O'Connell, A. N., J. L. Alpert, M. S. Richardson, N. G. Rotter, D. N. Ruble, and R. K. Unger. 1978. Gender-specific barriers to research in psychology. *JSAS Catalog of Selected Documents in Psychology, 8,* 80.

Oldham, G. R., J. R. Hackman, and J. L. Pearce. 1976. Conditions under which employees respond positively to enriched work. *Journal of Applied Psychology, 61,* 395–403.

Raynor, J. O. 1969. Future orientation and motivation of immediate activity. *Psychological Review, 76,* 606–610.

Raynor, J. O. 1970. Relationships between achievement-related motives, future orientation, and academic performance. *Journal of Personality and Social Psychology, 15,* 28–33.

Reiss, S., and L. W. Sushinsky. 1975. Overjustification, competing responses, and the acquisition of intrinsic interest. *Journal of Personality and Social Psychology, 31,* 1116–1125.

Runge, T. E. 1980. Work, leisure, and personality: A multivariate approach to life-satisfaction. Doctoral dissertation, University of Texas at Austin.

Sadd, S., M. Lenauer, P. Shaver, and N. Dunivant. 1978. Objective measurement of fear of success and fear of failure: A factor analytic approach. *Journal of Consulting and Clinical Psychology, 46,* 405–416.

Sanders, D. 1978. The relationship of attitude variables and explanations of perceived and actual career attainment in male and female businesspersons. Unpublished doctoral dissertation, University of Texas at Austin.

Schrank, H. T., and J. W. Riley, Jr. 1976. Women in work organizations. In J. M. Kreps (ed.), *Women and the American economy: A look to the 1980's.* Englewood Cliffs, NJ: Prentice-Hall.

Schuler, R. S. 1975. Sex, organizational level, and outcome importance: Where the differences are. *Personnel Psychology, 28,* 365–376.

Smith, C. P. (ed.). 1969. *Achievement-related motives in children.* New York: Russell Sage.

Smith, M. B. 1968. Competence and socialization. In J. A. Clausen (ed.), *Socialization and society.* Boston: Little, Brown.

Spence, J. T. 1970. The distracting effect of material reinforcers in the discrimination learning of lower- and middle-class children. *Child Development, 41,* 103–111.

Spence, J. T. 1971. Do material rewards enhance the performance of lower-class children? *Child Development, 42,* 1461–1470.

Spence, J. T. 1974. The Thematic Apperception Test and attitudes toward achievement in women: A new look at the motive to avoid success and a new method of measurement. *Journal of Consulting and Clinical Psychology, 42,* 427–437.

Spence, J. T., and R. L. Helmreich. 1978. *Masculinity and femininity: Their psychological dimensions, correlates and antecedents.* Austin: University of Texas Press.

Spence, J. T., and R. L. Helmreich. 1979. Comparison of masculine and feminine personality attributes and sex-role attitudes across age groups. *Developmental Psychology, 15,* 583–584.

Staw, B. M., B. J. Calder, and R. Hess. 1974. Situational norms and the effect of extrinsic rewards on intrinsic motivation. Unpublished manuscript, University of Illinois.

Stein, A. H., and M. M. Bailey. 1973. The socialization of achievement orientation in females. *Psychological Bulletin, 80,* 345–366.

Tresemer, D. *Fear of success.* New York: Plenum.

Trope, Y. 1975. Seeking information about one's own ability as a determinant of choice among tasks. *Journal of Personality and Social Psychology, 32,* 1004–1013.

Veroff, J., and S. C. Feld. 1970. *Marriage and work in America.* New York: Van Nostrand Reinhold.

Veroff, J., L. McClelland, and D. Ruhland. 1975. Varieties of achievement motivation. In M. T. S. Mednick, S. S. Tangri, and L. W. Hoffman (eds.), *Women and achievement: Social and motivational analyses.* Washington, DC: Hemisphere.

Vroom, V. H. 1964. *Work and motivation.* New York: Wiley.

Weiner, B. 1972. *Theories of motivation: From mechanism to cognition.* Chicago: Markham.

Weinstein, M. 1969. Achievement motivation and risk preference. *Journal of Personality and Social Psychology, 13,* 153–173.

White, R. W. 1959. Motivation reconsidered: The concept of competence. *Psychological Review, 66,* 297–333.

Zuckerman, M., and L. Wheeler. 1975. To dispel fantasies about the fantasy-based measure of fear of success. *Psychological Bulletin, 82,* 932–946.

2

Expectancies, Values, and Academic Behaviors

Jacquelynne Eccles (Parsons)

University of Michigan

With the assistance of Terry F. Adler, Robert Futterman, Susan B. Goff, Caroline M. Kaczala, Judith L. Meece, and Carol Midgley

EDITOR'S OVERVIEW

The beliefs that men and women ought to be accorded equal educational and vocational opportunities and that it is acceptable even for married women with children to work have gained increasing acceptance over the past decade. Despite these attitudinal changes and the substantial percentage of women who have paid employment, the labor force continues to exhibit marked segregation by sex. Prestigious, well-paying positions tend to be male-dominated, whereas female-dominated jobs tend to be relatively low in prestige and pay. These discrepancies in the vocational attainments of men and women and the factors that determine them have become a matter of social concern.

The proportion of women who enter careers in science, engineering, and related professions is particularly low. One contributory factor is insufficient training in mathematics. Although the genders perform equally well in mathematics during their grade-school years, females are less likely than males to elect courses in mathematics in high school and college. This, in turn, limits women's access to a variety of jobs that require a strong background in the subject matter.

In this chapter, Jacquelynne Eccles (Parsons) and her associates report the results of a cross-sectional and longitudinal study of students in the fifth through twelfth grades, their parents, and their teachers. The major purpose of the study was to discover the factors that contribute to these sex differences in math achievement. On a more theoretical level, the study was designed to test the investigators' general model of achievement behavior. This model, which is most directly influenced by theories in which the constructs of expectancy and value are prominent, focuses on the role of cognitive rather than motivational factors in determining achievement behaviors.

The model has two components: the first is a psychological component in which the interactions of various cognitive factors at one point in time are specified; the second is a developmental component. In the first component, the most immediate precursors of such performance variables as task choice and persistence are individuals' expectancies or subjective probabilities of success and the value they place on successful attainment. These expectancies and values, as they relate to children's school performance, are determined by such variables as the individuals' goals and self-concepts, their perceptions of parents' and teachers' expectations, their interpretations of the reasons for their past performance (e.g., their attribution of past success or failure to their own ability or lack thereof), and their perception of the difficulty of the task. The developmental component specifies the origins of individual differences in these psychological factors.

Past research has indicated that females are less likely than males to attribute their past successes to their ability and to have somewhat lower expectancy for future success, particularly on new tasks. The investigators' model thus has obvious implications for sex differences in math attainment. The model also incorporates sex differences in the value that males and females place on training in mathematics, females being hypothesized to perceive math as less important to their future plans than do males and as being a "masculine" activity and thus noncongruent with feminine roles.

Using path analyses and cross-lagged panel analyses as their statistical techniques, the investigators tested the interrelationships among the cognitive factors specified in their model and the contribution of these psychological variables to a measure with implications for actual achievement behavior: the students' intention to take additional math courses. These analyses confirmed the importance of children's self-concepts of ability, attributions for past performance, and perceptions of the beliefs of parents and teachers as determinants of expectancies, values, and course plans. Relatively few sex differences were found, but those that did appear confirmed the results of past investigations: females, in comparison with males, had lower confidence in their ability and perceived math as more difficult and less valuable. Such sex differences appeared to be related to parents' beliefs in the difficulty of math for their child.

W hy, given equivalent past histories of success and failure in a particular subject area, does one child approach the opportunity to take a new, more advanced course with enthusiasm and confidence, while another child approaches the same opportunity filled with self-doubt and anxiety, and yet another child avoids the opportunity altogether?

Why does one competent student fall apart in the face of failure, while another responds with renewed vigor?

Why do some good students conclude that they are able, while others doubt their abilities?

These questions and others like them have been the focus of my interests over the last decade. My colleagues and I have spent the last several years developing and refining a model for approaching these questions. We set ourselves the task of identifying the critical motivational/attitudinal mediators of achievement behaviors, of proposing causal relations among these beliefs, and of outlining the developmental origins of individual differences in these beliefs. In the spring of 1977, a project proposed by the National Institute of Education (NIE) was brought to our attention. The NIE wanted to fund research on sex differences in advanced mathematics course enrollment. Several reviews of the literature (Fennema, 1977; Fox, 1977; Sherman, 1977) had ruled out an innate ability difference as the primary causal determinant of the discrepancy in participation rates. Consequently, the NIE was particularly interested in studies of what were loosely called "math attitudes." Here was a golden opportunity to test our model of achievement behavior: a genuine achievement behavior (math course taking) showing fairly consistent individual differences that could not be explained by ability differences alone. Females, on the average, do not perform any more poorly in math than do males, and yet they are less likely to enroll in advanced high

The research reported in this chapter was supported by grants from the National Institute of Education (NIE-G-78-0022) and the National Institute of Mental Health (5R01-MH31724-01). We would like to express our appreciation to Richard Newman, Diane Ruble, and Peter Williams for their editorial comments on earlier versions of this chapter and to Toby Jayaratne for editorial comments and assistance on the final version. We are also thankful for the assistance of Kirby Heller for the development and design of observational measures and of Julie Karabenick for the development and design of parent and student questionnaires. We are particularly grateful to Diane Gromala for the preparation of figures. Finally, a note of thanks to Sabrina Flowers, Margaret Lepley, Carol Sionkowski, and Elizabeth Waggy for their typing assistance.

school math courses. Why? Needless to say, we set about translating our model into a field study of the determinants of math course plans and the developmental origins of individual differences in these determinants.

In this chapter, we outline the model and report the results of the study conducted to assess its predictive validity. The model presented in Figure 2-1 has two basic components: one psychological, and one developmental. We tested major portions of both components. In the first portion of the chapter, we discuss the psychological component and present the relevant findings from our study. The developmental component and its empirical test are discussed subsequently. Since the empirical study was conducted in the area of mathematics and since it focused on sex-differentiated achievement behaviors, particular attention is paid in this review to the relevant literature on mathematics achievement and sex differences.

PSYCHOLOGICAL COMPONENT OF ACHIEVEMENT MODEL

The search for an understanding of the motivational/attitudinal determinants of achievement-related behaviors is not new to psychology. Much of the work in the 1950s and 1960s was stimulated by the expectancy–value theory of Atkinson and his colleagues (e.g., Atkinson, 1958). This theory, the central tenets of which are outlined in Chapter 1 of this volume, focuses on individual differences in the motive to achieve and on the effects of subjective expectancy on both this motive and the incentive value of success. Some investigators, using new techniques to measure achievement motives, have continued to explore the implications of motivational mediators for achievement behaviors (e.g., Chapter 1, this volume). Much of the work of the last decade, however, has shifted attention away from motivational constructs to cognitive constructs, such as causal attributions, subjective expectancies, self-concepts of abilities, perceptions of task difficulty, and subjective task value. The theoretical and empirical work presented in this chapter fits into this tradition. Building on the seminal works of John Atkinson, Vaughn and Virginia Crandall, and Bernard Weiner, we have elaborated a model specifying the developmental and causal links among cultural factors, historical events, and one's expectancies, values, and achievement behaviors. We have proposed a detailed conceptualization of the mediators of expectancies and values. A general summary of these mediators and their relation to expectancies, values, and achievement behaviors is depicted in Figure 2-1. The model itself is built on the assumption that it is not reality itself (i.e., past successes or failures) that most

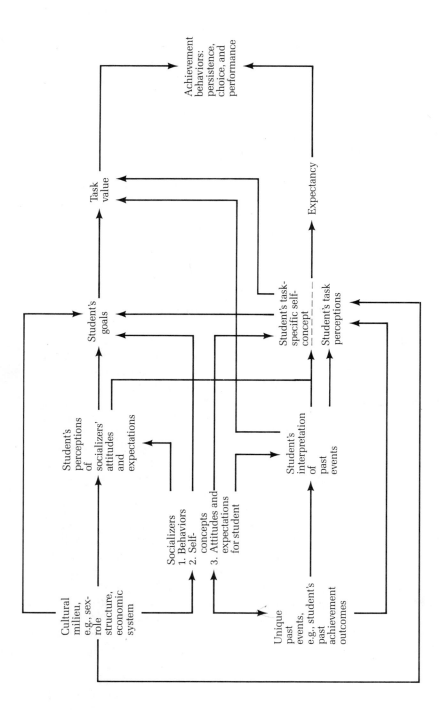

Figure 2-1
General expectancy–value and developmental model of achievement behaviors.

directly determines children's expectancies, values, and behavior, but rather the interpretation of that reality. The influence of reality on achievement outcomes and future goals is assumed to be mediated by causal attributional patterns for success and failure, the input of socializers, perceptions of one's own needs, values, and sex-role identity, as well as perceptions of the characteristics of the task. Each of these factors plays a role in determining the expectancy and value associated with a particular task. Expectancy and value, in turn, influence a whole range of achievement-related behaviors, e.g., choice of the activity, intensity of the effort expended, and actual performance.

In this section of the chapter, the psychological determinants of expectancies and values are discussed. In addition, specific hypotheses growing out of the psychological component of our model are presented, methodological procedures for the test of those hypotheses are outlined, and the findings of a longitudinal/cross-sectional study designed to test these hypotheses are summarized. The origins of expectancies are considered first.

Expectancies

The concept of expectancy or probability of success has long been recognized by decision and achievement theorists as an important variable in determining behavioral choice (Atkinson, 1964; Edwards, 1954; Lewin, 1938). Numerous studies have demonstrated the importance of expectancies for a variety of achievement behaviors including academic performance, task persistence, and task choice (e.g., Covington and Omelich, 1979a; Crandall, 1969; Diggory, 1966; Feather, 1966; Parsons, 1978; Veroff, 1969). Developmental studies indicate that the influence of expectancy on performance increases with age and may emerge earlier and more strongly in males than females (Crandall, 1969; Parsons and Ruble, 1977; Stein, 1971). By adolescence, however, expectancies are clearly related both to general achievement performance (e.g., Stein and Bailey, 1973) and to math achievement and course enrollment in particular (Armstrong and Kahl, 1978; Battle, 1966; Fennema and Sherman, 1978; Pedersen, Elmore, and Bleyer, 1979; Sherman, 1977; Sherman and Fennema, 1977). Not surprisingly, these studies have shown that students are more likely to enroll in advanced mathematics courses when they are confident of their performance.

Inconsistent findings, however, have been reported in studies examining sex differences in achievement expectancies. Laboratory studies, using somewhat novel tasks, generally have found females 8 years and older to have lower initial expectancies than males (Crandall, 1969; Dweck and Bush, 1976; Dweck and Gilliard, 1975; Montanelli and Hill, 1969; Parsons and Ruble, 1977). But when familiar tasks or actual school subjects are used, the findings have been less consistent (e.g., Parsons and Ruble, 1977; Stein, 1971). Inconsistent results have also been found in studies using measures of expectancies for math tests versus expectancies for future math courses (Fox, 1975; Fox, Brody, and Tobin, 1979; Heller, Futterman, Kaczala, Karabenick, and Parsons, 1978; Stein, 1971). Frieze, McHugh, Fisher, and Valle (1978) have interpreted this pattern of results as reflecting the difference between specific expectancies and generalized expectancies. They have argued that females' generalized expectances are lower than males', but that their specific expectancies, like those of males', are largely determined by performance history. Consequently, when males and females participate in a given achievement activity, one can expect their expectancies to be similar. It is generalized expectancies, however, that influence many decisions regarding future achievement behavior and, on these, females have lower expectancies than do males, in spite of similar past histories of achievement.

Since achievement expectancies play a significant role in students' academic choices, it is important to identify the factors shaping these expectancies. We propose that expectancies are influenced most directly by self-concept of ability and by the student's estimate of task difficulty. Historical events, past experiences of success and failure, and cultural factors are proposed to have indirect effects that are mediated through the individual's interpretations of these past events, perceptions of the expectancies of others, and identification with the goals and values of existing cultural role structures. Each of these influences is described briefly below.

Self-Concept of Ability   The importance of individuals' concepts of their abilities for their achievement behaviors has been discussed by several researchers (e.g., Brookover and Erickson, 1975; Covington and Beery, 1976; Covington and Omelich, 1979a, 1979b; Kukla, 1972, 1978; Meyer, Folkes, and Weiner, 1976; Nicholls, 1976; Purkey, 1970). Formed through a process of observing and interpreting one's own behaviors and the behaviors of others, self-concept of ability is defined as the assessment of one's own competency to perform specific tasks or to carry out role-appropriate behaviors. In the view of most authors, self-concepts of ability are key causal determinants of a variety of achievement behaviors.

Research assessing this view has yielded somewhat mixed results. Although several studies have demonstrated that those with higher estimates of their abilities to master a task in fact do better on the task, few have actually tested the causal direction of the relations. In a field study, Calsyn and Kenny (1977) found that academic achievement determines self-concept of ability rather than the reverse. In contrast, intervention procedures designed to raise students' confidence in their abilities in particular subject areas have been shown to induce gains in the students' subsequent achievement behaviors (e.g., deCharms, 1976; Dweck, 1975). These intervention studies suggest that, for some students at least, increases in self-confidence can produce increases in achievement.

Research specific to math achievement has yielded a consistent and positive relation between perception of mathematical ability and plans to enroll in advanced mathematics courses. For example, Kaminski, Erickson, Ross, and Bradfield (1976) and Armstrong and Kahl (1978) have demonstrated that students' ratings of their mathematical abilities predict the amount of math they plan to take in high school.

Furthermore, when sex differences emerge in measures of self-concept of math ability, females report lower estimates of their abilities than do males. These differences do not emerge with any consistency prior to junior high school but are frequently found at and beyond junior high, despite the fact that, during elementary school and junior high school, females perform just as well as males in math (e.g., Ernest, 1976; Fennema, 1974; Fennema and Sherman, 1977; Fox, 1975; Heller, Futterman, Kaczala, Karabenick, and Parsons, 1978; Kaminski, Erickson, Ross, and Bradfield, 1976).

While these studies indicate that self-concept of ability is related to such achievement behaviors as course plans and actual performance, its causal significance in explaining various forms of achievement behaviors is not clear. The one study that attempted to address this issue using path-analytic techniques found self-concept of ability to have only a small direct effect on course enrollment plans (Kaminski et al., 1976). Similarly, the causal role of self-concept in accounting for the sex differences in expectancies has received little direct attention. While adolescent females appear to have lower estimates of their math abilities than do adolescent males, the causal relation of this difference to sex differences in either expectancies, course plans, or actual course enrollment has yet to be tested. Researchers are often content to demonstrate a sex difference on a variable that is assumed to be causally related to achievement and then to conclude that the obtained sex difference is the cause of the sex difference in achievement. Such a conclusion is neither logically nor scientifically sound. Through the use of causal modeling procedures, we assessed the causal direction of the relation between confidence in ability and course plans. The results are summarized in a later section.

Perception of Task Difficulty   Intuitively, it seems that expectancies for success should be inversely related to perceived task difficulty. While little research has addressed this prediction directly, there is ample evidence that task choice in experimental settings is related to perceived task difficulty (e.g., Atkinson and Birch, 1970; Meyer, Folkes, and Weiner, 1976; Stallings and Robertson, 1979; Weiner, 1972, 1974). However, the relation between these two variables is not straightforward. In some situations and for some individuals, there is a curvilinear relationship between increasing task difficulty and the likelihood of both choice and persistence (Atkinson, 1958, 1964; Kukla, 1978; Meyer, Folkes, and Weiner, 1976; Weiner, 1972). Other investigators have suggested that these results may be generalizable to only a limited range of activities, namely, those that might be considered recreational or of limited long-range importance. For inherently difficult tasks with important future implications, such as school achievement, perceived task difficulty should be negatively related to enrollment plans. That is, the harder one judges a course to be, the less likely one will be to enroll in that course. The discrepancy between these two points of view may be a consequence of the variations in perceived difficulty levels of naturally occurring versus simulated achievement tasks. Most nontrivial, naturally occurring achievement tasks are probably perceived to be at the difficult end of the probability-of-success curve, while laboratory-simulated achievement tasks can be designed to span the full range of perceived difficulty. Furthermore, the very definition of success may differ markedly between these two domains, making comparison of results difficult. Raynor (1974) has made a similar point, suggesting that the discrepancy between these two viewpoints may be a function of how finely one divides up the sequence of events in naturally occurring achievement tasks. Nonetheless, we are left with two competing hypotheses regarding the nature of the relation between perceived task difficulty and naturally occurring achievement behaviors.

The few studies testing these predictions with regard to math in particular have not shed much light on this debate and have, in fact, yielded conflicting results. For example, a cross-cultural study of math achievement (Husen, 1967) did not find any relation between perceived task difficulty and math achievement. Stallings and Robertson (1979), in contrast, found perceived difficulty to be the most important variable in discriminating between females who planned to continue in math and those not planning to continue.

Few studies have tested for sex differences in perceived task difficulty. In our own studies, adolescent females rated future courses in mathematics as more difficult than did males (Heller, Futterman, Kaczala, Karabenick, and Parsons, 1978), suggesting that females' perceptions of task difficulty might work in conjunction with their lower self-concepts of math ability to lower their expectancies for success in future courses and to decrease the likelihood of their enrolling in advanced math courses. While there has been very little research directly testing this hypothesis, there are data suggesting that females more frequently than males select tasks that have been designated as easy by the experimenter (e.g., Crandall, 1969; Stein and Bailey, 1973; Veroff, 1969). Perhaps these results reflect a difference between males and females in their subjective assessments of task difficulty, coupled with a difference in their subjective assessments of their abilities. In support of this suggestion, females have been found to rate objectively similar tasks as more difficult than males (Foersterling, 1980). Consequently, females may actually be selecting tasks for themselves that they judge to be more difficult than the tasks the males are selecting for themselves.

The evidence reviewed is not especially encouraging for investigators hoping to predict achievement expectancies, plans, or other achievement behaviors exclusively from students' perceptions of the difficulty of the task. Findings from the few existing studies suggest that the effects of this variable are consistent but small. Of the two major mediators of expectancies discussed thus far, self-concept of ability appears to be the more critical construct. Perceptions of task difficulty, however, may influence self-concept of ability such that, over time, students who see a subject or task as more difficult develop lower estimates of their own abilities for that subject or task. For this reason, perceived task difficulty is included in our model of achievement behaviors as an important mediator of achievement expectancies, and its impact on math course plans and expectancies for success was assessed in our study.

Perception of Others' Expectations   The achievement literature has documented the importance of parents' and teachers' expectations and attitudes in shaping students' self-concepts and general expectancies of success (Brookover and Erickson, 1975; Brophy and Good, 1974; Parsons, Frieze, and Ruble, 1976; Rosenthal and Rosnow, 1969; Webster and Sobicozek, 1974). Studies investigating this relationship have yielded consistent results. Students for whom teachers and parents have high expectations also have high expectations for themselves and in fact do better in their course work. It seems only reasonable that this effect is mediated, in part, by students' perceptions of their parents' and teachers' expectations. In support of this suggestion, Poffenberger and Norton (1959) and Kaminski, Erickson, Ross, and Bradfield (1976) have found a significant positive relation between perceived parental evaluations and students' self-concepts and perceptions of task ease. However, the causal direction of this relation is unclear. While it is commonly assumed that the perceptions of the expectancies of others influence a student's self-concept of ability,

Calsyn and Kenny (1977) have found the reverse relationship to be stronger. Our study provides an additional test of the causal direction of this relationship.

Few studies have tested for sex differences in perceived parental expectations for achievement in mathematics. In general, when sex differences are evident, female students perceive their parents as having lower estimates of the females' math abilities than do male students (Fennema and Sherman, 1977; Fox, 1975; Kaminski et al., 1976). These differential perceptions of parental expectancies have been found to be related to students' intentions to take advanced mathematics courses. The relation of these perceptions to sex differences in expectancies has not been tested.

Perhaps the critical variable is the perception and internalization of the cultural stereotype of general female incompetence, rather than (or in addition to) the perceptions of the expectations of specific individuals. Several studies have documented the fact that women are viewed as less competent and are expected to do less well than men on a variety of different tasks (Broverman, Vogel, Broverman, Clarkson, and Rosenkrantz, 1972; Deaux and Emswiller, 1974; Feldman-Summers and Kiesler, 1974). Acceptance of these cultural stereotypes may be reponsible for females' lower expectancies.

Causal Attributions   Attribution theorists have suggested another set of variables as important mediators of individual differences in expectancies and perceptions of both one's ability and the difficulty of the task (Frieze, Fisher, Hanusa, McHugh, and Valle, 1978; Heider, 1958; Weiner, 1974). According to these theorists, it is not success or failure per se, but the causal attributions made for either of these outcomes that influence future expectancies. For example, if people attribute success to a stable factor such as ability, then they should expect continued success. If, on the other hand, they attribute success to an unstable factor such as effort or good luck, they should be uncertain about future outcomes. Similarly, attributing failure to stable factors should produce expectations of continued failure, while attributing failure to unstable factors should not. Consequently, individuals who attribute their success to an unstable factor such as task ease and their failure to a stable factor such as lack of ability should have lower expectancies than do individuals exhibiting the reverse attributional pattern, even if their performance histories have been identical.

Several studies have provided indirect support for these general hypotheses (e.g., Dweck, 1975; Dweck and Reppucci, 1973; Jackaway, 1974). The causal nature of these relations, however, has come under recent scrutiny (Covington and Omelich, 1979a, 1979b). Using path-analytic techniques, Covington and Omelich (1979a) tested the hypothesis that attributions for a failure experience on a college test mediate individual variations on both expectancies and retest performance. In comparing the effects of need-achievement motivation and attributions on subsequent expectancies and performances, they found that attributions added little predictive power and did not mediate the influence of need achievement on either expectancy or performance. Based on their findings, Covington and Omelich proposed that expectancy shifts are caused by students' initial self-concept of ability rather than by their causal attributions.

While in basic agreement with Covington and Omelich's conclusion regarding the importance of one's self-concept of ability, we maintain that attributions have a causal role in achievement expectancies. Extending the argument originally advanced by Weiner, Frieze, Kukla, Reed, Rest, and Rosenbaum (1971) into a developmental time frame, we hypothesize that attributions play a critical role in the formation of one's self-concept of ability and one's perceptions of task difficulty when confronted with novel tasks. Once individuals have formed a stable self-concept of ability at any particular task, however, attributions may well become an epiphenomenon rather than a causal influence on subsequent expectations and performance. In line with this developmental view, Kukla (1978) has suggested that it is primarily attributions to ability that influence subsequent achievement behavior. One could argue that the ability attribution plays a critical role during the period when an individual's self-concept of ability is forming. Once the self-concept has formed, however, attributions to ability may simply mirror one's self-concept.

Unfortunately, few studies have assessed this hypothesis. In a study in our laboratory, we compared the influence of attributions on expectancies for a familiar task (performance in one's current math course) with their influence for a novel task (an experimental task involving number sequences). Consistent with the findings of Covington and Omelich (1979a), we found that attributions were related minimally to expectations for performance in math class. In contrast, however, variations in the students' attributions of their math failures to lack of ability were critical mediators of their responses to the experimentally induced failure on the number-sequence task (Parsons, 1980). While only in its initial stages, this research provides encouraging support for our predictions.

Given our concern with sex-differentiated academic choices, examination of the studies assessing attributional differences between males and females is also in order. To the extent that males and females differ in their attributional patterns, females are more likely to exhibit low expectancy patterns, and in some studies their achievement behaviors are affected accordingly (e.g., Crandall, Katkovsky, and Crandall, 1965; Dweck, 1975; Dweck and Reppucci, 1973; Feather and Simon, 1973; Jackaway, 1974; McMahan, 1973; Nicholls, 1975). The pattern of results, however, is not as consistent as one might expect, given reviews of the field (e.g., Bar-tal, 1978; Dweck and Goetz, 1978; Parsons, Ruble, Hodges, and Small, 1976). For example, while some studies have reported that females attribute their failures more to lack of ability than do males (e.g., Dornbusch, 1974; Fennema, 1981; Nicholls, 1975; Parsons, 1980, 1981), other studies either have not found or have not reported sex differences (e.g., Beck, 1977–1978; Diener and Dweck, 1978; Dweck, Davidson, Nelson, and Enna, 1978; Dweck and Reppucci, 1973; Parsons, 1980). Still other studies have found that the nature of the sex differences varies depending on a variety of related variables such as the student's achievement level (Fennema, 1981), the point in the task at which the attribution is taken (Nicholls, 1975), the wording of the question, and the sex and age of the evaluator (Dweck and Bush, 1976). Thus, whether sex differences in attributions mediate sex differences in achievement behaviors remains an open question.

Locus of Control   Closely related to attribution theory is the work on locus of control. Based on the work of Rotter (1954), Virginia and Vaughn Crandall developed the construct of intellectual-achievement responsibility, arguing that the belief that one is responsible for or in control of achievement outcomes is both important and beneficial. Taking this construct one step further and building on the work of Seligman (1975), Dweck (1975) introduced the concept of academic learned helplessness to describe students who assume that they cannot control their failures. Attributional analysis of these concepts (Dweck and Goetz, 1978) has suggested the similarity of both of these constructs to the high and low attributional pattern analysis discussed earlier. Consequently, no further discussion of these constructs is included here except to note that:

1. Empirical evidence has demonstrated the important mediating role of locus of control and learned helplessness for achievement-related behaviors.

2. Sex differences have not been found consistently on either locus of control or learned helplessness.

3. The mediating role of learned helplessness in accounting for sex differences in achievement has yet to be established (Parsons, 1981).

Task Value

Consistent with the manner in which the causal pathways related to the expectancy component of our model were traced, the proposed causal pathways related to the value of an achievement task for the individual are now traced. In Atkinson's theory (1964), the value that an individual attaches to success or failure on a task is assumed to be a critical determinant of achievement motivation. Atkinson's definition of the concept (reviewed in more detail in Chapter 1, this volume) was narrow and based on objective task characteristics. Other theorists have used a broader, more individualistic concept of task value (Crandall, Katkovsky, and Preston, 1962; Parsons and Goff, 1978, 1980; Raynor, 1974; Spenner and Featherman, 1978). According to these theorists, the value of a task is determined both by the characteristics of the task and by the needs, goals, and values of the person. The degree to which the task is able to fulfill needs, facilitate reaching goals, or affirm personal values determines the value a person attaches to engaging in that task.

Elaborating on this more recent work, we suggest that the overall value of any specific task is a function of three major components: (1) the attainment value of the task, (2) the intrinsic or interest value of the task, and (3) the utility value of the task for future goals. Each of these components is discussed below.

Attainment value is the importance of doing well on the task. In its most basic form, this component coincides with the conceptualization of attainment value advanced by the Crandalls (e.g., Crandall, 1969; Crandall, Katkovsky, and Preston, 1962). In its broader form, it incorporates a variety of dimensions, including perceptions of the task's ability to confirm salient and valued characteristics of the self (e.g., masculinity, femininity, competence), to provide a challenge, and to offer a forum for fulfilling achievement, power, and social needs. The perceived qualities of the task determine its attainment value through their interaction with an individual's needs and self-perceptions. Consider, for example, a student who thinks of herself as "smart" and defines a certain course (e.g., advanced math) as both intellectually challenging and "the" course for "smart" students to take. The attainment value of such a course for this particular student should be high, precisely because doing well in it would affirm a critical component of her self-concept.

Intrinsic or interest value is the inherent, immediate enjoyment one gets from engaging in an activity. *Utility value*, on the other hand, is determined by the importance of the task for some future goal that might itself be somewhat unrelated to the process nature of the task at hand. For example, a high school student may want to be a veterinarian and may need to take a particular course (e.g., math) in order to gain entry into the appropriate graduate training program. Consequently, she may take advanced mathematics classes, even though she has little or no interest in math itself. In this case, the desirability of her career goal and the instrumentality of mathematics in helping her to achieve that goal would outweigh the student's neutral or even negative attitude toward the subject matter. The value of math in this case is high precisely because of its long-range utility.[1] This distinction between the intrinsic-value component and utility-value component coincides most closely to the distinction made between intrinsic and extrinsic motivation (Deci, 1975; Kruglanski, 1975; Lepper and Greene, 1978; Nicholls, 1979), namely, the distinction between "means" versus "ends" motivation. (This distinction is discussed in more detail in Chapter 1, this volume.)

In the literature specifically relevant to mathematics participation, there is some evidence to support the influence of *utility value* on course selection. Several researchers, for example, have reported that students' perceptions of the usefulness of mathematics are strongly related to their intentions to continue or discontinue their mathematical studies (e.g., Armstrong and Kahl, 1978; Brush, 1980; Fennema and Sherman, 1977; Sherman, 1980). Sex differences in students' math achievement values have also been uncovered. Males, as early as seventh and eighth grade, are more likely than females to perceive math as important to future career goals (Dornbusch, 1974; Fennema and Sherman, 1977, 1978; Fox, 1975; Hilton and Berglund, 1974; Wise, Steel, and MacDonald, 1979)—a belief that coincides nicely with reality. Professions demanding math are, in fact, dominated by males and, until recently, few women aspired to participate in them. High school males also place a higher importance on their grades in mathematics than do females (Dornbusch, 1974).

In sum, we are proposing that the value of a particular task to a particular person is a function of both the perceived qualities of the task and the individual's needs, goals, and self-perceptions. Individual differences on these variables are created by differential past experiences with that task or with similar tasks, by social stereotypes (e.g., the perception of math as a male domain), and by differential information from parents, teachers, or peers about the importance of or difficulty involved in doing well. Intuitively, three clusters of var-

---

[1]Raynor's (1974) work on future orientation has provided one example of the incorporation of utility value into the general need-achievement model.

iables seem to be particularly important mediators: (1) sex roles, (2) perceptions of the cost of success, and (3) previous affective experiences with similar tasks. Each of these is discussed below.

Sex-Role Identity and Personal Values   A sizable portion of both the empirical and the theoretical literature related to the processes of socialization has suggested that a variety of needs and values influence the form of an individual's achievement behavior (Hoffman, 1972; Mortimer and Simmons, 1978; Parsons and Goff, 1978, 1980; Spenner and Featherman, 1978; Stein and Bailey, 1973; Veroff, 1969, 1977). The importance of the centrality of values and needs to one's self-definition has been a recurring theme. Personal needs and values, it has been argued, operate in ways that both reduce the probability of engaging in roles that are perceived as inconsistent with these central values (Spenner and Featherman, 1978) and increase the probability of engaging in roles perceived as consistent with one's definition of self (Parsons and Goff, 1980).

One need, in particular, has received a great deal of attention: the need to behave according to a set of social prescriptions for sex-appropriate conduct, or sex-role identity. Proponents of the cognitive-developmental model of sex-role acquisition (e.g., Kohlberg, 1969; Parsons, 1977; Parsons, Frieze, and Ruble, 1976) have suggested that sex roles influence achievement behavior through their impact on perceived task value. Specific tasks are identified as either consistent or inconsistent with one's sex-role identity. The extent to which a task is consistent with one's sex-role identity influences the value of that task. In partial support of this view, several studies have documented the influence of sex labeling of tasks on students' performance and choice (e.g., Liebert, McCall, and Hanratty, 1971; Montemayor, 1974; Sherman, 1979). Studies of adolescent values have suggested that males become more oriented toward achievement in school with age, while females become more concerned with the potential conflict between their academic goals and their social goals (Beech and Schoeppe, 1974; Douvan and Adelson, 1966; Sherman, 1979; Stein and Bailey, 1973). Taken together, these studies have suggested a growing sensitivity to the congruence between anticipated adult sex-related roles and the current task demands that may influence the value of various tasks for the individual and, in turn, influence achievement-related behaviors.

Central to this line of argument is the assumption that sex-role identity and the sex stereotyping of particular achievement activities interact in influencing task value. That is, we are suggesting that the sex typing of the task will affect its perceived value only to the extent that one's sex role identity is a *critical* and *salient* component of one's self-concept. Conversely, sex-role identity should influence task value only to the extent the task is sex-typed by the individual. For example, the value of math should be low for a female who both sees math as a masculine activity and avoids masculine activities as one way to affirm her "femininity." Among those females who do not see mathematical competence as a masculine characteristic, sex-role identity should not be related to the perceived value of enrolling in a mathematics course. Similarly, for those females whose sex-role identity is not a central component of their self-identity ("sex-role aschematics," Markus, 1980), variations in the perception of mathematics as a masculine subject should not be related to variations in perceived task value. It is clear in these examples that effects of sex typing on task value are complex, depending not only on the subjective sex typing of the activity but also on the salience of sex-role identity to one's self-concept. Unfortunately, good measures of sex-role identity are not available. In addition, it may well be that sex-role identity is not a unitary concept, making measurement even more problematic.

The implications of sex typing on achievement behaviors has, nonetheless, received considerable attention in the area of math achievement. The results of these studies are mixed but, when math is stereotyped, it is seen as a male achievement domain by both male and female students. Males, however, typically consider math to be more of a male achievement domain than do females, and females, when asked, do not characterize greater participation in mathematics courses or competence in mathematics as unfeminine (Armstrong and Kahl, 1980; Boswell, 1979; Dwyer, 1974; Ernest, 1976; Fennema and Sherman, 1977; Fox, Brody, and Tobin, 1979; Nash, 1979; Stein and Smithells, 1969). For example, Fennema and Sherman (1977) have reported that the high school females in their studies stereotyped math as less of a male achievement domain than did males and did not show great concern about success in mathematics. Thus, it is not clear that females are stereotyping math as inappropriate for them, and it is even less clear that the sex stereotyping of math is lowering its attainment value for females.

Yet the hypothesized impact of the sex typing of math continues to be a favored explanation of sex-differentiated math course taking (e.g., Nash, 1979). If it is not the sex typing of high school math courses themselves that is responsible for this hypothesized link, how else might sex roles be influencing student decisions regarding math enrollment? While females may not be stereotyping mathematics as exclusively masculine, they may be stereotyping math-related careers as either masculine or unfeminine. In support of this suggestion, Boswell (1979) has found that career mathematicians are perceived as being decidedly unfeminine. It is not surprising, then, that females might not aspire to masculine-typed occupations and consequently would perceive advanced math courses as having low utility value, especially given the consistent view that advanced mathematics courses are difficult (e.g., Brush, 1980; Heller, Futterman, Kaczala, Karabenick, and Parsons, 1978). A number of articles have either reported or summarized distinct differences in the career interests of males and females, with females preferring occupations that require little math (Astin, 1969; Astin, Harway, and McNamara, 1976; Fox and Denham, 1974; Goff, 1978; Hawley, 1971, 1972; Lipman-Blumen and Tickameyer, 1975; Parsons, 1977; Parsons and Goff, 1980). Even in a study of high school math participation, Wise (1979) has found that a large proportion of the sex differences in participation could be accounted for by career interests in the ninth grade. Thus, it seems probable that it is the sex difference in career goals rather than the sex typing of math courses per se that is the major mediator of the sex difference in the perceived value of advanced math courses.

Sex differences in the perceived value of math could also result from sex differences in personal values and life goals. As noted earlier, several theoreticians have argued that one's values and life goals can influence the value one attaches to various activities such that activities consistent with these beliefs are seen as more valuable than activities that are inconsistent with or unrelated to one's personal value structure. In support of this argument, several recent studies have documented a relation between mathematics/science involvement and personal values. For example, Dunteman, Wisenbaker, and Taylor (1979) have found that being thing-oriented rather than person-oriented predicted becoming a math or science major. Similarly, Fox and Denham (1974) found that mathematically talented students are relatively low on social values and high on theoretical, political, and economic values. Furthermore, in both of these studies, females were less likely to hold the math- and science-related values than were males. Thus, it seems quite plausible that the sex difference in the perceived value of math is a function in part of the sex difference in personal value structure. The strength and causal direction of this prediction have yet to be tested.

Cost of Success or Failure The value of a task to an individual is also affected by a set of variables that can be conceptualized best as the cost of success or failure. Borrowing from exchange theorists (e.g., Thibaut and Kelley, 1959), we conceptualize the influence of cost on the value of an activity in terms of a cost/benefit ratio. Assuming that individuals have a conception of both the costs and the benefits of engaging in a variety of activities, then the value of each activity ought to be inversely related to this cost/benefit ratio. Variables influencing the benefit of an activity were discussed in previous sections. Variables influencing the cost of an activity include (1) the amount of effort needed to succeed, (2) the loss of time that could be used to engage in other valued activities, and (3) the psychological meaning of failure. Each of these is discussed briefly below.

1. *Effort.* Kukla (1972) has suggested that perceived effort needed for success may be a key determinant of achievement behavior. He has argued that a person calculates the minimal amount of effort needed to succeed on a task (i.e., to do as well as one considers essential), given the person's estimate of her or his ability and the difficulty of the task. The individual then exerts that minimal effort. If we assume that individuals have a sense of how much effort they think is worthwhile for various activities, then we could extend Kukla's argument to the following prediction: as the anticipated amount of effort increases in relation to the amount of effort considered worthwhile, then the value of the task to the individual should decrease. That is, as the cost/benefit ratio in terms of amount of effort needed to do well increases, the value of the task to the individual should decrease.

2. *Loss of valued alternatives.* Closely related conceptually to the cost of effort involved is the cost of a task in terms of the time lost for other valued activities. Students have limited time and energy. If they spend one hour on Task A, they have one hour less available for Task B. They must make choices among various activities. For example, imagine a female who likes math, knows it's hard, but also wants a boyfriend. To do as well in math as she feels she should, she thinks she'll have to do homework every night. She also believes that she can optimize her chance of getting a boyfriend by staying after school to watch the boy-of-her-dreams play basketball. Her parents, however, will not allow her to watch basketball practice unless her homework is finished, and she thinks she won't be able to finish her math homework in time. Despite its high incentive value, math poses an obstacle to success in her social goal. Consequently, the value of math for this female is decreased by its high cost in terms of the satisfaction of other important goals.

This analysis highlights the necessity of thinking about various achievement-related behaviors within the broad social array of behavioral options available to people. For example, the decision to try hard in math or not go to medical school, is not made in isolation of other salient life decisions that directly affect the perceived value of all of the available options.

3. *Psychological cost of failure.* Both the cost of success and the loss of valued alternatives are based on the assumption of anticipated

success. But what if a student is unsure of success or is certain of failure? How might that uncertainty affect the perceived value of the task? The common practice of avoiding courses that might lower one's grade-point average is a prime example of what can happen. Because students planning to attend college or graduate school know that they need high GPA's in order to compete, they often avoid courses that will add even a B to their academic records.

As another example, consider those students who view themselves as competent, have strong achievement needs, yet are unsure of their mathematical abilities and feel that they will have to try exceptionally hard to do well in their next math course. For these students, the cost of failure is high because failing to do well has important implications for their self-concept. In addition, these students would also be unsure of success and would believe that the amount of effort needed to do well was very high. Consequently, the perceived value of math should be lower for these students than for students who are either certain of success or do not find the prospect of failing as costly.

What does a student do when faced with these negative beliefs? If the option is available, he or she can avoid the activity altogether. But what if the student must engage in the activity, as is often the case in American schools? This is the situation given theoretical and empirical attention by Nicholls (1976), Covington and Beery (1976), and Covington and Omelich (1979a, 1979b). These theorists have suggested, and empirically demonstrated, that such a student would adapt by exerting the minimal effort necessary to get by. This strategy has two advantages. First, it prevents out-and-out failure; second, it provides the student with a face-saving attribution for lack of success; namely, "I didn't do better because I didn't try as hard as I could have." These theorists have argued that this attribution is psychologically less costly than the attribution to lack of ability that one would have to make if one had tried as hard as one could have and had still not "succeeded."

This analysis emphasizes the importance of the interaction among subjective definitions of success and failure (minimum standards), psychological cost of failure, perceptions of task demands, and expectations of success in determining task value. It is our contention that these variables interact to influence the perceived cost/benefit ratio and thus influence achievement behaviors. Whether or not this process is implemented at all, however, should depend, in part, on the initial levels of one's expectations for success and the perceived psychological cost of failure. To the extent that one's expectations are low or that the cost of failure is high, one should consider the cost/ benefit ratio very carefully. Conversely, to the extent that one's expectations are high or the cost of failure is low, other criteria should play a more critical role in determining achievement-related behaviors.

In summary, while past research on math achievement has not examined these cost variables, evidence from different lines of research provides support for our suggestions. Sex differences have not been examined for most of these variables. There have, however, been suggestions that females are not as likely to take risks as are males. This difference may reflect a differential sensitivity to the cost/benefit ratio discussed throughout this section. While these suggestions have not been tested in light of our model, they do provide support for our theoretical analysis and could add to the understanding of sex differences in achievement behaviors.

Affective Experiences   Achievement activities elicit a wide range of emotional responses. Past affect-laden experiences can influence one's responses to similar tasks in the present or future. For example, if one has had bad experiences with a math teacher in the past, one may be less positive in general toward current mathematics courses and mathematics teachers. To understand the value of various achievement activities, then, it is important to consider variations in the affective experiences students have had with different achievement activities. Variations in these experiences can take two quite different forms: (1) variations caused by overt, objective events like success, failure, and the responses or behaviors of major socializers such as parents and teachers, and (2) variations created by psychological factors such as causal attributions and individual differences in confidence or anxiety. A brief discussion of each of these follows.

1. *Objective events.* Past successes and failures themselves have been shown to elicit characteristic affective responses (e.g., Weiner, Russell, and Lerman, 1978). Success, especially on challenging tasks, leads to positive feelings; failure, especially on easy tasks, leads to negative feelings (Harter, 1980; Ruble, Parsons, and Ross, 1976). Other things being equal, these affective responses should influence the enjoyment or intrinsic value of subsequent related activities (Bandura, 1977). One should like activities that have been associated with positive feelings in the past more than activities that have been associated with negative feelings.

Both affect-laden behaviors of teachers and parents (e.g., praise, criticism, public ostracism, rejection) and more general experiences in school (e.g., test-taking procedures, curriculum variations) could have similar effects. Evidence documenting teacher and parent effects are discussed in a later section. Evidence documenting the impact of the more general school experience is abundant (e.g., see reviews by

Hill, 1977, on optimizing test-taking situations and by Nicholls, 1979, on optimizing motivation) and is not reviewed in detail in this chapter. One set of findings directly related to math achievement is, however, especially relevant for this discussion. Both Brush (1980) and Heller, Futterman, Kaczala, Karabenick, and Parsons (1978) have found a developmental decline in the perceived value and enjoyment of math. Brush interviewed students to assess the possible causes of this decline. Her students reported that high-level math courses are especially anxiety-provoking because students are called on and tested a great deal in these classes. Brush has speculated that this teaching style increases the negative experiences for the students and thus lowers the perceived value of these courses.

2a. *Psychological events: causal attributions.* Weiner (1972) has proposed that attributions of success and failure influence one's affective response to achievement tasks, such that attributing success and failure internally magnifies the associated affect. Thus, we should feel best about successes attributed to our abilities and efforts and feel worst about failures attributed to a lack of effort and/or ability. Evidence has supported this prediction (Ruble, Parsons, and Ross, 1976; Weiner, 1974). In more recent work, Weiner, Russell, and Lerman (1978, 1979) have provided empirical support for the link between attributions and affective responses. Weiner et al. (1978) have found that attributing one's success internally leads to feelings of pride, satisfaction, and competence, while attributing success externally leads to feelings of gratitude and surprise. Attributing one's failure to internal causes leads to feelings of guilt, resignation, and regret, while attributing failure to external causes leads to feelings of anger and surprise. Thus, it appears that attributions influence, in part, the affective responses one experiences in achievement settings. Individual differences in attributional patterns, consequently, should produce individual differences in the affect associated with similar tasks, which, in turn, should influence the value of these tasks.

2b. *Psychological events: individual differences in anxiety.* There has been a long tradition in the achievement literature of a concern with the effects of negative affective states on achievement-related behaviors, beginning with Atkinson's inclusion of a motive to avoid failure in his original model of need achievement (Atkinson, 1964) and related work on test anxiety (e.g., Sarason, 1972) and extending to more recent work on mastery orientation versus learned helplessness by Harter (1980) and Diener and Dweck (1979). Research in these areas has indicated that students classified as either high test-anxious or learned-helpless are more likely to label a given outcome as failure (Diener and Dweck, 1979), to blame themselves for their "failures"

(Diener and Dweck, 1978; Doris and Sarason, 1955), to experience more negative affect in general in testing situations that include both success and failure (Diener and Dweck, 1979; Mandler and Sarason, 1952), to suffer greater losses in self-esteem when confronted with evaluative situations (Diener and Dweck, 1979; Wine, 1971), to gain less in self-evaluation from success (Diener and Dweck, 1979), and to exhibit a range of debilitating behaviors reflecting anxiety in evaluative settings (e.g., Diener and Dweck, 1979; Ruble and Boggiano, 1980). This set of characteristics certainly would lead one to conclude that evaluative situations are particularly painful for some students. Since schools rely heavily on evaluative testing, we predict that the value of school-related achievement behaviors will decrease for these students as a consequence of the negative affect experienced during these evaluations.

The influence of negative affective states in achievement has received a great deal of attention in the area of math achievement. In particular, math anxiety has emerged as a popular explanation for sex differences in students' mathematics learning and course selection. Citing anecdotal evidence that more women than men openly admit feeling anxious about mathematics and enroll in math-anxiety clinics, some researchers (e.g., Lazarus, 1974; Tobias, 1978) have argued that women and men differ in their emotional reactions to mathematics and that women avoid math because it is anxiety-provoking.

Although there have been only a few studies that directly address affective outcomes of mathematics learning, and the findings have not been especially consistent, some support for this proposal is found in the literature. In terms of general affective responses to mathematics, expressed as a liking or preference for the subject matter, few differences are evident in males' and females' responses during elementary and junior high school. Sex differences in these variables do appear after junior high school, with males expressing more positive affective responses toward math (Aiken, 1970, 1976; Ernest, 1976; Fox, 1975, 1977). With respect to more negative affective responses to mathematics, the view that greater numbers of females are math-anxious has been supported by a few empirical studies (Brush, 1978; Dreger and Aiken, 1957; Suinn and Richardson, 1972). However, interpretation of these studies is problematic, given the possibility that males might be less willing to admit to feelings of anxiety, especially with regard to an area of achievement that is viewed as masculine, particularly by other males.

Fennema and Sherman have argued that math anxiety is psychologically equivalent to a lack of confidence in one's ability to learn mathematics. In support of this conclusion, they (1977) have reported a strong correlation between measures of students' confidence in math and their math anxiety. Meece (1980), however, has argued that equating math anxiety with lack of confidence in one's ability does not fully account for the intensity and range of students' emotional responses stemming from their lack of confidence in math. She has proposed instead that the affective reactions associated with math anxiety arise from a complex interplay of social and personal factors and are primarily a joint function of low expectancies for success and high psychological cost associated with failure in mathematics. If students believe that they have low mathematics ability and that low achievement in math is undesirable, then a reasonable emotional response would be to feel uneasy or anxious about math and, as a means of reducing this anxiety, to avoid mathematics. Research on the modification of test anxiety has provided some support for this hypothesis. Interventions designed to alter students' perceptions of task difficulty have had a beneficial effect on the performance of test-anxious subjects (Sarason, 1972; Weiner and Schneider, 1971). However, whether these manipulations worked because they reduced anxiety or because they raised expectations is not clear.

Summary Comment Our model proposes that task value is an important mediator of achievement-related behaviors that interacts with expectancies to influence these behaviors. In this section, we have discussed a set of factors that might influence task value. Unfortunately, less systematic research has been done on task value than on expectancies. Consequently, this section has been more speculative than the preceding section on expectancies and related mediators.

EMPIRICAL STUDY OF PSYCHOLOGICAL COMPONENT

In the previous sections, we identified a set of constructs as critical psychological mediators of students' achievement behaviors, and we suggested a model of the interrelations among these constructs. This model is summarized in Figure 2-2a, and the translation of the model into the domain of mathematics is summarized in Figure 2-2b. The model suggests that students interpret the external reality to which they are exposed and form concepts of their abilities and opinions about both the difficulty and the importance of various activities based on these interpretations. Previous research in the area of achievement has suggested many of the critical variables specified in Figures 2-2a and 2-2b, but has not explored in any depth the nature of the relations among these variables. Our model was designed to fill this gap. What follows in this section is a description of the project now in progress and a summary of our initial findings.

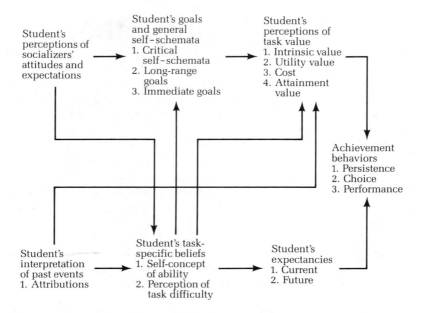

Figure 2-2(a)
Psychological model of achievement attitudes and behaviors.

As was discussed at the beginning of the chapter, the test of our model is being carried out as part of a larger study of the determinants of students', especially female students', decisions to enroll in advanced math courses. In keeping with this specific goal and with the tenets of our model, we administered specially developed measures of expectancies for success in current and advanced math courses, of perceived difficulty of current and future math courses, of self-concept of math ability, of attributional patterns for previous success and failure in math, of perceived interest value of math, of perceived utility value of math, of sex stereotyping of math, and of perceptions of the expectancies and values held by teachers and parents. In addition, we administered a test of sex-differentiating personality characteristics used in previous research on achievement.

Initial data collection took place in two waves during the years 1978 and 1979, designated as Year 1 and Year 2. The sample consisted of 668 students, in grades five through twelve, their parents, and their teachers. Data were collected in the following forms: student record data, student questionnnaires, parent questionnaires, teacher questionnaires, and classroom observations.

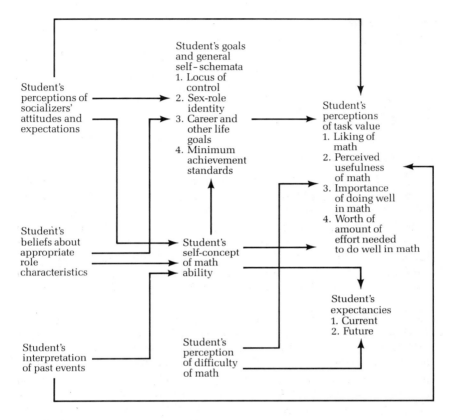

Figure 2-2(b)
Psychological model of mathematics attitudes and behaviors.

Data analysis proceeded in four distinct phases. Descriptive analyses comprised Phase 1. These analyses, in keeping with our interest in developmental trends and sex discrepancies, examined the distributions of variables in the sample as a whole as well as within each sex and within each grade level.

In Phase 2, bivariate and multivariate relations were examined. Correlation, regression, and single- and multiple-dimension contingency table analyses were used to assess relations among the variables and the relative importance of the student variables collected in Year 1 in predicting our major dependent variables: expectancies, values, course plans, and Year 2 math grades.

Phase 3 of analysis, that of model testing, integrated the knowledge obtained from prior analyses with our theoretical model in a test of the model's predictive power. The specific theoretical model tested is presented in Figure 2-2b. Multiple regression path analysis was the model-testing procedure used.

The final phase of our analysis involved the use of our longitudinal data to test causal hypotheses. The collection of data at two points in time strengthens one's ability to make inferences regarding the causal direction of correlational relations. We made use of cross-lagged panel analyses for these tests.

Descriptive Analyses

To assess the effects of year in school and sex on the student attitudinal variables, analyses of variance using year in school and sex as the independent variables were performed on each of the student scales. Table 2-1 summarizes the results of the analyses of variance for Year 1 and Year 2 separately. Effects significant at the .05 level or better are listed. Given the large number of analyses, one must be very cautious in interpreting the .05 probability findings. We call attention only to effects significant at the .01 level or better.

Sex Differences   Few sex differences emerged, but those that did confirmed previous findings. Compared with the females, males rated math as easier and more useful, felt math required less effort, and had higher expectations for their performance in future math courses, even though these males and females had done equally well in their previous math courses and on previous standardized math aptitude/achievement tests. In addition, males in Year 2 rated their math abilities higher than did the females. Males and females did not differ in expectations for performance in the current mathematics course, in estimates of current performance, in perceptions of parents' estimates of both the difficulty of the current math courses and the students' math abilities, and in liking of current or previous mathematics activities.

When asked to recall a previous success and failure on a mathematics examination, males and females provided different attributions for their performances (tested with chi-square analyses, $p < .05$). In both years, males attributed failure to ability less frequently and success to ability more frequently than did females; in contrast, females attributed success more frequently to consistent effort than did males. These sex differences were especially marked among those students with the highest expectations for their own performances.

This pattern of sex differences suggests that males and females have different perceptions of both the task demands and the value of math courses. This difference may be sufficient to explain, in part, the sex differences in students' decisions about enrolling in advanced math courses. For example, attributing one's success to constant effort rather than ability combined with the belief that future courses are more difficult, demanding even more effort, should reduce the likelihood of voluntary enrollment in advanced math courses, especially if there is some doubt about the value of the advanced math courses. Assuming that the amount of effort students can or are willing to expend has limits, perceptions of the need for greater effort would certainly have an adverse effect on their expectancies for future success in math and would predispose them against continuing to take math. Assuming that ability is not seen as a limited quantity like effort, the same dynamics would not apply to students who have attributed success to ability. Perceptions of increasing difficulty in math courses should not create concern over the effort needed to succeed if one believes ability is responsible for one's success.

Year in School   Year-in-school effects were both more numerous and stronger than sex effects. In general, these effects indicate that students become more pessimistic and negative about math as they grow older. The older students had lower expectancies for both their current and future math performances, rated both their math abilities and math performances lower, saw both their present and future math courses as more difficult, thought their parents shared these pessimistic views of their abilities and performance potentials, were less interested in math activities in general, liked their math teachers less, and rated the utility of advanced math courses lower than the younger students did. For most of these variables, there was a consistent downward linear trend as a function of grade level, with the females preceding the males (see Figure 2-3).

General Differences   Students in Year 1 rated math as more useful for males than for females. Students did not, however, rate males as having more math ability. The stereotyping of math as more useful for males (calculated by subtracting the usefulness-for-women score from the usefulness-for-men score; hereafter referred to as the stereotyping of math as a male domain) dropped from Year 1 to Year 2, due largely to an increase in the rating of the usefulness of math for women from Year 1 to Year 2.

In Year 2, the tenth- to twelfth-grade students were asked to rate the amount of encouragement to continue in math they had received from their fathers, mothers, last year's teachers, guidance counselors, older friends, siblings, and peers. Of these, fathers, mothers, and previous math teachers were perceived as having encouraged the students, while the other individuals were perceived as having neither encouraged nor discouraged the students. Contrary to the popular

Table 2-1

Summary of significant results from analyses of variance

Variables yielding significant sex effects	Effect	p^a
	Year 1	
Actual and required effort	$F > M^b$	.01
Expectancies for future math courses	$M > F^c$	.01
Difficulty of current math course	$F > M$	.01
Anticipated difficulty of future math	$F > M$	.01
Perception of task difficulty for self	$F > M$	.05
Stereotyping of math utility for females	$M > F$	.01
Femininity score on PAQ	$F > M$	.0001
Masculinity score on PAQ	$M > F$	.0001
	Year 2	
Self-rating of math ability	$M > F$	.01
Expectancies for future math courses	$M > F$	.01
Expectancies for current math course	$M > F$	.04
Actual and required effort	$F > M$	.01
Utility of advanced math	$M > F$	.001
Utility of basic math	$M > F$	.01
Stereotyping of math utility for females	$F > M$	.05
Femininity score on PAQ	$F > M$	.0001
Masculinity score on PAQ	$M > F$	.0001

[a] Only F's with $p < .05$ are summarized.
[b] $F > M$ = females greater than males.
[c] $M > F$ = males greater than females.

belief that peer pressure prevents some females from enrolling in difficult academic subjects, peers were not rated as having a negative influence on the students' enrollment decisions. One sex difference did emerge: males, in comparison with females, felt that their counselors had provided more encouragement ($p<.05$). Perceived counselor encouragement did not, however, predict future course plans.

The students also rated the importance of various reasons in influencing their decisions to take math. Three reasons emerged as the most influential: (1) preparation for either a college major or a career, (2) gaining admission to a prestigious college, and (3) the importance of math in a well-rounded education. Intrinsic properties of math, such as its challenge, ease, or interest value, were seen as

Table 2-1 (continued)

Variables yielding significant grade effects	Effect	p^a
Year 1		
Math aptitude score	$O > Y^{d,f}$	.01
Self-concept of math ability	$Y > O^e$	.001
Perception of task difficulty for self	$O > Y$	.0001
Perception of socializers' perception of math ability	$Y > O$	.0001
Perception of socializers' perception of task difficulty	$O > Y$	.01
Importance of math	$5th > O^g$	.01
Expectancies for current math course	$Y > O$	.01
Difficulty of current math course	$O > Y$	.001
Utility of advanced math	$Y > O$	.001
Interest in and liking for math	$Y > O$	.01
Liking of teacher	$Y > O$	.01
Year 2		
Stereotyping of math utility for females	$Y > O$	.0001
Stereotyping of math utility for males	$Y > O$	.0001
Stereotyping of math ability	$Y > O$	.001
Self-concept of math ability	$Y > O$	.0001
Perception of socializers' perception of task difficulty	$O > Y$	.0001
Perception of socializers' perception of math ability	$Y > O$	.0001
Expectancies for current math course	$Y > O$	.001
Difficulty of current math course	$O > Y$	.001
Utility of advanced math	$Y > O$	.001
Interest in and liking for math	$Y > O$	.01
Liking of teacher	$Y > O$	.0001
Anticipated difficulty of future math	$O > Y$	.0001

[d] $O > Y$ = linear trend increasing with age.
[e] $Y > O$ = linear trend decreasing with age.
[f] Not calculated for Year 2.
[g] Fifth-graders were significantly higher than children in all other grades.

less important. Again one sex difference emerged: males rated the importance of future plans (college or career) in their decisions higher than did females ($p < .01$).

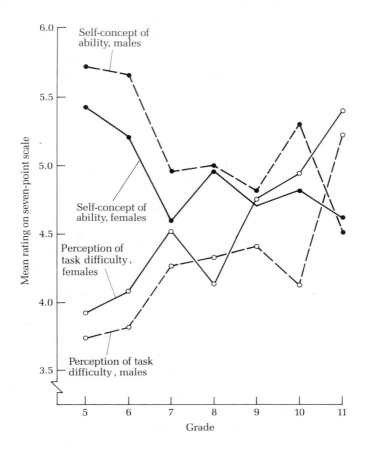

Figure 2-3
Developmental shifts in students' attitudes
toward their own abilities and the difficulty of math.

Relational Analyses

Sex-Role Measures It has been suggested by a variety of scholars
that sex differences in achievement behaviors are influenced by either
the sex typing of the task or the sex-role identity of the individual or
by some combination of these factors interacting with each other. Sex
typing of mathematics is fairly easy to measure. Sex-role identity, on
the other hand, is very difficult to conceptualize, much less to measure. We chose to focus instead on the relation of sex-related personality characters to mathematics achievement behaviors. Measures exist
for these constructs, and several theoreticians have suggested the

importance of personality characteristics for achievement choices. For example, Hoffman (1972) has suggested that females' lesser goal-oriented, instrumental qualities and greater affiliative needs and expressive orientations lead them to have weaker achievement strivings and to be less self-confident than males about certain academic tasks. To determine the role of these personality variables, we decided to use a simplified version of the Personal Attributes Questionnaire (PAQ) (Spence, Helmreich, and Stapp, 1975), a self-report measure containing a "masculinity" scale that taps instrumental personality traits and a "femininity" scale that taps expressive, interpersonally oriented traits. As has been found by other investigators, males perceived themselves as higher in "masculine" instrumentality and lower in "feminine" expressiveness than did females.

To evaluate both sex-typed personality characteristics and the effects of the stereotyping of math as a male domain on mathematics attitudes and course enrollment plans, we correlated the students' rating of the usefulness of advanced math for both males and females, their perception of math as a male domain, their sex stereotyping of math ability, and their ratings of themselves on a simplified version of the PAQ with the other student measures. Expressiveness, as measured by the PAQ, was not related to any of the student measures. Instrumentality, on the other hand, related consistently and positively to measures of expectancy and self-concept of math ability for both males and females. These results are consistent with data reported in Chapter 1, this volume.

To test more directly for the combined effects of "masculine" instrumentality and "feminine" expressiveness, we classified students on their joint scores on the two PAQ scales, using the median split method outlined by Spence et al. (1975). These variables, along with a measure of the degree of stereotyping of math as a male domain (neutral, moderately masculine, or highly masculine) and sex of student, were entered as predictor variables into a series of multivariate contingency table analyses. Self-concept of math ability, concept of task difficulty, concept of the value of math, estimate of the utility of math for future goals, and current expectancies were the dependent measures in these analyses. Neither a student's personality classification nor her or his degree of stereotyping of math as a masculine domain had any significant influence on these dependent measures. These findings, in conjunction with the correlational findings reported above, suggest that it is only the responses to the instrumental items on the PAQ that are related to self-concept of ability.

These findings do not, however, invalidate the significance of a student's sex-role identity as an influence in course selection. What they suggest is that the link between androgynous and feminine personality structures and achievement-related behaviors is weak at best. In addition, our data do not support the popular notion that sex typing of subject matter as masculine acts as a deterrent to female achievement.

Self- and Task-Concept Measures   To provide an initial test of our hypotheses regarding the relations among the student attitudinal items, we correlated Year 1 student attitudes with each other and with a composite score reflecting both past math grades and performance on either the California Achievement Test (CAT) or the Michigan Educational Assessment Program (MEAP), with their Year 2 math grades and with their plans to enroll in advanced math courses. A summary of these correlations is depicted in Table 2-2. Correlations for the sample as a whole and for females and males separately are listed.

As predicted, self-concept of ability was correlated positively with perceived value of math, with expectancies, with plans to continue in math, and with Year 2 math grades; self-concept of ability correlated negatively with ratings of task difficulty. Generally, these relations were true for both males and females. The relation of the math performance score (the composite score described above) to the other student measures varied, however, depending on the sex of the student. Measures of males' math performances were consistently related to their self-concept measures; the relations between the females' math-performance scores and their self-concept measures were neither as consistent nor as strong.

Model-Testing Analyses

Path Analysis   Path analysis was used to provide a more direct test of the psychological components of our model (Duncan, 1966; Wright, 1934). Theoretical models like ours specify the direct and indirect relations among variables; i.e., they specify variables that mediate the relations found between other variables. For example, our model specifies that the variables reflecting students' interpretation of their achievements mediate the relation between their past performance and expectancies for future success. Path analysis is a statistical procedure, based on multiple regressions, that allows one to estimate both direct and indirect relations among a set of variables. Its use provides a test for the relations hypothesized to exist in a causal model like ours. To the extent that significant paths (the coefficient of the relation between the predictor variable and the criterion variable) emerge where predicted, support is provided for one's theoretical model. To the extent that predicted paths are nonsignificant, the support for one's theoretical model is weakened. The path coefficients are estimated using a series of multiple regression equations. We have standardized our coefficients, so that the size of the coefficients provides an estimate of the relative strength of the relations specified by each path. Since multiple regression is used, these relative strengths are totally dependent on the set of variables entered into the analysis and should not be taken as absolute estimates of any given relationship.[2]

Figure 2-4 represents the reduced path model, with only those paths that are significant at $p<.05$ included. The percent of variance of each variable accounted for by the variables on which it was regressed is listed as the R^2 under the variable. This percent is the multiple R^2 for each of the unique regression equations. It indicates the percent of variance of the criterion variables accounted for by all of the variables in the columns to the left of the criterion variable.

As predicted, intention to take more math was directly influenced by students' perceptions of the value of math. Contrary to our predictions, combined expectancies (current and future) had a nonsignificant relation to students' intentions to take more math. However, values and expectations, as predicted, were related to both students' self-concepts of math abilities and their estimates of their parents' and teachers' beliefs regarding the students' abilities. Math performance did not have a direct effect on students' plans, expectancies, self-concepts of math abilities, or estimates of the difficulty of math. Finally, stereotyping of math as a male domain increased the value of math.

Separate stepwise multiple regression equations were calculated to assess the predictive power of our Year 1 data for Year 2 math grades. (Path analysis was not repeated, since only the last step of the analysis had changed.) Self-concept of math ability and performance emerged as significant predictors for both males and females $(p<.02)$. Perception of the value of math was also a significant predictor $(p<.03)$ for males.

In summary, the path-analytic procedures used provided support for our model. The Year 1 variables included in the model explained $68-78\%$[3] of the variance in expectancies, $32-46\%$ of the variance in

---

[2]Only those variables measured using interval scales and having significant zero-order correlations with the expectancy, value, or course-plan measure were used in these analyses. Path coefficients were calculated using a series of regression equations, with each variable regressed on the set of variables to its left (those theorized to have had a causal effect on it).

[3]The two values given represent the total percentage of variance accounted for by the two path analyses summarized in Figures 2-4 and 2-6.

Table 2-2

Zero-order correlation matrix of major student attitudinal and achievement variables

	Intention to take more math	Math grade: Year 1	Math grade: Year 2	Current and future expectancies in math	Perception of parents' aspirations	Perception of socializers' perception of task difficulty	Perception of socializers' perception of math ability	Self-concept of math ability	Perception of task difficulty	Value of math	Stereotyping of math as male domain	Masculinity score on PAQ
Intention to take more math	1.00											
Math grade: Year 1	.25**	1.00										
	.23**	1.00										
	.29**	1.00										
Math grade: Year 2	.11*	.42**	1.00									
	.12	.29**	1.00									
	.10	.54**	1.00									
Current and future expectancies in math	.39**	.48**	.35**	1.00								
	.46**	.39**	.27**	1.00								
	.31**	.59**	.45**	1.00								
Perception of parents' aspirations	.14*	.04	.06	.38**	1.00							
	.12	-.07	.08	.38**	1.00							
	.18*	.19*	.05	.38**	1.00							
Perception of socializers' perception of task difficulty	.17**	-.36**	-.21**	-.44**	-.12*	1.00						
	.18*	-.35**	-.11	-.42**	-.07	1.00						
	.16	-.38**	-.34**	-.46**	-.21*	1.00						

Variable												
Perception of socializers' perception of math ability	.20**	.43**	.26**	.72**	.32**	−.46**	1.00					
	.22**	.38**	.16*	.69**	.25**	−.51**	1.00					
	.19*	.50**	.37**	.75**	.41**	−.39**	1.00					
Self-concept of math ability	.35**	.53**	.39**	.93**	.33**	−.53**	.76**	1.00				
	.40**	.46**	.29**	.92**	.31**	−.53**	.77**	1.00				
	.30**	.63**	.50**	.94**	.36**	−.54**	.74**	1.00				
Perception of task difficulty	.05	−.31**	−.21**	−.45**	−.14*	.59**	−.41**	−.64**	1.00			
	.07	−.25**	−.10	−.45**	−.07	.53**	−.50**	−.67**	1.00			
	.04	−.38**	−.34**	−.43**	−.25**	.67**	−.29**	−.59**	1.00			
Value of math	.52**	.23**	.11*	.59**	.35**	−.19**	.42**	.53**	−.09	1.00		
	.55**	.11	.07	.55**	.30**	−.18*	.34**	.49**	−.05	1.00		
	.49**	.40**	.18*	.66**	.43**	−.19*	.54**	.59**	−.12	1.00		
Stereotyping of math as male domain	.22**	.04	.09	.24**	.17**	.02	.18**	.19**	.10	.51**	1.00	
	.30*	.02	.12	.30**	.18*	−.08	.21**	.24**	.08	.58**	1.00	
	.11	.04	.06	.20*	.18*	.15	.15	.16	.10	.43**	1.00	
Masculinity score on PAQ	.20**	.10	.12*	.34**	.14**	−.03	.19**	.29**	−.03	.21**	.10	1.00
	.28**	.12	.10	.38**	.12	.01	.16	.30**	−.03	.28**	.24**	1.00
	.10	.12	.17	.26**	.14	−.07	.22*	.24**	.05	.06	−.03	1.00
Past math performance	.25**	.65**	.40**	.39**	−.02	−.18**	.25**	.41**	−.27**	.18**	.09	.08
	.27**	.60**	.28**	.29**	−.11	−.11	.17	.31**	−.21*	.06	.02	.18*
	.24**	.70**	.52**	.52**	.09	−.26**	.33**	.52**	−.34**	.33**	.17	−.00

Notes: Within each row, there are three sets of correlations: the top set contains the correlation for all subjects; the middle set, the correlation for females; the bottom set, the correlation for males.

Boxed correlations contain a set of correlations in which the male and female correlations differ p<.05.

*p<.05.
**p<.01.

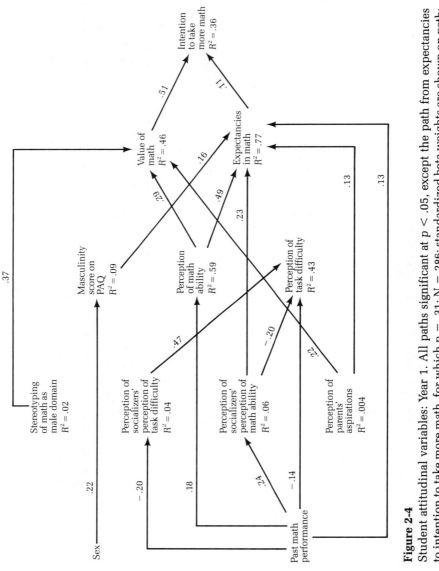

Figure 2-4

Student attitudinal variables: Year 1. All paths significant at $p < .05$, except the path from expectancies to intention to take more math, for which $p = .31$; $N = 286$; standardized beta weights are shown on path; R^2 = percent of variance accounted for on each criterion measure by all preceding predictor variables; each R^2 is listed under its criterion measure.

task value, 32–36% of the variance in course plans, and 13% (females)–40% (males)[4] of the variance in Year 2 math grades. In general, the predicted relations between the variables also emerged as significant paths. The path analysis also demonstrated that we can predict variation in expectancies better than we can predict variation in task value. Further conceptual work on the determinants of task value is needed. Interestingly, task value is the major predictor of plans to enroll in math, while self-concept of ability is the major predictor of subsequent grades. These data suggest that one's perception of the value of an activity is more important in determining one's decision to engage in that activity, while one's self-concept of ability is more important in determining one's actual performance once involved in the activity.

In summary, our model of the interrelations among these student achievement attitudes at one period of time provides a good representation of the data, especially for high school students. But how do these attitudes influence each other in the process of development? It is to this question that we now turn.

Longitudinal Analyses

Longitudinal data allow for more refined assessment of causal relations in correlational data sets. We used cross-lagged panel analyses for this purpose. Cross-lagged panel correlation (CLPC) is a technique used in evaluating evidence for causal inference (Kenny, 1975). The CLPC program examines correlations between pairs of variables collected at a minimum of two points in time. Significant differences between the values of the cross-lagged correlations (rx_1y_2 and rx_2y_1) suggest that one variable of the pair is causally dependent on the other. Using these analyses, we can infer the more probable causal direction in a correlational relation. The results of these analyses are given in Table 2-3.

In support of our predictions, future expectancy appears to be influenced by self-concept of ability and perceptions of task difficulty; self-concept of ability appears to be influenced by perceptions of task difficulty and of the amount of effort needed to do well; both the utility value and the intrinsic value of math appear to be influenced by perceptions of the worth of the effort needed to do well; one's estimate of the difficulty of future math courses appears to be influenced by one's perceptions of the estimates of future difficulty held by parents and teachers.

---

[4]These figures are based on the two stepwise multiple regression analyses reported above.

Table 2-3
Causal effects from cross-lagged panel analyses

Year 1	Year 2
Current math ability ⟶	Future expectancies
Difficulty of current math course ⟶(−)⟶	
Worth of effort needed to do well ⟶	
Current expectancies ⟶	Perception of socializers' perceptions of math ability
Self-concept of math ability ⟶	
Difficulty of current math course ⟶(−)⟶	
Actual and required effort ⟶(−)⟶	
Estimated performance in math ⟶	
Difficulty of current math course ⟶(−)⟶	Self-concept of math ability
Actual and required effort ⟶(−)⟶	
Difficulty of current math course ⟶(−)⟶	Estimated performance in math
Difficulty of current math course ⟶(−)⟶	Worth of effort needed to do well
Perception of socializers' perceptions of task difficulty ⟶	Difficulty of future math courses
Worth of effort needed to do well ⟶	Utility of math
Difficulty of future math courses ⟶(−)⟶	Interest in and liking for math
Worth of effort needed to do well ⟶	

Note: All causal effects lead to increases in Year 2 variables except where indicated by negative (−) sign, which indicates a causal effect leading to decrease in Year 2 variables.

Contrary to our predictions, perceptions of parents' and teachers' estimates of students' abilities did not have a causal influence on students' self-concepts or task variables. Instead, self-concept variables and perceptions of task difficulty appear to influence students' perceptions of the attitudes of parents and teachers. These latter results are consistent with the findings of Calsyn and Kenny (1977), who also found that students' self-concepts influenced their perceptions of others' opinions, rather than the reverse.

Summary Comment

What can we conclude from these results? These analyses provide reasonable preliminary support for our model. It is clear that self-concepts of ability and subjective task value are important mediators of achievement behavior. Furthermore, both the path-analytic results and the CLPC results indicate that we understand the determinants of self-concept of ability and expectancies better than we understand the determinants of task value. This could, however, be a consequence of the measures we used in these analyses. Since not all measures hypothesized to predict value were measured with ordinal scales, some important variables were not included in these analyses. For example, neither attributions nor math-anxiety measures were included.

With regard to sex differences, no single variable emerged as the critical mediator of sex-differentiated math achievement behaviors. Course plans and actual achievement in math are mediated by a complex set of interrelations for both males and females. While males and females do not differ greatly on any one variable, there are small but consistent sex differences on several of the important mediators: namely, self-concept of ability; expectancy (especially expectancy for future courses); perception of task difficulty; and attributions of success and failure to ability. In combination, these variables could mediate differential achievement behaviors. It should be noted, however, that we did not find sex differences in either course plans or grades. Whether actual enrollment differs by sex in this sample will require two more years of followup data. Nonetheless, the sex differences in achievement attitudes themselves are important phenomena to be studied, since these attitudes do play a significant role in future course plans and actual achievement and since we know, from national samples, that males and females differ in both course enrollment patterns and grades once they reach college.

One additional important sex difference emerged. Females' grades did not relate as highly to their attitudes and past performances as did males'. It has been speculated that females' expectations are more closely tied to their grades than are males' (Crandall, 1969). These data suggest just the opposite. Why this might be true is not apparent in this data set. Since the bulk of our sample was junior high school students, perhaps these results reflect the emergence of the conflict between social roles and achievement in the females. If this were true, then one would predict that females' school performance would be coming under the influence of variables we have not measured and would appear more erratic throughout this developmental period.

DEVELOPMENTAL COMPONENT OF ACHIEVEMENT MODEL

Developmental hypotheses comprise the second component of our model. Many theorists have suggested the important contributions of both parents and teachers to individual differences in children's concepts of their abilities, perceptions of task difficulty, expectancies, and values. The following three mechanisms of influence have emerged with some regularity in developmental research: (1) role modeling, (2) parent and teacher expectations, and (3) the shaping of activities through reinforcement and the provision of toys, clothes, and other experiences. The possible role of each of these processes in shaping students' achievement behaviors and attitudes is discussed in the following sections.

Socialization Effects of Role Modeling

Experimental research has established the importance of adult behavior as a standard or model for children's behavior. The process of "observational learning" is presumed to account for the efficiency with which children adopt social norms, particularly those associated with adult and sex-appropriate qualities of behavior (Bandura and Walters, 1963).

The effects of role modeling have received some attention in the literature on math achievement. For example, Ernest (1976) has reported that fathers are more likely to help their children with math homework than are mothers after the sixth grade; Fox (1977) has reported a tendency for more advanced math courses to be taught by males. This underrepresentation of appropriate female role models in math has been suggested as one reason for the underrepresentation of females in math courses.

Effects of Socializers' Expectations

Several studies have indicated that the expectations of socializers regarding a student's performance can influence actual performance (Brophy and Good, 1974; Rosenthal and Rosnow, 1969). The role of teacher expectancies in the formation of students' achievement expectancies and behaviors has been particularly well documented (Brophy and Good, 1974; Cooper, 1979). Similarly, throughout the achievement literature, parental expectancies have been linked to both high achievement motivation and high achievement behavior (e.g., Crandall, 1969; Parsons et al., 1976b; Winterbottom, 1958).

If expectancies of others mediate behavior, then the degree to which socializers hold differential expectancies for males' and females' performances in various achievement activities is an important factor to consider in understanding the origin of sex differences in achievement-related behaviors. Several studies have suggested that, in general, parents and teachers have higher educational expectancies for males than for females (e.g., Good, Sikes, and Brophy, 1973; Hilton and Berglund, 1974; Sears, Maccoby, and Levin, 1957), although these biases do not emerge consistently until students are older. In fact, during the elementary school years, parents and teachers generally expect females to do better than males (e.g., Maccoby and Jacklin, 1974). It is not until high school that teachers tend to express higher expectancies of academic performance for males than for females (Cooper, 1976; Good, Sikes, and Brophy, 1973).

Thus, while there is support for the suggestion that socializers hold differential achievement and performance expectancies for males and females, it is less clear how these expectancies are conveyed to students. There are undoubtedly a variety of indirect and direct means by which students learn what others expect of them. The nature of the evaluative feedback students receive about their academic performances and the causal attributions provided for students are two means that have received considerable recent attention.

Evaluative Feedback   One line of research assessing the impact of evaluative feedback has examined the overall pattern of feedback students receive in response to their achievement efforts. In a comprehensive review of the literature on teacher expectancies, Brophy and Good (1974) have identified several teacher behaviors (e.g., praise for good performance, criticism for bad performance, and student questioning patterns) that are related to students' expectancies and achievement. Additionally, Brophy and Good have found that teachers vary their use of evaluative feedback depending on characteristics of the student; in particular, high-potential males are more likely than females to receive reinforcement for their achievements.

Taking a slightly different tack, Dweck and her colleagues have suggested that it is the pattern of discriminate and indiscriminate feedback, rather than the absolute frequency of praise or criticism, that is the key determinant of sex differences found in students' achievement expectancies. Dweck, Davidson, Nelson, and Enna (1978) have argued that evaluative feedback has meaning to children only when it has been associated discriminately with the intellectual quality of their academic work. Thus, if teachers criticize males for both their work and their conduct, then negative feedback should lose its meaning for males and have relatively little effect on their achievement expectancies and performances. In contrast, if teachers criticize females primarily for their work, then negative feedback should have more meaning for females and, consequently, have a greater impact on them than on males. The main feature of this argument is that it is not the frequency of criticism or praise per se that is critical, but rather the ratio of discriminate to indiscriminate use. In fact, this is exactly what Dweck and her co-workers found. The teachers in their study used more indiscriminate criticism with males, addressing two-thirds of the total negative evaluation for males to intellectually irrelevant aspects of their academic performances. By comparison, over two-thirds of the negative evaluation of females was directed to the academic quality of their work. Extending this argument to the issue of more general individual differences, one would predict that the pattern of evaluative feedback received by a student would influence his or her expectancies. While this hypothesis has not been tested in the field, Dweck and her colleagues found support for the prediction in a laboratory simulation in which evaluative feedback was manipulated and self-expectancies served as the dependent measure.

Causal Attributions   In addition to patterns of feedback, socializers may vary in the causal explanations they provide students. Parents, teachers, and peers have ample opportunity to provide explanations like "You must have tried very hard," "You're really smart," or "Maybe this is too hard for you" for students' successes or failures. These explanations could influence students' self-perceptions in at least two ways. First, various causal explanations convey different information regarding the expectations parents and teachers have for the student. For example, attributing a student's failure to illness or insufficient effort tells the student that he or she can do the task. Conversely, attributing a student's success to hard work may inadvertently convey the message that the parent or teacher does not really think the student is very smart. Second, the attributions of parents and teachers could influence students' self-perceptions through the mechanisms associated with role modeling. Parents and teachers provide students with a model of relevant attributions that they may incorporate into their own attributional systems. For example, by attributing a student's failure to lack of effort, parents or teachers may be encouraging the student to attribute her or his failure to an unstable characteristic (i.e., to lack of effort or bad mood) and consequently may be discouraging the incorporation of failure experiences into the student's self-concept. In contrast, by attributing a student's failure to lack of ability or by overlooking or agreeing with a student's attribution of her or his failure to lack of ability, parents or teachers may be encouraging both a low expectancy attributional pattern and the incorporation of failure information into the student's self-concept. Indirect support for these hypotheses comes from experiments showing that, in general, people tend to attribute men's successful performances to their abilities and women's to hard work (Deaux and Emswiller, 1974; Etaugh and Brown, 1975; Feldman-Summers and Kiesler, 1974).

Differential Experiences

In addition to these more direct effects, parents and/or teachers could be influencing students' choices, self-concepts, and values by the types of general experiences they provide or encourage. Three types of experiences seem especially important. The first is the types of role models to which the student is exposed. The types of toys and recreational activities and the independence training the child receives are the other two. Each of these types of experiences has yielded rich theoretical discussion and some empirical study. For example, both Hoffman (1972) and Astin (1969) have suggested that males receive earlier independence training that do females, resulting in differentiated achievement patterns. Similarly, much of the thinking in role theory points to the importance of societal models in the formation of both self-concept and values.

Connor, Schackman, and Serbin (1978) have studied the impact of toys on spatial skills. They have suggested that "masculine" toys such as big wheels or large blocks encourage the development of spatial abilities in males, while "feminine" toys such as dolls fail to stimulate this skill in females. To support their hypothesis, they designed an intervention procedure for the preschool years that relied on exposure to certain "masculine" toys and other typically male play activities. Exposure to these activities produced an improvement in females' spatial skills. Since there is ample evidence that males and females are provided with sex-typed toys and develop an early preference for them, Connor and co-workers concluded their research report with the suggestion that socializers, especially parents, are not providing females with the necessary experiences for spatial skill acquisition.

Sex typing of toys and sports activities may also be creating deficits in females' experiences that impact on their subsequent achievement behaviors. For example, sex-differentiated participation in competitive sports programs during the elementary school years might be linked to later sex differences in response to failure experiences (e.g., Hennig and Jardim, 1976). Most bright females are exposed to few failure experiences in school. Consequently, they have little opportunity to experience public failure and to gain the knowledge that failure is often followed by continued social acceptance and by improvement in subsequent encounters. Bright males, on the other hand, are provided such opportunities if they play in organized competitive sports.

Summary Comment

We have argued in this section that parents and teachers influence students' achievement attitudes and behaviors through at least three processes: role modeling, communication of expectancies, and provision of differential experiences. Since their effects as role models and as expectancy socializers are assumed to be directly related to students' current achievement attitudes, we have chosen to focus on these two aspects of socialization in our study of math attitudes and behavior. It is to this part of our study that we now turn. The model guiding this portion of our research is depicted in Figure 2-5a; its specifications for the math study are depicted in Figure 2-5b.

EMPIRICAL STUDY OF DEVELOPMENTAL COMPONENT

To assess the developmental component of our model, we included in the study the parents and teachers of our student subjects and targeted the following sets of parent variables for study:

1. Parents as role models (assessed using measures of self-concept of ability, perceived task difficulty, perceived utility and intrinsic value of math, and estimates of amount of current use of math).

2. Parents as expectancy socializers (assessed using measures of parents' estimates of the following: their children's math abilities, the difficulty of math for their children, their children's liking for math, and their attributions for their children's math performances).

3. Parents as experience providers (assessed using measures of how important parents think it is that their children do well in and take math and how much encouragement in math they have given or planned to give their children).

To assess the impact of teachers as socializers, we made structured observations in classrooms and gave the teachers a brief questionnaire concerning each student. We identified the following teacher variables for study:

1. Teachers as reinforcers (assessed by using the amount of praise and criticism, pattern of praise and criticism, and frequency and type of teacher–student interaction).

2. Teachers as attitude socializers (assessed using public expectancy statements, public attributional statements, public responses to student errors, and written expectancies for and assessments of the relative abilities of students taken from the teacher questionnaire).

Teacher Effects

The effects of teachers' expectancies on their students' performance have been studied extensively since the publication of Rosenthal and Jacobson's *Pygmalion in the Classroom* (1968). Based on the studies of Brophy and Good (1974) and Dweck et al. (1978), we made the following hypotheses regarding the relation between teacher behaviors and student achievement attitudes:

1. Teachers' behaviors influence students' expectancies for success.

2. Teachers treat differently students for whom they have high versus low expectations.

3. Males receive more indiscriminate criticism (criticism toward both the quality and the form of their academic work and toward their conduct) than do females.

4. Females receive more discriminate criticism (criticism directed only to the quality of their work) and more indiscriminate praise than do males.

5. Teachers are more likely to attribute males' mistakes to lack of effort than they are females' mistakes.

These predictions were tested with analyses of variance using the classroom as the unit of analysis (Heller, 1978).

Few significant effects emerged from our analysis, and none of our hypotheses was supported as stated. There were significant sex effects on teachers' use of evaluation feedback: females received less work-related criticism than did males. In addition, teachers' expectancies, measured by the teacher questionnaire, were predictive of student expectancies, even when the effects of the students' past performances in math classes and on standardized tests were partialed out (partial $r = .26$).

Contrary to our predictions, however, teachers did not give more positive feedback to students in the high-expectancy group, and males and females did not differ in the amount of discriminate and indiscriminate praise and criticism they received for the quality or form of their work or for their conduct. In addition, teachers made similar attributions for males and females. Thus, no support was found for the suggestions of Dweck et al. (1978). Further, in a series of stepwise regression analyses, classroom observational measures did not emerge as significant predictors of student attitudinal variables. Thus, while the proposed relations between teachers' expectancies and students' expectancies were supported, the mediating effects of observational variables on expectancies were not demonstrated, suggesting that teacher behaviors in general have little effect on students' achievement-related attitudes (for full details, see Heller, 1978; Parsons, Kaczala, and Meece, 1982).

The analyses reported thus far were performed on the entire sample. It is possible that the effects of classroom behaviors are dependent on teacher style. For example, some teachers may treat males

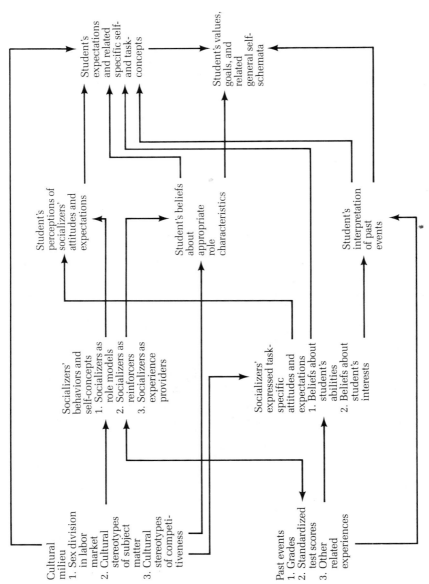

Figure 2-5(a)
Socialization model of achievement attitudes and behaviors.

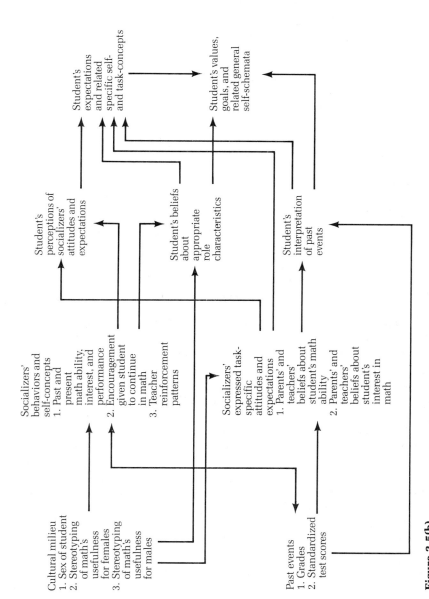

Figure 2-5(b)
Socialization model of mathematics attitudes and behaviors.

[123]

and females differently, while others may not. By collapsing across all of our teachers, these effects would have been masked. To explore this possibility, we selected from the sample the five classrooms with the largest sex differences in the students' self-reported expectancies and the five classrooms with no significant sex differences in expectancies. Then we reanalyzed the data using raw frequency scores (instead of the standardized scores used in the previous analysis) to allow for classroom comparisons (see Parsons, Kaczala, and Meece, 1982, for full details).

As was true for the previous analyses, most variables did not yield significant differences. None of the variables predicted by Dweck's model yielded classroom-type effects. Those effects that were significant were divided into three types:

1. Behaviors characteristic of teacher style (teacher behaviors under primary control of the teacher, e.g., use of praise following a correct answer).

2. Behaviors characteristic of student style (behaviors under primary control of the student, e.g., student-initiated dyadic interactions).

3. Behaviors dependent on both teacher and student style (behaviors requiring interactive responses of both the teacher and the student, e.g., total dyadics).

There were significant differences in the classroom dynamics observed in these two types of classrooms. Teachers in high sex-differentiated classrooms were more critical, were more likely to use a public teaching style and less likely to rely on private dyadic interactions, and were more likely to rely on student volunteers for answers rather than directing the class participation by calling on specific students ($p < .05$ in each case).

Table 2-4 summarizes the effects of student sex on classroom interactions as a function of classroom type. Females interacted more, received more praise, and had higher expectancies in the low sex-differentiated classrooms. Males, on the other hand, interacted more and received more praise in the high sex-differentiated classrooms and yet had similar expectancies across the two types of classrooms.

These data suggest that teacher praise is facilitative of females' expectancies for success in math. To test this hypothesis, we correlated teacher praise and the other teacher-style variables that discriminated the low from the high sex-differentiated classrooms with the following student attitudinal variables: future expectancies, current expectancies, self-concept of ability, interest in math, plans to continue in math, utility of advanced math, and ratings of the difficulty of present and future math courses. Few correlations were significant.

Table 2-4
Sex by classroom type: mean frequency per student per class period

Behavior	Classroom type			
	Low difference		High difference	
	Females	Males	Females	Males
Teacher-style behaviors				
Response opportunities yielding praise[a,b]	.043	.013[c]	.045	.085[c,d]
Total work praise[b]	.099	.032[c]	.066	.121[c,d]
Conduct criticism[a]	.089	.141	.179[d]	.274[d]
Teacher-initiated dyadics[a]	.094	.092	.035	.046
Total criticism[a]	.110	.164	.196	.334
Student-style behaviors				
Student-initiated interactions[b,e]	1.51	.61[c]	1.01	1.23[d]
Student-initiated dyadics[a]	.590	.375	.227	.329
Expectancies[f]	5.08	5.17	4.41[d]	5.24[c]
Joint-style behaviors				
Total response opportunities[a,b]	.536	.188[c]	.471	.842[c,d]
Total dyadics[a]	.684	.467[c]	.312[d]	.375[d]
Open questions[a,b]	.314	.017[c]	.271	.499[c,d]
Total interaction[b]	1.76	.80[c]	1.20[d]	1.52[d]

[a]Classroom type main effect significant: $p<.05$.
[b]Sex by classroom type interaction significant: $p<.05$.
[c]Sex differences within classroom type significant: $p<.05$.
[d]Classroom type effect within sex grouping significant: $p<.05$.
[e]Sex main effect significant: $p<.05$.
[f]Scored on a seven-point scale with 7 = highest expectancies.
Source: Parsons, Kaczala, and Meece (1982).

Teachers' expectancies as measured on the teacher questionnaire had the largest number of significant effects. However, the number of response opportunities and the number of open questions were positively and consistently related to how much students liked math.

We next divided the sample into two additional groups: those students for whom the teacher had high expectancies ("high" students), and those students for whom the teacher had low expectancies ("low" students). The results of these analyses are summarized in Table 2-5.

In general, we found that both high males and high females were

Table 2-5
Sex by classroom type by teacher expectancies[a]

	Low difference				High difference				Grand mean
	Low teacher expectancy		High teacher expectancy		Low teacher expectancy		High teacher expectancy		
	Females	Males	Females	Males	Females	Males	Females	Males	
Teacher-style behaviors									
Praise during response opportunities	.03	$.02^x$	.05	$.01^x$	$.11^Y$	$.02^x$	$.01^{x,y}$	$.12^X$	.05
Total praise for work	.08	$.02^x$	.12	$.04^x$	.14	.05	$.02^x$	$.17^X$	.08
Student-style behaviors									
Student-initiated procedure questions	$.05^x$	$.02^x$	$.09^x$	$.04^x$	$.24^X$	$.02^x$	$.03^x$	$.05^x$	.07
Student-initiated interactions	1.0	$.69^x$	1.9^x	$.56^{x,y}$	1.6^Y	$.88^x$	$.61^{x,y}$	1.4	1.1
Expectancies[b]	4.95^N	4.98	5.28^M	5.53	3.4^n	4.48^N	4.70^m	5.58^M	
Joint-style behaviors									
Open questions	.15	$.03^x$	.48	$.01^x$	.42	.28	.16	$.63^X$	.27
Response opportunities	$.32^x$	$.24^x$	.75	$.15^x$	.75	.50	$.29^x$	1.1^X	.51
Total interactions	1.23	1.00^x	2.15^X	$.67^{x,y}$	1.85^Y	1.15	$.76^{x,y}$	1.75^Y	1.33

Notes: Within each row, a capital letter (X, Y, Z) signifies a mean that is significantly greater than all means superscripted with a corresponding lowercase letter (x, y, z); significant differences were determined using Tukey's HSD, $p < .01$.

M, N and m, n: significant differences were determined using a priori t-tests at $p < .03$.

[a]All 3-way interaction terms significant: $p < .01$.

[b]Student questionnaire item; scale 1–7, 7 = highest.

Source: Parsons, Kaczala, and Meece (1982).

treated differently in each of the two classroom types. High females interacted the most, answered more questions, and received more praise for work and form and less criticism in the low sex-differentiated classrooms. In contrast, high males were accorded the most praise and interacted the most in the high sex-differentiated classrooms. High females in the high sex-differentiated classrooms were accorded less praise than most of the other eight student groups selected for comparison.

Since high females were treated so differently in these two classroom types, we did the correlational analyses outlined above separately for the samples of high and low females. For high females only, amounts of both praise and work criticism were predictive of perceptions of current and future math difficulty, and the total number of teacher-initiated interactions was predictive of both perceptions of future difficulty and plans to continue taking math. Apparently, high females who have a large number of teacher-initiated interactions followed by either praise or criticism see math as easier, and high females who have a large number of teacher-initiated interactions, regardless of the nature of the feedback, are more likely to plan to continue taking math.

Before concluding this discussion of teacher effects, three additional points are important to stress. First, the frequency rates of all these interactive variables were quite low. Second, interactional variables were not as predictive of students' expectancies as were other variables we measured, e.g., student sex and teacher expectancies. Third, the effects of classroom type may be mediated by the general social climate in the classroom rather than by the direct effects of one-to-one teacher–student interactions. Social climate is a function of both the teacher and the set of students in each particular class. Consequently, while classroom interactions may be having an effect on students' expectancies, the effects are not large and may be as much a function of the students as of the teachers.

Parent Effects

It was hypothesized that parents influence their children's achievement behaviors in two ways: through their roles as models, and through their roles as expectancy and value socializers. Tests of both of these hypotheses are discussed in this section.

Important models, especially parents, exhibit behaviors that children come to imitate and later adopt as part of their own behavioral repertoires. If mothers exhibit different behavior patterns than do fathers, then, it has been argued, females and males will acquire sex-differentiated behavioral patterns. With regard to math expectancies, it has been hypothesized that females exhibit more math avoidance and have lower math expectancies than do males because mothers are more likely than fathers to exhibit math-avoidance behaviors. To test this hypothesis, we compared the mathematics-relevant self-concepts of the mothers and fathers in our sample.

In comparison to mothers' self-evaluation responses, fathers' self-evaluations indicated that they felt that they were and always had been better at math, that math was and always had been easier for them, that they needed to expend less effort to do well at math, that they had always enjoyed math more, and that math had always been more useful and important to them. In sum, fathers had a more positive attitude toward math and had a more positive self-concept regarding their math abilities than mothers had. What is more, we found that these sex-differentiated beliefs were specific to math. Consistent with the fact that females on the average outperform males in school, mothers rated their general high school performances higher than did fathers (Parsons, Adler, and Kaczala, 1982).

In line with the modeling hypothesis, one might conclude at this point that we had identified a major cause of sex-differentiated math self-concepts. Males and females differ because their fathers and mothers differ. But one needs to demonstrate a relation between parents' behaviors and children's beliefs before this conclusion is justified. To test the modeling hypothesis more directly, we correlated the parents' self-concept variables with the children's responses to the student questionnaire and to their past-performance scale. None of the more than 100 correlations was significant. Thus, while parents' self-concepts do differ in the predicted direction, the influence of these differences on their children's math self-concepts is minimal.

The second hypothesized source of influence is the parents' expressed beliefs about either the math abilities of their children or the importance of math for their children. To assess the effects of this source, we compared the responses of parents of males and parents of females to questions regarding their perceptions of their children's math abilities, interests, and efforts, their expectancies for their children's future performances in math, and their perceptions of the relative importance of a variety of courses.

The sex of the child had a definite effect on parents' perceptions of their children's math abilities and on the parents' perceptions of the relative importance of various high school courses. While parents did not rate their daughters' math abilities significantly lower than their sons', they did think that math was more difficult for their daughters and that their daughters had to work harder to do well in math. Further, fathers exhibited more frequent sex-differentiated responses than did mothers (Parsons, Adler, and Kaczala, 1982).

That parents feel their daughters have to try harder to do well in math is of particular interest, given both our previous findings and a common finding in the attribution literature. As reported earlier, we found that females think they have to try harder than males to do well in math. Furthermore, on an experimental task, females actually rated their efforts as greater, even though an objective measure of effort did not reveal a sex difference (Parsons, 1978). Interestingly, women have been shown to attribute their success more to effort than do men (Frieze, Fisher, Hanusa, McHugh, and Valle, 1978). Taken together, these findings suggest that females *think* they have to try harder than males to receive a good grade. Our data suggest that parents are reinforcing this tendency. Whether parents initiate the bias or merely echo it is not clear, but they certainly are not providing their daughters with a counterinterpretation.

Is it necessarily harmful that both daughters and their parents think that females have to try harder to do well in math? It has been argued in the attribution literature that because attributions to effort do not contribute to a stable notion of one's ability in a particular domain, attributing one's success to effort is not as ego-enhancing as attributing it to ability. Attributing one's success to effort may also leave doubt about one's future performance on increasingly difficult tasks. If one is having to try very hard to do well now and one expects next year's math course to be even harder, one may not expect to do as well next year. In support of this suggestion, we found that perception of one's current effort is negatively correlated with both future expectancies and with estimates of one's ability and positively correlated with the perceived difficulty of the task ($p<.05$ in each case). If we add to this dynamic the fact that both daughters and their parents think that continuing math is less important for them than do sons and their parents, then a cognitive set emerges that certainly could produce a lower tendency in females to continue in advanced math courses.

Are these parental beliefs about their children's abilities and plans predictive of future math expectancies and future course plans? To answer this question, we correlated the major parent and child variables. The correlations are summarized in Table 2-6. Since the patterns of correlations were essentially the same for males and females, only the results from the entire sample will be discussed.

Children's plans, future expectancies, current expectancies, and perceptions of the importance and value of math were related consistently in the predicted direction to measures of their perceptions of their parents' beliefs and expectancies and to the parents' actual estimates of their children's abilities. Parents' beliefs about their children's abilities to do well in math were predictive of their children's

Table 2-6

Zero-order correlation of mother's and father's attitudes toward child and child's attitudes and perceptions of parents' attitudes

Mother's attitudes

	Past math performance	Intention to take more math	Current expectancies in math	Future expectancies in math	Self-concept of math ability	Perception of task difficulty	Value of math	Perception of parents' perception of math ability	Perception of parents' expectancies	Perception of parents' perception of task difficulty	Perception of parents' aspirations
Perception of importance of math	.41**	.35**	.41**	.44**	.46**	−.11	.42**	.46**	.25**	−.17**	.12
	.42**	.40**	.43**	.44**	.47**	−.09	.43**	.46**	.28**	−.20*	.11
	.39**	.29**	.40*	.50**	.47**	−.16	.43**	.48**	.21*	−.16	.15
Perception of child's math ability	.40**	.34**	.44**	.46**	.54**	−.31**	.33**	.54**	.33**	−.23**	.16*
	.38**	.38**	.45**	.49**	.58**	−.37**	.32**	.58**	.36**	−.29**	.14
	.43**	.27**	.44**	.42**	.49**	−.23*	.35**	.50**	.28**	−.15	.19
Perception of child's effort in math	−.32**	−.21**	−.32*	−.35**	−.47**	.49**	−.20**	−.38**	−.27**	.41**	−.18**
	−.20*	−.26**	−.25**	−.35**	−.44**	.48**	−.19*	−.34**	−.26**	.45**	−.11
	−.47**	−.15	−.40*	−.31**	−.48**	.47**	−.18	−.42**	−.29**	.33**	−.26*

Notes: Within each row, there are three sets of correlations: the top set contains the correlations for all subjects; the middle set, the correlations for females; the bottom set, the correlations for males.

Boxed correlations contain a set of correlations in which the male and female correlations differ $p < .05$.

* $p < .05$.

** $p < .01$.

Source: Based in part on Parsons, Adler, and Kaczala, 1982.

Perception of task difficulty	-.35**	-.27**	-.42**	-.47**	-.58**	.52**	-.29**	-.46**	-.31**	.43**	-.19**
	-.28**	-.27**	-.35**	-.45**	-.53**	.50**	-.23**	-.38**	-.27**	.42**	-.07
	-.46**	-.26**	-.51**	-.48**	-.64**	.51**	-.38**	-.58**	-.38**	.40**	-.37**
Perception of child's perception of importance of math	-.03	.02	.13*	.15*	.14*	-.08	.17**	.18**	.17**	-.07	.21**
	-.09	.11	.09	.10	.09	-.05	.20*	.13	.18*	-.03	.22**
	.04	-.12	.17	.18	.18	-.09	.09	.24*	.17	-.09	.17
Expectancies for child	.51**	.29**	.48**	.50**	.56**	-.33**	.28**	.55**	.36**	-.35**	.19**
	.53**	.28**	.45**	.50**	.56**	-.41**	.18*	.49**	.37**	-.34**	.17*
	.49**	.29**	.51**	.50**	.56**	-.22*	.41**	.63**	.34**	-.35**	.21*
Father's attitudes											
Perception of importance of math	.41**	.34**	.26**	.37**	.31**	-.02	.26**	.34**	.19**	-.10	.07
	.48**	.38**	.30**	.36**	.34**	-.06	.22**	.38**	.15	-.19*	.02
	.32**	.28**	.21*	.40**	.27**	.03	.35**	.28**	.25*	-.00	.17
Perception of child's math ability	.46**	.27**	.36**	.43**	.47**	-.28**	.26**	.48**	.24**	-.28**	.07
	.47**	.25**	.36**	.41**	.48**	-.33**	.18*	.43**	.19*	-.35**	-.01
	.44**	.31**	.34**	.45**	.45**	-.20	.38**	.55**	.29**	-.16	.19
Perception of child's effort in math	-.31**	-.20**	-.35**	-.39**	-.45**	.38**	-.25**	-.37**	-.21**	.34**	-.16*
	-.28**	-.22**	-.34**	-.38**	-.43**	.32**	-.17	-.30**	-.18*	.33**	-.11
	-.34**	-.17	-.33**	-.37**	-.43**	.41**	-.33**	-.43**	-.25*	.33**	-.18
Perception of task difficulty	-.36**	-.19**	-.43**	-.43**	-.53**	.40**	-.25**	-.50**	-.29**	.32**	-.12
	-.37**	-.17*	-.37**	-.35**	-.47**	.35**	-.14	-.42**	-.21*	.33**	.01
	-.35**	-.21	-.48**	-.49**	-.58**	.40**	-.38**	-.59**	-.37**	.27*	-.27*
Perception of child's perception of importance of math	-.02	.11	.06	.12	.03	.10	.17*	.06	.16*	.01	.18**
	-.07	.10	.05	.08	-.01	.13	.18*	.04	.21*	.04	.25**
	.03	.11	.06	.15	.06	.12	.10	.09	.04	.01	.00

(continued)

Table 2-6 (continued)

	Past math performance	Intention to take more math	Current expectancies in math	Future expectancies in math	Self-concept of math ability	Perception of task difficulty	Value of math	Perception of parents' perception of math ability	Perception of parents' expectancies	Perception of parents' perception of task difficulty	Perception of parents' aspirations
Expectancies for child	.53**	.22**	.30**	.40**	.39**	−.21**	.20**	.35**	.18**	−.21**	.09
	.57**	.21*	.30**	.40**	.38**	−.28**	.10	.28**	.15	−.22**	.07
	.49**	.24*	.30**	.42**	.40**	−.12	.34**	.43**	.22*	−.19	.11
Child's perceptions											
Perception of parents' perception of math ability	.34**	.32**	.61**	.64**	.72**	−.38**	.42**	1.00	.49**	−.36**	.25**
	.27**	.34**	.58**	.62**	.74**	−.44**	.35**	1.00	.45**	−.36**	.19**
	.42**	.29**	.64**	.65**	.69**	−.28**	.51**	1.00	.55**	−.36**	.33**
Perception of parents' expectancies	.10	.26**	.47**	.58**	.52**	−.21**	.45**	.49**	1.00	−.26**	.73**
	.04	.26**	.52**	.59**	.55**	−.21**	.41**	.45**	1.00	−.25**	.73**
	.17	.27**	.42**	.58**	.48**	−.21*	.50**	.55**	1.00	−.28**	.75**
Perception of parents' perception of task difficulty	−.13*	−.11	−.37**	−.32**	−.44**	.51**	−.15**	−.36**	−.26**	1.00	−.12*
	−.06	−.15	−.38**	−.29**	−.45**	.46**	−.16*	−.36**	−.25**	1.00	−.07
	−.22*	−.06	−.35**	−.34**	−.42**	.57**	−.13	−.36**	−.28**	1.00	−.18

course plans. Further, despite the greater sex typing by fathers, fathers' beliefs were not the stronger predictors of their children's self-concepts, expectancies, or plans (Parsons, Adler, and Kaczala, 1982).

In conclusion, parents had sex-differentiated perceptions of their children's math abilities, despite the similarity of actual performances of their sons and daughters. This difference was most marked for parents' estimates of how hard their children have to work to do well in math. Parents also thought advanced math was more important for their sons than for their daughters. Parents' perceptions of and expectations for their children were related to both the children's perceptions of their parents' beliefs and to the children's self-concepts, future expectations, and plans. Further, parents' beliefs and children's perceptions of these beliefs were more directly related to children's self-concepts, expectancies, and plans than were the children's own past performances in math. Finally, parents as role models of sex-differentiated math behaviors did not have a direct effect on their children's self-concepts, expectations, and course plans.

General Effects

As hypothesized, we found that parents' and teachers' beliefs are related to students' expectancies and plans. We predicted that this link would be mediated by students' perceptions of their parents' and teachers' beliefs rather than affected directly by the socializers' beliefs or by the shared knowledge of the students' math aptitudes. To assess these hypotheses, we performed a path analysis on the teacher, parent, and child scores. Results from this analysis are displayed in Figure 2-6.

In support of our predictions, the students' expectancies and plans were related most directly to their self-concepts of math abilities and to their perceptions of their parents' and teachers' beliefs about their math aptitudes and potentials. Furthermore, the influences of parents' and teachers' attitudes on students' math self-concepts, expectancies, and plans were mediated by the students' perceptions of these attitudes. Finally, while the zero-order correlations of the students' math-aptitude measure to the criterion measures occasionally were significant, the path coefficients, when other cognitive mediators were partialed out, were not significant. Thus, students' attitudes were more directly related to course plans and expectancies than either past objective measures of the students' performance or parents' actual attitudes. Any effect that these past objective measures might have had on the students' self-concepts was mediated by their impact on the perceptions of teachers and parents, rather than by their direct effect on the students' estimates of their own abilities.

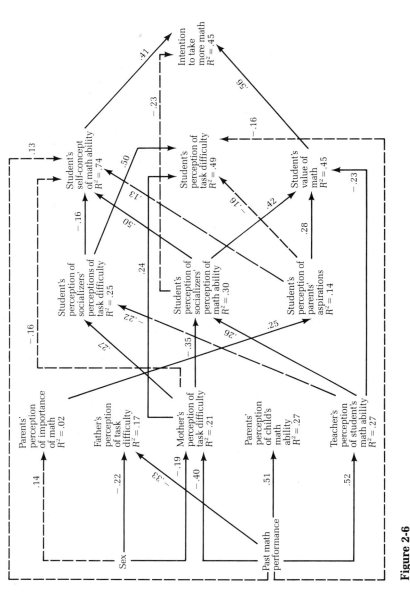

Figure 2-6

Reduced path-analytic diagram for test of socialization model. Dashed lines are significant at $p < .05$, solid lines at $p < .01$; $N = 156$; standardized beta weights are shown on path; $R^2 =$ percent of variance accounted for on each criterion measure by all preceding predictor variables; each R^2 is listed under its criterion measure.

With regard to the differential effectiveness of various socializers, mothers appear to have the strongest influence on students' beliefs and attitudes; fathers had no significant independent effect over and above that which they shared with mothers. Teachers, especially last year's teachers, had less effect than either mothers or parents in general.

SUMMARY AND DISCUSSION

In conclusion, let us review where we've been and what we've found. At the theoretical level, we identified key achievement-related psychological constructs and presented a developmental model of individual differences in those key constructs. This model, depicted in Figure 2-1, has two major components: a psychological component, in which the interrelations of the various psychological constructs at one point in time and within each individual are specified (depicted in more detail in Figure 2-2); and a developmental component, in which the origins of individual differences are specified (depicted in detail in Figure 2-5). Because sex differences have received so much attention in recent years, we made specific reference when appropriate to the applications of our model to an analysis of the origins and implications of sex-differentiated achievement-related belief systems.

In the theoretical sections, we tried to provide as full a picture as possible of the various factors included in our general model of achievement-related behaviors. We discussed a wide range of influences and specified various relations among them. Given the scope of the chapter, however, the discussion of each of these influences was brief, and only the most salient and global interrelations were considered in any detail.

In general, the studies reviewed supported the importance of the variables specified in our model. Achievement-related behaviors are related to self-concepts of abilities, expectancies, perceptions of task difficulty, perceptions of task value, personal goals and self-schemata, perceptions of parents' and teachers' beliefs and attitudes, parents' and teachers' actual behaviors, beliefs, and attitudes, and perceptions of the cultural stereotypes associated with particular activities. However, while the empirical work reviewed has provided some insights into the factors related to achievement-related behaviors, this body of literature has several shortcomings.

First, while broad, theoretical models have been developed and tested in the laboratory, the external validity of these findings has rarely been tested. Instead, field studies on academic achievement have been designed without the guidance of a broadly based, integrative, theoretical orientation. Applied researchers have tended to proceed piecemeal, each researcher investigating a subset of the possible causes. What has emerged resembles the proverbial blind men's description of the elephant: many conclusions but little understanding of the broader picture. As a consequence, two related research problems surfaced: imprecise definitions of the variables being studied, and a paucity of comprehensive studies designed to assess the interactions between and relative importance of the many variables that undoubtedly are involved. What was needed was a framework that would (1) provide more precise conceptualization of the components, (2) link the various pieces together, (3) suggest causal sequences, and (4) outline the relations between parent and teacher variables and students' actual beliefs and achievement-related behaviors. We designed our model with these concerns in mind.

Second, while an array of possible mediators has been proposed, many studies examining these variables have not tested the mediating hypotheses directly. Instead, many have tested for differences on the proposed mediators between high and low need achievers or between the sexes. But the demonstration of a sex difference or expectancy group difference on a variable does not support a conclusion regarding the causal importance of that variable in influencing achievement-related behaviors. At the very least, research should provide a direct test of the relation between the proposed mediator and the target achievement-related behavior. The optimal research program would include studies designed to estimate the causal direction of the relation between mediators and behavior. Included would be (1) longitudinal studies that provide tests of both the causal sequence of developmental change in the natural setting and the impact of the various socializers, (2) experimental studies designed to assess the internal validity and causal significance of various experiences and attitudes, and (3) correlational studies that employ statistical techniques for making causal inferences.

In the empirical sections, we summarized a large-scale longitudinal study designed to test major aspects of both of the components of this model through the use of two of these methods: longitudinal data, and statistical techniques of causal inference. In particular, the study relied on the use of path-analytic and cross-lagged panel correlational procedures to provide support for both our psychological and our developmental hypotheses.

With regard to the psychological hypotheses, we found support for the importance of the constructs we had identified as critical determinants of achievement-related behaviors. In particular, we found that students' interpretations of reality (i.e., attributions, self-concepts of abilities, and perceptions of the beliefs of parents and teachers) were more influential determinants of expectancies, values, and course plans than were objective indicators of past reality (i.e., previous grades and actual teachers' behaviors). In addition, self-concept of their ability was as powerful a predictor of subsequent grades as was their past performance in math.

Cross-lagged panel analyses provided a more rigorous test of our causal model. Expectancies were caused by self-concept of ability; self-concept of ability was determined by perceptions of both the effort required to do well and the difficulty of the task; and subjective task value was determined by the perceived cost of the effort needed to do well. Contrary to our predictions, however, perceptions of teachers' and parents' beliefs regarding one's abilities were determined by one's self-concept of ability and not vice versa.

We found few sex differences, but those that emerged indicated that females had a less positive self-concept of ability and felt that math was more difficult and of less value than did males. In addition, females were less likely to attribute their success to ability, more likely to attribute their failure to lack of ability, and more likely to attribute their success to stable effort than were males. Since no single variable emerged as the critical mediator of sex differences in expectancies or values, these findings suggest that sex-differentiated course enrollment is a joint function of perceived task difficulty, self-concept of one's ability, and the subjective value of math. Individual differences, especially sex differences, appear to be the result primarily of parents' beliefs regarding the difficulty of math for their children.

Turning to our developmental hypotheses, we found several intriguing results. First, parents, especially mothers, had a stronger influence on children's achievement-related beliefs than did teachers. Second, sex differences in expectancies were not mediated by teachers' use of discriminate or indiscriminate praise or criticism, as predicted by Dweck, Davidson, Nelson, and Enna (1978). Third, parents had little influence through their power as role models; instead, it was their role as direct socializers of achievement beliefs and attitudes that was important. Fourth, parents' beliefs regarding the amount of effort their children had to exert to do well and their beliefs about the importance of the activity for their children were the critical mediators of sex-differentiated self-concepts of math abilities and math expectancies. Finally, the effects of the students' sex and past academic histories on self-concepts and related achievement behaviors were mediated almost totally by the interpretation of these events made by socializers and by the students themselves.

REFERENCES

Aiken, L., 1970. Attitudes toward mathematics. *Review of Educational Research, 40*, 551–596.

Aiken, L. 1976. Update on attitudes and other affective variables in learning mathematics. *Review of Educational Research, 46*, 293–311.

Armstrong, J., and S. Kahl. 1978. *A national assessment of performance and participation of women in mathematics.* Prepared for National Institute of Education, Washington, DC.

Armstrong, J., and S. Kahl. 1980. *A national assessment of performance and participation of women in mathematics.* Final report to National Institute of Education, Washington, DC.

Astin, H. 1967. *The woman doctorate in America: Origins, career, and family.* New York: Russell Sage.

Astin, H., M. Harway, and P. McNamara. 1976. *Sex discrimination in education: Access to post-secondary education.* National Center for Education Statistics, Department of Health, Education and Welfare, Washington, DC.

Atkinson, J. W. (ed.). 1958. *Motives in fantasy, action, and society.* Princeton, NJ: Van Nostrand.

Atkinson, J. W. 1964. *An introduction to motivation.* Princeton, NJ: Van Nostrand.

Atkinson, J. W., and D. Birch. 1970. *A dynamic theory of action.* New York: Wiley.

Bandura, A. 1977. Self-efficacy: Toward a unifying theory of behavioral change. *Psychological Review, 84*, 191–215.

Bandura, A., and R. H. Walters. 1963. *Social learning and personality development.* New York: Holt, Rinehart and Winston.

Bar-tal, D. 1978. Attributional analysis of achievement-related behavior. *Review of Educational Research, 48*, 259–271.

Battle, E. 1966. Motivational determinants of academic task persistence. *Journal of Personality and Social Psychology, 4*, 634–642.

Beck, J. 1977–1978. Locus of control, task expectancies, and children's performance following failure. *Journal of Educational Research, 71*, 207–210.

Beech, R. P., and A. Schoeppe. 1974. Development of value systems in adolescents. *Developmental Psychology, 10*, 644–656.

Boswell, S. 1979. Nice girls don't study mathematics: The perspective from elementary school. Paper presented at meeting of American Educational Research Association, San Francisco.

Brookover, W. B., and E. L. Erickson. 1975. *Sociology of education.* Homewood, IL: Dorsey.

Brophy, J. E., and T. Good. 1974. *Teacher–student relationships: Causes and consequences.* New York: Holt, Rinehart and Winston.

Broverman, I. K., S. R. Vogel, D. M. Broverman, F. E. Clarkson, and P. S. Rosenkrantz. 1972. Sex-role stereotypes: A current appraisal. *Journal of Social Issues, 28*, 59–78.

Brush, L. 1978. A validation study of the mathematics anxiety rating scale (MARS). *Educational and Psychological Measurement, 38*, 485–490.

Brush, L. 1980. *Encouraging girls in mathematics: The problem and the solution.* Cambridge, MA: Abt Books.

Calsyn, R., and D. Kenny. 1977. Self-concept of ability and perceived evaluation of others: Cause or effect of academic achievement? *Journal of Educational Psychology, 69*, 136–145.

Connor, J. M., M. E. Schackman, and L. A. Serbin. 1978. Sex-related differences in response to practice on a visual–spatial test and generalization to a related test. *Child Development, 49*, 24–29.

Cooper, H. 1976. Teacher–student interaction. Paper presented at meeting of Eastern Psychological Association, New York.

Cooper, H. 1979. Pygmalion grows up: A model for teacher expectation communication and performance influence. *Review of Educational Research, 49*, 389–410.

Covington, M., and R. Beery. 1976. *Self-worth and school learning.* New York: Holt, Rinehart and Winston.

Covington, M., and C. Omelich. 1979a. Are causal attributions causal? A path analysis of the cognitive model of achievement motivation. *Journal of Personality and Social Psychology, 37*, 1487–1504.

Covington, M., and C. Omelich. 1979b. Effort: The double-edged sword in school achievement. *Journal of Educational Psychology, 71*, 169–182.

Crandall, V. C. 1969. Sex differences in expectancy of intellectual and academic reinforcement. In C. P. Smith (ed.), *Achievement-related behaviors in children.* New York: Russell Sage.

Crandall, V. C., W. Katkovsky, and V. J. Crandall. 1965. Children's belief in their own control of reinforcement in intellectual–academic achievement situations. *Child Development, 36*, 91–109.

Crandall, V. J., W. Katkovsky, and A. Preston. 1962. Motivational and ability determinants of young children's intellectual achievement behavior. *Child Development, 33*, 643–661.

Deaux, K., and T. Emswiller. 1974. Explanations of successful performance on sex-linked tasks: What's skill for the male is luck for the female. *Journal of Personality and Social Psychology, 29*, 80–85.

deCharms, R. 1976. *Enhancing motivation.* New York: Irvington.

Deci, E. L. 1975. *Intrinsic motivation.* New York: Plenum.

Diener, C. I., and C. S. Dweck. 1978. An analysis of learned helplessness: Continuous change in performance, strategy, and achievement cognitions following failure. *Journal of Personality and Social Psychology, 36*, 451–462.

Diener, C. I., and C. S. Dweck. 1979. An analysis of learned helplessness: II. The process of success. Unpublished manuscript.

Diggory, J. 1966. *Self-evaluation: Concepts and studies.* New York: Wiley.

Doris, J., and S. B. Sarason. 1955. Test anxiety and blame assignment in a failure situation. *Journal of Abnormal and Social Psychology, 50,* 335–338.

Dornbusch, S. M. 1974. To try or not to try. *Stanford Magazine, 2,* 51–54.

Douvan, E., and J. Adelson. 1966. *The adolescent experience.* New York: Wiley.

Dreger, R. M., and L. R. Aiken. 1957. Identification of number anxiety. *Journal of Educational Psychology, 47,* 344–351.

Duncan, O. D. 1966. Path analysis: Sociological examples. *American Journal of Sociology, 72,* 1–16.

Dunteman, G. H., J. Wisenbaker, and M. E. Taylor. 1979. Race and sex differences in college science program participation. Report to National Science Foundation, Washington, DC.

Dweck, C. S. 1975. The role of expectations and attributions in the alleviation of learned helplessness. *Journal of Personality and Social Psychology, 31,* 674–685.

Dweck, C. S., and E. Bush. 1976. Sex differences in learned helplessness: I. Differential debilitation with peer and adult evaluations. *Developmental Psychology, 12,* 147–156.

Dweck, C. S., W. Davidson, S. Nelson, and B. Enna. 1978. Sex differences in learned helplessness: II. The contingencies of evaluative feedback in the classroom; III. An experimental analysis. *Developmental Psychology, 14,* 268–276.

Dweck, C. S., and D. Gilliard. 1975. Expectancy statements as determinants of reactions to failure: Sex differences in persistence and expectancy change. *Journal of Personality and Social Psychology, 32,* 1077–1084.

Dweck, C. S., and T. E. Goetz. 1978. Attributions and learned helplessness. In J. H. Harvey, W. Ickes, and R. F. Kidd (eds.), *New directions in attribution research.* Vol. 2. Hillsdale, NJ: Lawrence Erlbaum.

Dweck, C. S., and N. D. Reppucci. 1973. Learned helplessness and reinforcement responsibility in children. *Journal of Personality and Social Psychology, 25,* 109–116.

Dwyer, C. A. 1974. Influence of children's sex-role standards on reading and arithmetic. *Journal of Educational Psychology, 6,* 811–816.

Edwards, W. 1954. The theory of decision making. *Psychological Bulletin, 51,* 380–417.

Ernest, J. 1976. *Mathematics and sex.* Santa Barbara: University of California Press.

Etaugh, C., and B. Brown. 1975. Perceiving the causes of success and failure of male and female performers. *Developmental Psychology, 11,* 103.

Feather, N. T. 1966. Effects of prior success and failure on expectations of success and subsequent performance. *Journal of Personality and Social Psychology, 3,* 287–298.

Feather, N. T., and J. G. Simon. 1973. Fear of success and causal attributions for outcome. *Journal of Personality, 41,* 525–542.

Feldman-Summers, S. A., and S. B. Kiesler. 1974. Those who are number two try harder: The effects of sex on attributions of causality. *Journal of Personality and Social Psychology, 30,* 846–855.

Fennema, E. 1974. Mathematics learning and the sexes: A review. *Journal for Research in Mathematics Education, 5,* 126–139.

Fennema, E. 1977. Influences of selected cognitive, affective, and educational variables on sex-related differences in mathematics learning and studying. *Women and mathematics: Research perspectives for change.* NIE Papers in Education and Work, No. 8.

Fennema, E. 1981. Attribution theory and achievement in mathematics. In S. R. Yussen (ed.), *The development of reflection.* New York: Academic.

Fennema, E., and J. Sherman. 1977. Sex-related differences in mathematics achievement, spatial visualization and affective factors. *American Educational Research Journal, 14,* 51–71.

Fennema, E., and J. Sherman. 1978. Sex-related differences in mathematics achievement and related factors: A further study. *Journal for Research in Mathematics Education, 9,* 189–203.

Foersterling, F. 1980. Sex differences in risk taking: Effects of subjective and objective probability of success. *Personality and Social Psychology Bulletin, 6,* 149–152.

Fox, L. 1975. Career interests and mathematical acceleration for girls. Paper presented at meeting of American Psychological Association, Chicago.

Fox, L. 1977. The effects of sex-role socialization on mathematics participation and achievement. *Women and mathematics: Research perspectives for change.* NIE Papers in Education and Work, No. 8.

Fox, L., L. Brody, and D. Tobin. 1979. Sex differences in attitudes and course taking in mathematics among the gifted: Implications for counseling and career education. Paper presented at meeting of the American Educational Research Association, San Francisco.

Fox, L. H., and S. A. Denham. 1974. Values and career interests of mathematically and scientifically precocious youth. In J. C. Stanley, D. P. Keating, and L. H. Fox (eds.), *Mathematical talent: Discovery, description and development.* Baltimore: Johns Hopkins University Press.

Frieze, I. H., J. Fisher, B. Hanusa, M. McHugh, and V. Valle. 1978. Attributing the causes of success and failure: Internal and external barriers to achievement in women. In J. Sherman and F. Denmark (eds.), *Psychology of women: Future directions of research.* New York: Psychological Dimensions.

Goff, S. 1978. Career plans and life goals of college students. Paper presented at meeting of American Psychological Association, Toronto.

Good, T., J. N. Sikes, and J. E. Brophy. 1973. Effects of teacher sex and student sex on classroom interaction. *Journal of Educational Psychology, 65,* 74–87.

Harter, S. 1980. A model of intrinsic mastery motivation in children: Individual differences and developmental change. *Minnesota Symposium on Child Psychology.* Vol. 14. Hillsdale, NJ: Lawrence Erlbaum.

Hawley, P. 1971. What women think men think: Does it affect their career choice? *Journal of Counseling Psychology, 18,* 193–199.

Hawley, P. 1972. Perceptions of male models of femininity related to career choice. *Journal of Counseling Psychology, 19,* 308–313.

Heider, F. 1958. *The psychology of interpersonal relations.* New York: Wiley.

Heller, K. A. 1978. Expectancies for success in mathematics: The effects of students' attributions, teachers' expectancies, and teacher–student interactions. Doctoral dissertation, University of Michigan.

Heller, K., R. Futterman, C. Kaczala, J. D. Karabenick, and J. Parsons. 1978. Expectancies, utility values, and attributions for performance in mathematics. Paper presented at meeting of American Educational Research Association, Toronto.

Hennig, M., and A. Jardim. 1976. *The managerial woman.* New York: Doubleday.

Hill, K. T. 1977. The relation of evaluative practices to test anxiety and achievement motivation. *Educator, 19,* 15–22.

Hilton, T. L., and G. W. Berglund. 1974. Sex differences in mathematics achievement: A longitudinal study. *Journal of Educational Research, 67,* 231–237.

Hoffman, L. W. 1972. Early childhood experiences and women's achievement motives. *Journal of Social Issues, 28,* 129–155.

Husen, T. (ed.). 1967. *International study of achievement in mathematics.* Vols. 1 and 2. New York: Wiley.

Jackaway, R. 1974. Sex differences in achievement motivation, behavior, and attributions about success and failure. Doctoral dissertation, State University of New York, Albany.

Kaminski, D., E. Erickson, M. Ross, and L. Bradfield. 1976. Why females don't like mathematics: The effect of parental expectations. Paper presented at meeting of American Sociological Association, New York.

Kenny, D. A. 1975. Cross-lagged panel correlation: A test for spuriousness. *Psychological Bulletin, 82,* 887–903.

Kohlberg, L. 1969. Stage and sequence: The cognitive–developmental approach to socialization. In D. A. Goslin (ed.), *Handbook of socialization theory and research.* New York: Rand McNally.

Kruglanski, A. W. 1975. The endogenous–exogenous partition in attribution theory. *Psychological Review, 82,* 387–406.

Kukla, A. 1972. Foundations of an attributional theory of performance. *Psychological Review, 79,* 454–470.

Kukla, A. 1978. An attributional theory of choice. In L. Berkowitz (ed.), *Advances in experimental social psychology.* Vol. 2. New York: Academic.

Lazarus, M. 1974. Mathophobia: Some personal speculations. *The Principal, 53,* 16–22.

Lepper, M. R., and D. Greene (eds.). 1978. *The hidden costs of reward: New perspectives on the psychology of human motivation.* Hillsdale, NJ: Lawrence Erlbaum.

Lewin, K. 1938. *The conceptual representation and the measurement of psychological forces.* Durham, NC: Duke University Press.

Liebert, R. M., R. B. McCall, and M. A. Hanratty. 1971. Effects of sex-typed information of children's toy preference. *Journal of Genetic Psychology, 119,* 133–136.

Lipman-Blumen, J., and A. R. Tickameyer. 1975. Sex roles in transition: A ten-year perspective. In A. Inheles (ed.), *Annual Review of Sociology.* Vol. 1. Palo Alto, CA: Annual Reviews.

Maccoby, E. E., and C. N. Jacklin. 1974. *The psychology of sex differences.* Stanford, CA: Stanford University Press.

McMahan, I. 1973. Relationships between causal attributions and expectancy for success. *Journal of Personality and Social Psychology, 28,* 108–114.

Mandler, G., and S. B. Sarason. 1952. A study of anxiety and learning. *Journal of Abnormal and Social Psychology, 47,* 166–173.

Markus, H. 1980. The self in thought and memory. In D. M. Wegner and R. R. Vallacher (eds.), *The self in social psychology.* New York: Oxford University Press.

Meece, J. 1980. A theoretical framework for studying students' course selection in mathematics. Paper presented at meeting of American Educational Research Association, Boston.

Meyer, W. U., V. Folkes, and B. Weiner. 1976. The perceived informational value and affective consequences of choice behavior and intermediate difficulty task selection. *Journal of Research in Personality, 10,* 410–423.

Montanelli, D. S., and K. T. Hill. 1969. Children's achievement expectations and performance as a function of two consecutive reinforcement experiences, sex of subject, and sex of experimenter. *Journal of Personality and Social Psychology, 13,* 115–128.

Montemayor, R. 1974. Children's performances in a game and their attraction to it as a function of sex-typed labels. *Child Development, 45,* 152–156.

Mortimer, J. T., and R. G. Simmons. 1978. Adult socialization. In *Annual Review of Sociology.* Vol. 4. Palo Alto, CA: Annual Reviews.

Nash, S. C. 1979. Sex role as a mediator of intellectual functioning. In M. A. Wittig and A. C. Petersen (eds.), *Sex-related differences in cognitive functioning: Developmental issues.* New York: Academic.

Nicholls, J. G. 1975. Causal attributions and other achievement-related cognitions: Effects of task outcomes, attainment value, and sex. *Journal of Personality and Social Psychology, 31,* 379–389.

Nicholls, J. G. 1976. Effort is virtuous, but it's better to have ability: Evaluative responses to perceptions of effort and ability. *Journal of Research in Personality, 10*, 306–315.

Nicholls, J. G. 1979. Quality and equality in intellectual development: The role of motivation in education. *American Psychologist, 34*, 1071–1084.

Parsons, J. 1977. Attributional patterns and women's career choices. Paper presented at meeting of American Psychological Association, San Francisco.

Parsons, J. 1978. Cognitive mediation of the effects of evaluative feedback on children's affect and expectancy for success. Paper presented at meeting of American Educational Research Association, Toronto.

Parsons, J. 1980. Attributions: Cause, effect or mediator of attitudes toward mathematics. Paper presented at meeting of American Educational Research Association, Boston.

Parsons, J. 1981. Attributions, learned helplessness, and sex differences in achievement. In S. R. Yussen (ed.), *The development of achievement.* New York: Academic.

Parsons, J., T. Adler, and C. Kaczala. 1982. Socialization of achievement attitudes and beliefs: Parental influences. *Child Development, 53*, 310–321.

Parsons, J. E., I. H. Frieze, and D. N. Ruble. 1976. Introduction. *Journal of Social Issues, 32*, 1–5.

Parsons, J. E., and S. B. Goff. 1978. Achievement and motivation: Dual modalities. *Journal of Educational Psychology, 13*, 93–96.

Parsons, J. E., and S. B. Goff. 1980. Achievement motivation: A dual modality. In L. J. Fyans (ed.), *Recent trends in achievement motivation: Theory and research.* New York: Plenum.

Parsons, J., C. Kaczala, and J. Meece. 1982. Socialization of achievement attitudes and beliefs: Teacher influences. *Child Development, 53*, 322–339.

Parsons, J. E., and D. N. Ruble. 1977. The development of achievement-related expectancies. *Child Development, 48*, 1075–1079.

Parsons, J. E., D. N. Ruble, K. L. Hodges, and A. W. Small. 1976. Cognitive–developmental factors in emerging sex differences in achievement-related expectancies. *Journal of Social Issues, 32*, 47–61.

Pedersen, K., P. Elmore, and D. Bleyer. 1979. A study of the attitudes toward mathematics of junior high school students. Paper presented at meeting of American Educational Research Association, San Francisco.

Poffenberger, T., and D. Norton. 1959. Factors in the formation of attitudes toward mathematics. *Journal of Educational Research, 52*, 171–176.

Purkey, W. W. 1970. *Self-concept and school achievement.* Englewood Cliffs, NJ: Prentice-Hall.

Raynor, J. O. 1974. Future orientation in the study of achievement motivation. In J. W. Atkinson and J. O. Raynor (eds.), *Motivation and achievement.* Washington, DC: Winston.

Rosenthal, R., and L. Jacobson. 1968. *Pygmalion in the classroom: Teacher expectations and pupils' intellectual performance.* New York: Holt, Rinehart and Winston.

Rosenthal, R., and R. L. Rosnow. 1969. *Artifacts in behavioral research.* New York: Academic.

Rotter, J. B. 1954. *Social learning and clinical psychology.* Englewood Cliffs, NJ: Prentice-Hall.

Ruble, D. N., and A. K. Boggiano. 1980. Optimizing motivation in an achievement context. In B. Keogh (ed.), *Advances in special education.* Vol. 1. Greenwich, CT: Jai Press.

Ruble, D. N., J. E. Parsons, and J. Ross. 1976. Self-evaluative response of children in an achievement setting. *Child Development, 47,* 990–997.

Sarason, S. B. 1972. Experimental approaches to test anxiety: Attention and the uses of information. In C. D. Spielberger (ed.), *Anxiety: Current trends in theory and research.* Vol. 2. New York: Academic.

Sears, R. R., E. E. Maccoby, and H. Levin. 1957. *Patterns of child rearing.* Evanston, IL: Row, Peterson.

Seligman, M. E. P. 1975. *Helplessness: On depression, development, and death.* San Francisco: W. H. Freeman and Company.

Sherman, J. 1977. Effects of biological factors on sex-related differences in mathematics achievement. *Women and mathematics: Research perspectives for change.* NIE Papers in Education and Work, No. 8.

Sherman, J. 1979. Predicting mathematics performance in high school girls and boys. *Journal of Educational Psychology, 71,* 242–249.

Sherman, J. 1980. *Women and mathematics: Summary of research from 1977–1979.* Final report to National Institute of Education, Washington, DC.

Sherman, J., and E. Fennema. 1977. The study of mathematics by high school girls and boys: Related variables. *American Educational Research Journal, 14,* 159–168.

Spence, J. T., R. L. Helmreich, and J. Stapp. 1975. Ratings of self and peers on sex-role attributes and their relation to self-esteem and conception of masculinity and femininity. *Journal of Personality and Social Psychology, 32,* 29–39.

Spenner, K., and D. L. Featherman. 1978. Achievement ambitions. *Annual Review of Sociology, 4,* 373–420.

Stallings, J., and A. Robertson. 1979. Factors influencing women's decisions to enroll in advanced mathematics courses. Prepared for National Institute of Education, Washington, DC.

Stein, A. H. 1971. The effects of sex-role standards for achievement and sex-role preferences on three determinants of achievement motivation. *Developmental Psychology, 4,* 219–231.

Stein, A. H., and M. M. Bailey. 1973. The socialization of achievement orientation in females. *Psychological Bulletin, 80,* 345–366.

Stein, A. H., and T. Smithells. 1969. Age and sex differences in children's sex-role standards about achievement. *Developmental Psychology, 1,* 252–259.

Suinn, R., and F. Richardson. 1972. The mathematics anxiety scale: Psychometric data. *Journal of Counseling Psychology, 19,* 551–554.

Thibaut, J. W., and H. H. Kelley. 1959. *The social psychology of groups.* New York: Wiley.

Tobias, S. 1978. *Overcoming math anxiety.* New York: Norton.

Veroff, J. 1969. Social comparison and the development of achievement motivation. In C. P. Smith (ed.), *Achievement-related behaviors in children.* New York: Russell Sage.

Veroff, J. 1977. Process vs. impact in men's and women's motivation. *Psychology of Women Quarterly, 1,* 283–292.

Webster, M., and B. Sobicozek. 1974. *Sources of self-evaluation: A formal theory of significant others and social influence.* New York: Wiley.

Weiner, B. 1972. *Theories of motivation: From mechanism to cognition.* Chicago: Markham.

Weiner, B. 1974. *Achievement motivation and attribution theory.* Morriston, NJ: General Learning Press.

Weiner, B., I. Frieze, A. Kukla, L. Reed, S. Rest, and R. M. Rosenbaum. 1971. *Perceiving the causes of success and failure.* Morristown, NJ: General Learning Press.

Weiner, B., D. Russell, and D. Lerman. 1978. Affective consequences of causal ascriptions. In J. H. Harvey, W. Ickes, and R. F. Kidd (eds.), *New directions in attribution research.* Vol. 2. Hillsdale, NJ: Lawrence Erlbaum.

Weiner, B., D. Russell, and D. Lerman. 1979. The cognition–emotion process in achievement-related contexts. *Journal of Personality and Social Psychology, 37,* 1211–1221.

Weiner, B., and K. Schneider. 1971. Drive versus cognitive theory: A reply to Boor and Harmon. *Journal of Personality and Social Psychology, 18,* 258–262.

Wine, J. 1971. Test anxiety and direction of attention. *Psychological Bulletin, 76,* 92–104.

Winterbottom, M. 1958. The relation of need for achievement in learning experiences in independence and mastery. In J. W. Atkinson (ed.), *Motives in fantasy, action, and society.* Princeton, NJ: Van Nostrand.

Wise, L. 1979. Long-term consequences of sex differences in high school mathematics education. Paper presented at meeting of American Educational Research Association, San Francisco.

Wise, L., L. Steel, and C. MacDonald. 1979. Origins and career consequences of sex differences in high school mathematics achievement. Prepared for National Institute of Education, Washington, DC.

Wright, S. 1934. The method of path coefficients. *Annals of Mathematical Statistics, 5,* 161–215.

3

Achieving Styles in Men and Women: A Model, an Instrument, and Some Findings

Jean Lipman-Blumen
University of Maryland

Alice Handley-Isaksen

Harold J. Leavitt
Stanford University

EDITOR'S OVERVIEW

In previous chapters, the authors have focused on psychological models that describe the nature and intensity of individuals' achievement-related motives and the expectations and values they bring to particular types of tasks and that relate these psychological characteristics to such behaviors as task persistence, task choice, and quality of task performance. The authors of this chapter, Jean Lipman-Blumen, Alice Handley-Isaksen, and Harold J. Leavitt, note that these and other well-known psychological approaches fail to specify the means that individuals prefer to use in their attempts to realize their achievement goals, or, as they have labeled these characteristic strategies, individuals' *achieving styles*. They present a conceptual model in which achieving styles are divided into three domains: direct, instrumental, and relational—each with three substyles.

Individuals using a *direct* achievement style are described as confronting tasks directly and achieving through their own efforts. Within the direct domain is the *intrinsic* substyle, in which the individual pits himself or herself against an impersonal standard of performance excellence; the *competitive* substyle, in which the individual's goal is to best others; and the *power* substyle, in which the individual assumes leadership and controls others as a means to accomplish achievement goals.

The *instrumental* style refers to the use of the self or others as the means to goals. Within the instrumental domain, individuals who trade on their status, influence, reputation, and other social and personal characteristics to reach their goals are described as employing a *personal* substyle. Those who use relationships with other individuals (such as cultivating friendships and developing networks of associates) to accomplish their goals are described as employing a *social* substyle. Individuals who lack faith in their own efficacy and depend on others for direction and help are described as using a *reliant* substyle.

The third, *relational* style stands in contrast to the direct style, referring to the individual's preference for achieving through contributing actively or passively to the accomplishment of another. Thus, individuals employing the *collaborative* substyle prefer group efforts to individual ones, but contribute actively to the achievement of group goals and expect to accept their share of both responsibility and credit for the group's accomplishments. Those using a *contributory* substyle prefer a more secondary role, meeting their achievement needs by facilitating and helping other achievers. And, finally, the *vicarious* substyle is employed by those who are content to identify with achieving others and to satisfy their own needs by sharing in their success.

The nine substyles have varying degrees of compatibility or correlation with each other, the authors proposing that a circular conceptual representation best describes the relationships among them. Although the authors suggest that most individuals primarily employ one or two adjacent substyles, they also propose that individuals differ both in the range of the nine substyles they are comfortable in using and in the flexibility of their stylistic behavior, i.e., their capacity to vary their behavior according to situational demands.

As the flexibility notion implies, the characteristics of the setting in which individuals manifest or attempt to realize their achievement goals—that is, the particular role or position they occupy—can be expected to be related to the achieving styles that individuals exhibit. Role requirements differ, tolerating or encouraging and rewarding some of the achieving styles described by the authors and discouraging others. The conceptual model proposed by the authors, considered in conjunction with the approach they have taken to the validation of their model and their operational measures, thus appears to have elements of both a personality theory and a role theory, particularly of occupational roles, though closer to the former. They suggest that achieving styles are behavioral tendencies acquired relatively early in life; as such, they could be expected to be coordinated with or consequences of achievement-related traits. Indeed, as the authors imply in their literature review, there are several correspondences between their achieving styles and achievement-related motives proposed by personality theorists. This is most conspicuous in the case of the instrumental domain, the intrinsic and competitive orientations having obvious parallels with the mastery and competitive motives of Spence and Helmreich (Chapter 1, this volume) and the power orientation having parallels with such notions as dominance and the power motive. To the extent that temporally stable dispositions are involved, individuals' preferred styles could be expected to be related to their role choices (e.g., occupation) and their successes within these roles. At the same time, individuals can be expected to mold their behaviors to the requirements of their role and to become adept at new styles as opportunities present themselves. Changes in achieving styles are most obvious in instances in which individuals climb within an occupational hierarchy, e.g., rise from junior executive (with low status, limited responsibility, and few subordinates) to company president. Individuals' preferred styles at any given time may thus represent an amalgam of stable behavior dispositions and the particular strategies they have found to be effective in their current role. Useful insights may be provided by examining the profiles of styles employed by successful individuals in various occupations or occupational strata.

The bulk of this chapter is devoted to describing the psychometric properties of the self-report instrument the authors currently use to measure achieving styles and their initial attempts to validate their instrument and the conceptual model on which it is based. Although the results of their analyses suggest to the authors that further work is needed to perfect several of their scales, the data confirm the overall outlines of their conceptual model and its implications for the achievement-related strategies of various groups.

$\boxed{T}$ he long tradition of achievement research has emphasized the motive to achieve. In contrast, the focus of the research reported in this chapter is on the achieving process—on the characteristic ways people go about reaching whatever goals they seek to achieve. This orientation toward implementation, toward action, seems to us both a neglected and an extremely important issue in human affairs. The styles that people use in their efforts to achieve whatever they want, we propose, are reasonably stable descriptors of those individuals. In addition, such achieving styles represent important aspects of both their roles and the socialization that they have undergone. These styles are probably significant contributors to success in human striving.

Such achieving behavior (as distinct from achievement per se) has been largely ignored for understandable reasons. This is not the first time in the history of social science that an ingenious conceptualization of a phenomenon has determined the direction of scientific investigation for a very long time. Such a formulation is like a spotlight illuminating a conceptual space previously unnoticed. Two general consequences commonly ensue: (1) the newly defined conceptual space is intensely explored, spawning many efforts to support or refute the concept's formulation; and (2) at least for a time, other possible formulations are almost totally neglected.

In the field of achievement research, the important work of McClelland, Atkinson, and their colleagues (1953, 1955) had such an effect for several decades. Their conceptualization of achievement motivation and its projective measurement by Murray's Thematic Apperception Test (TAT) sparked countless research efforts, providing important insights into one critical dimension of the achievement puzzle (Atkinson, 1958a, 1958b, 1960; Atkinson and Feather, 1966; French, 1955, 1958; Jones, 1961; Veroff, Atkinson, Feld, and Gurin,

Much of the work reported in this paper was conducted while Jean Lipman-Blumen was a Fellow at the Center for Advanced Study in the Behavioral Sciences, Palo Alto, California, and was partially funded under a grant from the National Endowment for the Humanities and the Spencer Foundation. The contribution of Alice Handley-Isaksen was supported by a National Research Service Award (NIMH Grant 5T32 MH15149). This research program has been helped enormously by our ongoing research group at the Graduate School of Business, Stanford University, whose members have included Roger Awad, Robert Bies, Inez Brunner, Jeffrey Feinberg, Joan Kofodimos, Ellen Mandinach, Kerry Patterson, Edward Reynolds, Nancy Roberts, Nancy Sherman, and by Kathy Bostick's administrative assistance.

151

1960; Weiner, 1966). In the process, however, the boundaries of achievement research were rather narrowly delineated.

This constriction now appears to have been dysfunctional in at least four ways:

1. As Veroff, McClelland, and Ruhland (1975) have noted, achievement motivation per se is a significantly more differentiated phenomenon than the original conceputalization suggested. The part has been taken for the whole.

2. The conceptualization and measurement of achievement motivation in the McClelland–Atkinson tradition never accounted satisfactorily for the behavior of more than half of the general population: the female half. Its failure to explain female data (McClelland, Atkinson, Clark, and Lowell, 1953) first led to various efforts to specify conditions under which it might do so (Alper and Greenberger, 1967; Angelini, 1955; Crandall, 1969; French and Lesser, 1964; Heilbrun, 1963; Lesser, 1973; Lesser, Krawitz, and Packard, 1963). Failing any widely confirmed results, Horner's work, following in the McClelland tradition, then stimulated nearly a decade of research on women's "fear of success" (Alper, 1973, 1974; Fleming, 1977; Frieze, 1975; Hoffman, 1974; Levine and Crumrine, 1975; Lockheed, 1975; Mednick and Puryear, 1976; Tresemer, 1974, 1976). This "motive to avoid success," popularized as the "fear of success," dominated much of the achievement research in the 1970s, leading to diverse and inconclusive findings (Levine and Crumrine, 1975; Tresemer, 1974, 1976).

3. The McClelland–Atkinson tradition of achievement research focused almost exclusively on motives, and, hence, on *what* individuals wanted or felt a *need* to achieve—power (n *Pow*), affiliation (n *Aff*), or excellence of achievement (n *Ach*)—rather than on *how* they went about achieving whatever objectives they valued or sought. Thus, the strength and correlates of an individual's need for power, affiliation, or achievement were the primary foci of concern, while the *strategies* by which individuals sought to achieve any of these or other goals were largely ignored. In the process, distinctions among goals, motives, behaviors, and traits were seriously blurred.

4. The TAT method, yielding a host of coding and other technical problems, persisted as the major methodological approach (Bellak, 1942, 1944; Cattell, 1949; Coleman, 1947; Combs, 1946a, 1946b, 1973; MacFarlane, 1941; Sargent, 1945). The emphasis on this projective technique, promoted in subsequent research by the quest for comparability, obscured (even discouraged) necessary efforts to develop more direct and useful measures to tap achievement phenomena.

As illustrated by several chapters in this volume, the past decade has witnessed several significant departures from the McClelland–Atkinson tradition. A number of investigators have essentially abandoned the concept of achievement motivation, conceived as a stable disposition to achieve performance excellence, in favor of expectancy or attributional theories (see, e.g., Vroom, 1964; Weiner, 1972, 1980; also Chapter 2, this volume). Other investigators have retained the sense of the concept of achievement motivation, but have sought more objective measures than the TAT or have conceptualized achievement motivation as multidimensional rather than unidimensional (see, e.g., Chapter 1, this volume). Current research and theory have also been designed to apply to both sexes or to illuminate observed differences between males and females in achievement behaviors.

The research reported here departs from past achievement research by investigating achieving styles rather than achievement motivation. It focuses on means rather than ends. In this chapter, we first present a three-factor model of achieving styles—characteristic ways in which individuals approach achievement goals (regardless of the substantive nature of those goals). The three factors are called *direct, instrumental*, and *relational* achieving styles. Each factor or domain subsumes three styles, resulting in nine individual achieving styles.

Next we describe the origins and major characteristics of an instrument for measuring achieving styles, the L-BLA Achieving Styles Inventory. This Likert-scale instrument, the result of extensive testing and revising, has been used to collect data from a diverse set of populations. And, third, data from several samples are presented and discussed in the final section of this chapter.

RELATED RESEARCH TRADITIONS

This research on achieving styles draws on a wide and diverse set of research traditions, some of which are detailed in other chapters of this volume. Only the most directly related work is reviewed in this chapter. Besides the voluminous research on achievement motivation, the achieving-styles concept is also linked to need theory, social-learning theory, small-group research, sex-role stereotypes, and women's achievement, as well as to research on leadership and personal styles.

Need Theories

Murray's (1938) complex taxonomy of needs explicated the concept of an underlying set of human needs and presented the Thematic Apperception Test (TAT) as a projective means of tapping them. Using

Murray's methodology, McClelland, Atkinson, Clark, and Lowell (1953) offered an "affective arousal" model of motivation, specifically achievement motivation. Achievement motivation was characterized by learned standards of excellence, "competition" with or "attempts to meet" these standards, and positive or negative affect, depending on success or failure of such efforts.

Personal responsibility, uncertainty about actual outcomes, but anticipation of clearly defined success or failure were all key concepts in the early work on need for achievement. Thus, a learned need for achievement was treated as a drive triggered by environmental cues, leading to need-fulfilling (or drive-reducing) behavior. Later efforts sought to relate need for achievement to entrepreneurial behavior (McClelland, 1961), as well as to delineate its cross-cultural variations. But the strategies characteristically used for achieving were not emphasized in the McClelland et al. paradigm. If they were acknowledged at all, they were viewed as indicators of needs rather than as styles. Thus, for example, competitive behavior in TAT stories is treated as one of several indicators of the presence of n Ach.

Other variations of need theory also claimed their intellectual inheritance from Murray's central formulation. Maslow's (1954) hierarchy of needs, culminating in self-actualization, evoked its own research tradition. The need for personal efficacy, a concept delineated by White (1959), stemmed from the same general orientation. The need for personal control, studied by deCharms (1968), is still another research initiative falling within the need-theory perspective.

Cognitive Approaches

Reevaluations of traditional need theory (e.g., Salancik and Pfeffer, 1977) have questioned the utility of need theory and emphasized the contributions of more cognitive approaches. Numerous cognitive theorists have focused on the role of expectations in achievement behavior. The importance of expected outcomes learned from prior experience (Atkinson and Raynor, 1974; Vroom, 1964) or from social comparisons (Abramson, Seligman, and Teasdale, 1978; Bandura, 1977) has been emphasized in these cognitive formulations. Expectations concerning one's ability to behave in a given way or to achieve a vital goal are seen as critical determinants of the level of achievement behavior.

Attribution theorists (Kelley, 1967, 1971; Ross, 1977; Weiner, 1972, 1974, 1979; Weiner and Kukla, 1970) have studied the impact of attributions of success and failure on achievement performance, while learned-helplessness investigators (Dweck, 1975a, 1975b; Dweck and Reppucci, 1973; Seligman, 1975) have documented the process by which individuals come to relinquish expectations of influencing their own destinies. Within the attribution tradition, studies of intrinsic/extrinsic motivation (Deci, 1975) describe how behavior varies with source of motivation, as well as with intensity.

Other theorists have begun to criticize the concepts of motive and need and their link to traits or enduring personality dispositions. In 1968, Mischel argued that the conceptualization of traits as broad response dispositions (Allport, 1937, 1965; Murray, 1938) had not been substantiated and that social-learning paradigms more accurately modeled how individuals learn, aspire, and achieve. More recently, Mischel (1977) has acknowledged the value of examining "person variables" as well as environmental variables. While his person variables are by no means equivalent to traits, they do include such properties of the individual as "construction competencies," methods of "categorization," and "expectancy" patterns. While classical need theory, then, appears to be less widely accepted than previously, the underlying question of what the person brings to the situation remains a focus of active debate.

Small-Group Research

Small-group research has brought increased attention to the influence of group processes. It has focused largely on role-embedded behavior emanating from the natural evolution of groups. Bales and Slater (1955), in their laboratory observations of undergraduate groups, have reported that natural group processes produce two kinds of leadership roles, without regard to the specific personality traits of group participants: (1) an instrumental or task leader, whose function is to enable the group to achieve a given goal; and (2) an expressive or socioemotional leader, whose function is to sustain group cohesion by binding the social/emotional wounds inflicted in the course of group task accomplishment.

This binary orientation, tasks versus people, or the instrumental/expressive dichotomy, has been applied, not always correctly, to a wide range of leadership and achievement phenomena. Task orientation, particularly, has become synonymous with achievement. Perhaps the most problematic application of the instrumental/expressive dichotomy has been to family gender roles (Parsons and Bales, 1955). Reevaluations of that dichotomy have seriously questioned this application (e.g., Lipman-Blumen and Tickamyer, 1975).

Gender Stereotypes

The instrumental/expressive role dichotomy finds a parallel in stereotypes about gender differences in personality (Broverman, Vogel,

Broverman, Clarkson, and Rosenkrantz, 1972). Not only are females seen as warmer, more expressive, and people-oriented, and males as more competent, assertive, rational, and task-oriented, but these male "instrumental" characteristics are perceived as more socially desirable than those ascribed to women (Broverman et al., 1972). More recent work has confirmed the existence of such gender differences (Spence and Helmreich, 1978). Moreover, male-associated character- istics of competence, task orientation, and rationality serve as cor- nerstones of Western achievement. These gender stereotypes, prob- ably learned in early childhood (Hartley, 1960; Hartley and Hardesty, 1964; Kohlberg, 1966; Maccoby and Jacklin, 1974), affect the differ- ential assessment of female and male competence (Goldberg, 1968) and appropriateness in various occupational roles (Schein, 1973, 1975).

Other research has related women's self-concept and sex-role ide- ology to their achievement aspirations. In a study of female college graduates, "mode of achievement satisfaction" emerged as the critical link between gender-role ideology and educational aspirations (Blu- men, 1970; Lipman-Blumen, 1972). Mode of achievement satisfaction was measured by an active to passive continuum, whose polar posi- tions were "vicarious" and "direct" achievement (Lipman-Blumen, 1973). Individuals relying primarily on vicarious achievement derive their achievement satisfaction through the accomplishments of other individuals with whom they identify. Direct achievers look to them- selves for such achievement satisfaction.

Still other research has investigated "two-person careers" (Papa- nek, 1973) and "greedy institutions" (Coser and Rokoff, 1971)—two related phenomena in which wives are expected to contribute their achievement efforts to their husbands' careers without explicit reward or acknowledgment. The dynamics of individual female achieve- ment, except in gender-appropriate roles, remained an elusive phenomenon.

Female achievement motivation was not a major concern for McClelland et al. (1953), who briefly reported and then ignored the failure of standard male cues to arouse achievement motivation in women. By the 1960s, a small cadre of researchers, puzzled by wom- en's unexplored achievement behavior, sought to specify the condi- tions generating n Ach in female subjects (Alper and Greenberger, 1967; Baruch, 1967; Crandall, 1969; French and Lesser, 1964; Horner, 1968; Lesser, Krawitz, and Packard, 1963). Differential expectations of success, social rather than cognitive cues, occupational interest and choice, and subject or task relevance were just a few of the many variables investigated as correlates or conditions of women's achieve- ment motivation. More recently, Spence and Helmreich (1978) have addressed achievement motivation within the context of masculinity and femininity.

Horner's (1968) efforts to explicate a "motive to avoid success" in women caught the imagination of researchers and lay public alike. The questions Horner's work raised about women's "fear of success" were addressed by a host of researchers, with conflicting results (Alper, 1973, 1974; Breedlove and Cicerelli, 1974; Fleming, 1977; Frieze, 1975; Hoffman, 1974; Horner, 1972; Lockheed, 1975; Mednick and Puryear, 1975; Puryear and Mednick, 1974; Watson, 1970; Weston and Mednick, 1970). Subsequent critiques of the fear-of-success paradigm (Levine and Crumrine, 1975; Tresemer, 1974, 1976) and persisting replication difficulties have called into question the efficacy of this theoretical thrust. In addition, the emphasis on the dichotomous acceptance or rejection of success obscured the importance of investigating differentiated types of achievement (Veroff, McClelland, and Ruhland, 1975), including competence motivation (Smith, 1968) and group achievement orientation (Zander, 1971).

Leadership Styles

A differentiated model of achievement should take into account differing styles—personal styles, leadership styles, and achieving styles. The literature on personal styles has dealt with such issues as authoritarianism (Adorno, Frankel-Brunswick, Levinson, and Sanford, 1950) and Machiavellianism (Christie and Geis, 1970). The work on authoritarian personality has investigated both acquiescence to and use of authority. The more recent Machiavellian behavior research has focused on manipulative interpersonal strategies, enhanced by competition and power, as avenues to achievement.

Much leadership research has attended to styles of leadership, beginning with the early work of Lewin, Lippit, and White (1939), who explored the relationship between leadership styles and group dynamics. In their leadership studies, Lewin et al. found that neither the authoritarian nor the laissez-faire leadership style is as likely as democratic leadership to encourage group members' satisfaction and productivity. A consistent demand of later leadership research has called for some balance between task and people orientation on the part of the leader (Bass and Dunteman, 1963; Blake and Mouton, 1969; Fiedler, 1978; Fleishman, 1971; Likert, 1961; Stogdill and Coons, 1957; Vroom and Yetton, 1973), although the exact nature of the balance has remained a matter of serious controversy.

People orientation (or affiliative styles) also became the subject of intense scrutiny (Atkinson, Heyns, and Veroff, 1954; Atkinson and

Walker, 1956; Schachter, 1959). Affiliation's relationship to group productivity and organizational structure aroused additional debate (deCharms, 1957; French, 1955; Harris, 1969; Weiner and Rubin, 1969). Boyatzis' (1972, 1974) distinction between "affiliative interest" and "affiliative assurance" represented an effort to clarify the ambiguities regarding the effectiveness of people-oriented leaders or managers.

Despite such enormous research attention, the distinction between people orientation or affiliation and the use of relationships as the medium for achieving has not been elucidated in the leadership literature. The model of achieving styles presented here draws such a distinction, recognizing that liking or needing people—as people orientation and affiliation needs usually imply—is not necessarily isometric with perceiving and using relationships as the means to achievements. This model contrasts (1) achieving styles that actively or passively contribute to achievement through relationships, with (2) achieving styles that are more directly task-oriented, and with (3) achieving styles that approach achievement instrumentally, using relationships or aspects of the self to accomplish goals.

A MODEL OF ACHIEVING STYLES

The present research makes several assumptions about the etiology of achieving styles, those characteristic modes of achieving that are the focus of this chapter. First, we assume that there are three major types of needs: (1) physical needs, (2) social needs, and (3) egoistic needs. Whereas physical needs are mostly innate, both social and egoistic needs are learned.

Social and egoistic needs, we assume, are learned initially from differentially successful and unsuccessful outcomes of attempts to satisfy physical needs. Dependency on parents and others in the child's early environment is presumed to be the primary mechanism through which both social and egoistic needs are acquired.

Satisfactory experiences in meeting needs through other individuals reinforce a relational achieving orientation. Failures, delays, and other negative experiences of the dependent child push toward one of two related predilections: (1) an orientation to eschew relationships as the avenues for meeting one's own needs and to look instead toward the self's direct confrontation with the environment to get what one wants (a direct achieving orientation); or (2) an orientation toward manipulating relationships, aspects of the self, or situational factors to get what one wants (an instrumental achieving orientation).

Achieving styles, then, refer to characteristic ways individuals learn to use in approaching achievement goals or tasks. Achieving styles are the preferred strategies or means individuals employ to accomplish tasks, to achieve, to implement their plans, to "get things done." Our achieving-styles model identifies the three major orientations toward achievement mentioned above: direct, instrumental, and relational orientations (Leavitt and Lipman-Blumen, 1980; Leavitt, Lipman-Blumen, Schaefer, and Harris, 1977; Lipman-Blumen and Leavitt, 1976, 1978, 1979; Lipman-Blumen, Leavitt, and Handley-Isaksen, 1980; Lipman-Blumen, Leavitt, Patterson, Bies, and Handley-Isaksen, 1980). The model emanates from earlier work on "mode of achievement satisfaction" (Blumen, 1970; Lipman-Blumen, 1972) and "vicarious achievement" (Lipman-Blumen, 1973).

The current achieving-styles model, as well as the L-BLA Achieving Styles Inventory (ASI) (Form 10), which is described in the following section of this chapter, represents refinements in conceptualization and instrumentation that have occurred over an eight-year period (1974–1982). The original model was conceived as a linear continuum (Lipman-Blumen and Leavitt, 1976) that described "vicarious" and "direct" achieving styles. Working interactively between theory and empirical data, we have refined the model into three major domains—direct, instrumental, and relational—each subsuming three substyles of achieving. Evidence from earlier versions of the L-BLA Achieving Styles Inventory suggested that a circular, rather than a linear, conceptualization provided a better representation of the achieving-styles phenomenon. A graphic representation of this conceptualization is shown Figure 3-1.

Direct Achieving Styles

The direct achieving styles are characterized by direct confrontation of the achievement task or challenge through an individual's personal efforts. Using direct styles, individuals act to accomplish the task by addressing the challenge in toto individually or by overtly delegating and controlling subordinate components of task performance by others, while retaining overall responsibility. Three subcategories of the direct achieving style have been defined: (1) intrinsic-direct, (2) competitive-direct, and (3) power-direct.

Individuals who exhibit a strong *intrinsic-direct* style prefer to approach the task individually and directly, taking satisfaction from performing the task well and measuring their performance against an internalized standard of excellence. They derive satisfaction from the intrinsic demands and challenge of the task and their own indi-

Figure 3-1
A model of achieving styles.

vidual ability to meet that challenge. Pitting oneself directly against a task, or one's own previous performance, rather than against another individual, distinguishes the intrinsic-direct style from the competitive-direct style.

The *competitive-direct* style is characterized by a tendency to compare oneself to another or to another's accomplishments. For the individual who uses the competitive-direct style, doing well at the task is not quite enough. Doing better than anyone else—doing the best—is what counts. The satisfaction of achieving comes from besting all challengers. Competition, for users of this style, adds a necessary, even zesty, ingredient to the achieving process.

The *power-direct* style's hallmark is the use of power and control over other individuals, resources, and situations as a means of accomplishing tasks. A power-direct achieving style involves actively and overtly controlling and organizing individuals, situations, and resources—in effect, taking charge and directing. Users of the power-direct achieving style, without relinquishing control, often assign or delegate part of the task to others. Individuals who favor a power-direct style tend to perceive leadership roles as their natural milieu.

Instrumental Achieving Styles

The second major achieving style domain is instrumental achieving, which also subsumes three subcategories: (1) personal-instrumental, (2) social-instrumental, and (3) reliant-instrumental. These instrumental achieving styles reflect a two-stage process in which the instrumental achiever usually, but not necessarily covertly, uses achievement-related aspects of self and others as means to goal accomplishment. Such behavior is often quite conscious and explicit on the part of the instrumental achiever, so that even others in the situation may be aware of the instrumentality. For some instrumental achievers, however, the instrumental style is so much a modus vivendi that they may be essentially unaware of it. For individuals using instrumental achieving styles, various dimensions of relationships and of self are evaluated in terms of their potential benefit to the individual achiever in promoting still other achievements.

The *personal-instrumental* achieving style characteristically involves using one's earlier or present achievements or attributes—personal accomplishments, status, financial resources, political clout, family position, personal charisma, educational or occupational background—as instrumental means to new achievements. The individual who uses this style usually explicitly recognizes the process, which itself is generally covert. Prior accomplishments, present achievement efforts, or characteristics of self are valued to the degree that they serve as gateways to future achievements. This style is commonly used by individuals who highly value external approval. The Secretary of State who regretted leaving office because he perceived official status as the "greatest aphrodisiac," as evidenced by a coterie of romantic admirers, is an illustration of the personal-instrumental style.

The *social-instrumental* achieving style's hallmark is the use of (versus the contribution to) relationships and other individuals as means to further achievements. Relationships, even acquaintanceships, are cathected and evaluated primarily in terms of their utility as avenues to accomplishment. The lobbyist who cultivates connections with congressional staff to ensure passage of favorite legislation is employing this style. The social-instrumental style is exemplified in salespersons' dictum to establish warm relationships with their customers before trying to sell their products. Social-instrumental achievers[1] have faith in their own efficacy. A substantial core of this faith is based on the knowledge that they have and know how to use a wide network of relationships to accomplish their goals. Again, a social-instrumental style usually, but not invariably, implies conscious use of an indirect or covert process. On occasion, however, the process may be used overtly in a reciprocal manner by two or more individuals who engage in symbiotic interactions. Informal networks in formal organizations often operate according to social-instrumental principles.

The *reliant-instrumental* achieving style finds its essence in the expectation that others will take responsibility for fulfilling one's achievement goals. The individual who characteristically uses the reliant-instrumental style looks to others—sometimes even rather openly—to implement plans or perform tasks for the reliant-instrumental achiever. Individuals who consistently turn to others for help and direction, who cannot or will not act directly in their own behalf, who seek others to carry the ball, are employing the reliant-instrumental style. It is important to note that reliant-instrumental achievers not only seek help from others, but also relinquish responsibility for selecting the means to be used.

The distinction between the social-instrumental and the reliant-instrumental styles is subtle. *Social*-instrumental achievers believe in their own capacities to accomplish things. They simply see other people as the best, most natural, and perhaps the easiest means of accomplishing their ends. The "well-connected" father who approaches influential friends to facilitate his child's admission to a good university is using a social-instrumental style. Deliberately targeting a specific individual as the means to a certain accomplishment or set of accomplishments is characteristic of the social-instrumental style. By contrast, the reliant-instrumental achiever perceives virtually everyone in his or her environment in a more diffuse way as a possible avenue for accomplishment, as long as they are willing to serve an instrumental purpose.

Reliant-instrumental achievers have relatively little faith in their own efficacy. Such individuals feel a clear and present need for others to "do it for them." Reliant-instrumental achievers tend to define their own goals, but depend on others to accomplish those goals. The stu-

---

[1]Technically, while there are distinguishable achieving styles, individuals rarely are characterized by only one style. Rather, individuals tend to use some subset of achieving styles, showing primary predilection for one or two. Thus, our use of terms such as "social-instrumental achievers" is merely for expositional ease.

dent who has not learned to type and expects a friend or spouse to type his or her paper is practicing a reliant-instrumental style. So is the child who expects Dad to get him or her into college.

It may be worth noting that, in American culture, reliant-instrumental behavior so contradicts the basic value of individualism as to be virtually socially undesirable. Thus, despite the fact that the paradigm itself implies no normative valuation of the various achieving styles, most people raised in this culture probably would prefer not to perceive themselves as depending on others through reliant-instrumental behavior. In other cultures this may not be so.

Relational Achieving Styles

The third major achieving style domain is relational achieving. Relational achievers contribute actively or passively to relationships as part of their own accomplishments. Again, three subcategories are delineated: (1) collaborative-relational, (2) contributory-relational, and (3) vicarious-relational.

The *collaborative-relational* achieving style is archetypically exemplified by the team player, the individual who prefers to approach tasks through group effort. The synergism generated through group endeavors is both the special fuel and the reward on which the collaborative-relational achiever thrives. The individual who repeatedly uses this style expects a proportionate share of credit, as well as responsibility. The collaborative-relational's contribution is to the group goal, which the collaborative-relational achiever accepts as his or her own objective.

The *contributory-relational* achievers meet their achievement needs primarily by contributing actively to the success of another achiever(s), who define(s) both the means and the goal. Assisting, helping, or encouraging the other achiever in his or her task, while playing essentially a secondary role, typifies the contributory-relational style. People whose primary achievement satisfaction comes from helping others succeed fall within the definition of the *contributory*-relational achieving style. A political candidate's spouse who campaigns actively, writes speeches, and helps develop policy positions for the political aspirant exemplifies a contributory-relational style.

Individuals who prefer a *vicarious-relational* style identify with another achiever and perceive the other's accomplishments as their own. The vicarious-relational achiever does not participate in the other's task performance. Identifying with and/or being in a relationship with certain other achievers is the passive role the vicarious-relational achiever most typically plays. This indirect or vicarious approach meets the achieving needs of the vicarious-relational achiever, who takes pleasure from others' accomplishments as if they were his or her own. "My son the doctor" are words commonly spoken by vicarious-relational achievers.

Range, Flexibility, and Intensity

The foregoing discussion has described heuristically the nine sub-categories of achieving styles as if they were discrete phenomena. Indeed, we do distinguish conceptually and operationally between and among the styles. Nonetheless, their deliberately ordered placement on the circular achieving-styles diagram (in Figure 3-1) is an effort to represent the theoretical and empirically-demonstrated closeness of contiguous styles.

Many individuals operate at the interface of one or more pairs of styles. It is the very combination of achieving styles that individuals or groups use that adds to both the complexity and the interest of the model. The ability to access or use multiple styles is what we have described elsewhere as *range* (Lipman-Blumen, Leavitt, and Handley-Isaksen, 1980; Lipman-Blumen, Leavitt, Patterson, Bies, and Handley-Isaksen, 1980). A related concept, *flexibility*, refers to the ease with which the individual can move from one achieving style to another in response to situational cues. *Intensity*, the strength of preference for a particular achievement style relative to other styles, may vary within any individual's range and across individuals with access to the same style.

As Figure 3-1 suggests, we conceive of degrees of self-, other-, and task-orientation varying as we move around the diagram (cf. Bass and Dunteman, 1963). Generally, the styles in the upper portion of the diagram share a lower self-orientation, focusing more on performing tasks or contributing to and identifying with others. The styles in the lower portion tend to focus more on the self and what may be gained for the self from relationships.

Given this conceptual model, we next describe the development and testing of an instrument for measuring these achieving styles.

DESCRIPTION OF L-BLA ACHIEVING STYLES INVENTORY

We have described elsewhere the stages in the development of the L-BLA Achieving Styles Inventory (Lipman-Blumen, Leavitt, and Handley-Isaksen, 1980; Lipman-Blumen, Leavitt, Patterson, Bies, and Handley-Isaksen, 1980). The Achieving Styles Inventory (Form 10), after several revisions and iterations, constitutes a 45-item Likert-scale instrument, requiring approximately 10 minutes to complete.[2] Most items are descriptive statements of behaviors used in accomplishing or implementing goals. In a few cases, the statements describe feelings about particular ways of accomplishing goals.[3] Nine scales of five items each are logically and empirically keyed to each of the achieving styles described in our model (Figure 3-1). Subjects are asked to respond along a seven-point Likert-type continuum ranging from "never" (1) to "always" (7).

The instrument is scored by summing the subject's responses over the five items of each scale and dividing by the number of items answered. Three *domain* scores are also calculated by averaging the scores of the three individual scales subsumed under each domain. Thus, the average of the three direct scales (1, 2, 3) constitutes the *direct* domain score; the average of the three instrumental scales (4, 5, 6) is the *instrumental* domain score; and the average of the three relational scales (7, 8, 9) becomes the *relational* domain score. The test-item mean is calculated by averaging over all 45 items.

We report below on (1) the reliability and factorial validity of the L-BLA Achieving Styles Inventory (Form 10), (2) the fit of empirical data to our circular conceptualization of the achieving-styles model, and (3) the instrument's effectiveness in correctly classifying gender, age, and occupational groups.

Samples

In our study, 3294 participants from 18 individual exploratory samples were pooled to examine the test characteristics of the L-BLA Achieving Styles Inventory (Form 10). Table 3-1 presents demographic data for the entire pool, by sample.

Samples 1–4 in Table 3-1 are high school students from eight San Francisco Bay Area high schools: 1029 of the students are male, 1200 female, and 23 did not indicate gender. The total of 2252 high schoolers (ninth through twelfth grades) represents 68.4% of the total sub-

---

[2] After this chapter was completed, the L-BLA Achieving Styles Inventory underwent four additional revisions in an effort to overcome deficiencies reported here. The final form (13), which eliminates numerous problems reported here, is now available, along with a user's manual.

[3] The following are five examples of the 45 items on the ASI:

1. For me, the most gratifying thing is to have solved a tough problem.
2. I want to be the leader.
3. The more competitive the situation, the better I like it.
4. Real team effort is the best way for me to get a job done.
5. I achieve my goals through contributing to the success of others.

Table 3-1
Demographics of sample pool for L-BLA Achieving Styles Inventory (Form 10)

Sample	N	Identification	Male N^a	Female N^a	Mean age	S.D. (age)	Mean educational level	S.D. (educational level)
1	1651	S.F. Bay Area high school	805	827	15.75	2.16	10.58	1.12
2	490	S.F. Bay Area high school	185	302	16.64	1.05	11.45	.50
3	54	S.F. Bay Area high school	20	34	16.30	.59	11.05	.19
4	57	S.F. Bay Area high school	19	37	17.28	.49	11.95	.40
5	26	Graduate students in education	11	11	33.37	9.04	16+	N.A.
6	52	Graduate students in business	33	19	25.62	3.64	17.01	1.12
7	48	Graduate students in business	35	13	24.41	6.59	16.53	.54
8	111	Graduate and undergraduate students in engineering course	92	19	22.61	5.49	16.05	2.46
9	220	Senior executives/spouses (1979)	130	90	44.88	5.80	15.81	2.43
10	189	Senior executives/spouses (1980)	112	73	42.23	5.22	15.96	2.22
11	61	Middle-level executives/spouses	34	27	36.36	5.39	16.36	1.58
12	34	Upper-level executives	34	—	37.12	5.79	16.26	1.36
13	31	Technical supervisors	29	2	39.48	7.12	18.26	1.93
14	48	Credit managers	35	13	43.67	10.72	14.81	2.12
15	15	University administrators	7	8	43.53	6.64	16.80	1.08
16	69	Adult social-club members	33	36	59.41	10.25	13.36	2.09
17	56	Family therapists	18	38	39.89	9.97	18.41	1.77
18	82	Clients of women's resource center	—	82	38.10	9.14	16.52	1.45
Total	3294		1632	1631	23.67	12.75	12.55	2.91

Note: Samples 9 and 11 were administered L-BLA Achieving Styles Inventory (Form 8), consisting of 54 items, 41 of which were identical to Form 10. In this chapter, data from these two samples were limited to those 41 items. Scale scores between senior executives in 1979 (41 items) and senior executives in 1980 (45 items) were compared. No significant differences on scale-score means were found between the groups. About half the participants ($N = 26$) in sample 17 received Form 11A, which had some slightly different items for scale 6. Means for this scale were higher than scale means for subjects receiving Form 10. Means on the other scales of the instrument were not different. The group mean of subjects taking Form 10 on scale 6 was assigned to subjects taking Form 11A, so that error from this measurement was regressed to the mean.

[a]Male and female *N*'s do not sum to sample total because some subjects failed to indicate gender.

ject pool. Most of the high schools are located in mid- to high socio-economic communities.

The next four groups (samples 5–8) are university graduate and undergraduate students in business, education, engineering, and the social sciences: 171 are males; 62 are females (4 did not report gender). The total of 237 students represents 7.1% of the subject pool.

The next three samples (9–11) were drawn from 1979 and 1980 classes of a senior-executive program at a western university and one 12-month middle-level-executive education program. The samples include executives in these programs, as well as their spouses. Combined, these groups include 276 males and 190 females (plus 4 not reporting gender), for a total of 470, representing 14.3% of the total sample pool. Of the females in this group, 154 reported being full-time homemakers, while 36 reported careers outside the home. Approximately 24% of this group were not U.S. citizens.

The next four samples (12–15) are also managerial groups. Sample 12 is from an upper-level executive program at an eastern university. Sample 13 is composed of first-level supervisors from a single, large research and development organization in the private sector. Sample 14 was collected at a credit managers' conference, and sample 15 from a year-long managerial training program for administrative employees of a western university. The total number of subjects in these four samples is 128. These 105 males and 23 females represent 3.9% of the sample pool.

Sample 16 is comprised of 69 older citizens of the San Francisco Bay Area, including 33 husband-and-wife pairs, plus 3 additional females. They represent 2.1% of the subject pool. Both males and females from this sample reported a variety of occupations. A few were retired.

Sample 17 was collected at a professional symposium of family therapists: 18 are males, 38 are females, for a total of 56, representing 1.7% of the subject pool. Most of these participants were mental-health practitioners, although 3 had full-time academic appointments, 5 were students in training, and 10 reported administrative posts.

The final sample (sample 18) of 82 women was drawn from the client population of a community resource center for women. Of these women, 60% reported seeking job advancement, and the remaining 40% planned to reenter the job market. A variety of occupations was reported. This sample represents 2.5% of the subject pool.

For the most part, the total sample pool is composed of well-educated individuals of high socioeconomic status. Occupations of male subjects were concentrated in business management and administration. Samples 16 and 17, however, do represent other careers.

Occupations of women respondents covered a wider range, but fell mostly within teaching, medical-health occupations, management, sales, and homemaking. Thus, the sample pool is by no means representative of the general population.

Data Collection

Data from the following samples were collected from intact groups on site in a single sitting: 1–7, 12–14, and 17. Data from sample 8 were collected by having subjects respond to a computer command at a computer terminal. Data from samples 9–11 and 16 were collected by mail. Data from sample 15 were collected by handout in a training session and returned by mail, and data from sample 18 were collected by having subjects pick up research materials from a booth at the resource center, to be returned by mail. All subjects, except those in sample 16, received feedback about the global characteristics of their own sample and an individual profile of their own scores.

Younger subjects are both overrepresented in our study populations and present a relatively distinctive factor structure. For purposes of analysis, therefore, we have split the respondent pool into two subsamples: those 30 years old or more, and those under 30 years old. Table 3-2 specifies some demographic characteristics of these age-split pooled samples.

For some of the occupational analyses, a sample pool of female managers ($N = 61$) was created. All women who reported they were managers or administrators were pooled and removed from their original samples to eliminate duplication of data.

Table 3-2
Demographics of age-split subpool samples used to evaluate test characteristics of the L-BLA Achieving Styles Inventory (Form 10)

Age group	Sample N	Male N^a	Female N^a	Age range	Mean age	S.D. (age)	Mean educational level	S.D. (educational level)
30 +	783	437	343	30–77	43.67	8.76	16.08	2.28
< 30	2511	1195	1288	13–29	16.81	2.87	11.22	1.71
Total	3294	1632	1631	13–77	23.19	12.75	12.55	2.91

[a]Male and female N's do not sum to sample total because some subjects failed to indicate gender.

Test Characteristics

Reliability of the L-BLA Achieving Styles Inventory was estimated by Cronbach alpha procedures and by Pearson r's between test and retest scores. *Validity* of the instrument was demonstrated by SPSS PA1 Factor Analysis, with oblique rotation, of both items and scales. Scale validities were further estimated by reliability of difference scores.

Predictive ability of the instrument was demonstrated by cross-validation using gender as a criterion in discriminant function analysis. Age and occupational groups were also subjected to discriminant function analysis. The F-tests for scale means, provided by the one-way analysis of variance of these analyses, were used to examine gender, age, and occupational differences among groups. All analyses were conducted using raw scores, with a significance criterion of $p = .05$.

RESULTS WITH L-BLA ACHIEVING STYLES INVENTORY: RELIABILITY AND VALIDITY

Consistency and Stability of Scales

For the 30+ age group, the lowest Cronbach alpha (.75) is on the reliant-instrumental scale, while the highest is on power-direct (.89) (Table 3-3). Cronbach alphas for the nine scales in the < 30 age group range from .72 on reliant-instrumental to .84 on collaborative-relational. The domain-stratified alphas exceed .80 for both samples, and the test-item mean alpha exceeds .90.

A 15-week test/retest of 90 high school students (Table 3-3) shows internal consistency estimates for both test and retest very similar to estimates from the larger samples. Across time, alphas range from .66 to .90 for scales and from .79 to .95 for domains. The stability coefficients range from .58 on intrinsic-direct to .73 on both competitive-direct and social-instrumental. The domain coefficients are in the mid-.70's range.

Factor Analyses of Items

Principal Component Factor Analyses, with oblique rotation, were performed on the two age-split pooled samples. Table 3-4 displays the results.

Table 3-3
Reliability estimates for scales of the L-BLA Achieving Styles Inventory
(Form 10), Cronbach alphas and 15-week Pearson product-moment
coefficients

Scale	Internal consistency Cronbach alpha		15-week test/retest		
			Internal alphas		Pearson r
	Age 30+ N = 783	Age < 30 N = 2511	Test	Retest	Test/ Retest
			Age mean = 16.0 N = 90		
1 Intrinsic direct	.79	.80	.83	.86	.58
2 Competitive direct	.87	.79	.79	.85	.73
3 Power direct	.89	.80	.86	.89	.67
4 Personal instrumental	.77	.75	.79	.75	.63
5 Social instrumental	.82	.76	.73	.83	.73
6 Reliant instrumental	.75	.72	.66	.75	.59
7 Collaborative relational	.88	.84	.86	.90	.63
8 Contributory relational	.87	.79	.78	.84	.69
9 Vicarious relational	.85	.81	.81	.86	.68
10 Direct domain	.86*	.82*	.79*	.81*	.74
11 Instrumental domain	.86*	.86*	.86*	.95*	.75
12 Relational domain	.85*	.85*	.82*	.87*	.73
13 Test-item mean	.92*	.93*	.91*	.87*	.73

*Stratified alpha.

For the 30+ age group, nine factors, accounting for 63.7% of the total item variance, were extracted and named in order:

1. Power-direct.
2. Vicarious-relational.
3. Reliant-instrumental.
4. Collaborative-relational.
5. Competitive-direct.
6. Intrinsic-direct.
7. Personal-instrumental.
8. Social-instrumental.
9. Contributory-relational.

Most items logically keyed to a scale are loaded on by a single factor. Exceptions are the following: the power-direct factor loaded at the criterion level on power-direct scale items, but also on one intrinsic and one competitive-direct item. The social- and personal-instrumental items are not independent of each other. Although the vicarious- and contributory-relational items are loaded on separately by two factors, each of the factors also loads moderately on all the items of these two scales (most of the loadings on the nonkeyed items are in the .4 range). Also, in this age group, the competitive-direct factor loads moderately on the items keyed to the power-direct scale.

For the < 30 group, eight factors account for 58.8% of the total item variance. The factors, in order of extraction, were named:

1. Social-instrumental.
2. Contributory- and vicarious-relational.
3. Reliant-instrumental.
4. Collaborative-relational.
5. Intrinsic-direct.
6. Competitive-direct.
7. Power-direct.
8. Personal-instrumental.

For the most part, again, items logically keyed to scales were loaded on by a single factor. Close inspection of the matrix, however, shows that two items logically keyed to the personal-instrumental scale are loaded on at the criterion level (.50 or higher) by the social-instrumental factor. And the personal-instrumental factor loads on only two of the items logically keyed to that scale. Further, the items log-

Table 3-4

L-BLA Achieving Styles Inventory (Form 10), SPSS PA1 factor analysis, oblique rotation

	Factor									
Item	1	2	3	4	5	6	7	8	9	Scale
	Age group 30 + (N = 783)[a]									
1	.00	.04	−.07	−.07	−.25	.76	−.13	−.11	−.16	
8	.44	−.04	−.14	−.17	−.21	.66	−.14	−.06	−.27	
17	.33	.04	−.14	−.13	−.29	.81	−.11	−.12	−.17	1
33	.54	.07	−.13	−.15	−.15	.58	.00	−.22	−.28	
43	.16	.18	−.08	−.14	−.19	.80	−.03	−.21	−.12	
4	.34	.11	.12	−.14	−.76	.19	−.24	−.27	−.12	
11	.26	.05	.07	−.15	−.85	.25	−.26	−.23	−.10	
14	.31	.09	−.04	−.21	−.83	.30	−.16	−.21	−.21	2
22	.56	.16	.14	−.12	−.69	−.21	−.23	−.29	−.02	
37	.42	.12	.00	−.27	−.80	.31	−.15	−.33	−.21	
7	.78	−.10	−.08	−.25	−.49	.35	−.22	−.22	−.25	
10	.77	−.10	−.14	−.25	−.47	.34	−.19	−.25	−.26	
21	.78	−.13	−.11	−.22	−.47	.27	−.21	−.32	−.19	3
28	.79	−.04	−.04	−.19	−.41	.26	−.17	−.33	−.15	
38	.63	.06	.11	−.16	−.53	.16	−.21	−.43	−.10	
6	.17	.00	.09	−.20	−.19	.18	−.79	−.30	−.13	
13	.07	.16	.29	−.12	−.27	.04	−.86	−.37	−.08	
27	.14	.15	.34	−.17	−.23	.04	−.77	−.55	−.07	4
30	.13	.20	.22	−.11	−.25	.18	−.34	−.57	−.10	
39	.28	.11	.15	−.21	−.20	.14	−.32	−.69	−.19	
2	.21	−.14	.24	−.16	−.33	.19	−.36	−.68	−.14	
20	.09	−.02	.42	−.15	−.20	−.03	−.30	−.67	−.10	
26	.15	−.03	.26	−.19	−.23	.13	−.40	−.80	−.14	5
35	.35	.07	.15	−.40	−.29	.18	−.16	−.67	−.27	
40	.15	.11	.33	−.23	−.19	.12	−.26	−.77	−.09	

[a]63.7% of the total item variance explained by the matrix.

Table 3-4 (continued)

Item					Factor					Scale
	1	2	3	4	5	6	7	8	9	

Age group 30 + (N = 783)[a]

Item	1	2	3	4	5	6	7	8	9	Scale
5	−.25	.02	.57	−.11	−.14	−.15	−.30	−.20	−.08	
18	.03	.04	.75	−.20	−.07	−.07	−.19	−.29	−.19	
25	.05	.08	.71	−.25	−.09	−.15	−.12	−.32	−.13	6
31	.16	.23	.62	−.13	.13	−.11	−.22	−.14	.08	
44	.12	.16	.81	−.21	−.10	−.05	−.21	−.30	−.06	
9	.10	.08	.19	−.79	−.20	.08	−.18	−.13	−.30	
15	.06	.16	.22	−.84	−.23	.10	−.16	−.15	−.37	
24	.12	.21	.19	−.84	−.16	.12	−.06	−.18	−.35	7
36	.18	.17	.07	−.78	−.10	.19	−.15	−.30	−.32	
45	.16	.22	.18	−.81	−.06	.06	−.09	−.21	−.35	
3	.11	.24	.04	−.37	−.18	.18	−.11	−.17	−.77	
16	.02	.40	.09	−.42	−.05	.15	−.15	−.07	−.83	
23	.24	.42	.16	−.40	−.12	.14	−.09	−.14	−.77	8
34	.21	.44	.08	−.41	−.17	.22	−.01	−.21	−.79	
41	.14	.35	.15	−.34	−.11	.22	−.07	−.25	−.73	
12	−.12	.70	.07	−.18	−.09	.07	−.15	.03	−.39	
19	.16	.63	.27	−.20	−.19	.10	−.15	−.10	−.22	
29	−.03	.83	.05	−.26	−.08	.10	−.08	−.08	−.41	9
32	−.16	.79	.12	−.23	−.08	.10	−.04	−.04	−.44	
42	−.05	.82	.03	−.31	−.09	.13	−.04	−.18	−.46	

(continued)

Table 3-4 (continued)

Item	factor									Scale
	1	2	3	4	5	6	7	8	9	
Age group < 30 (N = 2511)[b]										
1	.03	.17	−.12	.06	.73	.11	.15	.17		
8	.10	.23	−.20	.03	.70	.31	.33	.05		
17	.08	.25	−.04	.00	.80	.14	.24	.03		1
33	.18	.35	−.03	.06	.70	.26	.33	−.07		
43	.13	.29	−.05	.11	.75	.21	.22	.03		
4	.24	−.01	.20	.05	.07	.70	.38	.22		
11	.18	.10	.09	.19	.12	.77	.30	.20		
14	.23	.16	−.09	.12	.30	.75	.25	.09		2
22	.21	−.03	.18	.01	.15	.63	.48	.17		
37	.27	.17	−.01	.20	.33	.77	.35	.03		
7	.19	.14	−.04	.09	.30	.38	.83	.19		
10	.19	.19	−.06	.17	.28	.31	.83	.12		
21	.27	.18	−.02	.09	.28	.33	.85	.12		3
28	.29	.14	.03	.04	.28	.33	.82	.10		
38	.48	.07	.22	.04	.10	.42	.61	−.01		
6	.31	.15	.13	.14	.20	.30	.27	.73		
13	.45	.18	.24	.18	.11	.33	.29	.73		
27	.62	.11	.31	.11	.08	.36	.34	.48		4
30	.43	.20	.06	.11	.22	.24	.23	.17		
39	.76	.16	.31	.15	.09	.30	.33	.12		
2	.57	.14	.13	.10	.15	.25	.28	.24		
20	.67	.09	.45	.11	−.03	.20	.22	.12		
26	.75	.15	.21	.18	.09	.22	.19	.15		5
35	.70	.19	.34	.24	.13	.23	.31	−.01		
40	.69	.09	.21	.14	.07	.18	.20	.11		

[b]58.8% of the total item variance explained by the matrix.

Table 3-4 (continued)

					Factor					
Item	1	2	3	4	5	6	7	8	9	Scale
				Age group < 30 (N = 2511)[b]						
5	.14	.10	.62	.15	−.04	−.01	.02	.30		
18	.36	.05	.68	.12	−.11	.13	.06	−.07		
25	.22	.06	.78	.18	−.14	.04	.00	.03		6
31	.12	.17	.49	.19	−.04	.01	−.02	.20		
44	.33	.08	.75	.23	−.06	.12	−.04	.05		
9	.07	.10	.20	.75	−.05	.08	.06	.12		
15	.15	.25	.15	.79	.04	.24	.09	.13		
24	.17	.26	.20	.83	.06	.16	.11	.07		7
36	.19	.35	.05	.73	.16	.09	.11	−.03		
45	.20	.37	.17	.77	.12	.08	.08	−.02		
3	.23	.49	.08	.18	.29	.06	.20	.15		
16	.08	.69	.03	.34	.27	−.03	.10	.03		
23	.17	.64	.12	.28	.24	.18	.24	−.01		8
34	.25	.75	.09	.30	.36	.15	.17	−.04		
41	.33	.68	.13	.30	.22	.06	.15	−.13		
12	−.10	.63	−.03	.20	.18	.00	.06	.27		
19	.19	.59	.23	.12	.19	.12	.19	.19		
29	.12	.75	−.01	.21	.27	.09	.21	.11		9
32	.07	.76	.02	.27	.23	.07	−.01	.03		
42	.14	.80	.04	.29	.29	.05	.09	.02		

ically keyed to the vicarious- and contributory-relational scales are loaded on by only one factor. Although three items do not have criterion-level (.50) loadings on any factor, they are close (.49, .43, and .49, respectively).

Factor Analyses of Scales

The results of Principal Component Factor Analyses on the nine scale scores for each age-split sample are presented in Table 3-5.

In the 30+ age group, three factors, accounting for 68.1% of the total variance, were extracted and named:

1. Instrumental domain.
2. Direct domain.
3. Relational domain.

In this sample pool, the domain factors exhibit qualities of independence.

Table 3-5

Scales of L-BLA Achieving Styles Inventory (Form 10), SPSS PA1 factor analyses, oblique rotation, factor structure

Age group 30+ (N = 783)[a]				Age group < 30 (N = 2511)[b]			
	Factor				Factor		
Scale	1	2	3	Scale	1	2	3
1	−.05	−.73	.25	1	.54	.50	−.42
2	.36	−.77	.22	2	.79	.17	.04
3	.31	−.85	.12	3	.81	.24	−.08
4	.79	−.34	.22	4	.75	.29	.48
5	.82	−.39	.20	5	.65	.27	.58
6	.75	.26	.29	6	.15	.20	.83
7	.37	−.21	.67	7	.18	.59	.43
8	.19	−.25	.87	8	.29	.89	.08
9	.11	−.05	.83	9	.19	.87	.02

[a]68.1% of the total item variance explained by the matrix.
[b]68.4% of the total item variance explained by the matrix.

In the $<$ 30 age group, three factors, accounting for 68.4% of the total variance, were named in order:

1. Direct domain.
2. Relational domain.
3. Instrumental domain.

The direct factor loads at the criterion level on the first five scales of the achieving-styles model. The relational factor loads on the three relational scales of the model and on the intrinsic-direct scale. The instrumental factor loads on the social- and reliant-instrumental scales. The personal- and social-instrumental scales have moderate or criterion-level loadings on both the direct and the instrumental factors. The intrinsic-direct scale is also loaded on at the criterion level by the direct and the relational factors. Thus, unlike the 30+ group, independence of domain scores is not demonstrated in this pool of subjects.

Reliability of Difference Scores

When subscale scores are used as a profile, they should show reliable differences from each other if predictions from the separate scores are to be made (Gulliksen, 1950). Our results are shown in Table 3-6.

For the 30+ age group, the lowest coefficient among the reliability of difference scores was between the personal- and the social-instrumental scales (.46). For this group, six other coefficients ranged between .64 and .69. Most of these also occurred between adjacent scales. For this age sample, 80% of the reliability of difference score coefficients were equal to or exceeded .70 (36% exceeded .80).

For the $<$ 30 age group, the reliability of difference scores ranged from a low of .28, again between personal- and social-instrumental, to .80 between competitive-direct and reliant-instrumental, competitive-direct and vicarious-relational, and power-direct and reliant-instrumental. Only 6 of the coefficients had values below .65. Only 16, however, were .70 or above. The highly "unreliable" coefficients were between the personal- and social-instrumental scales (.28) and the vicarious- and contributory-relational scales (.35). These are the same two pairs of scales that exhibited lack of independence in the factor analyses. Both of them are pairs of adjacent scales in the model.

The circular conceptualization of the model assumes moderate correlations between adjacent scales. Thus, the lower than usual reliabilities of differences between adjacent scales are not surprising.

Table 3-6

L-BLA Achieving Styles Inventory (Form 10), reliability of difference
scores among scales

	Scale	Factor								
		1	2	3	4	5	6	7	8	9
		Age group 30 + (N = 783)								
1	Intrinsic direct	(.79)								
2	Competitive direct	.73	(.87)							
3	Power direct	.72	.68	(.89)						
4	Personal instrumental	.80	.82	.74	(.77)					
5	Social instrumental	.79	.82	.71	.46	(.82)				
6	Reliant instrumental	.80	.88	.83	.67	.64	(.75)			
7	Collaborative relational	.80	.84	.78	.74	.69	.69	(.88)		
8	Contributory relational	.78	.84	.78	.74	.72	.78	.76	(.87)	
9	Vicarious relational	.80	.86	.83	.75	.76	.78	.82	.67	(.85)
		Age group < 30 (N = 2511)								
1	Intrinsic direct	(.80)								
2	Competitive direct	.69	(.79)							
3	Power direct	.67	.64	(.80)						
4	Personal instrumental	.74	.67	.65	(.75)					
5	Social instrumental	.76	.73	.69	.28	(.76)				
6	Reliant instrumental	.77	.80	.80	.62	.57	(.72)			
7	Collaborative relational	.78	.78	.77	.68	.65	.63	(.84)		
8	Contributory relational	.67	.79	.74	.66	.63	.74	.69	(.79)	
9	Vicarious relational	.69	.80	.77	.69	.68	.75	.72	.35	(.81)

Note: Parentheses indicate Cronbach alpha of scale.

The correlation matrices of the nine scales for the age-split pooled samples (Table 3-7) show general congruence with these assumptions of stronger relationships between scales closer together in our model. In the older sample, however, the relationship between intrinsic-direct and vicarious-relational is much weaker than desired. In both age groups, the collaborative-relational scale correlates less with the reliant-instrumental scale than one would ideally wish.

As a further check on validity, the factor analyses of scale scores were examined. As discussed earlier, three dimensions emerged from the analysis of each age sample. In the 30 + sample, scales theoretically belonging to one domain are clearly loaded on by a single factor. In the younger sample, the factor loadings on the sets of scales defined as separate domains were not entirely independent. Nevertheless, the more highly correlated scales are adjacent to one another, consistent with the circular model. It is clear, however, that the very low reliability of differences between the social- and personal-instrumental scales in both age groups (.46 for 30 +, .28 for < 30) indicates that more work is needed on those two scales. In contrast, the reliability of difference between the vicarious- and contributory-relational scales, while very low (.35) in the < 30 group, is considerably higher (.67) in the 30 + group. It is possible that these styles become more differentiated as people age.

The reliant-instrumental scale shows lower internal consistency (.72, .75) than do other scales and is currently being revised; and the overly high correlations between it and the social-instrumental scale contributes to the low reliability of difference scores (.57 for < 30, .64 for 30 +). Further, mean scores on reliant-instrumental are low across all samples, suggesting a negative response bias. (More recent samples, using a revised reliant-instrumental scale, show higher mean scores.)

Summary Comment

These findings concerning reliability and validity of the L-BLA Achieving Styles Inventory (Form 10) can be summarized as follows: First, the instrument exhibited good to excellent internal scale consistency and adequate stability over a 15-week interval in a sample of high school students. Second, the test exhibited strong factorial validity for seven of the nine scales in both age-split samples. Results from both pooled subsamples, however, indicate that the instrumental scales need more work, which has since been completed. Items of the personal-instrumental scale are loaded on by the social-instrumental scale, and the reliant-instrumental scale (because of its very low endorsement and lack of any significant differences between

Table 3-7

Correlation matrix of L-BLA Achieving Styles Inventory (Form 10), scale scores

Scale	Factor								
	1	2	3	4	5	6	7	8	9
Age group 30+ (N = 783)									
1 Intrinsic direct	1.00								
2 Competitive direct	.38	1.00							
3 Power direct	.40	.63	1.00						
4 Personal instrumental	.16	.38	.34	1.00					
5 Social instrumental	.19	.37	.42	.62	1.00				
6 Reliant instrumental	−.17	.06	−.06	.37	.41	1.00			
7 Collaborative relational	.14	.23	.24	.22	.31	.28	1.00		
8 Contributory relational	.24	.22	.23	.21	.22	.18	.48	1.00	
9 Vicarious relational	.14	.17	−.01	.19	.09	.18	.31	.58	1.00
Age group < 30 (N = 2511)									
1 Intrinsic direct	1.00								
2 Competitive direct	.33	1.00							
3 Power direct	.38	.52	1.00						
4 Personal instrumental	.22	.47	.45	1.00					
5 Social instrumental	.15	.35	.38	.66	1.00				
6 Reliant instrumental	−.10	.11	.02	.35	.40	1.00			
7 Collaborative relational	.09	.20	.14	.24	.26	.28	1.00		
8 Contributory relational	.38	.17	.25	.27	.28	.16	.39	1.00	
9 Vicarious relational	.35	.12	.17	.22	.16	.12	.33	.69	1.00

groups) shows strong indications of negative response bias. Third, the reliability of difference between most scale scores on this version of the Achieving Styles Inventory is in the good range for research purposes, but falls short of meeting the criterion for use as a clinical tool. Further, in the younger age group, there is no reliable difference between the vicarious- and contributory-relational scales and, for both samples, no reliable difference between the personal- and social-instrumental scales. These problems have been overcome on a subsequent revision of the instrument. Fourth, factorial validity of the domain scores are more accurate for older persons than for younger ones.

RESULTS WITH L-BLA ACHIEVING STYLES INVENTORY: PREDICTABILITY

Discriminant Analyses to Predict Gender and Age

Discriminant function analyses were used to examine the predictive ability of the scale scores on the Achieving Styles Inventory. Using the nine scale scores as independent predictors, we first attempted to predict gender as a dependent variable.

We chose gender as the dependent variable for several reasons. Studies of early gender-role socialization have shown both differences and similarities in achievement orientations taught to males and females (Crandall, 1963; Crandall and Battle, 1970; Hoffman, 1972; Stein, 1971; Stein and Bailey, 1973). Put simply, males are socialized toward competitive and leadership behaviors (direct achieving styles), while females are encouraged to be helpers, placing others before themselves (relational achieving styles). They are also socialized to vicarious achievement and status emanating from their relationships with others. But, for both genders, American culture has strongly reinforced and valued the intrinsic-direct style—jobs well done and the dignity of work.

For such reasons, we hypothesized (1) that men would score higher on direct than on relational scales, (2) that women would show higher relational than direct scores, and (3) that both groups would score relatively high on the intrinsic-direct style. Further, because women traditionally have occupied more dependent roles, we believed they would show higher reliant-instrumental scores than would men. On the other hand, we were less certain about the social- and personal-instrumental scales. We felt that perhaps women, consistent with their derivative achievement socialization, would score higher on the social-instrumental, tending more to use relationships as mechanisms for other achievements; while men might be more personal-instrumental, parlaying direct achievements to other ends.

Each of the age-split pooled samples was randomly stratified by gender into two groups. In each case, group 1 was used to compute a single significant canonical discriminant function, which then was used to predict gender in group 2 (Table 3-8).

In the older group, about three out of four people were correctly classified; while in the younger sample, approximately two out of three people were correctly classified. These rates are, of course, significantly higher than the 50% chance level. The shrinkage of R^2 is negligible, as indicated by the small differences in the overall percentage of cases correctly classified between the computational and cross-validated groups.

The distributions of discriminant scores for men and women in both age-split pooled samples were normal, although the women's distributions were flatter in both age groups. Further, the overlap between the genders was considerably greater in the younger group than in the older group. Since these data are entirely cross-sectional, we are uncertain about whether these age-group differences are attributable to cohort differences, aging, or other factors.

Table 3-8
Cross-validation of predictive validity of the L-BLA Achieving Styles Inventory (Form 10), percentage of cases correctly classified by gender, prior probability = 50%

	Group 1 (computational)				Group 2 (cross-validational)		
	N	Males	Females		N	Males	Females
Age group 30+ (N = 780)							
Males	224	74.1%	25.9%	Males	213	78.9%	21.1%
Females	167	24.0%	76.0%	Females	176	24.4%	75.6%
Overall percentage of cases correctly classified: 74.94%							
Age group < 30 (N = 2483)							
Males	583	68.4%	31.6%	Males	612	71.9%	28.1%
Females	650	32.9%	67.1%	Females	638	39.2%	60.8%
Overall percentage of cases correctly classified: 67.72%							

Table 3-9 shows F-test results of one-way analyses of variance for the discriminant function analyses of the two age groups. In the older age group, men scored significantly higher than women on all scales except the reliant-instrumental and vicarious-relational scales. These two scales failed to show significant differences between women and men. While the generally higher scores given by men are consistent with similar patterns reported in the psychometric literature, sampling error may be partially responsible. Of the men in this older subsample, 88% were business executives. Their high endorsement of most styles may represent a special attribute, perhaps self-confidence, of occupants of such roles. Indeed, in a recent study (Awad, 1980), male and female M.B.A. students showed no significant differences from one another on any scale, while both scored significantly higher across the board than the several sets of other college majors tested.

In our older age group, the intrinsic-direct style was given the highest scores by both genders. Older males' next most preferred style was power-direct. For females in the 30 + group, the cluster of relational styles were next most preferred after intrinsic-direct. These data generally support our expectations about distributions of scores within gender groups, but the two higher absolute relational scores of men were something of a surprise.

In the <30 group, statistically significant differences were found between men and women for all except the reliant-instrumental and collaborative-relational scales. These differences between young men and women also tend to support our general hypotheses. Women showed significantly higher contributory- and vicarious-relational scores and a near-significantly higher score on collaborative-relational. Also as predicted, males showed significantly higher means on all the direct scales. Further in accordance with our predictions, both genders scored high on the intrinsic-direct scale. This scale, again, was given the highest mean of all scales by both men and women. Our expectation, however, that females would give a higher reliant-instrumental mean than males was not borne out. As noted earlier, this scale received very low endorsement from all samples, so its failure to discriminate may be due to other characteristics. Finally, on both the personal- and the social-instrumental scales, men scored significantly higher than women.

Table 3-10 presents the significant standardized canonical discriminant function coefficients explaining 100% of the variance for the two age-split samples by gender. By applying the function coefficients to the mean scores shown in Table 3-9, we see that, in the 30 + age group, the dominant discriminating variable for separating

Table 3-9
Results of analyses of variance from discriminant function analyses, age-split subsamples

	Scale	Male		Female		F	P
		Mean	S.D.	Mean	S.D.		
	Age group 30+ (N = 780)						
1	Intrinsic direct	5.19	.89	4.92	1.22	20.96	.000
2	Competitive direct	4.69	1.01	3.44	1.17	249.00	.000
3	Power direct	5.08	1.03	4.01	1.37	183.90	.000
4	Personal instrumental	3.95	1.16	3.48	1.19	24.07	.000
5	Social instrumental	3.52	1.07	2.99	1.17	51.50	.000
6	Reliant instrumental	2.85	1.07	2.91	1.03	.24	.624
7	Collaborative relational	4.68	1.11	4.31	1.22	49.61	.000
8	Contributory relational	4.59	1.02	4.21	1.17	41.96	.000
9	Vicarious relational	4.70	1.06	4.52	1.39	43.28	.038
	Age group < 30 (N = 2483)						
1	Intrinsic direct	4.63	1.03	4.54	1.05	8.16	.004
2	Competitive direct	4.39	1.17	3.84	1.17	155.50	.000
3	Power direct	4.23	1.24	3.76	1.33	71.42	.000
4	Personal instrumental	4.05	1.08	3.59	1.09	777.40	.000
5	Social instrumental	3.41	1.14	2.91	1.08	104.20	.000
6	Reliant instrumental	2.79	.97	2.72	.94	.96	.328
7	Collaborative relational	4.09	1.20	4.21	1.21	3.69	.055
8	Contributory relational	3.88	1.04	4.06	1.05	14.54	.000
9	Vicarious relational	4.02	1.12	4.48	1.12	86.63	.000

Table 3-10

Significant standardized canonical discriminant function coefficients for separate analyses of two age-split samples by gender

Scale	Analysis 1 Age group 30 + Function 1	Analysis 2 Age group < 30 Function 1
1 Intrinsic direct	.29	.08
2 Competitive direct	− .82	.39
3 Power direct	− .29	.15
4 Personal instrumental	.08	.26
5 Social instrumental	− .14	.46
6 Reliant instrumental	.20	− .10
7 Collaborative relational	− .10	− .20
8 Contributory relational	− .21	− .04
9 Vicarious relational	.05	− .68

males from females is the high competitive-direct scale score for males. Younger men are also separated from younger women by their higher competitive-direct scores and by higher social-instrumental and lower vicarious-relational scores.

A discriminant analysis was also performed to determine whether the Achieving Styles Inventory could correctly predict membership in the 30 + and < 30 age groups without regard to gender. We believed that relational styles, particularly the vicarious-relational style, would tend to be used more by older people, as the variety of their relational experiences grew. While direct styles of achieving should increase as people enter and advance through their careers, older people, having achieved some of their primary occupational goals, may be expected to move away from competitive- and power-direct styles toward more relational styles. Older individuals, regardless of gender, are also "socialized" as they grow even older, away from task-oriented direct-ness toward more vicarious- and contributory-relational styles. Fur-ther, we expected younger persons to use more personal- and social-instrumental styles than would older persons, since they are in the process of actively searching for a place in the world, often through the aid of and connections with more powerful others.

As Table 3-11 shows, 68.2% of the sample was correctly classified into the 30 + and < 30 age groups. Examination of the single signif-icant discriminant function explaining 100% of the variance shows

Table 3-11
Predictive ability of the L-BLA Achieving Styles Inventory (Form 10),
percentage of cases correctly classified by age, prior probability = 50%

Age group	N	< 30	30 +
30 +	783	31.4	68.6
< 30	2511	68.0	32.0

Overall percentage of cases correctly classified: 68.2%

that age groups are distinguished from each other by a pattern of negative coefficients for the intrinsic-direct, power-direct, and reliant-instrumental scales, and positive coefficients for the personal-instrumental and competitive-direct scales. These differences were, of course, presaged (Table 3-9) by younger people's lower intrinsic-direct, power-direct, and reliant-instrumental scores and higher personal-instrumental scores. The higher competitive-direct score for younger women relative to older women also contributed to the discrimination between age groups. This difference is not particularly difficult to explain, given the more assertive orientation endorsed by the women's movement, whose influence is felt most strongly by younger women.

Our expectations about age differences are only partially supported, however. Older persons do show, as expected, higher mean scores on the relational scales, with the difference greater for males than for females. And younger persons do show slightly higher personal-instrumental scores. But social-instrumental scores are fairly constant across groups, and the competitive-direct mean is lower with age among women, but higher among men.

In summary, the predictive ability of the instrument was shown to be considerably better than chance in classifying subjects by gender and age, and the discriminating variables and direction of results tend grossly to fit our a priori predictions. The predictions about gender were more accurate for persons 30 + than < 30. The clearer differences within older age groups may be due to developmental processes, cohort effects, sampling, role differences, or some combination of these, or indeed, to other causes. Our cross-sectional data inevitably shed little light on that question.

Intercorrelations among scales are generally consistent with our circular model of achieving styles. Factor analyses of the scale scores also pick up three dimensions consistent with the model's three domains. While there are several instances of multiple loadings in the < 30 subjects, the domains are highly differentiated in the 30 + group.

Data from Occupational Groups of Men and Women

In order to explore further the relationship among ASI scores, salient characteristics of various occupational groups, and gender, we selected eight homogeneous subpopulations from the larger sets described in the previous section. We were particularly interested in (1) differences across levels and types of management (e.g., how senior managers compared on, say, power-direct styles with junior managers) and (2) differences, if any, between the genders when both are engaged in similar occupations (e.g., whether male middle managers show significantly different profiles from female middle managers).

To take a first cut at these questions, we isolated five sets of men and three sets of women as follows:

1. *Senior* managers ($N = 242$) drawn from the 1979 and 1980 senior-executive programs of a western university. These men averaged 44.8 years of age and 16.7 years of education. Typically, they held titles such as Vice President or General Manager in large corporations. Estimated mean annual income: $90,000 to $100,000. They are the males from groups 9 and 10 in Table 3-1.

2. *Upper* male managers ($N = 34$) from a 1979 executive program at an eastern university. They are younger (mean age = 37.1), from slightly lower organizational levels than group 1 above, and typically from smaller companies. Average education for this group was 16.3 years. Estimated mean annual salary: $60,000. They are the males from group 12 in Table 3-1.

3. *Middle* male managers ($N = 34$) who were Fellows in a one-year degree program at a western university in 1980. They are younger (mean age = 37.0) and generally of lower organizational rank than group 1 or 2. Average education was 16.9 years. Estimated mean annual salary: $40,000. They are the males from group 11 in Table 3-1.

4. *Technical* managers ($N = 29$) who were all technical supervisors in a large, private research and development organization in 1980. Their average age was 40.3; average education, 18.3 years. Estimated average salary: $40,000. They are the males from group 13 in Table 3-1.

5. *Staff* managers ($N = 35$) who were credit managers and loan officers from banks and other business organizations in a 1980 sam-

ple. Their average age was 34.8; average education, 15.1 years. Salaries unknown. They are the males from group 14 in Table 3-1.

We also selected three female groups, as follows:

6. *Homemakers* (N = 154), most of whom were the wives of the men in groups 9, 10, 11, and 18 in Table 3-1. Their average age was 43.5; their average education covered 14.3 years. These women identified themselves as full-time homemakers.

7. *Career* women (N = 146) who were nonmanagerial working women drawn from groups 9, 10, 11, and 18 of Table 3-1. Their average age was 40.7 years, and average education was 16.2 years. Incomes were not recorded.

8. *Managers* (N = 61) who were drawn from groups 9, 10, 11, 13, 14, and 18 of Table 3-1. These women coded their occupations as managers or administrators. Their average age was 39.5; their average education, 15.9 years. Their incomes are not known.

Table 3-12 shows mean scores, standard deviations, and *F* ratios from one-way analyses of variance for those eight groups on the nine scales of the Achieving Styles Inventory.

Analysis of Male Scores   The salient findings from groups 1–5 are these:

1. The intrinsic-direct and reliant-instrumental scales showed little variation and uniformly high and low means, respectively. These scales have been modified in a subsequent revision of the L-BLA Achievement Styles Inventory (Form 13).

2. An analysis of variance over the means of all scales showed significant differences among groups on competitive-direct, power-direct, personal-instrumental, collaborative-relational, and vicarious-relational scales, and near-significance ($p = 0.07$) on the social-instrumental and contributory-relational scales.

3. The technical managers ranked fifth of the five groups on each of the three direct scales and each of the three instrumental scales, while the middle managers ranked fifth on each of the three relational scales. Moreover, senior managers and upper managers gave higher raw mean scores on *every* scale than did the technical managers. That the technical supervisors showed the lowest scores almost across the board may indicate either less "intensity" of style, less self-confidence, or, perhaps stereotypically, greater caution than other groups about giving extreme responses. That the technical managers were the least direct and instrumental of the male groups may also suggest a less macho, more balanced set of styles than exhibited by the other male managerial groups.

4. These uniformly high scores for some groups and low scores for others warrant separate consideration of the *pattern* of any group's scale scores relative only to itself. We, therefore, examined raw rank orders across scales for each group. Since all groups gave very consistent low ranks to the three instrumental scales, we considered differences among the groups on only the direct and the relational scales.

The within-group patterns now emerge more clearly. The middle managers gave their three highest ranks to the three direct styles, with low ranks given to contributory-, collaborative-, and vicarious-relational scales. The technical managers, in contrast, showed a pattern of preference for the intrinsic-direct style (rank 1), followed by all three relational scales, with their lowest (of these six) ranks going to the competitive- and power-direct scales. The senior managers gave their highest ranks to the power- and intrinsic-direct styles, and then spread their third rank over three scales: competitive-direct, and collaborative- and vicarious-relational.

5. Overall, the results with male managers are at least consistent both with our own experience and with commonly held stereotypes. The senior general managers showed the highest power-direct orientation, but they were also moderately high on the relational styles (highest of all male groups in their collaborative and vicarious scores). They were the only group to show a lower intrinsic- than power-direct orientation. This picture seems consistent with the senior-management role, which involves several components: organization and control of others with relatively little directly targeted individual work, and significant elements of coaching and peer collaboration.

The slightly younger and slightly lower-level upper managers came through as more direct on all three direct scales than did the senior managers, and also less relational on two of the three relational scales. They fit more closely the aggressive, competitive executive stereotype, while the older senior managers reflected something closer to a strong, benevolent fatherly image.

The still younger and even lower-level middle managers put forward a clear "young tiger" pattern. They scored high on the direct styles: intrinsic, competitive, and power. The difference between their average direct-domain and average relational-domain scores was .86, almost twice as large as that displayed by any other group. But these subjects were fairly recent entrants into the managerial world, so perhaps such a "muscular" set of orientations is to be expected.

The technical managers also fulfilled stereotypic expectations. They gave cautiously low scores across all nine scales; but, within their own group, their highest ranks were reserved for the task-centered intrinsic-direct style and the contiguous altruistic vicarious-

Table 3-12

Results of one-way analysis of variance including raw scale means and standard deviations, eight occupational groups (5 male, 3 female), L-BLA Achieving Styles Inventory (Form 10)

Group	N	Gender	Direct								Instrumental			
			Intrinsic 1		Competitive 2		Power 3		Personal 4		Social 5		Reliant 6	
			$\overline{X}$	S.D.	$\overline{X}$	S.D.	$\overline{X}$	S.D.	$\overline{X}$	S.D.	$\overline{X}$	S.D.	$\overline{X}$	S.D.
1. Seniors	242	M	5.27	.86	4.96	.93	5.38	.81	3.78	1.25	3.44	1.06	2.85	1.00
2. Uppers	34	M	5.44	.94	5.25	.80	5.46	.78	4.49	.82	3.87	.90	2.92	1.09
3. Middles	34	M	5.49	.85	4.71	.99	5.29	.86	3.77	1.23	3.69	.92	2.82	1.00
4. Techs	29	M	5.22	.90	4.26	1.03	4.47	1.14	3.73	.92	3.21	1.06	2.60	.84
5. Staffs	35	M	5.52	.67	4.73	.83	5.02	.87	4.35	.98	3.67	1.30	2.69	1.05
F			1.30		5.57		8.73		4.30		2.22		.63	
P			.27		.00		.00		.00		.07		.64	
6. Homemakers	154	F	4.70	1.19	3.30	1.20	3.46	1.39	3.35	1.27	2.60	1.14	2.96	1.06
7. Careers	146	F	5.04	1.10	3.48	1.05	4.22	1.23	3.51	1.18	3.04	1.16	2.94	1.10
8. Managers	61	F	5.56	.89	3.84	1.55	4.83	.91	3.77	1.18	3.64	.99	2.75	1.01
F			13.99		4.99		30.18		2.67		19.35		.96	
P			.00		.01		.00		.07		.00		.38	

Group	N	Gender	Relational						Domain							
			Collaborative 7		Contributory 8		Vicarious 9		Direct		Instrumental		Relational		Total test	
			$\bar{X}$	S.D.	$\bar{X}$	S.D.	$\bar{X}$	S.D.	$\bar{X}$	S.D.	$\bar{X}$	S.D.	$\bar{X}$	S.D.	$\bar{X}$	S.D.
1. Seniors	242	M	4.97	1.02	4.78	.97	4.95	.97	5.20	.68	3.36	.92	4.90	.84	4.49	.60
2. Uppers	34	M	4.87	1.23	5.07	.97	4.86	1.14	5.39	.69	3.76	.77	4.94	.96	4.69	.52
3. Middles	34	M	4.17	1.10	4.39	1.19	4.33	1.32	5.16	.66	3.43	.75	4.30	.98	4.29	.44
4. Techs	29	M	4.68	.72	4.67	.85	4.79	.95	4.65	.76	3.18	.78	4.71	.59	4.18	.54
5. Staffs	35	M	4.45	1.15	4.85	1.05	4.81	1.08	5.09	.63	3.57	.90	4.70	.87	4.46	.56
			F 6.05		2.21		2.70		$\bar{X}$(1–5) 5.16	.69	3.41	.89	4.82	.87	4.46	.58
			P .00		.07		.03									
6. Homemakers	154	F	4.06	1.31	4.20	1.19	4.98	1.36	3.82	.94	2.97	.94	4.41	1.01	3.73	.68
7. Careers	146	F	4.21	1.21	4.09	1.16	4.18	1.31	4.25	.87	3.16	.93	4.16	.91	3.86	.61
8. Managers	61	F	4.65	1.06	4.60	.94	4.53	1.08	4.74	.74	3.83	.79	4.60	.74	4.24	.49
			F 5.22		4.46		14.13		$\bar{X}$ (6–8) 4.15	.94	3.12	.92	4.34	.94	3.87	.65
			P .01		.01		.00									

[191]

relational style. While they showed lower overall mean scores than did any other group in both the direct and the instrumental domains, they were considerably higher in the total relational domain and in each of its three substyles. The technical managers came through, then, as reasonable purists, targeted toward task, supportiveness, and group effort, rather than toward power, competition, and political ploys.

The staff managers, a group of credit and loan officers, had the widest age spread. They showed a mixed achieving styles pattern. Like the middle managers, their highest scores were in the intrinsic- and power-direct areas, with lower scores on the competitive-direct scale. Compared to other groups, they were also among the higher scorers on the personal- and social-instrumental scales, suggesting a tendency to get things done by indirection—a phenomenon frequently associated with staff positions in organizations.

The data on these five male groups, while far from definitive, do seem grossly to match expectations about the behaviors associated with their respective organizational roles.

Analysis of Female Scores[4]   In the three occupational groups of women (groups 6, 7, and 8 described earlier), the prominent results (Table 3-12) are these:

1. Again, we found low means and low group-to-group variations on the three instrumental scales, contrary to manipulative and dependent stereotypes of women.

2. An analysis of variance across scales showed significant differences among groups on seven scales, near-significance ($p = .07$) on the personal-instrumental scale, and nonsignificance only on the reliant-instrumental scale.

3. A comparison of ranks across scales for female occupational groups provides a crude picture of patterns of response within these three groups. The top three ranks for homemakers were the vicarious-relational, intrinsic-direct, and contributory-relational scales. For both groups of working women, the top three ranks went to the intrinsic-direct, power-direct, and collaborative-relational scales, respectively.

---

[4]For an analysis of differences in achieving styles among four female groups (teenage students, full-time homemakers, women in traditional "feminine" occupations, and female managers) and several male groups, see Lipman-Blumen, Leavitt, and Handley-Isaksen, 1980.

4. The managerial women scored highest of the three groups on seven of the nine scales and lowest only on the reliant-instrumental scale. Thus, these managers also had the highest overall test mean of the female groups. The homemakers, by contrast, were the lowest scorers on six scales, including the three direct scales, two instrumental scales, and one relational scale. They were highest on the vicarious-relational and reliant-instrumental scales. Likewise, their overall test mean was the lowest of the three female groups. The managerial women differed from the homemakers in their much higher power-direct and social-instrumental scores and in their relatively lower vicarious-relational scores. The career women who occupy mostly traditional female work roles gave the lowest vicarious-relational score of any group. The career women scored between the homemakers and managers on seven of the nine scales and on the total test mean. The two scales on which the career women did not have a position midway between the homemakers and managers were the contributory- and vicarious-relational scales; in fact, they scored lowest on both.

5. The patterns within women's groups conform to some, but not all, stereotypical expectations. As we expected, homemakers gave their four highest ranks to all three relational styles, as well as to the intrinsic-direct style. Contrary to stereotypes, they gave lowest ranks to social- and reliant-instrumental scales. Nonetheless, they showed somewhat stronger reliant patterns than did their female counterparts in the paid labor force, although the differences were not quite significant. Homemakers' reliant-instrumental scores were only slightly higher than those of careerists, but noticeably higher than the managerial women's reliant-instrumental scores. Compared to their managerial and careerist sisters, the homemakers gave particularly lower scores to the power-direct and social-instrumental scales, but the greatest differences among the female groups, as one might expect, were those between the managerial women and the homemakers. On all but one scale—the vicarious-relational—the differences between the homemakers and the managerial women were greater than between the homemakers and the career women employed in traditional feminine jobs.

Both groups of women in paid employment gave first rank, as well as higher absolute scores than did homemakers, to the intrinsic-direct scale. They also ranked and scored the power-direct scale higher than did homemakers. And although managerial women are more competitive than their homemaking and careerist sisters in both rank order and scores, they gave the competitive-direct scale a much lower rank (6) and consistently lower scores than did their male counterparts.

These findings, with exceptions, are mostly consistent with expectations about role demands on managers and homemakers, suggesting a possible selection mechanism moving persons with appropriate styles toward consonant roles, and perhaps also some further honing of achieving styles appropriate to one's role. Moreover, some of these roles may provide few opportunities and little encouragement for experimenting with other styles outside of that subset. For example, one might argue that the homemakers' environment, other things being equal, provides a narrower range of situations and a smaller number of opportunities to practice alternative styles than some other occupational environments. The homemakers' consequent lower overall scale scores may result from more tentative and conservative answers to scale items than those given by groups that operate in wider experiential and/or self-confidence-evoking contexts. Further, any given role within an environment may provide structured opportunities for developing a particular subset of achieving styles.

Comparison of Males and Females   A joint consideration of the five groups of men and three groups of women provides the following comparisons:

1. The total raw test-item means (Table 3-12) were considerably higher for the men (4.46) than for the women (3.87). The men also scored higher on each of the three domains and on all but the reliant-instrumental scale.

2. Separate examination of the data from all eight groups indicates that the lower test scores for women were generated primarily by the homemaker group. They scored lowest of all eight groups on six of the nine scales and seventh on one more. But they scored highest (by a very small margin) on the reliant-instrumental and vicarious-relational scales—the two scales probably most closely associated with traditional "feminine" behavior.

On the other hand, the women managers, themselves a diverse group, are not easily distinguishable from male groups 1 (seniors), 2 (uppers), or 3 (middles), except on the competitive- and power-direct scales. There are considerable differences on the competitive-direct scale, with female managers giving much lower scores than did male managers. The differences in power between male and female managers are weaker, but discernible. All but one male group scored higher on power-direct than did the female managers. The female managers' raw scores ranked highest among all eight groups on the intrinsic-direct scale and higher than at least one of the male groups on six other scales.

3. Considering patterns of ranks within groups, the total set of women gave intrinsic-direct their highest rank, vicarious-relational second, with the other two relational scales (contributory and collaborative) tied for third. The men also gave the number 1 slot to intrinsic-direct, but second rank went to power-direct. Third place was a tie between the competitive-direct and vicarious-relational styles.

Only the *overall* men's and women's patterns, then, generally fit prevailing stereotypes: the "warm, supportive" women were vicarious-, contributory-, and collaborative-relational; they rejected the power- and competitive-direct styles. The "cold, hard" men were power-oriented and competitive-direct. Nonetheless, both genders (perhaps primarily in the highly task-oriented American tradition) showed high intrinsic-direct achievement orientations.

Two apparent contradictions of traditional gender-role stereotypes appear: the relatively high vicarious-relational status of the men's groups, especially the older, male managers of higher rank; and, as noted above, the relatively low social-instrumental scores of women in traditional roles, who stereotypically are seen as achieving through manipulating relationships.

4. Finally, if we plot (Figure 3-2) standard (T) scores for four special groups, intragroup patterns show up more clearly. The homemakers showed an essentially U-shaped pattern: high on intrinsic-direct, lower in the remaining direct scales and the three instrumental scales, then peaking again on the relational scales. The male senior managers were high on the direct scales, dipped sharply in the instrumental scales, then came back partway on all the relational scales. The male middle managers' pattern, in contrast, was very high on the direct scales and low on the relational styles. The managerial women looked most like the male senior managers, ranking intrinsic- and power-direct high and vicarious-relational low, but showing a much sharper drop from intrinsic- to competitive-direct than either male group.

We draw no definitive conclusions from these exploratory occupational data. The findings do point up problems with several scales, which, as we have indicated, have since undergone four revisions. They raise the painful question of high and low response biases (tentatively associated here both with line management and gender). Beyond those methodological questions, the data are consistent with contemporary expectations about male managers and female homemakers. But the scoring patterns of both female labor-force groups and male technical supervisors make it clear that gender alone cannot account for our findings.

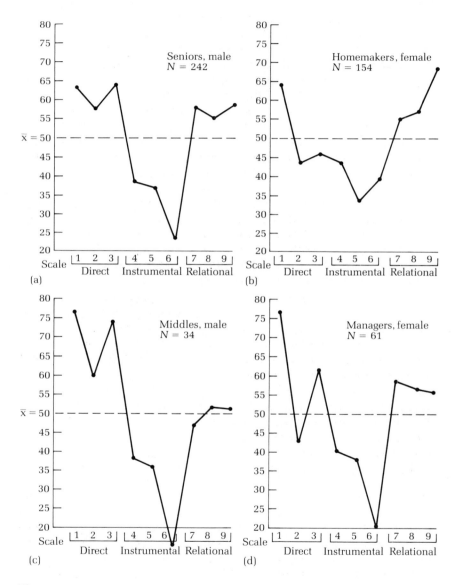

Figure 3-2
T scores, Achieving Styles Inventory (Form 10), four occupational groups $(\overline{x} = 50; S.D. = 10)$.

SUMMARY AND DISCUSSION

In summary, we have developed and presented a three-factor model of achieving styles, built on the assumption that individuals learn more or less preferred methods for trying to achieve—to implement, to get things done. These preferred styles, we believe, are learned fairly early in life as a consequence of differential reinforcement of the individual's search for solutions. Adult roles may be selected that are perceived as consonant with an individual's preferred achieving-style profile. Often, the role further hones the individual's pattern. Moreover, people may become so well attuned to and skilled in the use of particular styles that other possible styles may no longer even be perceived or may be considered infeasible. As a consequence, styles familiar to the person may be used, even when deemed inappropriate by observers. Style, once formed, may then drive the definition or selection of achieving situations. Individuals then perceptually may redefine situations, enacting a world compatible with their preferred styles, thereby constructing more comfortable perceived realities. Indeed, analogous phenomena often take place at organizational and societal levels.

We have also developed a nine-scale self-report instrument, the L-BLA Achieving Styles Inventory, designed to measure the nine achieving styles identified in the model. Preliminary findings on the validity and reliability of the instrument are reassuring. We are currently in the process of relating the L-BLA Achieving Styles Inventory to other conceptually proximate psychometric instruments and to more direct behavioral measures. The achieving-styles paradigm may provide a useful lens for viewing gender roles, organizational behavior, and cross-cultural differences. We have already undertaken preliminary work in each of these areas (Leavitt and Lipman-Blumen, 1980; Lipman-Blumen and Leavitt, 1978, 1979). For example, we are comparing ASI performance at several levels of management and in several specialized functions. We have collected data on occupation, age, and gender groups in Singapore and Taiwan, and we expect soon to have data from comparable groups in Brazil, Scandinavia, South Africa, Italy, and Israel. In addition, several doctoral dissertations on various aspects and applications of achieving styles are in progress at present.

The genesis of this research emanated from a concern about gender differences in achieving styles. That interest continues with planned or ongoing studies of age, gender, and cohort differences. The interactions among age, gender, and occupation seem particularly intriguing as women increasingly move into traditionally male occupational roles. Further inquiry is also under way both into the life-style correlates of individual patterns of achieving styles and possible programs for helping individuals expand their style repertoires. Such tailor-made programs might encourage individuals to become more sensitive to situational cues and more flexible in their responses. Other applications in the areas of group dynamics, including team building and conflict resolution, as well as family therapy and occupational counseling, offer possible additional avenues of exploration.

REFERENCES

Abramson, L. Y., M. E. D. Seligman, and J. D. Teasdale. 1978. Learned helplessness in humans: Critique reformulation. *Journal of Abnormal Psychology, 87,* 49–74.

Adorno, T. W., E. Frankel-Brunswik, D. J. Levinson, and R. N. Sanford. 1950. *The authoritarian personality.* New York: Harper.

Allport, G. W. 1937. *Personality: A psychological interpretation.* New York: Holt.

Allport, G. W. 1965. Traits revisited. *American Psychologist, 21,* 1–10.

Alper, T. G. 1973. The relationship between role-orientation and achievement motivation in college women. *Journal of Personality, 11,* 9–31.

Alper, T. G. 1974. Achievement motivation in college women: A now-you-see-it-now-you-don't phenomenon. *American Psychologist, 29,* 194–203.

Alper, T. G., and E. Greenberger. 1967. Relationship of picture structure to achievement motivation in college women. *Journal of Personality and Social Psychology, 7,* 362–371.

Angelini, A. L. 1955. Un novo metedo para avaliar a motivacao humano. (A new method of evaluating human motivation.) *Boletin Facildade de Filosefice Ciences,* Saõ Paolo, No. 207.

Atkinson, J. W. 1958a. Thematic apperception measurement of motives within the context of a theory of motivation. In J. W. Atkinson (ed.), *Motives in fantasy, action, and society.* Princeton, NJ: Van Nostrand.

Atkinson, J. W. (ed.). 1958b. *Motives in fantasy, action, and society.* Princeton, NJ: Van Nostrand.

Atkinson, J. W. 1960. Personality dynamics. *Annual Review of Psychology, 11,* 255–290.

Atkinson, J. W., and N. T. Feather. 1966. *A theory of achievement motivation.* New York: Wiley.

Atkinson, J. W., R. W. Heyns, and J. Veroff. 1954. The effect of experimental arousal of the affiliative motive on thematic apperception. *Journal of Abnormal and Social Psychology, 49,* 400–410.

Atkinson, J. W., and J. O. Raynor (eds.). 1974. *Motivation and achievement.* Washington, DC: Winston.

Atkinson, J. W., and E. L. Walker. 1956. The affiliation motive and perceptive sensitivity to faces. *Journal of Abnormal and Social Psychology, 53,* 38–41.

Awad, R. 1980. Suggested relationships between academic major and achieving styles. Unpublished manuscript, Stanford University.

Bales, R. F., and P. Slater. 1955. Role differentiation in small decision making groups. In T. Parsons and R. F. Bales (eds.), *Family socialization and interaction process*. Glencoe, IL: Free Press.

Bandura, A. 1977. *Social learning theory.* Englewood Cliffs, NJ: Prentice-Hall.

Baruch, R. 1967. The achievement motive in women: Implications for career development. *Journal of Personality and Social Psychology, 5,* 260–267.

Bass, B., and G. Dunteman. 1963. Behavior in groups as a function of self, interaction and task orientation. *Journal of Abnormal Social Psychology, 66,* 419–428.

Bellak, L. 1942. An experimental investigation of projection. *Psychological Bulletin, 39,* 489–490.

Bellak, L. 1944. The concept of projection. *Psychiatry, 7,* 353–370.

Blake, R. P., and J. S. Mouton. 1969. *Building a dynamic corporation through grid organization development.* Reading, MA: Addison-Wesley.

Blumen, J. (Lipman). 1970. Selected dimensions of self-concept and educational aspirations of married women college graduates. Unpublished doctoral dissertation, Harvard University.

Boyatzis, R. E. 1972. A two-factor theory of affiliation motivation. Unpublished doctoral dissertation, Harvard University.

Boyatzis, R. E. 1974. The need for close relationships and the manager's job. In D. A. Kolb, I. M. Rubin, and J. M. McIntyre (eds.), *Organizational psychology: A book of readings.* 2nd ed. Englewood Cliffs, NJ: Prentice-Hall.

Breedlove, J. J., and V. G. Cicerelli. 1974. Women's fear of success in relation to personal characteristics and types of occupation. *Journal of Psychology, 86* (2nd half), 181–190.

Broverman, I. K., S. R. Vogel, D. M. Broverman, F. E. Clarkson, and P. S. Rosenkrantz. 1972. Sex-role stereotypes: A current appraisal. *Journal of Social Issues, 28,* 59–78.

Cattell, R. B. 1949. Projection and the design of projective test of personality. *Character and Personality, 12,* 177–194.

Christie, R., and F. R. Geis. 1970. *Studies in Machiavellianism.* New York: Academic.

Coleman, W. 1947. The thematic apperception test: I. Effect of recent experience. II. Some qualitative observations. *Journal of Clinical Psychiatry, 3,* 257–264.

Combs, A. W. 1946a. A method of analysis for the thematic apperception test and autobiography. *Journal of Clinical Psychology, 2,* 161–174.

Combs, A. W. 1946b. The validity and reliability of interpretations from the thematic apperception test and autobiography. *Journal of Clinical Psychology, 2,* 240–247.

Combs, A. W. 1973. A comparative study of motivations as revealed in thematic apperception stories and autobiography. In D. C. McClelland and R. S. Steele (eds.), *Human motivation: A book of readings.* Morristown, NJ: General Learning Press.

Coser, R. L., and G. Rokoff. 1971. Women in the occupational world: Social disruption and conflict. *Social Problems, 18,* 535–554.

Crandall, V. C. 1969. Sex differences in expectancy of intellectual and academic reinforcement. In C. P. Smith (ed.), *Achievement-related motives in children.* New York: Russell Sage.

Crandall, V. C., and E. S. Battle. 1970. The antecedents and adult correlates of academic and intellectual achievement effort. In J. P. Hill (ed.), *Minnesota symposia on child psychology.* Vol. 4. Minneapolis: University of Minnesota Press.

Crandall, V. J. 1963. Achievement. In H. W. Stevenson (ed.), *Child psychology.* National Society for the Study of Education. Yearbooks series #62, part 1. Chicago: University of Chicago Press.

deCharms, R. 1957. Affiliation motivation and productivity in small groups. *Journal of Abnormal and Social Psychology, 55,* 222–226.

deCharms, R. 1968. *Personal causation: The internal affective determinant of behavior.* New York: Academic.

Deci, E. L. 1975. *Intrinsic motivation.* New York: Plenum.

Dweck, C. S. 1975a. Children's interpretations of evaluative feedback: The effect of social cues on learned helplessness. In C. S. Dweck, K. T. Hill, W. H. Reed, W. M. Steihman, and R. G. Parke (eds.), *The impact of social cues on children's behavior.* Special issue of *Merrill–Palmer Quarterly, 22,* 83–123.

Dweck, C. S. 1975b. The role of expectations and attributions in the alleviation of learned helplessness. *Journal of Personality and Social Psychology, 31,* 674–685.

Dweck, C. S., and N. D. Reppucci. 1973. Learned helplessness and reinforcement responsibility in children. *Journal of Personality and Social Psychology, 25,* 109–116.

Fiedler, F. F. 1978. The contingency model and the dynamics of the leadership process. In L. Berkowitz (ed.), *Advances in experimental social psychology.* Vol. 11. New York: Academic.

Fleishman, E. A. 1971. Twenty years of consideration and structure. Paper presented at Southern Illinois University Leadership Conference, Carbondale.

Fleming, J. 1977. Predictive validity of the motive to avoid success in black women. *Humanitas, 13,* 225–244.

French, E. G. 1955. Some characteristics of achievement motivation. *Journal of Experimental Psychology, 50,* 232–236.

French, E. G. 1958. The interaction of achievement motivation and ability in problem solving success. *Journal of Abnormal and Social Psychology, 57,* 306–309.

French, E. G., and G. S. Lesser. 1964. Some characteristics of the achievement motive in women. *Journal of Abnormal and Social Psychology, 68,* 119–128.

Frieze, I. H. 1975. Women's expectations for and causal attributions of success and failure. In M. T. S. Mednick, S. S. Tangri, and L. W. Hoffman (eds.), *Women and achievement: Social and motivational analyses*. Washington, DC: Hemisphere.

Goldberg, P. 1968. Are women prejudiced against women? *Trans-action, 5,* 28–30.

Gulliksen, H. 1950. *Theory of mental tests*. New York: Wiley.

Harris, H. 1969. An experimental model of the effectiveness of project management offices. Unpublished master's thesis, Massachusetts Institute of Technology.

Hartley, R. E. 1960. Children's concepts of male and female roles. *Merrill–Palmer Quarterly, 6,* 83–91.

Hartley, R. E., and F. P. Hardesty. 1964. Children's perceptions of sex roles in childhood. *Journal of Genetic Psychology, 104,* 43–51.

Heilbrun, A. B., Jr. 1963. Sex-role identity and achievement motivation. *Psychological Report, 12,* 483–490.

Hoffman, L. W. 1972. Early childhood experiences and women's achievement motives. *Journal of Social Issues, 28,* 129–156.

Hoffman, L. W. 1974. Fear of success in males and females: 1965 and 1972. *Journal of Consulting and Clinical Psychology, 42,* 353–358.

Horner, M. S. 1968. Sex differences in achievement motivation and performance in competitive and non-competitive situations. Unpublished doctoral dissertation, University of Michigan.

Horner, M. S. 1972. Toward an understanding of achievement-related conflicts in women. *Journal of Social Issues, 28,* 147–176.

Jones, M. R. (ed.). 1961. *Nebraska symposium on motivation*. Vol. 9. Lincoln: University of Nebraska Press.

Kelley, H. H. 1967. Attribution theory in social psychology. In D. Levine (ed.), *Nebraska symposium on motivation*. Vol. 15. Lincoln: University of Nebraska Press.

Kelley, H. H. 1971. *Attribution in social interaction*. Morristown, NJ: General Learning Press.

Kohlberg, L. 1966. A cognitive-developmental analysis of children's sex-role concepts and attitudes. In E. E. Maccoby (ed.), *The development of sex differences*. Stanford, CA: Stanford University Press.

Leavitt, H. J., and J. Lipman-Blumen. 1980. A case for the relational manager. *Organizational Dynamics,* Summer, 27–41.

Leavitt, H. J., J. Lipman-Blumen, S. Schaefer, and R. Harris. 1977. Vicarious achievement orientation. Paper presented at meeting of American Psychological Association, San Francisco.

Lesser, G. S. 1973. Achievement motivation in women. In D. C. McClelland and R. S. Steele (eds.), *Human motivation: A book of readings*. Morristown, NJ: General Learning Press.

Lesser, G. S., R. N. Krawitz, and R. Packard. 1963. Experimental arousal of achievement motive in adolescent girls. *Journal of Abnormal and Social Psychology*, *66*, 59–66.

Levine, A., and J. Crumrine. 1975. Women and the fear of success: A problem in replication. *American Journal of Sociology*, *80*, 964–974.

Lewin, K., R. Lippit, and R. K. White. 1939. Patterns of aggressive behavior in experimentally created social climates. *Journal of Social Psychology*, *10*, 271–299.

Likert, R. 1961. *New patterns of management*. New York: McGraw-Hill.

Lipman-Blumen, J. 1972. How ideology shapes women's lives. *Scientific American*, *266*, 34–42.

Lipman-Blumen, J. 1973. The vicarious achievement ethic and non-traditional roles for women. Paper presented at meeting of Eastern Sociological Society, New York.

Lipman-Blumen, J., and H. J. Leavitt. 1976. Vicarious and direct achievement patterns in adulthood. *Counseling Psychologist*, *6*, 26–32.

Lipman-Blumen, J., and H. J. Leavitt. 1978. Socialization and achievement patterns in cross-cultural perspective: Japanese and American family and work roles. Paper presented at International Sociological Association, 9th World Congress, Uppsala, Sweden.

Lipman-Blumen, J., and H. J. Leavitt. 1979. Sexual behavior as an expression of achievement orientation. In H. A. Katchadourian (ed.), *Human sexuality*. Berkeley: University of California Press.

Lipman-Blumen, J., H. J. Leavitt, and A. Handley-Isaksen. 1980. A model of achieving styles: Implications for women's occupational roles. Presented at Women and the World of Work, A NATO Symposium, Lisbon.

Lipman-Blumen, J., H. J. Leavitt, K. J. Patterson, R. J. Bies, and A. Handley-Isaksen. 1980. A model of direct and relational achieving styles. In L. J. Fyans (ed.), *Achievement motivation*. New York: Plenum.

Lipman-Blumen, J., and A. R. Tickamyer. 1975. Sex roles in transition: A ten-year review. in A. Inkeles (ed.), *Annual Review of Sociology*. Palo Alto, CA: Annual Reviews.

Lockheed, M. 1975. Female motive to avoid success: A psychological barrier or a response to deviancy? *Sex Roles*, *1*, 41–50.

McClelland, D. C. 1961. *The achieving society*. New York: Van Nostrand.

McClelland, D. C. (ed.). 1955. *Studies in motivation*. New York: Appleton-Century-Crofts.

McClelland, D. C., J. W. Atkinson, R. A. Clark, and E. L. Lowell. 1953. *The achievement motive*. New York: Appleton-Century-Crofts.

Maccoby, E. E., and C. N. Jacklin. 1974. *The psychology of sex differences*. Stanford, CA: Stanford University Press,.

MacFarlane, J. W. 1941. Critique of projective techniques. *Psychological Bulletin*, *38*, 746.

Maslow, A. H. 1954. *Motivation and personality*. New York: Harper.

Mednick, M. T. S., and G. R. Puryear. 1975. Motivation and personality factors related to career goals of black college women. *Journal of Social and Behavioral Sciences, 24,* 1–30.

Mednick, M. T. S., and G. R. Puryear. 1976. Race and fear of success in college women: 1968 and 1971. *Journal of Consulting and Clinical Psychology, 44,* 787–789.

Mischel, W. 1968. *Personality and assessment.* New York: Wiley.

Mischel, W. 1977. On the future of personality measurement. *American Psychology, 32,* 246–254.

Murray, H. A. 1938. *Explorations in personality.* New York: Oxford University Press.

Papanek, H. 1973. Men, women and work: Reflection on the two-person career. *American Journal of Sociology, 78,* 852–870.

Parsons, T., and R. F. Bales (eds.). 1955. *Family socialization and interaction process.* Glencoe, IL: Free Press.

Puryear, G. R., and M. T. S. Mednick. 1974. Black militancy, affective attachment, and fear of success in black college women. *Journal of Consulting and Clinical Psychology, 2,* 263–266.

Ross, L. 1977. The intuitive psychologist and his shortcomings: Distortions in the attribution process. In L. Berkowitz (ed.), *Advances in experimental social psychology,* Vol. 10. New York: Academic.

Salancik, G. R., and J. Pfeffer. 1977. An examination of need-satisfaction model of job attitudes. *Administrative Science Quarterly, 22,* 427–456.

Sargent, H. 1945. Projective methods, their origins, theory, and application to personality research. *Psychological Bulletin, 42,* 257–293.

Schachter, S. 1959. *The psychology of affiliation.* Stanford, CA: Stanford University Press.

Schein, V. E. 1973. The relationship between sex-role stereotypes and requisite management characteristics. *Journal of Applied Psychology, 57,* 95–100.

Schein, V. E. 1975. Relationship between sex-role stereotypes and requisite management characteristics among female managers. *Journal of Applied Psychology, 60,* 340–344.

Seligman, M. E. P. 1975. *Helplessness: On depression, development, and death.* San Francisco: W. H. Freeman and Company.

Smith, M. B. 1968. Competence and socialization. In J. Clausen (ed.), *Socialization and society.* Boston: Little, Brown.

Spence, J. T., and R. L. Helmreich, 1978. *Masculinity and femininity: Their psychological dimensions, correlates and antecedents.* Austin: University of Texas Press.

Stein, A. H. 1971. The effects of sex-role standards for achievement and sex-role preferences on three determinants of achievement motivation. *Developmental Psychology, 4,* 219–231.

Stein, A. H., and M. M. Bailey. 1973. The socialization of achievement orientation in females. *Psychological Bulletin, 80,* 345–366.

Stogdill, R. M., and A. E. Coons (eds.). 1957. *Leader behavior: its description and measurement.* Columbus: Bureau of Business Research, College of Commerce and Administration, Ohio State University.

Tresemer, D. 1974. Fear of success: Popular but unproven. *Psychology Today, 7,* 82–85.

Tresemer, D. (ed.). 1976. *Fear of success.* Special issue of *Sex Roles, 2,* No. 3.

Veroff, J., J. W. Atkinson, S. C. Feld, and G. Gurin. 1960. The use of thematic apperception to assess motivation in a nationwide interview study. *Psychological Monograph, 94* (Whole No. 499).

Veroff, J., L. McClelland, and D. Ruhland, 1975. Varieties of achievement motivation. In M. T. S. Mednick, S. S. Tangri, and L. W. Hoffman (eds.), *Women and achievement: Social and motivational analyses.* Washington, DC: Hemisphere.

Vroom, V. H. 1964. *Work and motivation.* New York: Wiley.

Vroom, V. H., and P. W. Yetton. 1973. *Leadership and decision-making.* Pittsburgh: University of Pittsburgh Press.

Watson, R. 1970. Female and male responses to the succeeding female cue. Unpublished manuscript, Harvard University.

Weiner, B. 1966. Achievement motivation and task recall in competitive situations. *Journal of Psychology, 3,* 693–696.

Weiner, B. 1972. *Theories of motivation: From mechanism to cognition.* New York: Rand McNally.

Weiner, B. 1974. *Achievement motivation and attribution theory.* Morristown, NJ: General Learning Press.

Weiner, B. 1979. A theory of motivation for some classroom experiences. *Journal of Educational Psychology, 71,* 3–25.

Weiner, B. 1980. *Human motivation.* New York: Holt, Rinehart and Winston.

Weiner, B., and A. Kukla. 1970. An attributional analysis of achievement motivation. *Journal of Personality and Social Psychology, 15,* 1–20.

Weiner, H. A., and I. M. Rubin. 1969. Motivation of research and development entrepreneurs. *Journal of Applied Psychology, 53,* 178–184.

Weston, P. J., and M. T. S. Mednick. 1970. Race, social class, and the motive to avoid success in women. *Journal of Cross-Cultural Psychology, 1,* 203–291.

White, R. W. 1959. Motivation reconsidered: The concept of competence. *Psychological Review, 66,* 297–333.

Zander, A. 1971. *Motives and goals in groups.* New York: Academic.

4

Achievement and Intellectual Functioning of Children in One-Parent Households

E. Mavis Hetherington
University of Virginia

Kathleen A. Camara
Tufts University

David L. Featherman
University of Wisconsin

EDITOR'S OVERVIEW

The authors of this chapter, E. Mavis Hetherington, Kathleen A. Camara, and David L. Featherman, begin with a disturbing set of figures: due largely to the climbing divorce rate, nearly half of all children born at the beginning of the 1980s can be expected to spend some part of their lives prior to age 18 in a one-parent household. Although men are now more frequently awarded custody of their children than in earlier years, the vast majority of these households are headed by women.

Public acceptance of divorce has largely removed its stigma, but not its traumatic effects. Marital dissolution brings in its wake emotional distress in parents and children alike, disruption of the patterns of family life, and economic changes. Children from "broken homes," it has often been conjectured, are likely to suffer long-lasting emotional disturbance, behavior problems, or disruptions in intellectual functioning and school performance.

In this chapter, the authors have set themselves the important tasks of reviewing the voluminous and often methodologically flawed research literature to discern what is known about the relationship between children's academic achievements and their rearing in a one-parent home and of developing a social-psychological model that describes the relationships this research has revealed.

They conceive of divorce as setting off a sequence of life changes, often over a period of years, with children and each of their parents confronting different stresses and challenges at each stage. Many factors, such as the age, sex, and temperament of the child, the characteristics of the parents and their relationships to each other and their children after the divorce, economic circumstances, and extrafamilial sources of support, can all be shown to moderate or exacerbate the stresses associated with the divorce and its sequels and to influence the child's adjustment.

Their analyses allow the authors to reach several major conclusions. Most heartening of these is that, when the family socioeconomic status is taken into account, only small differences are typically found between the scores of children from one-parent homes and those of children from two-parent homes on IQ tests and standardized tests of academic achievement. Apparently, relatively few children in one-parent homes suffer any serious, long-term intellectual deficit. On the other hand, greater discrepancies are found between these two groups of children in school grades. The authors suggest that these data are subject to several interpretations. Circumstances within the one-parent household sometimes result in children becoming more disruptive in the classroom, less efficient in their study habits, and less likely to be willing or able to attend school regularly. These behaviors, which are particularly likely to occur when there is a relative lack in both the home and the school of a responsive, caring atmosphere and of consistently enforced standards and rules of behavior, may depress children's school performance. However, the lower evaluations these children receive from their teachers may reflect, not the quality of their academic performances per se, but the documented tendency of teachers to rate more favorably children who are obedient, industrious, and generally well-behaved. (The significance of teachers' linkage between what they consider appropriate classroom behavior and their treatment of students is also explored in the concluding chapter of this volume, on the academic problems of Black children.)

A second major finding that emerges from the present analysis of the literature is that boys are more likely than girls to be adversely affected in intellectual functioning by being reared in single-parent homes, particularly on tests of quantitative aptitude and achievement. These results, the authors observe, parallel the outcome of numerous studies in which it has been shown that the impact of divorce on boys is more severe and long-lasting than on girls and is more likely in boys to be manifested in behavioral and interpersonal problems. They add an important qualification to this finding: in most studies, the custodial parent is the mother. Recent evidence indicating that girls in father-custody homes exhibit many of the same social problems suggests that separation from the same-sex parent may be particularly stressful for children.

One of the authors' final statements deserves particular emphasis: "Most children find divorce to be a stressful life transition, but the long-term effects of marital disruption on children may be modified by effective family functioning and by positive experiences of the child in extrafamilial settings such as the school, peer group, neighborhood, or work."

ecent studies of the impact of family disruption
on children's academic functioning reflect trends
in marital dissolution and the growing numbers of children living in
one-parent homes. At least one-third and perhaps nearly one-half of
all children born in 1979 are expected to spend some portion of their
lives prior to age 18 in a one-parent household (Bumpass and Rindfuss, 1978; Glick, 1979) due largely to the increasing divorce rate. In
1960, nearly one-half of all children in one-parent families lived with
a divorced or separated parent; in 1980, nearly two-thirds did.

Although the social and psychological implications of rearing
children in one-parent households are not fully understood, numerous reports have suggested a relationship between divorce and children's intellectual functioning and academic achievement. What kinds
of effects does divorce have on academic performance and achievement behavior? What are the sociocultural variations in family life
after divorce that mediate the effects on children's cognitive functioning? Parents, educators, and professionals working with families
in transition need information about the effects of divorce that has
been verified through rigorous research. Attempts at providing answers
to these questions have been limited severely by the use of inadequate
research designs and methods that fail to take into account the complex changing patterns of family life surrounding divorce. It is our
intent in this chapter to describe separation and divorce as experienced by parents and their children and to review research that has
examined the relationship between one-parent rearing and intellectual functioning of children.

LIMITATIONS OF PREVIOUS RESEARCH

Early research on the effects of family disruption in children focused
on "father absence." The conceptualization of one-parent households
as father-absent households was due in part to the large numbers of
one-parent homes headed by women and to the influence of psychoanalytic theories that stressed the importance of the father in the
development of a child's sex role and behavior. Little attention was
paid to variations in individual or cultural factors or to variations in

life experiences and family interaction in one-parent homes that could modify the outcomes of divorce for children.

Research on the effects of parental separation on achievement has been plagued by methodological problems. These have been identified in previous reviews of father-absent literature (Camara, Baker, and Dayton, 1980; Herzog and Sudia, 1973; Hetherington, Cox, and Cox, 1978b; Shinn, 1978). Primary among the problems is the failure to identify the reason for parental separation: death, divorce, or desertion. Factors such as the sex, age, and developmental status of the child at the onset of separation, as well as the length of separation or the presence of parent surrogates, are frequently not specified in the designs of these studies.

Sampling procedures used in research designs have posed additional problems in interpreting and generalizing results from studies. Individuals may be selected from clinic populations that are not representative of the total range of divorced families, since not all families in which parents divorce seek clinical assistance. Samples drawn from different periods or on the basis of the duration of a child's living in a one-parent household are also susceptible to distortion and misrepresentation of the social-demographic character of divorce. For example, the contemporary context of research on children's experiences of divorce is different from that of the 1960s. Reasons for living in one-parent families have changed, as have the characteristics of children who encounter this form of family life.

Another limitation in the existing knowledge of the effects of divorce stems from the tradition of exclusive focus on comparing group means. This procedure has led to a distorted and simplistic view of divorce and the one-parent family structure. The variability in the responses of adults and children to divorce and to life in a single-parent household needs to be examined in relation to other conditions within the family, such as changes in economic status, stages of development of parents within the family life cycle, and the availability of other support systems in the family and in the child's social environment. Simple comparisons of academic performance of children in divorced and nondivorced households have yielded little information on the intrafamilial and extrafamilial conditions that influence the impact of divorce on children.

Our discussion of the limitations of research in this area is by no means exhaustive, but is intended to serve as a guide for the reader in evaluating studies of the effects of divorce and life in a one-parent household on children's intellectual functioning. The inadequacies of methods, coupled with changing social contexts of family disruption, have contributed to the apparently noncumulative nature of "findings" and to the inability of researchers to derive consistent and replicable conclusions.

A SOCIAL-PSYCHOLOGICAL MODEL
OF DIVORCE AND ACHIEVEMENT

In this chapter, an attempt is made to develop a comprehensive social-psychological model of the effects of divorce and the one-parent family environment on achievement behavior. Economic and sociological contexts of family life after divorce and the interactional family processes that may be linked to achievement behavior are described. Obviously, not all literature linking achievement to home or social contexts can be reviewed in this chapter. There is an extensive literature for which reviews are available (Featherman, 1980; Ruble and Boggiano, 1980; Spenner and Featherman, 1978). We focus on achievement studies that appear to be related to the structural and functional aspects of family life in divorced one-parent households.

Our conceptualization of the impact of divorce is based on the notion that divorce is not a single event, but a process involving a sequence of changes in life circumstances extending over a period of many years. At different points in this sequence, children and parents are confronted with different stresses and adaptive tasks. Our review includes a summary of the qualitative conditions of family life after divorce.

The Experience of Divorce for Adults

The dissolution of marriage and the transition to a new family life involve considerable personal and emotional disorganization and stress for all family members. Most theories of divorce propose that divorce is a life transition involving a series of stages in which certain emotional and social problems must be solved (Bohannan, 1970; Goode, 1956; Hetherington, 1981; Hetherington, Cox, and Cox, 1978a, 1981; Krantzler, 1973; Smart, 1977; Waller, 1967; Wallerstein and Kelly, 1980; Weiss, 1975; Wiseman, 1975). Almost all models of divorce are based on crisis theory and include several common stages. An initial stage of alienation and conflict is associated with disruption in family functioning and the decision to divorce. This is followed by a stage of family and personal disequilibrium when separation first occurs and family members begin to adjust to new roles, tasks, and identity changes. Finally, a stage of reorganization emerges, which involves an acceptance of the divorce and a reorientation of identity.

In the period immediately preceding and following divorce, separated adults frequently report feelings of loneliness, guilt, depression, anger, rejection, helplessness, frustrated dependence, incompetence, and lowered self-esteem (Goode, 1956; Hetherington, Cox, and Cox, 1978b, 1979c; Hunt, 1966; Waller, 1967; Wallerstein and Kelly, 1980; Weiss, 1975). Symptoms that frequently accompany the trauma of divorce include the inability to work effectively, sleeplessness, lethargy, poor health, weight changes, and increased smoking, drinking, and drug use (Goode, 1956; Hunt, 1966; Waller, 1967).

Perhaps because it is usually the father who leaves the home and suffers the trauma of separation from children, divorced fathers seem to undergo greater initial changes in self-concept and report more emotional distress than do divorced mothers (Fulton, 1978; Hetherington, Cox, and Cox, 1978b; Kitson and Sussman, 1976). Divorced fathers complain of not knowing who they are, being rootless, isolated, and having no structure in their lives. Divorced mothers complain of feeling physically unattractive and of having lost the identity and status associated with being a married woman (Hetherington, Cox, and Cox, 1978a).

The emotional problems of custodial parents are particularly important in determining the adjustment of children in single-parent homes (Hetherington, Cox, and Cox, 1979a; McCord, McCord, and Thurber, 1962). Children of depressed, anxious, or dissatisfied mothers are more likely to feel rejected and unhappy (Zill, 1978). Since divorced mothers are more likely to be emotionally distressed than are married mothers (Briscoe, Smith, Robins, Marten, and Gaskin, 1973; Guttentag and Salasin, 1979; Hetherington, 1972; Hetherington, Cox, and Cox, 1979a; Pearlin and Johnson, 1977), children in divorced families are at increased risk of encountering parent–child relationships associated with adverse emotional outcomes.

The Experience of Divorce for Children

Studies that have examined the responses of children in the immediate period surrounding separation and divorce have usually found indicators of emotional distress such as fearfulness, inhibition, habit disturbances, and neediness (Fulton, 1978; Hess and Camara, 1979; Hetherington, Cox, and Cox, 1979b; Kelly and Wallerstein, 1976; Wallerstein and Kelly, 1974, 1975, 1976, 1980). Although divorce may be the best solution to a destructive family relationship and may offer the child an escape from one set of stresses, almost all children experience the transition of divorce as painful (Camara, 1979; Fulton, 1978; Hetherington, Cox, and Cox, 1979a, 1979b, 1981; Kelly and Wallerstein, 1979; Weiss, 1975). Even children who are later able to recognize the constructive outcomes of the divorce initially undergo considerable emotional distress. The most common early responses of children to divorce are anger, fear, depression, loneliness, and guilt (Wallerstein, 1978). It is not usually until after the first year following divorce that there appears to be a reduction in tension and an emergence of a sense of well-being.

As with adults, there is wide variability in the quality and intensity of responses and adaptations of children to divorce. Some children exhibit severe or sustained disruptions in development; others seem to move easily through a turbulent divorce and emerge as competent, well-functioning individuals. Although there is increasing interest in the relative vulnerability of children to psychosocial stress (Garmezy, 1975; Rutter, 1979a, 1979b), this issue has not been explored systematically in relation to divorce. It seems likely that the child's temperament, past experience, and developmental status all contribute to individual differences in coping with family disruption. Temperamentally difficult children have been found to be less adaptable to change and more vulnerable to adversity than are temperamentally easy children (Chess, Thomas, and Birch, 1968; Graham, Rutter, and George, 1973; Rutter, 1979a, 1979b).

There is also evidence that children who have been exposed to chronic stress or to several concurrent stresses may be at greater psychiatric risk than are children who experience only a single stressful event (Rutter, 1979b). Extrafamilial factors such as stresses or supports offered by others, the quality of housing, the availability of child care, the need for the custodial parent to work, economic status, and residential mobility moderate or potentiate stresses associated with divorce (Coletta, 1978; Hodges, Wechsler, and Ballantine, 1978).

The adaptation of the child also varies with his or her developmental status. The limited cognitive and social competencies of the young child and the child's dependency on parents are associated with different responses from those of the more mature and self-sufficient older child, who has available a wider variety of social supports.

The young child, compared with the older child, is less able to appraise accurately the divorce situation, the motives and feelings of parents, and his or her own role in the divorce. The egocentrism and restricted cognitive and social skills lead the young child to be more self-blaming in interpreting the cause of divorce and to distort perceptions of the parents' emotions and behavior (Tessman, 1978; Wallerstein and Kelly, 1974, 1975). In addition, regressive behavior, irritability, and anxiety seem most common in preschool children, and dramatic increases in aggressive and destructive behavior, particularly in young boys, are often observed (Hetherington, Cox, and Cox,

1979a; McDermott, 1968, 1970). Although older children are distressed and depressed at separation, they are better able to be sympathetic to the difficulties experienced by their parents.

Most adolescents experience considerable pain and anger when their parents divorce. However, when the immediate trauma of divorce has passed, they are able to assign accurately responsibility for the divorce, to resolve loyalty conflicts, and to assess and cope with economic and other practical exigencies (Wallerstein and Kelly, 1974, 1975). This process is often accompanied by premature disengagement from the family. However, adolescents, more than younger children, do have the option of seeking support elsewhere if the home situation is particularly painful.

The age status of children is important not only in relation to variations in cognitive and social competencies but also because of the increased salience of social networks outside the family for older children. For the young child, stress and turmoil in the family are inescapable; disruptions in parent–child relations may undermine the only important bonds in a child's life. Older children spend much time in other social settings—the neighborhood, the school, the church, and, for some adolescents, the work situation. Thus, older children have more opportunities to find support systems outside the home that may mitigate the deleterious effects of divorce.

A crisis model of divorce may be most appropriate in conceptualizing the short-term effects of divorce on children. In the period surrounding the divorce of parents, children may be responding to changes in their family lives—the loss of a parent, marital discord, family disorganization and changes in parent–child relations associated with temporary distress and emotional neediness of family members, and to other real or imagined threats to the well-being of the children elicited by the uncertainty of the situation. The research evidence suggests that most children can cope with and adapt to the short-term crisis of divorce within a few years. However, if the crisis is compounded by multiple stresses and continued adversity, disruptions in development may occur.

The long-term adjustment of children is more likely to be related to sustained conditions associated with the quality of life in a household with only one parent. These include changes in family functioning, the increased salience of the custodial parent, the lack of availability of the noncustodial parent, and the presence of fewer adults in the household to participate in decision making, to assume responsibility for household and child-care tasks, and to serve as models and socialization agents in helping children learn effective work and play skills.

Most custodial parents remarry within five years of divorce, so that children reenter a two-parent family involving a stepparent. It is important to recognize that the point at which we tap into the sequence of events and changing processes associated with divorce modifies our view of the adjustment of children to divorce and of the factors that influence that adjustment.

Changes in Family Life After Divorce

In going through the dissolution of marriage and adapting to life in a one-parent household, each family member must cope with changes and problems in family life. The main areas in which transition and stress are experienced are in the practical problems of everyday living and in the changes that take place in family functioning and parent–child interaction.

The practical problems of family life after divorce can be grouped into two clusters: those associated with economic changes, and those associated with changing family roles and responsibilities.

Economic Status   Some of the most pervasive stresses confronting members of divorcing families are those associated with finances and downward economic mobility. Divorce and separation are associated with a marked drop in income for women, by as much as 30% (Hoffman, 1977). Although divorce results in reduced income for women, it does not for most men (Bane, 1976; Hoffman, 1977; Hoffman and Holmes, 1976). This is in part attributable to the fact that less than one-third of ex-husbands contribute to the support of their families (Kriesberg, 1970; Winston and Forsher, 1971). Also, since divorced women typically retain custody of children, the women's income-to-needs ratio is effectively lower at each income level. It should be noted that fathers' financial statuses are in fact less adversely affected by divorce even among those who continue to pay child support or alimony.

The downward economic mobility of mother-headed families after divorce may entail a return to work and reduced contact between mother and children, a lower standard of living, relocation into a combined household, usually with the mother's family of origin, and a shift to more modest housing in a poorer neighborhood (Brandwein, Brown, and Fox, 1974). Research on the effects of maternal employment suggests that if a divorced mother works and if adequate provisions are made for child care and household maintenance, maternal employment may have no adverse effects on children (Hetherington, Cox, and Cox, 1978a). However, a study by Coletta (1978) has shown that a substantial number of mothers in low-income, but not moderate-income, one-parent families experience stress in coordinating their roles as mothers and employees. Greater task overload is experienced by working divorced mothers of young children. Furthermore, if the mother begins to work at the time of divorce or shortly thereafter, preschool children seem to experience the loss of both parents, which is reflected in a higher rate of behavior disturbances (Hetherington, Cox, and Cox, 1978a).

Relocation is experienced by most people as a psychological stress (Weissman and Paykel, 1972). For children of divorce, moving means not only loss of friends, neighbors, and a familiar educational setting, but often greater contact with delinquency, fewer recreational facilities, and inadequate schools. Each of these factors may affect the child's academic functioning, since the child is likely to experience reduced contact with a parent, who might otherwise offer encouragement and assistance in school-related work, and a deprived educational environment with few enriching resources and experiences.

Roles and Responsibilities   Divorce means assuming new roles and responsibilities. Many divorced women feel that they have neither the time nor the energy to deal competently with routine financial tasks, household maintenance, child care, and occupational or social demands. When a single parent undertakes the tasks usually accomplished by two parents, and other support systems are not available, the burden can be mammoth. This is particularly true in families with more than one child or with young children.

The task overload experienced by the divorced mother is sometimes associated with family disorganization, in which roles and responsibilities are not well delineated and many routine chores do not get accomplished. Low-income mothers in one-parent families, even with preschool children, are likely to expect more independence and help from their children than do middle-class mothers (Coletta, 1978). Many children of divorced parents receive less adult attention, are more likly to have erratic mealtimes and bedtimes, and are apt to be late for school (Hetherington, Cox, and Cox, 1978a). In addition, playful interactions associated with caretaking such as bathing, eating, or reading to children at bedtime are less likely to be prolonged. With school-aged children, task overload may be associated with early assignment of responsibilities to children (Weiss, 1978).

When fathers have custody of children, they report many of the same feelings of being overburdened that are found in custodial mothers (Ferri, 1976; George and Wilding, 1972; Spanier and Castro, 1979). However, men are more likely to be helped with household tasks by female friends or relatives or by a paid housekeeper (Brandwein, Brown, and Fox, 1974; Hetherington, Cox, and Cox, 1978a).

Parent–Child Interaction   It has been proposed that one of the ways in which divorce or life in a one-parent family can affect the development of children is through changes in parent–child relations. Recent studies of one-parent families have focused on qualitative changes in the family after divorce, including the effects of the loss or unavailability of the father, of conflict between parents, and of parent–child relations on children's adjustment.

1. *Loss or unavailability of the father.* Since mothers generally gain custody of children, most children are confronted with the loss or relative unavailability of the father following divorce. Although some fathers increase the frequency of their contacts with their children in the period immediately following divorce, in most families contacts rapidly decrease over time (Hetherington, Cox, and Cox, 1978a; Kelly and Wallerstein, 1979). Fathers maintain more frequent contacts with sons than with daughters; visits with sons are of longer duration than those with daughters; and fathers are more likely to continue child-support payments when they have sons (Hess and Camara, 1979; Hetherington, Cox, and Cox, 1978a, 1981).

Most children want to maintain contact with their fathers, and, in preschool children, fantasies of reconciliation may continue for several years (Hetherington, Cox, and Cox, 1978b; Tessman, 1978; Wallerstein and Kelly, 1975). Unless the father is very poorly adjusted or there is continued, intense child-involved conflict between the parents, availability of the father is associated with positive adjustment, especially in male children (Hess and Camara, 1979; Hetherington, Cox, and Cox, 1978b; Wallerstein, 1978; Westman, Cline, Swift, and Kramer, 1970).

The father may have a unique contribution to make to family functioning and to the development of the child. Some of the roles the father plays are indirect and serve to support the mother in her role. The father in the nuclear family indirectly supports the mother in a number of ways—with economic aid, with assistance in household and childrearing tasks, and with support, encouragement, and appreciation of her performance as a mother. In nuclear families, high mother–child involvement and sensitive, competent, affectionate mother–infant relationships have been found when the father is supportive of the mother (Feiring, 1976; Pederson, Anderson, and Cain, 1977). Similarly, a mutually supportive relationship between parents and involvement of the father with the child have been found to be the most effective support for preschool children and their divorced mothers (Hetherington, Cox, and Cox, 1978b).

The father may also have a direct and active role in shaping the child's behavior through discipline, direct tuition, or acting as a model.

For example, in both divorced and nuclear families, children are more likely to obey fathers than mothers (Hetherington, Cox, and Cox, 1978a). A mother and father are likely to exhibit wider-ranging interests, skills, and attributes than does a single parent (Pedersen, Rubenstein, and Yarrow, 1979). Finally, one parent can serve as a protective buffer between the other parent and the child in a nuclear family. In a nuclear family, a loving, competent, or well-adjusted parent can help counteract the effects of a rejecting, incompetent, or emotionally unstable parent (Hetherington, Cox, and Cox, 1979a; Rutter, 1979a). When the father is not available in a single-parent, mother-headed family, the constructive or pathogenic behaviors of a divorced mother are funneled more directly on the child, and the quality of the mother–child relationship is more directly reflected in the adjustment of the child than it is in a nuclear family (Hetherington, Cox, and Cox, 1979a, 1981).

2. *Conflict between parents.* Children who are exposed to parental quarreling, mutual denigration, and recrimination are placed in a situation of conflicting loyalties. This may result in demands for a decision to reject one parent. The vast majority of children want to maintain relations with both parents and are unable or unprepared to reject one parent over the other. Conflict between parents also gives children the opportunity to play one parent against the other and, in some children, to develop exploitative manipulative skills (Tessman, 1978; Wallerstein, 1978; Westman, Cline, Swift, and Kramer, 1970).

Research findings have been consistent in showing that children in single-parent families function more adequately than children in conflict-ridden nuclear families (Hetherington, Cox, and Cox, 1979a; McCord, McCord, and Zola, 1959; Nye, 1957; Rutter, 1971, 1979a). The eventual escape from conflict may be one of the most positive outcomes of divorce for children. However, children in divorced families where there is continuing conflict and resentment between parents several years after the divorce are even more severely disturbed than children in conflictful nuclear families (Hetherington, Cox, and Cox, 1981).

3. *Parent–child relations.* Most studies have reported some stress or alteration in parent–child relations during the crisis period of separation and divorce (Hetherington, Cox, and Cox, 1978b; McDermott, 1970; Kelly and Wallerstein, 1979; Tessman, 1978; Weiss, 1975). How long such effects endure is not clear. In the period immediately surrounding separation and divorce, parents are often preoccupied with their own depression, anger, and emotional neediness and may be unable to respond sensitively to the needs of the child. Two longitudinal studies of divorce have suggested that there may be a period

when parent–child relations deteriorate markedly following separation (Hetherington, Cox, and Cox, 1981; Wallerstein and Kelly, 1980).

It is important to note that the relationship with the custodial mother and noncustodial father differs, and the parent–child relationship varies with the age and sex of the child. With young children in the first year following divorce, divorced parents communicate less well with their children, make fewer demands for maturity, and are less affectionate than parents in nuclear families. Divorced mothers and sons in particular are likely to become involved in escalating cycles of conflict and coercion. Greater use of restrictive, power-assertive disciplinary methods (Coletta, 1978; Kriesberg, 1970; Phelps, 1969) and negative sanctions (Burgess, 1978; Hetherington, 1972) has been noted in mothers in one-parent families.

On the other hand, divorced mothers are likely to rely on their children for emotional support and assistance with the practical problems of daily life (Kelly and Wallerstein, 1979; Weiss, 1979). Greater participation in family decision making and added responsibility for household tasks lead to children's accelerated self-sufficiency (Weiss, 1979), but can also lead to their feeling overwhelmed and resentful about the lack of support and the unavailability of the mother (Kelly, 1978; Wallerstein, 1978).

Divorced fathers become increasingly less available to their children, particularly their daughters (Hess and Camara, 1979). After divorce, most fathers want to minimize the dissension in contacts with their children, so they begin by being indulgent and permissive, but gradually they increase in restrictiveness (Hetherington, Cox, and Cox, 1978b).

Although almost all studies of parent–child relations in one-parent families have been done on mother-headed families, a few studies of fathers with custody have reported some of the same concerns expressed by mothers in one-parent families: homemaking, setting schedules, responding to children's emotional needs, and supervising children (Gasser and Taylor, 1976; George and Wilding, 1972; Mendes, 1976; Orthner, Brown, and Ferguson, 1976; Schlesinger and Fordres, 1976). In addition, a study by Santrock and Warshak (1979) has reported that family relations and the social adjustment of children are better following divorce if children are living with the parent of the same sex.

ACHIEVEMENT, DIVORCE, AND ONE-PARENT STATUS: A CRITICAL STRATEGY

Research on the development of achievement in children in two-parent households has suggested that high achievement, leadership, social confidence, and assertiveness in children are related to authoritative control and demands for mature, independent behavior by warm, involved parents. The pattern and relative salience of these factors varies for males and females. Females' achievement, in contrast to males', benefits from moderate rather than high levels of parental warmth, whereas paternal availability and control are more important for males (for reviews of this literature, see Dweck, in press; Huston, in press; Ruble and Boggiano, 1980).

Few studies have dealt directly with the relation between family functioning and achievement following divorce. Since life experiences and family interaction differ in divorced and nondivorced families, it seems possible that different factors contribute to the achivement of children in one- versus two-parent households. Some of the conditions of family life that shape achievement outcomes may be relatively direct. The increased responsibilities and decreased availability of both the custodial and the noncustodial parent to participate in educational activities, such as reading to children or attending school functions, may also result in decreased emphasis on school-related performance and fewer opportunities for engaging in learning activities outside the school. Depressed income can also mean fewer resources, both educational and social, available to children. These include the quality of the available educational system, the purchase of books, and participation in school field trips or in summer or other supplemental educational programs. Other factors may be less direct and may be related to changes in motivation, social adjustment, self-concept, personality, and the attitudes of others that are associated with divorce.

In the following sections, we review the effects of divorce and life in a one-parent household on scholastic and career achievements. Wherever possible, we attempt to focus on one-parent households resulting from separation or divorce. Since much of the literature does not separate the reasons for one-parent home status, we have had to include studies that do not specify the reason for one parent's absence.

Our generic definition of achievement includes two aspects. The first is a set of behaviors or performance in roles and settings that are achievement-related. Examples of these are scores on intelligence and aptitude tests, teacher-assigned grades, and grade-point averages. The second referent of achievement is the attainment of a position or social role that is subject to social evaluation by peers. An example of this definition is the amount or level of education a person completes. Our review focuses on both types of achievement and includes a review of learning and social conditions that may affect achievement-related performance.

In our search for relevant studies, we have reviewed empirical and descriptive work found in journal articles, unpublished research reports, and dissertations; we have described the designs and results of the studies in summary tables (Hetherington, Camara, and Featherman, 1982). We have included studies that report both significant and nonsignificant results. Since sample sizes and effect sizes are usually small, the power of statistical tests in determining the presence of an effect in most studies is generally low. The procedure of reviewing studies that yield only significant results can distort the conclusions drawn from data (Lane and Dunlap, 1978).

Alternative approaches to the synthesis of research studies, other than the usual counting of studies reporting statistically significant results, have been developed. Glass (1978) has described a procedure for calculating an effect size for each study and combining these to produce an overall estimate of effect size. Such a procedure requires access to group means, standard deviations, and other descriptive data for each research study.

The method we have selected for combining results when complete data on means and standard deviations are not available is a "sign count" procedure (Hedges and Olkin, 1980). This method involves a tally of studies in which the target-group mean is different from the control-group mean, although this difference may not be reported as a significant difference. Studies are grouped into positive-difference, negative-difference, or no-difference categories.

In our review, after each study was analyzed and the direction of effects noted, results (signs) were tabulated. When there was a sufficient number of studies on a particular dimension, a sign test (Siegel, 1956) was used to determine whether there was a significant number of studies reporting positive differences compared with those reporting negative differences or no differences. In all instances, the null hypothesis that was tested is that one-parent and two-parent groups do not differ. The hypothesis described at the top of each summary table is the alternate hypothesis that was tested.

The conclusions we reach must be stated as provisional. Research on the connection of family structure to achievement—especially in the case of one-parent families—has often been flawed in design and execution. As we discuss and categorize studies, the reader should not presume that the studies were without methodological faults.

MEASUREMENT OF ACHIEVEMENT
BY STANDARDIZED TESTS

Most studies of the effects of one-parent rearing on children's intellectual functioning have used intelligence tests or standardized tests of achievement as indices of academic performance. Both types of tests offer useful information with which to describe scholastic achievement. In general, intelligence or aptitude tests measure general abilities or aptitudes that are predictive of future achievement. The Scholastic Aptitude Test (SAT) and the American College Entrance Examination (ACEE) are examples of fairly valid and reliable measures of academic potential. Achievement tests generally are thought to be measures of an individual's past academic achievements. Many primary and secondary schools use some form of achievement test to assess the learning of basic skills or knowledge. Some examples of achievement tests used in studies of differential effects of family structure are the California Achievement Test, the Iowa Test of Basic Skills, the Metropolitan Achievement Tests, the Stanford Achievement Tests, and the Science Research Associates Achievement Series.

The advantage of using standardized measures is that they have been statistically refined, so that information on their reliability and validity is available. In addition, these tests provide normative information on an individual's performance. However, there are some important limitations to the use of test scores as the sole measure of individual or group academic functioning. First, while it is true that these tests have high predictability for academic success based on a total population, the tests are not necessarily predictive of the academic performance of an individual or a subset of a population. The specific predictive validity of such tests for children reared in one-parent homes is unknown. Second, there are data to support the notion that scores on intelligence or aptitude tests that are normally stable may fluctuate during times of disturbance in the lives of those being tested. However, no longitudinal studies have examined intraindividual shifts of intellectual performance among children experiencing parental loss; few studies have identified or taken into account the time at which separation occurred. In general, most studies have grouped children together cross-sectionally on the basis of a father-absent or one-parent status, with little attention paid to the time, onset, or duration of one-parent status. Children who are in the midst of family disruption are mixed with those who experienced a change in their family lives several years before they participated in a research study. This approach makes it impossible to detect temporary changes in intellectual functioning or test performance due to stressful experiences in family lives and those that are due to family conditions related to long periods of one-parent rearing.

Studies of the effects of family disruption and one-parent rearing on children's academic functioning measured by standardized tests were located. For the analysis in this paper, these studies were divided into three areas: those that measured performance based on IQ or aptitude tests, those that measured overall performance or total scores on tests of achievement, and those that examined patterns of intellectual performance relating to quantitative–verbal differences or analytic and divergent thinking styles.

IQ and Aptitude Tests

Thirty studies using a measure of IQ or aptitude in the study of differences in intellectual performance based on family structure were identified. The results of the synthesis of research are presented in Table 4-1. The ages of subjects in these studies ranged from infancy to college-age. Seventeen of these studies focused on preschool and elementary school children; five of these studies extended to junior high age students. Eleven studies included junior or senior high students; six studies were based on college-age or high-school-graduate samples. Only one study (Pedersen, Rubenstein, and Yarrow, 1973) explored cognitive functioning in infants from mother-headed homes. One-third of the studies gathered data from working-class or lower-income families, and another third of the studies used a mixture of lower- and middle-income families. Only two studies reported using a middle- or upper-middle-income group; eight studies failed to report the socioeconomic backgrounds of the families.

The studies varied in the racial backgrounds of participants, with seven studies using a mixed sample of Black and White subjects, eight studies using a sample of Black subjects, and three studies using a sample of White subjects. Twelve studies failed to identify the racial or ethnic background of families. A majority of the studies (twenty-three) used mixed groups of male and female children or students; six studied males exclusively. Only one investigation studied females exclusively.

Looking at directional differences (and not just statistically significant differences) between the means of scores of those in one- and two-parent family groups, we find that nineteen of the thirty studies reported that children from one-parent homes received lower scores on IQ and aptitude tests than did children in two-parent homes. Two studies reported reverse findings (Herzog, 1974; Oshman, 1975); one found no differences between groups; and three studies that reported only significant results found no significant differences between groups. Five studies reported mixed findings depending on variables related to one-parent status, such as the time and duration of father absence, the sex of the child, or the presence of a father surrogate or siblings. Further discussion of these studies generally is restricted to studies that have made some effort to use adequate methodological controls, namely, the use of comparison groups of two-parent families and attempts to match subjects on sociocultural background or the selection of subjects from homogeneous backgrounds.

Similar trends are found when the different age, racial, and socioeconomic groups represented in the studies are examined, although differences are less marked for older age groups studied. For example, using age of the child as an organizing factor for analyzing the results of studies, we find that the studies of preschool and infant children consistently reported depressed test scores for children in one-parent homes (Broman, Nichols, and Kennedy, 1975; Hetherington, Cox, and Cox, 1979a; Ilardi, 1966; Pedersen, Rubenstein, and Yarrow, 1973; Willerman, Naylor, and Myrianthopoulos, 1970). Broman, Nichols, and Kennedy (1975) studied 26,094 White and Black 4-year-olds from father-present and father-absent homes matched on race, sex, and socioeconomic status. The authors found significant differences between mean IQ scores of children in family groups, particularly for White children, although the effects were no longer significant after socioeconomic status and mother's educational level were taken into account. Differences were found between IQ scores of one- and two-parent groups of Black 4-year-olds from lower-income families (Ilardi, 1966) and 4-year-olds from interracial matings (Willerman, Naylor, and Myrianthopoulos, 1970). Hetherington, Cox, and Cox (1979a) reported significant differences in the IQ scores of preschool children from divorced and nondivorced middle-income White families two years following the divorce. Pedersen, Rubinstein, and Yarrow (1973) reported differences for father-absent compared with father-present children, although the differences were significant only for Black 5- to 6-month-old males.

Eight of the thirteen studies of children of elementary school age reported lower scores on intelligence tests of groups of children from one-parent homes compared with those from two-parent homes (Collins, 1969; Cortes and Fleming, 1968; Deutsch and Brown, 1964; Douglas, Ross, and Simpson, 1968; Edwards and Thompson, 1971; Hess, Shipman, Brophy, Bear, and Adelburger, 1969; Rees and Palmer, 1970; Solomon, Hirsch, Scheinfeld, and Jackson, 1972).

Six studies of the eleven that included students of junior high school or high school age found differences between scores of children in family groups (Collins, 1969; Douglas, Ross, and Simpson, 1968; Feldman and Feldman, 1975; Jaffe, 1965; Stetler, 1959; Sutherland, 1930); three studies obtained mixed results (Kandel, 1971; Lessing, Zagorin, and Nelson, 1970; Maxwell, 1961); one study reporting only significant results found no differences between groups (Wilson, 1967). Findings for college-age students are less clear-cut. Only two studies reported depressed scores on aptitude tests for stu-

Table 4-1
Research synthesis of one-parent household status and standardized tests
of aptitude and ability

OP = one-parent home. TP = two-parent home. FA = father-absent. FP =
father-present. (s) = no means reported, only significant findings.

Hypothesis: Children from one-parent homes receive lower scores on tests
of IQ and aptitude than do children from two-parent homes ($OP < TP$).

Study	Direction of difference	Sign
Broman, Nichols, and Kennedy (1975)	$OP < TP$	+
Carlsmith (1973)	$OP = TP$ (males)	0
Chapman (1977)	$OP < TP$ (males)	+ *
	$OP > TP$ (females)	−
Collins (1969)	$OP < TP$	+
Cortes and Fleming (1968)	$OP < TP$	+
Deutsch and Brown (1964)	$OP < TP$	+
Douglas, Ross, and Simpson (1968)	$OP < TP$	+
Edwards and Thompson (1971)	$OP < TP$	+
Feldman and Feldman (1975)	$OP < TP$	+
Herzog (1974)	$OP > TP$	−
Hess, Shipman, Brophy, Bear, and Adelburger (1969)	$OP < TP$	+
Hetherington, Cox, and Cox (1979a)	$OP < TP$	+ *,a
Ilardi (1966)	$OP < TP$	+
Jaffe (1965)	$OP < TP$	+
Kandel (1971)	$OP > TP$ (males)	−
	$OP < TP$ (females)	+
Lessing, Zagorin, and Nelson (1970)	$OP < TP$ performance IQ	+ *
	$OP < TP$ verbal IQ (lower-income group)	+
	$OP > TP$ verbal IQ (middle-income group)	−

*Differences are significant.
[a]In this study, differences were significant at 2 years following divorce on certain subscales of
WPPSI.

Table 4-1 (continued)

Study	Direction of difference	Sign
Mackie, Lloyd, and Rafferty (cited in Shinn, 1978)	No significant difference	(s)
Maxwell (1961)	No relationship (FA before age 5)	0
	OP < TP (after age 5 on WISC subtests)	+
Nielson (1971)	No significant difference	(s)
Oshman (1975)	OP > TP (females, FA first 5 years)	−
Pedersen, Rubinstein, and Yarrow (1973)	OP < TP (males and females)	+ *,b
Rees and Palmer (1970)	OP < TP (males, females)	+
Santrock (1972)	OP < TP (FA, divorce)	+
	OP > TP (FA, death)	−
Solomon, Hirsch, Scheinfeld, and Jackson (1972)	OP < TP	+
Stetler (1959)	OP < TP	+
Sutherland (1930)	OP < TP	+
Sutton-Smith, Rosenberg, and Landy (1968)	OP < TP	+ *
Thomas (1969)	OP < TP (FA less than 5 years)	+ *
Willerman, Naylor, and Myrianthopoulos (1970)	OP < TP	+
Wilson (1967)	No significant difference	(s)

[b]This study revealed significant differences between groups for 3 of 16 measures.
Summary: Nineteen studies reported OP < TP. Five studies reported mixed results. Two studies reported OP > TP. Four studies reported no significant differences (means not available).
Conclusions: Although a majority of studies report OP < TP, the differences reported are always small. Several studies have noted that differences are decreased when socioeconomic status is taken into account. Therefore, we conclude that the differences on aptitude tests that exist between one- and two-parent groups of children are slight.

dents in one-parent homes (Sutton-Smith, Rosenberg, and Landy, 1968; Thomas, 1969). Chapman (1977) obtained mixed findings; Carlsmith (1973) and Nielson (1971) found no differences between family groups on aptitude, and Oshman (1975) reported higher scores for females in father-absent families.

Although many studies have yielded differences in mean scores of students from one- and two-parent homes, it should be noted that these differences are usually small, ranging from less than 1 point to 7 points between the group mean scores on IQ tests. In the general population, the standard deviation of IQ's is about 15 points. By that criterion of variation, the effect of one-parent rearing is very slight. Further, several studies have reported that the differences are decreased when socioeconomic status is taken into account (Broman, Nichols, and Kennedy, 1975; Deutsch and Brown, 1964; Wilson, 1967).

Achievement Tests

Eleven studies that examined differences in overall or total scores for tests of achievement were identified. The results of the research synthesis are presented in Table 4-2. Studies of achievement that have focused on specific abilities, such as verbal or quantitative performance, are discussed in the section on patterns of cognitive functioning.

Of the eleven studies using measures of standardized achievement, six used samples of elementary school children and five used junior or senior high school students. All but two of the studies included both males and females in the sample; the two remaining studies focused only on males' performance. Five of the studies investigated lower-income families; three included mixed socioeconomic groups, and three did not include information on social-class backgrounds. Only one study focused primarily on White students; four studies used samples of Black children; one study contained a mix of racial and ethnic groups. Five studies did not provide information on the racial or ethnic background of participants.

Of the eleven studies on achievement, seven reported differences between test scores of groups of students from one- and two-parent homes. Children from one-parent homes received lower scores on standardized tests of achievement than did children from two-parent homes. Three studies that reported only significant results showed no differences between groups; one study found that children in the one-parent group received higher scores. Trends of lower scores among children in one-parent homes appeared in studies of both elementary and junior high samples.

As mentioned in studies of aptitude, differences in achievement-

Table 4-2
Research synthesis of studies of one-parent household status and
standardized achievement tests

OP = one-parent home. TP = two-parent home. (s) = no means reported,
only significant findings.

Hypothesis: Children from one-parent homes receive lower scores on
standardized tests of achievement than do children from two-parent homes
($OP < TP$).

Study	Direction of difference	Sign
Clarke (1961)	$OP > TP$	−
Coleman, Campbell, Hobson, McPartland, Mood, Weinfeld, and York (1966)	No significant difference	(s)
Crescimbeni (1965)	$OP < TP$	+ *
Deutsch (1960)	$OP < TP$	+ *
Essen (1978)	$OP < TP$	+[a]
Fowler and Richards (1978)	$OP < TP$	+
Jaffe (1965)	$OP < TP$	+
Keller (1968)	No significant difference	(s)
McNeal (1973)	No significant difference	(s)
Santrock (1972)	$OP < TP$	+ *
Solomon, Hirsch, Scheinfeld, and Jackson (1972)	$OP < TP$	+

*Differences are significant.
[a]In this study, significant differences between groups disappeared when controls for socioeconomic status were introduced.
Summary: Seven studies reported $OP < TP$. Three studies reported nonsignificant differences. One study supported $OP > TP$ for females.
Conclusions: Differences are present, but the overall effect size is small.

test scores between groups of children in different family structures are small and are reduced when adequate controls for socioeconomic status are introduced (Essen, 1978; Ferri, 1976; Smith, 1972; Wilson, 1967).

Our review of studies using aptitude and achievement tests as measures of cognitive functioning suggests that children in one-parent homes score lower on standardized tests than do children from two-parent homes. However, these differences are usually small (less than 1 year's difference). More importantly, we are unable to establish

clear associations between one-parent status and depressed achievement, since many studies have not provided adequate controls for
socioeconomic status or for racial or ethnic background, and most
have not provided information on factors that might be associated
with test performance, namely, onset, reasons and duration of parental separation, or on the quality of family relationships after separation. A detailed analysis of some of these studies and factors that are
associated with performance is included in a later section of this
chapter.

Patterns of Cognitive Performance

Total test scores do not provide any information on the processes of
intellectual functioning that may be affected by family disruption.
Some researchers have proposed that growing up in a one-parent
household may result in patterns of cognitive performance that differ
from the patterns of children in two-parent households. It has been
suggested that quantitative problem solving and analytic thinking of
children in one-parent, father-absent families is depressed relative to
performance on verbal tests or measures of global thinking. We now
examine the research on specific components of intellectual functioning among children in different family structures: quantitative–
verbal differences, field-independent and analytic thinking, and
creativity.

Quantitative–Verbal Differences   The analysis of sex differences
in performance on aptitude and achievement tests has revealed that,
in general, females are superior to males in verbal areas, whereas
males are superior to females in quantitative tasks. The problem-
solving style of females is likely to be more global and to be characterized by less clear discrimination of stimuli. In contrast, males use
an analytic approach to problems, distinguished by a clear discrimination of stimuli and a disregard for extraneous material. The analytic approach of males is reflected in their superior ability to solve
mathematical and spatial-perception problems, which require different skills in discrimination and differentiation than are required by
tests of verbal ability.

Two hypotheses have been offered to explain a high-verbal/low-
quantitative pattern of performance on cognitive tests. The first is
the "identification hypothesis" proposed by Carlsmith (1964). Carlsmith has suggested that differences in cognitive styles and problem-
solving strategies are part of the larger process of sex-role typing and
identification. When children identify with the same-sex parent, they
incorporate not only the parent's sex-typed attitudes, values, and social
behaviors, but also the parent's cognitive style. Carlsmith has sug-

gested that, in homes where the father is absent, children identify with the more global and verbal cognitive style of the mother. Disruptions in cognitive style are unlikely to occur in females in mother-headed households. However, males who do not have an analytic, problem-solving father with whom to identify may exhibit a "feminine" cognitive style, reflected by a high-verbal/low-quantitative pattern of test performance.

The second explanation is the "anxiety interference" hypothesis proposed by Nelson and Maccoby (1966). They have suggested that the loss of a parent is a stressful event that produces considerable anxiety for children. High levels of anxiety interfere more with the cognitive functions basic to problem-solving and mathematical skills (e.g., focusing, maintaining attention, retention of symbols, and sequential reasoning) than with those in verbal areas such as vocabulary, reading, or creative writing. Nelson and Maccoby have proposed that stress might even enhance verbal performance by the child's attempts to escape tension through fantasy and reading. Loss of a father or mother is only one stressful event that may impact on the pattern of cognitive performance. Conflict among family members whether or not parents are divorced and changes in economic conditions or the working statuses of parents are examples of other stressors that could suppress performance on quantitative, problem-solving tasks. According to this hypothesis, there is no reason to expect that males in father-absent homes, as compared with females, would show more disruptions in problem solving. The quantitative scores of both should be lower than those of their nonstressed peers of the same sex. However, Nelson and Maccoby have proposed that conflict over sex-role identification may be another type of stressor that results in high levels of anxiety and depressed quantitative scores.

Several methods have been used to assess differences in quantitative–verbal patterns among children from one-parent homes. One method involves computing an index of differential abilities by subtracting raw verbal scores from raw quantitative scores. As Shinn (1978) has stated in her review, studies of cognitive patterns using a quantitative–verbal (Q–V) difference score cannot tell us whether the difference is due to lowered quantitative performance, improved verbal performance, or both. A more illuminating procedure would be to construct separate deviation scores for verbal and quantitative abilities by subtracting the mean from each individual's score. In that manner, one could determine whether "verbal enhancement" or "math enhancement" was more likely for persons with different family patterns. However, Q–V difference scores do provide us with information about the magnitude of difference among those in one- and two-parent groups and are worth examining for this reason. Characterizing their work as both "tentative" and "exploratory," Nelson and

Maccoby (1966) gathered Scholastic Aptitude Test scores and family-history data from students in the 1959 and 1960 entering freshman classes at Stanford University. Difference scores between Q and V were computed for individuals. The magnitude of Q–V differences among females in the one-parent group was larger than among females in the two-parent group. The reverse was true for males. College males from one-parent homes had smaller differences in Q–V scores than did those from two-parent families.

Information from males about how frequently the father was away from home lends support to the notion that father absence may have a nonrandom relationship to relatively large Q–V differences. The most "masculine" (i.e., higher quantitative, lower verbal) patterns appeared for those replying "never" or "occasionally," and the largest difference was recorded for those indicating a year or more of father absence. However, the groups were identical in math scores; group differences occurred because verbal scores were higher in the group with the more extensive father absence.

Nelson and Maccoby have acknowledged the inconclusive evidence for predictions based on either the sex-identification theory or the tension-interference theory. They have also cited research by Alpert (1957) at Stanford that failed to confirm the tension-interference hypothesis.

Carlsmith (1964, 1973) calculated Q–V difference scores on the Scholastic Aptitude Test for a set of Massachusetts high school males and a sample of Harvard University sophomores whose fathers were absent from home because of wartime service abroad. Those whose fathers were away for at least a year or who had left early in their sons' lives (before age 1) had smaller Q–V differences. That is, the father-absent males displayed a less superior score in mathematics, relative to the verbal score, than did the father-present group of males. Carlsmith has interpreted this pattern as more "feminine" or as indicating a more global and less analytic cognitive style.

It is important to note that Carlsmith focused on the difference scores between group means, not on the individual difference scores. If one focuses on the separate patterns of Q and V scores, rather than on either the total scores or the difference scores, comparisons between control groups and the various groups experiencing father absence have less clear interpretations. For example, in the Harvard class of 1964, the average verbal score of the total class (677) is above the average verbal score of males whose fathers were absent for a year or less at some time in their lives (660). The average score for men without fathers for 30 or more months was well above either of these (690). In isolation, this information might suggest some verbal enhancement as a function of paternal absence. This same group scored below the mean math score of the class (661 versus 695), whereas males who experienced shorter periods of paternal absence were within 10 points of the overall mean but consistently below it. Given admission procedures that select for high total scores, it is not surprising that males with the lowest Q scores (and longest periods of father absence) must also have high verbal scores. Verbal enhancement is therefore not a justifiable conclusion. Further, verbal enhancement is not evident in the less intellectually selective high school samples, in which one- to five-year periods of paternal absence were associated with lower Q and V scores than were obtained by young males whose fathers were not abroad in military service.

We cannot conclude, therefore, from the data reported by Carlsmith that math aptitude suffers relatively more than verbal aptitude from periods of father absence. Such a comparison requires standardized individual scores in terms of the respective Q and V distributions. The use of simple arithmetic differences assumes that the Q and V scores are similarly distributed. Moreover, an analysis of Q–V scores assumes an interval scale with a fixed zero point, so that a Q score of 400 is the same as a V score of 400, and a Q–V difference of 50 is constant at all levels of Q or V. These properties of the SAT have not been substantiated.

The sum of other research is no less ambiguous with regard to the presence of a Q–V difference, to the enhancement of verbal aptitude versus interference with quantitative performance, or to a causal explanation for whatever pattern of differential cognitive skill is manifest among children experiencing paternal absence. Funkenstein (1963) purposively chose, from a class of 1100 Harvard College freshmen, 40 students who represented extreme Q–V differences on the SAT (i.e., a Q score of at least 1 standard deviation larger than the V score, and vice versa). The "feminine" or global pattern of scores was associated with paternal absence from home during World War II for at least a year during the son's first five years. The two extreme groups of high verbal/low quantitative (Vq) and high quantitative/low verbal (Qv), both in good academic standing, manifested different academic interests, with the Qv extreme majoring in mathematics, engineering, or the natural sciences and the Vq extreme studying the humanities or the social sciences.

Altus (1958) compared the Q and L (linguistic) subscales of the American College Entrance Examination (ACEE) for 25 male college freshmen whose parents had divorced with those of a control group of males from nondivorced families. While the averages of the Q scores for the two groups were approximately equal (.72 point difference), the mean of the L scores was higher in the group of males from divorced families. The group means of males from nondivorced families on the Q and L scores were almost equal, whereas the group mean L scores for males from divorced homes was 6.28 points higher than the mean Q score. This "feminine" pattern positively correlated with the *Mf* (masculinity–femininity) subscale of the Minnesota Multiphasic Personality Inventory (MMPI).

A study by Bernstein (1976) of 117 fifth-grade students from middle-income families has shown differences in cognitive patterns between a father-present group and a group with absent fathers due primarily to divorce. Using the Iowa Test of Basic Skills, Bernstein examined the math–verbal discrepancy in the individual scores of each student. Both father-absent males and father-absent females had lower mathematics percentile scores than did the students in the father-present group, although the difference was significant only for females. On the other hand, Jones (1975) has found no consistent association between father absence and a "feminine" versus "masculine" pattern of intellectual functioning on the Henmon–Nelson Test among students at Michigan State University. Jones compared the quantitative and verbal test scores of 30 students who had fathers living at home with another 30 students whose fathers had been absent for at least two years before the students turned 12 because of separation or divorce. "Early" father absence was connected with a feminine pattern of intellectual functioning, but "later" father absence was not. In fact, males in the "late" father-absent group achieved significantly higher scores in verbal and mathematical aptitudes than did those in the father-present and "early" father-absent groups.

Chapman's (1977) research among University of Virginia students has found that, for males, father absence was significantly associated with lower total SAT scores and lower verbal scores, but the Q–V differences that can be computed from his published data present a different pattern from that reported by Carlsmith at Harvard. Whereas males without fathers (because of death or divorce) for two years prior to age 18, those with stepfathers, and those in nuclear families all had Q scores exceeding V scores, the Q–V difference was smaller in the nuclear group and largest in the father-absent group. Females from intact families had lower verbal and total SAT scores than did either the stepfather or father-absent groups. Females in stepfather families received slightly higher scores on verbal tests than did females in father-absent families, and lower scores on quantitative tests than did either the father-absent group or the intact family group of daughters. The results generally were not consistent with any predictions about the effects of father absence on differential cognitive aptitudes or performance.

Fowler and Richards (1978) have similarly found differences in the overall cognitive functioning of Black, lower-income father-absent and father-present males and females. Father-present females and males received higher scores in mathematics, reading, and language arts of the Science Research Associates Achievement Series administered in the second grade. The mean scores for each group were highest for the reading subtest. However, computations of the Q–V difference scores based on the published data reveal greater differences among the scores of father-present males compared with father-absent males, and greater differences among father-absent females compared with father-present females where the reading and math scores were nearly equal.

The synthesis of findings from research studies that have examined quantitative verbal differences in intellectual functioning (measured by aptitude and standardized achievement tests) of children from one-parent homes is presented in Table 4-3. Four main questions are analyzed in these tables:

1. Are Q–V difference scores in one-parent groups larger than those in two-parent groups?

2. Within the group of one-parent children, are scores on verbal tests higher than scores on quantitative tests?

3. Do children in one-parent groups score lower on quantitative tests than do children in two-parent groups?

4. Do children in one-parent groups compared to those in two-parent groups score higher on verbal tests?

Attempts were made to analyze the studies on the basis of the sex of subjects and to separate results of IQ or aptitude tests from those derived from achievement tests.

We conclude from the analysis of directional (as opposed to only significant) findings that there is no evidence to suggest that the magnitude of Q–V differences of students from one-parent families is larger than that of students from two-parent families. There is an equal number of studies supporting both positions based on the aptitude-test scores of those in selected college populations. The one study measuring differences in quantitative–verbal functioning on achievement tests (using test results from a group of second-grade Black children) has found a larger difference in the Q–V mean difference scores of one-parent females than of two-parent females. A similar trend appears in the synthesis of aptitude-test studies; i.e., Q–V differences for females in one-parent families tend to be larger than for those in two-parent families. However, too few studies have been completed with female populations to provide any conclusive evidence.

Second, within the group of students reared in one-parent households, the synthesis of research studies yields no evidence that verbal scores on aptitude tests are higher or lower than quantitative scores.

Table 4-3

Research synthesis of studies of one-parent household status and Q–V cognitive patterns

OP = one-parent home. *TP* = two-parent home. *FA* = father-absent. *V* = verbal scores. *Q* = quantitative scores. (*s*) = no means reported, only significant findings.

Problem 1

Hypothesis: Q–V differences in scores of one-parent household groups are larger than those in two-parent groups (*OP* > *TP*).

Study	Direction of difference	Sign
IQ and aptitude		
Altus (1958)	*OP* > *TP* (males)	+
Carlsmith (1973)	*OP* < *TP* (males)	−
Chapman (1977)	*OP* > *TP* (males, females)	+
Nelson and Maccoby (1966)	*OP* < *TP* (males)	−
	OP > *TP* (females)	+
Standardized achievement		
Fowler and Richards (1978)	*OP* > *TP* (females)	+
	OP < *TP* (males)	−

Summary: On IQ and aptitude tests, two studies support and two studies fail to support the hypothesis *OP* > *TP* for males. Two studies report *OP* > *TP* for females. Only one achievement study supports *OP* > *TP* for females and fails to support *OP* > *TP* for males.

Conclusions: These studies reveal mixed results. There is not enough evidence to conclude that *OP* and *TP* differ. *Trends:* Q–V differences for females in *OP* families tend to be larger than for females in *TP* families.

Problem 2

Hypothesis: Within the one-parent group, scores on verbal tests are higher than scores on quantitative test (*V* > *Q*).

Study	Direction of difference	Sign
IQ and aptitude		
Carlsmith (1973)	*V* > *Q* (males)	+
Chapman (1977)	*V* > *Q* (females)	+
	V < *Q* (males)	−
Funkenstein (1963)	*V* > *Q* (males)	+
Gregory (1965)	*V* < *Q* (males, females)	−
Nelson and Maccoby (1966)	*V* < *Q* (males)	−
	V > *Q* (females)	+
Standardized achievement		
Bernstein (1976)	*V* > *Q* (males, females)	+
Fowler and Richards (1978)	*V* > *Q* (males, females)	+

Summary: For aptitude tests, two studies support and two studies fail to support the hypothesis *V* > *Q* for males. Two studies support and one fails to support *V* > *Q* for females. All studies use samples from a college or university that generally requires a minimum total aptitude, suggesting that by definition a lower quantitative score must be balanced by a higher verbal score. For achievement tests, there are only two studies, both of which support the hypothesis *V* > *Q* for males and females.

Conclusions: These studies show mixed results. Problems associated with the use of selective samples in the studies of aptitude and the small number of studies using tests of achievement provide too little evidence to conclude that *OP* and *TP* differ.

Table 4-3 (continued)

Problem 3

Hypothesis: Children from one-parent homes receive lower scores on quantitative tests than do children from two-parent homes ($OP < TP$).

Study	Direction of difference	Sign
IQ and aptitude		
Carlsmith (1973)	$OP < TP$ (males)	+
Chapman (1977)	$OP < TP$ (males)	+
Collins (1969)	No differences	(s)
Jones (1975)	$OP < TP$ (early *FA* males)	+
	$OP > TP$ (late *FA* males)	−
Landy, Rosenberg, and Sutton-Smith (1969)	$OP < TP$ (females)	+
Lessing, Zagorin, and Nelson (1970)	$OP < TP$ (males)	+
	$OP > TP$ (females)	−
Sutton-Smith, Rosenberg, and Landy (1968)	$OP < TP$ (males, females)	+
Standardized achievement		
Blanchard and Biller (1971)	$OP < TP$ (high *FP* males)	+
	$OP > TP$ (late *FA* males, low *FP*)	−
Deutsch (1960)	$OP < TP$ (males, females)	+
Essen (1978)	$OP < TP$	+
Ferri (1976)	$OP < TP$ (males, females; effect is small when socioeconomic status is controlled)	+
Fowler and Richards (1978)	$OP < TP$ (males, females)	+
Lambert and Hart (1976)	$OP < TP$	+
Solari (1976)	$OP < TP$ (males, females)	+

Summary: For tests of IQ and aptitude, five studies support the hypothesis $OP < TP$ for males (one of these for early *FA* only). For females, two studies support and one fails to support the hypothesis $OP < TP$. For tests of achievement, six studies report $OP < TP$ for males. Only one study fails to support the hypothesis $OP < TP$ for late *FA* males compared to high *FP* males. No study fails to support $OP < TP$ for females.

Conclusions: For IQ and aptitude tests, $OP < TP$ for males ($p < .01$). The results are mixed for females, and there is not enough evidence to reject the null hypothesis $OP = TP$ for females. For achievement tests, *OP* males and *OP* females score lower than the *TP* groups on quantitative tests. Several studies report that the effects of *OP* status are small when adjustments are made for socioeconomic status.

(continued)

Table 4-3 (continued)

Problem 4

Hypothesis 1 (H_1):   Children from one-parent homes receive higher scores on verbal tests than do children from two-parent homes (*OP* > *TP*).

Hypothesis 2 (H_2):   Children from one-parent homes receive lower scores on verbal tests than do children from two-parent homes (*OP* < *TP*).

Study	Direction of difference	Sign
IQ and aptitude		
Altus (1958)	*OP* > *TP* (males)	+
Carlsmith (1973)	*OP* > *TP* (males)	+
Chapman (1977)	*OP* < *TP* (males)	−
	OP > *TP* (females)	+
Collins (1969)	No difference	(s)
Jones (1975)	*OP* > *TP* (late *FA* males)	+
	OP ≈ *TP* (early *FA* males)	0
Lessing, Zagorin, and Nelson (1970)	*OP* > *TP* (females and middle-income groups)	+
	OP < *TP* (males and low-income groups)	−
Maxwell (1961)	*OP* > *TP* (*FA* after age 5; males, females)	+
	No difference (*FA* before age 5; males, females)	(s)
Oshman (1975)	*OP* > *TP* (females)	+
Sutton-Smith, Rosenberg, and Landy (1968)	*OP* < *TP* (males, females)	−
Standardized achievement		
Birnbaum (1966)	No difference (males)	(s)
Blanchard and Biller (1971)	*OP* > *TP* (high *FP* males)	+
	OP < *TP* (low *FP* and late *FA* males)	−
Camara (1979)	*OP* < *TP* (males, females)	−
Deutsch (1960)	*OP* < *TP* (males, females)	−
Essen (1978)	*OP* < *TP* (when adjustments for socioeconomic status are made, *OP* > *TP*)	+
Ferri (1976)	*OP* < *TP* (effect is small when socioeconomic status is controlled)	−
Fowler and Richards (1978)	*OP* < *TP* (males, females)	−

Table 4-3 (continued)

Study	Direction of difference	Sign
Hess, Shipman, Brophy, Bear, and Adelberger (1969)	$OP < TP$	−
Kelly, North, and Zingle (1965)	$OP < TP$ (males, females if breakup during first to third grades)	−
	$OP > TP$ (males, females if breakup during fourth to sixth grades)	+
Lambert and Hart (1976)	$OP < TP$	−
Malmquist (1958)	No significant relation to reading	(s)
Mueller (1975)	$OP < TP$ (in more "disadvantaged" group)	−
Oshman (1975)	$OP > TP$ (females, FA first 5 years)	+
Sciara and Jantz (1975)	$OP < TP$ (males, females)	−
Solari (1976)	$OP < TP$ (males, females)	−

Summary: For IQ and aptitude tests, four studies support H_1 for males (two of these for late FA conditions). Three studies support H_2 for males. Four studies support H_1 for females; one study supports H_2 for females. On tests of achievement, four studies support H_2 for groups of children in studies where means for separate sex groups were not provided. Five studies support H_2 for groups of male and female children; one study supports H_1 for groups of male and female children when adjustments are made for socioeconomic status; and one study supports H_1 for early FA females. One study finds mixed results depending on the degree of FP and onset of FA.

Conclusions: For IQ and aptitude tests, there are mixed results for OP males. There is not enough evidence to conclude that OP and TP differ for males. OP females > TP females on tests of verbal aptitude ($p < .19$; all but one of five studies support H_1: $OP > TP$). For achievement tests, there is evidence to support H_2, that children in OP groups receive lower scores on verbal tests than do children in TP groups ($p < .01$ when the nine studies reporting negative effects are compared with one study reporting positive effects; $p < .11$ when the five studies reporting negative effects for males are compared with one study reporting positive effects; and $p < .23$ when five studies reporting negative effects for females are compared with two reporting positive effects).

Only two studies have used scores on achievement tests to examine potential verbal and quantitative differences. Both these studies have supported the hypothesis that children from one-parent homes have higher verbal scores than mathematics scores on achievement tests.

The synthesis of studies analyzing between-group differences of those in one-parent versus two-parent homes on quantitative-test scores suggests that one-parent males, but not females, score lower on quantitative-aptitude tests than do males in two-parent families. On the other hand, one-parent females, but not males, score higher on verbal-aptitude tests than do their two-parent female counterparts. On achievement tests, both male and female children in one-parent groups receive lower scores on verbal and quantitative tests than do children in two-parent groups.

Field-Independent and Analytic Thinking   Several studies relating the absence of a father to cognitive functioning in children have focused on the development of differentiated or field-independent thinking. Field independence is an analytic, problem-solving style that refers to the extent to which an individual's perception of an item is separate from the organized context in which it occurs. Evidence of analytic ability is usually derived from tests such as the Embedded Figures Test and the Rod and Frame Test developed by Witkin, Dyk, Faterson, Goodenough, and Karp (1962). In the Embedded Figures Test, the individual is asked to locate a previously seen geometric figure within a complex figure designed to embed it. The Rod and Frame Test requires the individual, who is seated in a darkened room, to adjust a lighted rod within a tilted frame to a position he or she perceives as upright. The extent to which individuals can ignore contextual cues in solving each of these problems is the measure of their field independence. Other tests loading on the same factors that have been shown to be related to these measures are the Block Design, Picture Completion, and Object Assembly tests of the Wechsler Intelligence Scale for Children, a test of children's IQ.

Sex differences in performance on tests of field independence have reflected, in general, a superior analytic style for males compared with a more global, less discriminating style for females. Absence of a father or father figure in the home has been thought to lead to a less differentiated style of intellectual functioning, particularly for males. However, studies of field-independent functioning of children in one-parent homes have offered inconclusive support for this purported association.

Barclay and Cusumano (1967) have studied field-independent functioning of 20 Black and 20 White male adolescents. In each of these groups, 10 individuals experienced the absence of a biological or surrogate father since the age of 5. Field independence was assessed through four Rod and Frame Tests. The authors have found that males in father-absent families are significantly more field-dependent than males in father-present families. Although Black children are more field-dependent than White children, there is not a significant interaction between race and father absence. In other words, regardless of race, the father-absent condition is associated with a less analytic cognitive style. To support the hypothesis that father-absent males may develop a closer identification with the mother, the researchers have reported that, on the Gough Femininity Scale, the father-absent group of males scored higher on femininity scores than did the father-present group, although these differences are not statistically significant.

Chapman (1977) has similarly reported that father-absent males are more field-dependent than males from either intact or stepfather families. Results for females show very small differences or are inconsistent with any predictions about the effects of father absence on differential cognitive aptitudes. Maxwell's (1961) study of 8- to 13-year-olds from a clinical sample has shown that lack of a paternal figure after age 5 is associated with lower scores on only one analytic subtest of the WISC test (Picture Completion). Paternal absence before age 5 is not associated with test scores.

Two studies reporting data on the field-independent style of middle-income children from divorced and intact families have not supported the relationship between analytic ability and rearing in a one-parent, mother-headed home. Camara (1979) has reported no differences in scores on the Embedded Figure Test for 9- to 11-year-olds whose parents had separated two to three years prior to participation in the study. Hetherington, Cox, and Cox (1979a) have similarly found no differences in field-independent scores between preschool children in divorced and intact families. In both studies, the mother had custody, and the divorced father remained in contact with the children. The results of these studies have suggested that differences in analytic reasoning are not simply the function of the presence or absence of the father in the household. For example, Mertz (1976) has found no apparent relationship between the length of time a father was in the household and the level of differentiation in one-parent families. One study has suggested that the cognitive styles of children are related to maternal differentiation (Goldstein and Peck, 1973).

In summary, the research we have reviewed does not permit conclusions about depressed analytic ability as a function of the one-parent household. However, it should be noted that the two studies that found males from father-absent homes to be more field-dependent involved the oldest samples of subjects. Sex differences in field independence do not usually emerge until the late elementary school years or even early adolescence. It may be only when such sexual cognitive differentiation would normally occur that differences between children in father-absent and father-present homes can be identified. As we mentioned earlier, stress associated with parental loss or separation or with changes in family functioning may have a greater impact on motivational processes that are related to performance on achievement tests or to school grades than on the general cognitive abilities or cognitive patterns of children measured by tests of IQ, aptitude, or analytic style.

Creative and Flexible Thinking   There is probably more contradictory evidence regarding the antecedents of creative and flexible thinking than any other aspect of intellectual functioning. Although there have been only a few studies directly relating parental absence and the development of creativity, there is some empirical evidence suggesting that distance in the parent–child relationship may have a liberating effect on children and may stimulate their creative activity.

Two lines of thought have guided research in this area. The first, proposed by Becker (1974), has suggested that highly involved fathers may suppress creative achievement in their children, whereas mothers are more likely to foster creative activity. Studies of family conditions related to the creative expression of children have pointed to a home environment that allows opportunities for exploration and decision making, with a mother who encourages independence, individual freedom, and autonomy (Domino, 1969; Nichols, 1964; Schaefer, 1965). Several studies have reported a stronger relationship between creativity and time spent with the mother than time spent with the father (Dreyer and Wells, 1966; Eisenman and Foxman, 1970).

Becker has studied the relationship between father absence and perceived parental influence on the creative performance of 60 undergraduate college students at the City University of New York. Students were divided into three groups: those who had experienced loss of a father by death, divorce, separation, or abandonment before age 12; those with both parents present where the mother was perceived by the student as having a stronger influence than the father; and those with both parents where the father was perceived as having a stronger influence than the mother. Creativity was measured by scores on the Unusual Uses Test on dimensions of fluency, flexibility, and originality. Becker found that students from the two-parent, high father-influence group scored the lowest on all three measures. Those from the father-absent and two-parent, high mother-influence groups generated a larger number of ideas, were more flexible in identifying a broad range of categories, and provided more uncommon or original responses than did the two-parent, father-influenced group. He concluded that perceived influence and not absence of a father accounted for differences in creativity among students.

A second hypothesis relating parental loss to creative performance has been offered by Gregory (1965). Gregory has suggested that loss of a parent by death may present children with a challenging life experience that leads to exceptional striving for achievement. A number of studies have reported childhood loss of a father in the family histories of gifted, "extraordinary," and highly creative individuals (Albert, 1971; Eisenman and Foxman, 1970; Eisenstadt, 1978).

Only one study has reported evidence contradictory to the conclusions reached by Becker. Schooler (1972) interviewed 3101 men employed in civilian occupations and analyzed their family histories for incidence of parental loss. Using respondents' analyses of hypothetical problems based on economic or social issues as a measure of ideational flexibility and rigidity of attitude, Schooler has found that males raised in homes with no male adults were more rigid and less flexible than were father-present males. Schooler has reported no information on the validity or reliability of the instrument used, so it is difficult to assess the quality of data gathered or conclusions reached.

In conclusion, there have been too few well-designed studies on the relationship between parental absence and the development of creative thought to come to any firm conclusions regarding this issue. We have included this section in our review in order to recommend an area of inquiry that needs further attention. Studies based on a deficit model of parental loss have failed to examine potential benefits or positive outcomes for children as a result of family change. Most research in the area has been based on the assumption that stress due to family disruption and rearing in a one-parent home environment leads to adverse consequences for children. More systematic studies of the conditions surrounding transitions in family life may offer evidence that stress due to changes in family structure or functioning may, for some children, lead to the development of positive coping strategies and striving for achievement.

TEACHER EVALUATIONS

Teacher-assigned grades and grade-point averages are another important index of scholastic achievement of children. Achievement in this sense is defined by how well a student can meet the objectives set by teachers and school staff and is represented by letter or number grades. Grades differ from standardized tests in that the latter are generally measures of broad knowledge that is dissociated from specific course content. Grades, on the other hand, are measures of learning in limited areas of study peculiar to a given course or teacher. The evaluation of success in learning may be based on teachers' judgments of the students' ability to master skills and knowledge, to apply knowledge to novel situations, and to be productive in the classroom. Grade-point averages (GPA) in high school are highly predictive of college success, even better predictors than are scores on college entrance examinations (Lindgren, 1980). Many educators have argued that grades offer a more useful evaluation of student progress than do standardized achievement tests because they include teachers' informal observations and impressions of how the students think and solve problems.

There are, however, numerous problems with the use of teacher-assigned grades as a measure of student achievement. For one thing, schools and communities differ in their concepts of what constitutes a good education. The interpretation of student grades in various subject areas may differ among schools and prevent meaningful comparisons of student achievement across communities. Second, there is considerable variation among teachers as well as within the standards of an individual teacher in grading students' work (Akeju, 1972; Educational Testing Service, 1961; Starch, 1927; Valin, 1961).

There is also evidence that teachers may be influenced by variables other than actual performance in grading student progress (Ebel, 1968; Markham, 1976). For example, even when levels of achievement measured by standardized tests are the same, females characteristically receive higher marks than do males (e.g., Hilker, 1976), and students who are obedient, conforming, and industrious tend to receive higher grades than those who are perceived by teachers as rebellious and lazy (e.g., Morrison, 1969). Ebel (1968) has suggested that teachers base grades on social behaviors, such as cooperation, and not on mastery of subject matter.

Although grades may not be true indicators of intellectual performance, they may, as Lindgren (1980) has suggested, provide an index of scholastic adjustment, i.e., the ability of a student to adapt his or her behavior to the expectations of teachers. With this distinction in mind, let us turn to a review of studies that have compared the teacher-graded performance of students from one- and two-parent homes.

Studies of the scholastic performance of students in different family environments offer some evidence that children in one-parent homes receive lower GPA's than do children in two-parent homes. As we shall see later, this should not be interpreted to imply a causal relation between one-parent family status and depressed school grades.

The most recent and perhaps most controversial study comparing achievement and behavior records of children from one-parent and two-parent homes was conducted by the Kettering Foundation and the National Association of Elementary School Principals. Statistical data on students' class standing in low, average, or high achievement groups based on GPA's were gathered from a total of 18,244 students. The preliminary reports of the analysis based on 8556 students (Brown, 1980) has revealed differences between family groups, with a larger proportion of children from one-parent households appearing in the low achievement groups compared with those who lived with both parents or with one biological parent and a stepparent. In the published report of findings, Brown (1980) used percentages to describe the differences in achievement and behavior among family groups. The large differences in numbers of one- and two-parent families (the ratio of two-parent children to one-parent children was 3.75 to 1 at the elementary level, and 5.26 to 1 at the secondary level) made it difficult to interpret the percentage comparisons between groups. In a later report prepared by Evans and Neel (1980), a multivariate analysis was performed to determine differences between the family groups at elementary and secondary levels. Separate analyses were conducted for children from lower-income families, determined by participation in a free-lunch program, and for those who did not participate in the free-lunch program. Significant differences were found between one- and two-parent groups of children when income was not controlled. Elementary and secondary students from one-parent homes were placed in the low achievement group significantly more often than were children from two-parent homes. However, the authors failed to report whether differences in achievement status remained significant when the two income groups were analyzed separately. A severe criticism of this study is the authors' implication of a causal relationship between one-parent status and achievement. No information is provided about the background characteristics of the population, such as race or ethnicity, reasons for one-parent family status, or recency of one-parent status. The high rate of mobility in the population reported by the authors suggests the presence of stressors other than parental separation. In addition, the school records used to determine one-parent status may not have been a reliable source of information on family background.

The failure to control or account for either socioeconomic status or ethnic background of subjects is a methodological problem common to several studies of this type that have reported depressed achievement among one-parent children (Feldman and Feldman, 1975; Hess, Shipman, Brophy, and Bear, 1968; Jaffe, 1965; McNeal, 1973; Shelton, 1968; Stetler, 1959; Webb, 1970). We cannot determine whether low achievement is linked to family status or to the differences in the economic circumstances between family groups. However, the studies that have controlled or compared sociocultural backgrounds of families have reported lower achievement by children in one-parent homes compared with children in two-parent homes. Blanchard and Biller (1971) have examined the effects of father availability and absence on the GPA's of third-grade males from working-class and lower-middle-income White families. The academic performance of the high father-present group was superior to that of the group who had experienced father absence, whether before or after age 5. Kandel (1971) has reported larger percentages of high school students from intact families in the top quarter in GPA of their class. This finding held for Black and White females and for White males but not for Black males.

Collins' (1969) study of Black fourth-, sixth-, and eighth-graders has found differences in teachers' ratings of reading and mathematics, although significant differences favoring the intact family group were found only for sixth-grade mathematics. Herzog's (1974) study of boys in three socioeconomic family groups has also reported higher scores on teacher-graded exams for those in the father-present group. Similar findings have been reported by Wasserman (1972) in his study of 10- to 15-year-old Black youths from one- and two-parent families in public housing. Most of the studies of the effects of parental absence on school achievement have been based on teacher reports of Black children from lower-income families (Hetherington, Camara, and Featherman, 1982). Two studies that controlled for or used IQ as a covariate (but did not report data on socioeconomic or ethnic background) have reported significant differences in the achievement grades of upper elementary and junior high school students, favoring those from intact families (Keller, 1968; Shelton, 1968). Four studies have reported no significant differences between scholastic grades of one- and two-parent students (Atkinson and Ogston, 1974; Birnbaum, 1966; Kitano, 1963; Mackler, 1969). However, group means were not available, so it is not possible to identify the direction of differences.

A synthesis of research studies on parental absence and teacher-rated achievement is presented in Table 4-4. Even when we eliminate studies that have failed to use adequate controls for background variables such as socioeconomic status or ethnicity, we find evidence to suggest that, compared with two-parent children, students in one-parent homes receive lower GPA's. More studies are needed before we can report any conclusive evidence for depressed achievement for middle- or upper-middle-income families. However, preliminary studies would suggest differences among family types for these groups as well.

As shown in our earlier review of studies that have measured

Table 4-4
Research synthesis of studies of one-parent household status and teacher-rated achievement and grade-point average

OP = one-parent home. TP = two-parent home. (s) = no means reported, only significant findings.

Hypothesis: Children from one-parent homes receive lower scores on teacher-rated achievement than do children from two-parent homes ($OP < TP$).

Study	Direction of difference	Sign
Atkinson and Ogston (1974)	No significant difference	(s)
Birnbaum (1966)	No significant difference	(s)
Blanchard and Biller (1971)	$OP < TP$	$+$ *
Brown (1980)	$OP < TP$	$+$ *
Collins (1969)	$OP < TP$ (sixth-grade mathematics; no significant difference on other measures)	$+$
Feldman and Feldman (1975)	$OP < TP$	$+$ *
Herzog (1974)	$OP < TP$	$+$
Hess, Shipman, Brophy, and Bear (1968)	$OP < TP$	$+$ *,a
Jaffe (1965)	$OP < TP$	$+$
Kandel (1971)	$OP < TP$	$+$
Keller (1968)	$OP < TP$	$+$ *
Kitano (1963)	No significant difference	(s)
Mackler (1969)	No significant difference	(s)
McNeal (1973)	$OP < TP$	$+$ *
Shelton (1968)	$OP < TP$	$+$ *
Solomon, Hirsch, Scheinfeld, and Jackson (1972)	$OP < TP$	$+$
Stetler (1959)	$OP < TP$	$+$
Wasserman (1972)	$OP < TP$	$+$
Webb (1970)	$OP < TP$	$+$
Weitz and Wilkinson (1957)	$OP < TP$	$+$

*Differences are significant.
[a]This study reported significant differences in teacher grades for 5 out of 14 subjects.
Summary: Twenty studies provide data on students from one- and two-parent homes. Of these, sixteen studies reported lower academic achievement among children in OP homes. Four studies in which means were not available reported no significant differences.
Conclusions: There is striking evidence to support the hypothesis $OP < TP$. A significant number of studies show depressed teacher-rated achievement among children in OP homes ($p < .001$).

aptitude or overall achievement scores on standardized tests, it is unlikely that the differences in grades received by children in one- and two-parent homes are due to differences in intellectual ability. One possible explanation for the depressed achievement ratings by teachers may be that these children lack, or appear to lack, interest or motivation to learn in the school setting. As we discuss in a later section, teachers' perceptions of students' willingness to cooperate and "try hard" can affect their evaluations of student work.

YEARS OF SCHOOLING COMPLETED

Completed years of schooling is another important index of scholastic achievement. Featherman and Hauser (1978) have analyzed the relationship between family structure and years of school completed in a large sample of males residing in the United States who were born between 1907 and 1951. Their results are summarized in Table 4-5. Compared with males who lived with both parents, biological or adoptive, through age 15, males reared in a one-parent family for most of their first 16 years completed about three-quarters of a year less schooling. This relative deficit reflects statistical controls for socioeconomic status and race.

Across successively younger birth cohorts, starting with the 1907–1911 cohort and moving down to younger ones, the handicap of one-parent family structure shows a small irregular decline in magnitude from .85 year to about .6 year. Interestingly, this decline is coincident with a rise in the mean educational level of males during this period and a decline in the variability around the mean (indicated by cohort means and standard deviations). Declining variability in the education of successive birth cohorts has reduced the predictive importance of many aspects of social background for scholastic achievement of this kind, including the effects of rearing in a one-parent household. Still, the net impact of a one-parent family structure is apparent, even though its manifestation throughout the range of schooling is undergoing change. For example, among cohorts born prior to 1937, the handicap of rearing in a one-parent household was larger among persons completing 12 or fewer years of schooling than for those completing some college. In subsequent cohorts, the relative effects were reversed, so that the handicap of one-parent rearing was greater for persons matriculating in postsecondary education (Featherman and Hauser, 1978).

Despite the fact that the data in Table 4-5 and the study from which they are drawn do not permit us to assay the effects of the reason for family disruption (e.g., death, divorce, separation, or unmarried parent) or its timing or duration, they do suggest that the experiences of living in one-parent family structures are not homogeneous in their consequences. When we examine, within each cohort, the achievement of men reared by both parents, by mother or other female head, or by father or other male head in relation to the grand mean for the cohort, we find that male-headed, one-parent families are the least advantageous for the education of male offspring. Males reared by their fathers or other male figures complete a year less schooling than the average in their cohort. (Note, however, that, unlike the coefficients for "one-parent," the coefficients for the three family structure types—two-parent, female-headed, and male-headed—do not reflect controls for socioeconomic status or race.) Rearing in a female-headed family is associated with a lesser disadvantage of about a half-year below the cohort average, while the most beneficial arrangements are within two-parent families.

Rearing by one parent for a significant portion of preadult life is linked to the socioeconomic status and race of the family—at least in historical perspective. Given the linkage between both socioeconomic status and race to length of schooling and other forms of scholastic achievement, it is not surprising that the unique impact of family structure among statistically equivalent groups in family socioeconomic status and race is less than the gross impact. For example, among American males born after World War II, the total gross educational differential between those reared by both parents and those reared in a male-headed family was about a year; this difference was reduced to about one-half year when adjustments were introduced for race, number of siblings, and socioeconomic status (Featherman and Hauser, 1978). Although these correlates of family structure reduce the significance of rearing in a one-parent versus a two-parent family for education, they do not eliminate it. Neither do they fully attenuate the differential disadvantage associated with a male- versus female-headed family.

For males born after the Great Depression, the net effect of race on schooling has been smaller than the net effect of rearing in a one-parent family. The differential disadvantage of those reared by one parent, relative to those reared in Black families, actually has been increasing since World War II among cohorts of males equated statistically for family size, socioeconomic status, and farm background. Blacks reared in one-parent families obviously are placed under the most severe disadvantage. This striking finding can be illustrated by the comparison of the net effect of being Black (versus White or non-Black) with the net effect of a one-parent family background on years of school completed, as reported by Featherman and Hauser (1978). In the 1932–1936 birth cohort, those reared in one-parent households

Table 4-5
Family structure and years of school completed, U.S. males aged 21–65 in March 1973

OP = one-parent home. TP = two-parent home. FH = female-headed.
MH = male-headed.

Year of birth	Proportion	Schooling variables			
		Years of schooling[a]	Graded schooling[b]	College education[c]	Cohort means/ S.D. (years of schooling)
1907–1911					9.87/3.74
OP[d]	.177	−.85[g]	−.70[g]	−.15[g]	
TP[e]	.823	.20[h]			
FH[e]	.102	−.76[h]			
MH[e]	.075	−1.15[h]			
1912–16					10.55/3.49
OP	.172	−.75	−.65	−.10	
TP	.828	.18			
FH	.093	−.52			
MH	.079	−1.24			
1917–1921					11.03/3.42
OP	.184	−.90	−.71	−.19	
TP	.816	.19			
FH	.111	−.35			
MH	.073	−1.60			
1922–1926					11.45/3.38
OP	.168	−.87	−.64	−.23	
TP	.832	.16			
FH	.101	−.57			
MH	.067	−1.11			

[a]Years of regular or formal school completed, 0–17 +.
[b]Years of elementary and secondary school completed, 0–12.
[c]Years of postsecondary education completed, 1–5.
[d]Dichotomy indicating whether or not the son lived with both parents most of the time up to age 16.
[e]Three mutually exclusive and exhaustive categories of family structure indicating (1) lived with *both* parents (natural or adoptive) most of the time up to age 16, (2) lived with only mother or other *female-headed* family, or (3) lived with only father or other *male-headed* family.
[f]In 1973, this cohort had not entirely completed its schooling; data are to be interpreted with caution.
[g]Coefficients for "broken family" (versus intact) are *net* deviations from the cohort means of the various schooling variables, controlling for family head's occupation and education, race, farm versus nonfarm status, and number of siblings.
[h]Coefficients for the three family structure types (two-parent, female-headed, and male-headed) are *gross* deviations about the cohort means.

Source: Featherman and Hauser (1978).

Table 4-5 (continued)

Year of birth	Proportion	Schooling variables			
		Years of schooling[a]	Graded schooling[b]	College education[c]	Cohort means/ S.D. (years of schooling)
1927–1931					11.72/3.39
OP	.169	−.71	−.37	−.34	
TP	.831	.15			
FH	.105	−.63			
MH	.064	−.93			
1932–1936					12.02/3.31
OP	.165	−.78	−.42	−.36	
TP	.835	.17			
FH	.105	−.69			
MH	.060	−1.21			
1937–1941					12.40/3.01
OP	.171	−.66	−.30	−.36	
TP	.829	.16			
FH	.105	−.63			
MH	.066	−.99			
1942–1946					12.76/2.76
OP	.140	−.61	−.24	−.36	
TP	.860	.12			
FH	.087	−.57			
MH	.053	−1.04			
1947–1951[f]					12.14/2.38
OP	.132	−.56	−.21	−.35	
TP	.868	.12			
FH	.086	−.79			
MH	.046	−.85			

completed about three-quarters of a year less schooling than did males in intact families with equivalent socioeconomic status, number of siblings, farm or nonfarm background, and race. On the other hand, the effect of being Black in the same comparison was about a half-year deficit. In the cohort born between 1942 and 1946, the net effect of a one-parent home was a 0.61 year deficit, while the net deficit associated with race was about 0.09 year (Featherman and Hauser, 1978, Table 5.9). Thus, whereas the impact of race on the education of cohorts that would have completed their schooling since the mid-1950s has been declining, the disadvantages of one-parent rearing for continuation of schooling have declined much more slowly across successive cohorts.

These relationships have been replicated for Canadian males and females in nationally representative samples taken at the same time as the United States study described in Table 4-5 (Featherman and Hauser, 1978). The interpretation of these results is far from clear. It cannot be concluded from these data that relatively premature termination of schooling is necessarily the result of earlier or cumulative academic failure or deficiency in intellectual performance. One could entertain the view that achievement on tests and teacher evaluations and the completion of additional years or grade levels of schooling may be linked to nonidentical sets of antecedent conditions. For example, young adults from one-parent backgrounds may acquire less schooling than their counterparts because of economic circumstances that require entry into the work force at earlier ages. It is interesting to note, in this connection, that Duncan and Duncan's (1969) study of family stability and occupational success has reported that males reared in one-parent, female-headed households began work at an earlier age than did males of the same race reared in two-parent families (1.2 years for Blacks and 0.8 year for non-Blacks). The patterns of formal schooling completed by the males in this study were consistent with the trends reported by Featherman and Hauser. Despite our inability to disentangle causal antecedents at differential lengths of schooling, the evidence clearly indicates a substantial disadvantage from rearing for lengthy periods during childhood in arrangements that do not include two (biological or adoptive) parents.

FACTORS ASSOCIATED WITH ACHIEVEMENT

Throughout our review of the literature on the intellectual functioning and achievement of children, we have referred to several dimensions along which the effects of one-parent rearing appear to vary. These include:

1. The reason for one-parent household status.

2. The duration of one-parent rearing and the age of the child at onset.

3. The mediating influences of parent surrogates.

4. The age or maturational level of the child.

5. The presence of siblings.

6. The socioeconomic status of the family or residence household.

7. The ethnic or racial background of the family.

In this section we reexamine studies that have provided information on how these dimensions may affect the cognitive performance of children in one-parent homes.

Reasons for One-Parent Status

Most investigations confound the analysis of the effects of one-parent rearing by combining all nonintact family groups into an undifferentiated category of "broken" or "one-parent" homes. One-parent status in these studies may refer to families who have experienced parental death, divorce, separation, desertion, or temporary father absence due to employment or military service, or it may refer to families where the mother has never married. Only five studies have examined the differential effects of family living arrangements according to the reasons for parental absence (Crescimbeni, 1965; Essen, 1978; Ferri, 1976; Gregory, 1965; Santrock, 1972).

Crescimbeni (1965) has analyzed the Metropolitan Achievement Test scores of children in second to sixth grade. He has reported significant differences between the mean scores of groups of children in two-parent and father-absent groups, favoring the intact-family children. Differences between intact- and divorced-family children were largest, followed by absence due to parental death and to desertion or separation.

Ferri's (1976) longitudinal study of British children has shown that, on standardized reading tests administered at age 11, children who lived in mother-headed families because of marital breakdown scored below all other family types—nuclear, mother-headed due to paternal death, and motherless primarily due to maternal death. However, after adjusting the data for social class, all significant effects of family structure were eliminated, and the achievements of motherless children were below all others. Arithmetic scores at age 11 were affected by family structure within all social classes. Those who were father-absent due to marital breakdown scored less than 2 points below children from nuclear families. Similarly, eleventh-grade scores in arithmetic and reading showed small differences favoring children from nuclear families. On the other hand, Essen (1978), reporting on the same British children in Ferri's study at age 16, has found that the reason for parental absence was not a significant factor influencing scores. Differences between intact and one-parent groups were no longer significant after adjustments were made for socioeconomic status.

Gregory (1965) has reported that the largest differences between quantitative and verbal scores on the American College Entrance Examination occurred among students who had experienced parental divorce or among those who had experienced parental loss before age 10.

Santrock (1972) has offered contradictory findings regarding the consequences of paternal death, divorce, or separation for elementary school students. For example, comparisons of the third- and sixth-grade Otis IQ scores and Stanford Achievement Test scores for males and females reared by widowed mothers versus separated, deserted, or divorced mothers favored the children of widows when paternal death occurred after age 6 (Santrock, 1972, Table 1). Developmental changes in scores between third and sixth grades are conflicting. For example, for males in intact families, mean IQ increased 1.2 points, and mean SAT increased 2.7 points. For males who lost a father because of marital dissolution between the ages of 6 and 9, the mean IQ rose 2.3 points, and mean SAT rose 3.6 points. For males experiencing parental death during the same period of their lives, the gain in SAT was about equal to that of males from intact families and less than that of the one-parent group of males, but the mean IQ declined 2.2 points. For males losing a father by marital breakdown at age 6–11, mean IQ dropped less than 1 point, but SAT increased 30 points. For males losing a father by death, mean IQ dropped 2.2 points, and SAT increased 2.7 points. Males whose fathers left the family when the sons were age 12–13 suffered a mean loss of 5.6 points in IQ, but a gain of 3.4 points in SAT. Females fatherless because of marital dissolution gained nearly 3 points in IQ, whereas those in intact families dropped 2 points on the Otis IQ test. These and other inconsistencies in the matrix of data reported by Santrock do not offer a defensible conclusion that divorce, compared with parental death, has more harmful consequences for school-related cognitive performance of children in elementary school.

When we look at all the studies that have examined reasons for parental absence, it appears that children of divorced parents are performing at lower levels on tests of achievement and IQ. However, an examination of gains in scores over time in Santrock's data suggests that children in one-parent homes may progress at a pace similar or better than those in nuclear families depending on the age of the child at the time of separation and the reasons for separation.

Duration of Absence and Age at Onset

There is no clear evidence of a relationship between duration of parental absence and children's cognitive functioning, although such a relationship has been suggested in a previous review by Shinn (1978). While it is reasonable to expect that longer periods of living in a one-parent household may produce more severe effects on academic performance, no study to date has confirmed this relationship. One difficulty with studies in this area is that the age of the child at onset and the duration of parental absence have been frequently confounded, particularly in studies using age or birth cohorts of children who have been reared since onset in a one-parent household. The investigations of Douglas, Ross, and Simpson (1968) and Ferri (1976), both longitudinal studies of representative British populations, have failed to find systematic patterns of deficit as a function of the age of the child at onset or the duration of absence. Similarly, Sutton-Smith, Rosenberg, and Landy (1968) have reported no significant association between the number of years of father absence and ACEE scores for female students.

Two studies have suggested that duration of absence may not be the most influential factor in determining outcomes. Living in a one-parent home does not necessarily mean total absence of the father, nor does father presence necessarily mean high levels of contact between father and children. Blanchard and Miller (1971) have found significant differences in achievement-test scores of third-grade White boys when a comparison was made of those in complete father-absent and high father-present groups. However, children from low father-present families (based on the physical presence and involvement of the father in child care) received lower scores than did children from the late (after age 5) father-absent group. Landy, Rosenberg, and Sutton-Smith (1969) have found that duration of partial father absence due to night-shift work was negatively related to aptitude-test scores of college-age females, but this difference was fully a function of the difference between the quantitative scores of females experiencing no father absence and those of females whose fathers were totally absent for 10 or more years. That males and females with the most extreme circumstances of father absence should differ from others with the most favorable circumstances of parent availability is not surprising, although causal relations cannot be inferred from these studies.

Similarly, a relationship between age of child at the time of parental separation and cognitive performance has not been clearly established. Some studies have reported more detrimental effects if parental absence occurs before the age of 5 (Blanchard and Biller, 1971; Landy, Rosenberg, and Sutton-Smith, 1969; Santrock, 1972). Some studies have reported that children in first to third grades, compared with preschool or later grades at the time of parental separation, were doing most poorly (Kelly, North, and Zingle, 1965; Maxwell, 1961; Shelton, 1969). One study has reported a curvilinear trend for an age analysis of children in the 3- to 5-year-old group doing better than those younger or older (Santrock and Wohlford, 1970). In the more tightly controlled British studies (Ferri, 1976; Douglas, Ross, and Simpson, 1968), no effects of age were found. The inconsistent findings and methodological problems of studies discussed earlier do not allow us to form any conclusions about the effects of age of child at time of separation on cognitive functioning.

Parent Surrogates

Almost 80% of divorced individuals remarry, although the rate is lower for women. For the child, remarriage of parents presents some distinctive problems. Research on family relations in remarried families has been meager and has been based on verbal, often retrospective reports of parents. These reports have suggested that the role of a stepparent is poorly defined and may be particularly ambiguous in families where there is active involvement of the children with the noncustodial parent. The adjustment of children to stepparents seems to be better if remarriage occurs when children are young than when they are preadolescents or early adolescents (Bowerman and Irish, 1962; Hetherington, Cox, and Cox, 1981).

Studies of the cognitive functioning of children in stepparent (particularly stepfather) families have been based on the opinion that the presence of a father surrogate in the home may alleviate some of the effects of father absence by providing a role model with whom male children can identify. A surrogate father also may offer additional economic and emotional support for the children and the mother. Having a father surrogate to share household and family responsibilities may allow more time to be spent with the children and provide an additional adult resource to help and encourage children in their school work.

It seems likely that in remarriage, as in parental divorce or death, there may be an initial crisis and readjustment period that involves a transition between family forms, followed by an eventual restabilizing of family functioning in the stepparent family. The point at which one taps into this sequence of changing family patterns is reflected in the image obtained of family relations, adjustment, and academic functioning of children. Unfortunately, data on the time of remarriage or family experiences before remarriage (e.g., parental separation or death) have not been used in analyses of the intellectual functioning of children. It is thus not surprising that findings on the mediating effects of a surrogate father have been highly mixed.

Chapman (1977) has reported that female college students from stepfather families scored significantly higher on the SAT than did father-absent females, but did less well than females from intact families. On the other hand, Essen's (1978) longitudinal study of British children has found that children with a substitute parent figure received lower achievement-test scores than did those whose parents had remained alone, and Blanchard and Biller (1971) have found no relationship between the availability of a parent surrogate and achievement in males from White lower-income and working-class families.

Still further complexity is suggested by Lessing, Zagorin, and Nelson (1970) in a study of 9- to 15-year-olds. In working-class families, mean scores for the father-present children were above both the father-surrogate and father-absent groups. In the middle-class sample, however, the father-present children scored below both groups. The means of the father-surrogate and father-absent groups in the working-class and middle-class samples were similar (1970, Table 5). These anomalous results for the middle-income children may have been due to the "wide range of personality and behavior problems" (1970, p. 183) observed in this group.

Gordon (1972), in a reanalysis of a portion of the national Coleman study, has found higher verbal ability among ninth-grade White children in families with no male adult than among children in "weak" male-headed families (i.e., those with a surrogate father who is not employed). In the working-class and lower-income families, the mother-headed children and the employed-father children were equally more likely to score in the top one-third of the verbal-ability distribution than were children reared by neither parent or in a family with an unemployed father.

The results of these studies have suggested that the availability of a father surrogate does not necessarily mean superior achievement by children when compared with those in father-absent, mother-headed families. In fact, the presence of a stepfather may, in some cases, portend a less advantageous situation for cognitive abilities than that of a mother rearing children alone.

Age of Child

Several longitudinal studies have suggested that the effects of one-parent rearing on children's cognitive functioning may not emerge fully in the preschool years or that test scores and academic achievement of young children are not so strongly affected as the achievement levels of those tested at later ages. However, a closer examination of these studies yields no evidence to support such a conclusion.

Hess and his associates (1968, 1969) followed a small group of urban Black families and their 3-year-olds through the children's second grade in school. A comparison was made between the working-class families where the father was absent and those where he was present. In both groups, the family head was in an unskilled occupation. In the father-absent group, the families were receiving Aid to Dependent Children payments, whereas father-present, working-class families were not receiving welfare support. At age 4, the group means for IQ scores of the children in both working-class groups were equal. Although the differences between groups in reading readiness and reading primer scores were significant at age 7, the arithmetic difference in actual scores between the father-absent and father-present groups became smaller over time, and in all cases the absolute gains or improvements in grades favored the father-absent group (1969, Table III-1). There were, however, increasing differences between ages 4 and 7 for the two groups on teacher-assigned grades for conduct, arithmetic, and writing, but not reading. The relationship between grades in conduct and socioeconomic status and family structure suggests that part of the difference in grades may have reflected some global teacher reaction to the child's behavior in the classroom.

Rees and Palmer (1970), synthesizing data from several longitudinal studies, have reported a trend toward an association between one-parent family status and IQ at age 12 but not at age 6. Males but not females were affected. However, since Rees and Palmer have not specified the time of family disruption in the synthesis of data, the difference could indicate a somewhat later (between the ages of 6 and 12) occurrence of parental separation than some delayed effect of one-parent rearing.

Longitudinal studies including an analysis of intraindividual changes in achievement and IQ of different age cohorts experiencing parental separation may provide evidence needed to assess the effects of the maturational level of the age of child at the time of study. Until these data are available, no firm conclusions can be made regarding the presence or absence of delayed effects of one-parent rearing on achievement.

Presence of Siblings

The small number of studies and the lack of consistent findings do not allow us to form any conclusions about the possible modifying effects of siblings on the cognitive performance of children in one-parent homes. For example, Ilardi (1966) and Sutherland (1930) have found that the presence of siblings was not a significant factor influencing IQ scores of one-parent children. Chapman (1977) has reported enhanced verbal ability among college females in stepfather families with same-sex siblings compared with those with opposite-sex siblings. Sutton-Smith, Rosenberg, and Landy (1968) have also reported that first-born children compared with second- or third-born children in one-parent families and those in larger families compared with children in smaller families were more adversely affected. This suggests that the experience of one-parent rearing may be different for children in various family configurations. Older or first-born children in one-parent homes may be required to assume some of the household and family responsibilities. The added responsibility for care of younger siblings and for household duties could take time away from academic study. Further studies are needed on how children in one-parent families organize and spend their time before we can assess the effects of varied family configurations and how they interact with one-parent family status.

Sex of Child

Because of the preoccupation with father absence and its impact on sons, research on one-parent rearing frequently has been confined to one-sex samples. In most instances where both sexes have been studied, males seem to have suffered greater deficits in cognitive performance, although, as we discussed earlier, the differences in cognitive performance on tests between children in one- and two-parent families were generally small and usually not significant. However, when directional differences have been noted, males from one-parent families generally scored lower on quantitative-aptitude tests, compared with males from two-parent families, and females from one-parent families scored higher than females from two-parent families on verbal-aptitude tests. On achievement tests and teacher-assigned grades, males from one-parent homes were more likely than females to receive lower scores.

We discussed previously the sex-identification and tension-interference explanations for differences in the cognitive functioning of children in one-parent homes. Our synthesis of research on tests of aptitude and achievement and classroom grades suggests that neither theory by itself offers a sufficient explanation for the differences reported. Perhaps the stress of family disruption and change in family environment may reduce the typically superior quantitative scores compared with verbal scores achieved by males, but the pattern of higher quantitative and lower verbal scores for males remains intact. In most cases, mean scores in quantitative measures for males are higher than those for one-parent females. The difference lies in the magnitude of difference between same-sex peers in the two family groups. In other words, the difference between mean quantitative scores of males in one- and two-parent homes is larger than the difference between mean quantitative scores of females in one- and two-parent homes. This suggests that males are more adversely affected than females in one area of cognitive functioning—the area in which they usually excel compared with females. On the other hand, females in one-parent families show enhanced verbal aptitude, even above that normally shown when females' verbal scores are compared with males'.

It is possible that a combination of factors is responsible for these findings. Males, compared with females, appear to have a tendency to excel in quantitative areas of test performance. Males who have lost a salient male figure with whom to identify and interact may be without the necessary environmental conditions that lead to the development of this aptitude for superior quantitative performance. In contrast, females, compared with males, appear to have a tendency to excel in verbal areas. Parental loss, specifically the absence of a father, does not interfere with the development of this verbal potential and may even enhance environmental conditions leading to the development of verbal aptitude by providing increased interaction with the female parent.

The sex-identification and environmental-interaction theories do not, however, explain depressed performance on achievement scores in both verbal and mathematical areas for males and females. A more appropriate explanation may be one similar to the tension-interference hypothesis discussed earlier. It seems likely that stress may interfere with performance on tests that measure *actual* learning and not affect performance on tests that measure ability or aptitude for learning. The stress accompanying parental conflict or marital dissolution may interfere with the day-to-day academic functioning of children and result in depressed performance on achievement tests. The lower grades received by males compared with females in one-parent homes may be due to other factors, such as classroom behavior, which influence teacher ratings of performance. This possibility is discussed in more detail in a later section.

In summary, our synthesis of research studies on effects of one-parent rearing suggests that the academic performance of males compared with that of females is more adversely affected, but it must be emphasized that the reported differences are small.

Socioeconomic Status

As Shinn (1978) has pointed out, the large majority of American studies on the effects of one-parent families have been conducted with lower- and working-class families. Some studies that have examined socioeconomic factors have found small net effects of family structure when proper controls for socioeconomic status are introduced (e.g., Ferri, 1976; Lambert and Hart, 1976). However, nearly all investigations have either failed to introduce any controls for social class or constructed improper and insufficient indices of socioeconomic variation. For example, it is common practice to measure the social class of a household by the occupation of the head and to categorize such information into broad occupational strata like manual/nonmanual or lower-class/working-class. These broad designations mask large socioeconomic heterogeneity within the categories—variations in education, income, and other factors that may have separate and nonidentical socioeconomic effects on the relationship between family structure and cognitive performance. Even when composite indices of social class, such as the Hollingshead scale, are used, there remain potential nonidentical effects of class categories.

Controlling or categorizing families by social class is even more problematic with studies of divorced one-parent families (Mueller and Parcel, 1981). For example, Ferri (1976) has measured social status in terms of the family status before divorce and has assessed economic level in terms of the family situation after divorce. In contrast, Santrock (1972) has measured social class after parental separation and has used the mother's occupation as an indicator when information on the father's occupation was not available. In addition, the comparison of heads of nuclear families, who typically are men, with the heads of divorced and separated families, who typically are women, is not an equal one; the same nominal occupational title does not entail the same economic attributes for females as it does for males.

Apart from imprecise measurement of socioeconomic level, research on the consequences of divorce and one-parent rearing on children's achievement has been hampered by inattention to changes in level that are associated with family dissolution (Herzog and Sudia, 1973). Divorce entails changes in income and in the distribution of economic resources, even if the household head retains the same occupation. Hampton (1975), reporting on 5000 American families that were interviewed annually over a six-year period, has shown a larger reduction in the economic circumstances of separated wives than of their former husbands.

Elder (1974) has demonstrated that sudden changes in economic fortunes, even in families not undergoing shifts in social class or experiencing marital discord or dissolution, can have marked consequences for the personality development and achievement of even adolescent children. However, research on a broader range of possible effects of changed economic circumstances following divorce has not found consistent results (e.g., Coletta, 1978; Fulton, 1978; Hetherington, Cox, and Cox, 1979a).

Although several studies have suggested a close connection between economic factors and the effects of one-parent rearing on scholastic achievement, the relationship among these factors is a complex one. For example, even when we find that all of the variance predicted by family structure can be explained by the socioeconomic status of the family, we cannot clearly identify the causal links in the process. Divorce or death of a spouse may create the low socioeconomic conditions within the family. These conditions in turn can impact on children's achievement. It is likely, therefore, that both the socioeconomic status of the family and divorce play a part in scholastic achievement.

Race of Child

A considerable body of literature has been accumulated regarding the achievement of children in Black one-parent families. This may be due in part to the large numbers of Black children in one-parent homes. Whereas roughly 15% of all children under age 18 were Black in 1978, fully 36% of all children in one-parent households in that year were Black. These children constituted 20% of all those under age 18 living with a divorced mother, 33% of those living with a widowed mother, 44% of those living with a separated mother, and 75% of those living with a never-married mother. The larger proportion of one-parent Black families within the Black population, compared with the proportion of one-parent White families within the White population, has led to the stereotype of a typical Black family as being fatherless and on welfare. In actuality, most Black children are raised in two-parent families.

The research on Black families has been based largely on an unsubstantiated model of family functioning. Over a decade ago, the Moynihan report (1965) alleged a major connection between the "disorganized," "matriarchal" Black family and the lower scholastic achievement of the Black minority. However, evidence is lacking that Black families headed by a female constitute less beneficial environments for the learning of achievement values and the development of high cognitive abilities than do nuclear or intact families. Most studies of Black children reveal small and nonsignificant effects of one-parent rearing on achievement tests (e.g., Shinn, 1978; Solomon, Hirsch, Scheinfeld, and Jackson, 1972).

Fowler and Richards (1978) have compared lower-income Black second-graders from intact homes with those from homes where the father had been absent since the child was age 4 and there was no father surrogate or extended family. Controlling for social class, Fowler and Richards have found father absence related to depressed scores on standardized tests in mathematics, but not on tests of language arts or reading. By contrast, kindergarten tests of educational readiness at age 4 revealed no comparative disadvantage for lower-class Black children as a function of father absence—a finding that corroborates Hess, Shipman, Brophy, and Bear (1968).

The small effects of one-parent rearing on achievement in Black children could arise from a number of sources, including the smaller variability in test scores (e.g., Deutsch and Brown, 1964), the prevalence of one-parent rearing, or the substitution of child care from other kin or a parent surrogate. Studies of parental characteristics have found that Black mothers whose marriages have been terminated or who were never married were no less aspiring for the educational achievement of their children than were mothers in intact marriages (e.g., Kandel, 1971). Kandel has also found that "matriarchy," whether defined as a structural feature of the family or as an interactional feature of family relations, was unrelated to educational aspirations, IQ scores, self-reported grades, and school records of class rank. More descriptive data on the processes of childrearing in one- and two-parent Black families are needed before we can draw any conclusions about the relation between Black family structure and children's achievement. As we have suggested, the experience of living in a Black one-parent family may be very different from the experience of living in a White one-parent family. The presence of extended kin and community networks among Black families may be one factor influencing the experience for children. This and other potential differences in one-parent family environments among different racial and ethnic groups are discussed in a later section.

SCHOOL BEHAVIORS AND WORK PATTERNS

In this section, we summarize what is known about school behaviors and school work patterns that may be associated with achievement of children from one-parent homes. This topic has seldom been studied independently but has usually been addressed as part of a larger question regarding school achievement. The studies we have reviewed have focused on a range of grade levels and have varied in procedures used to obtain information from schools and teachers. The types of information have included descriptive data on school attendance, tardiness, and discipline referrals and teachers' ratings of students' attitudes toward school and their study behaviors within the school setting.

The adequate measurement of study and social behaviors is even more difficult and controversial than the assessment of achievement. Most studies of school behavior have relied on teacher ratings. Direct observations of behavior and standardized measurement instruments have rarely been used in gathering information about the work and interaction patterns of children from one-parent households. There is evidence that teacher and peer ratings of children from one-parent homes have been subject to bias. For example, teachers, peers, and parents have continued to view the behavior of preschool boys from divorced families in an unrealistically negative fashion even after their behavior has improved markedly in the years following divorce (Hetherington, Cox, and Cox, 1979b). It should be noted, however, that even at two years following divorce, observations have shown that, although the behavior of boys from divorced families had improved, the boys were still showing more verbal aggression, dependency, attention-seeking behavior, shorter attention spans, lower task persistence, and less helping behavior than were boys from nondivorced families. The lag in teacher perception of positive changes has not occurred with reference to females from divorced families.

Teacher bias has been substantiated to some extent in an experimental study by Santrock and Tracy (1978), in which teachers were asked to view and rate the same videotaped behavior of a child who was presented as coming from an intact or a divorced home. Teachers rated the child of divorced parents more negatively than the child of nondivorced parents on the dimensions of happiness, emotional adjustment, and the ability to cope with stress, but not on other factors, such as anxiety and aggression. However, teachers' perceptions of children's behavior and attitude toward school may be important information in itself, despite its questionable relation to actual behavior. It is possible that teachers' negative evaluations of academic achievement might be related to the children's disruptive behavior in the classroom. Parents, teachers, and peers react negatively to uncontrolled, impulsive behaviors; their responses may influence the experiences of children both in the home and in the school.

The studies we have reviewed have been divided into three general areas of children's functioning in the school setting: attendance, conduct or social behavior, study patterns and attitudes toward school.

Attendance

Studies comparing children of one- and two-parent households have reported consistent differences in school absenteeism, tardiness, and truancy. In an effort to study patterns of achievement and school behaviors of children from one-parent homes, the Kettering Foundation and National Association of Elementary School Principals gathered data from school records of approximately 18,000 students in fifteen elementary and secondary schools. In a preliminary report of findings, Brown (1980) and Evans and Neel (1980) have reported significant differences in the number of absences and incidents of truancy and tardiness among students in one-parent homes compared with those living with both parents or with one biological parent and a stepparent. Differences among family groups were greater for students in secondary schools. For example, the average number of absences for 1 year at the secondary level for students in one-parent families was 17.8 days compared with 12.6 days for students in two-parent homes. Significant differences in the socioeconomic backgrounds of children in the one- and two-parent groups did not permit us to attribute these difficulties solely to one-parent family status. Results of the analysis for students from lower-income families were not presented, nor were data on the ethnic or racial backgrounds of students reported. However, several studies that have provided adequate controls for sociocultural background have reported fewer absences and fewer instances of tardiness among children in two-parent compared with one-parent homes (Collins, 1969; Hetherington, Camara, and Featherman, 1982; Kelly, North, and Zingle, 1965; McNeal, 1973; Scott, 1974).

Reasons for absence or tardiness have not been specified in these studies, but one could speculate that the reasons for not attending school are different for students in one- and two-parent homes. Hetherington, Cox, and Cox (1981) have found that children of divorced parents were more likely than children in nuclear families to have erratic home schedules for meals and bedtimes. Single parents burdened with child care, work, and household responsibilities were more likely to rely on children, particularly adolescents, for emotional support and for assistance with the practical problems of daily life, such as household tasks and taking care of younger siblings (Kelly and Wallerstein, 1979; Weiss, 1978). It might also be necessary for these students to take on part-time jobs while attending school in order to assist with the financial support of the family or, on occasion, to stay home from school to assist with household and family responsibilities.

The relation between school absence or tardiness and academic performance is not clearly established. Interestingly, a study by Scott

(1974) has found a significant association between school absence and achievement for children in intact families but not for children in one-parent homes. However, it is not unreasonable to assume that absence from school for whatever reason can have direct as well as indirect effects on school performance. Time away from the class-room can mean less time spent in learning basic skills and developing knowledge needed for more advanced study. Absences and tardiness also create additional disruptions for school administrators and classroom teachers. Failure to attend school or to arrive on time may be interpreted by school personnel as lack of motivation and interest on the part of students and parents. These impressions may influence the evaluations of students from one-parent homes and teachers' expectations for performance. The responses of teachers may deter-mine how successful the school environment can be in helping chil-dren learn to work and play effectively.

Conduct

Studies comparing the classroom social behavior of students from one- and two-parent homes have consistently described children from one-parent homes as being more disruptive, aggressive, immature, and less self-controlled (Cox, 1975; Hetherington, Cox, and Cox, 1979b; Santrock, 1975; Santrock and Tracy, 1978). These children were more likely to be referred for discipline problems and to receive detentions or suspensions from school for problems in conduct (Brown, 1980; Evans and Neel, 1980; Herzog, 1974).

Felner, Stolberg, and Cowan (1975) have collected teachers' rat-ings of adjustment for school children from nuclear families, those from families where parents had separated or divorced, and those who had lost a parent through death. The three groups of children were matched on sex, grade in school, school location, socioeconomic status, and previous participation in a primary mental-health project. Marked differences were found between groups on the measures of self-control. Children from divorced or separated families had higher overall maladjustment scores and were rated as being more restless, impulsive, obstinate, and disruptive in class than were children from nuclear families.

A similar pattern of observed and teacher-rated impulsiveness, distractibility, oppositional behavior, tantrums, and aggression in preschool children from divorced homes has been found by Heth-erington, Cox, and Cox (1979b). The differences on observational measures between children in divorced and nuclear families dimin-ished over the two-year period following divorce. However, males from divorced families continued to exhibit more maladaptive behavior than did other groups and were so rated by their teachers and peers. Authoritative control by the mother plus a high degree of household organization immediately following divorce were related to self-control of children one year after divorce. These factors, in turn, were correlated with scores on performance and problem-solving scales of the WPPSI two years after divorce. This result suggests that, under stressful conditions, young children may require a more structured and orderly environment in order to function effectively. Under conditions of low stress or with older children who are better able to organize their environments, these factors may not be so critical.

Lack of self-control has also been found with older subjects from father-absent homes. Siegman (1966) has found that groups of male law and medical students who had been without a father for at least one year from age 1 through 4 scored higher on such self-reported antisocial behaviors as parental disobedience, property damage, and drinking than did males whose fathers had been continuously present.

From these and other studies, we can conclude that children from one-parent families, particularly separated or divorced families, are perceived and labeled by their teachers and others as having conduct problems and difficulties in peer relations (Gregory, 1965; Hardy, 1937; Hess and Camara, 1979; Hetherington, Cox, and Cox, 1979b; Holman, 1953; Layman, 1961; Leiderman, 1953; McDermott, 1968; Miller, 1961; Mitchell and Wilson, 1967; Pemberton and Benady, 1973; Wallerstein and Kelly, 1976). The difficulties these children experience socially could be another factor leading to problems in school academic performance. Disruptions in the class interfere with time spent on teaching and learning. Single parents may be able to reduce some of these difficulties by providing a predictable, structured home environment for children during times of stress. Teachers' reactions to disturbances in the classroom may also determine how supportive the school environment is for these children. The stress accompanying family change and the added responsibilities associated with living in a one-parent household coupled with a nonsupportive school environment may affect not only children's performance on achievement tests but also their attitudes toward school and their motivation to learn.

Study Patterns and School Attitudes

The relation of study behaviors to learning and academic performance has not been well documented. Although most educators would agree that factors such as preparedness, concentration on tasks, persistence, and enthusiasm for learning are important qualities for a successful learner, there have been few empirical studies that provide us with any reliable information on how these factors relate to achievement. The measurement of study behaviors is also problematic: most studies have relied on teacher reports or ratings of students' work styles in the classroom. The validity and reliability of these estimates have seldom been examined. Despite the problems of method and definition, descriptive data on children's work or study styles in the classroom may provide evidence of interference in cognitive functioning due to high levels of stress or anxiety. One may reasonably expect that teachers' perceptions of behaviors may influence evaluations of performance that are represented in grade-point averages.

Studies that have examined the responses of children in the immediate period surrounding separation and divorce have usually found indicators of anxiety, such as fearfulness, inhibition, worry, regressive behaviors, habit disturbances, and neediness (Hess and Camara, 1979; Hetherington, Cox, and Cox, 1979a; Kelly and Wallerstein, 1976; Wallerstein and Kelly, 1974, 1975, 1976). These effects are related to parental conflict, to the quality of the mother–child and father–child relationship, and to the time lost in the presence of the father. Jacobson (1978a, 1978b) has found these relationships to be more marked for 7- to 13-year-olds than for 3- to 6-year-olds. Wallerstein and Kelly (1974, 1975, 1976) have reported that the form anxiety takes varies with the age of the child. Preschool children exhibited regressive behavior, separation anxiety, and irritability; elementary school children manifested sadness; and adolescents were anxious about their futures. In any case, high levels of anxiety often interfere with learning and performance (Hill, 1977; Ruble and Boggiano, 1980). Thus, high levels of anxiety may be one factor that explains differences in children's style of study and performance on tests.

The few studies of children's classroom work behavior have reported differences in the study habits of children from one- and two-parent families. In general, one-parent children were described by their teachers as having greater difficulty in concentrating and attending to tasks, completing tasks within a specified time period, and working independently (Herzog, 1974; Hess and Camara, 1979; Hetherington, Cox, and Cox, 1981; McNeal, 1973).

Hess and Camara (1979) have compared teacher ratings of 9- to 11-year-olds from divorced and intact family groups on scales of concentration, attention, completion of tasks, and preference for group versus independent activity. Children were matched on age, sex, and classroom assignment. Significant differences were found in the ratings of teachers who perceived children in divorced families to have less effective work styles than those of children from intact families.

Although males in general scored lower on these dimensions, the differences between females' scores in the two family groups were most striking. Females from divorced families compared with those from intact families were seen as less competent in their study patterns in the school setting. This is not in accord with the findings of the Hetherington, Cox, and Cox (1981) study of preschool children, which reported more distractibility and less task persistence for males than for females from divorced parents as obtained both by observation and by teacher and parent reports.

Frequently, these differences in study behaviors are interpreted by teachers as representing a lack of motivation by these youngsters. Teachers in Herzog's (1974) study distinguished between father-absent and father-present males in terms of their attitudes toward school work. Males whose fathers were absent during the first 5 years of the child's life or during the ages of 2 to 4 were more often labeled "lazy" than those with fathers present during those years. Males in the father-present group were described as quiet, cooperative, and as "trying hard." Teachers described the males with a history of continuous father absence as "troublesome" and unwilling to conform to school expectations. Interestingly, teachers' ratings of children's attitudes and behaviors were significantly correlated with scores on teacher-graded examinations in comprehension, composition, and arithmetic, and on a standard reading test but were not correlated with performance on standardized tests of IQ.

Two studies have failed to find significant differences between the school work habits of children in lower- and lower-middle-income broken and intact families (Birnbaum, 1966; Collins, 1969). However, reasons for broken-home status and duration of living in a one-parent household were not analyzed in these studies. The effects of divorce on children's study habits may not be long-lasting unless there are continued conflict and family disorganization. However, temporary stress that interferes with children's ability to concentrate and attend to tasks in the early grades could result in a failure to learn basic skills needed for study in later grades. This could produce lags in achievement that last beyond the time of stress. Further research is needed before any conclusive statements can be made about the causal connections among family structures, children's study habits, and school performance.

Summary Comment

To summarize, our review of research studies on school behaviors and school work patterns reveals that, compared with children in two-parent homes, children from one-parent households are absent from school more frequently, are more disruptive in the classroom, and may have less effective study styles in their school work, particularly in the two- to three-year period surrounding the time of family disruption. All of these factors may explain in part differences in teacher evaluations of children's achievement and in grade-point average. Teachers' reports of depressed achievement among children from one-parent households may be based on their reactions to disruptive classroom behaviors and to classroom work styles that do not conform to school expectations rather than on the actual academic performance of these children. We have little information on the relation between teachers' evaluation or students' grade-point averages and performance on standardized achievement tests. However, school evaluations of student work may have their own unique impact on achievement in the students' school setting. For example, negative evaluations, particularly during times of stress, may affect the motivation to learn and the decision of whether or not to continue schooling. Depressed grade averages may also reduce students' eligibility for scholarship assistance for further schooling and may affect future academic opportunities.

SUMMARY AND DISCUSSION

In each of the sections of our review, we drew attention to the often contradictory and inconsistent state of accumulated research on the effects of one-parent rearing on children's achievement and intellectual functioning. We have noted the rapid changes in the social context of divorce and one-parent rearing as an experience of childhood that may restrict the applicability of all but the most recent research to contemporary American society. In addition, generalizations from past research have been limited because of methodological shortcomings. Based on the analysis of all available research, several themes do emerge concerning the relation of intellectual functioning and one-parent household status.

Standardized Versus Teacher Ratings

First, differences between groups of one-parent and two-parent children on tests of intelligence and aptitude are usually small and decrease when socioeconomic status is taken into account. Children in one-parent homes tend to score on IQ tests an average of approximately 3 to 4 points lower than do children in two-parent families. Scores on achievement tests between groups usually reflect less than 1-year difference. However, an overwhelming number of studies have reported lower grade-point averages and teacher-assigned grades for children in one-parent homes compared with those in two-parent homes. Given the data available on intellectual test performance of these children, it is unlikely that children reared in one-parent homes are experiencing any serious intellectual deficit.

What does account for the depressed evaluations of performance in the school setting? In our review, we have suggested a complex interaction among student attitudes and behaviors, teacher attitudes, and home conditions that may result in poorer achievement performance as measured by teacher-assigned grades and grade-point averages. Children in divorced and other one-parent families tend to be more disruptive in the classroom, have less efficient work or study habits, and tend to be absent, truant, or tardy more often than children who live in homes where two adults are present. These behaviors may interfere with application of knowledge as evidenced in the poorer quality of classroom work and the failure to complete assignments or attend to tasks.

A second interpretation is that children who do not conform to school routines and requirements are perceived by their teachers as less competitive. Research evidence on teachers' assessment of student performance has pointed to factors other than intellectual ability or quality of work in determining student evaluations. For example, papers with better handwriting receive higher marks from teachers, regardless of the quality of their content (Markham, 1976). Other data tended to show that students who are obedient, conforming, and industrious receive higher grades than those who are rebellious, nonconforming, and lazy (Lindgren, 1980).

An alternative explanation is that the conditions of family life surrounding separation and divorce affect children's functioning in the school setting and that the outcomes of family disruption are modified by characteristics of the home and school. For example, the study by Hetherington, Cox, and Cox (1978b) has shown that mothers' maturity demands and their authoritative control, combined with a high degree of household organization following divorce, were correlated with measures of children's attention span, persistence, and self-control one year following divorce. These, in turn, were correlated with performance on arithmetic and problem-solving scales on a standardized IQ test two years after divorce. These authors have suggested that, under stressful conditions, children may require external controls provided by a structured and orderly environment since they may have difficulty exerting self-control.

This study has found a remarkable similarity in the attributes of the home and the school that were associated with more rapid and satisfactory adjustment of children from divorced families. In both settings, an organized, predictable environment, with clearly defined and consistently enforced standards, roles, and responsibilities, and a responsive, nurturant atmosphere were associated with effective cognitive functioning, low rates of behavior disorders, and more adaptive behavior in children. These home and school characteristics are similar to those of authoritative parent behaviors described by Baumrind (1971). The role of structure, organization, rule enforcement, and assignment of responsibilities or maturity demands was more important for children from divorced than from nondivorced families. These characteristics in the school were also associated with greater self-control in children from nondivorced families with high levels of parent–child or marital conflict. This seems to support the position that young children who have undergone the stress, inconsistency, and transitions associated with divorce or high rates of family conflict require a more predictable and structured environment than do children not exposed to such difficult life experiences. The structure and control factors were more salient for males; responsiveness, warmth, and maturity demands were more salient for females. However, all of these factors in the school were significantly related to positive outcomes in children of both sexes from divorced families two years after divorce.

Until very recently, there has been a pervasive pessimism about the effects of schooling on child development. Since the time of the original Coleman (1966, 1975) reports and the work of such investigators as Bernstein (1970) and Jencks and his colleagues (Jencks, Smith, Acland, Bane, Cohen, Gintis, Heyns, and Michelson, 1972), family influences, particularly early family influences, have been thought to dominate the development of children. It is only recently, in the work of such people as Rutter and some of his British co-workers (Rutter, Maughan, Mortemore, Ouston, and Smith, 1979) that the characteristics of schools have been found to attenuate adverse outcomes such as delinquency that might have been expected for children coming from disorganized households and economically deprived neighborhoods. Similar results for children of divorce have been reported in the Hetherington, Cox, and Cox (1981) study.

Some researchers have speculated that the occurrence of stressful events such as the loss of a parent or adverse environmental factors associated with life in a one-parent family may contribute to a sense of lack of personal determinism (Hetherington, 1972; Rotter, 1966). In many theories of achievement, perceived internal control has been viewed as an essential prerequisite to achievement striving. Although the relationship among family structure, locus of control, and achievement is obviously complex, it is a topic that warrants further study.

Attitudes toward the self, particularly as they relate to self-determination, are also associated with academic achievement (Coopersmith, 1967), problem-solving strategies, and responses to success and failure. High self-esteem is associated with authoritative parent behaviors (Coopersmith, 1967). Studies of the self-esteem of children in mother-headed, one-parent households have yielded inconsistent results. These ranged from no differences in self-esteem between children in nuclear and mother-headed families (Rubin, 1974; Thomes, 1968) to lower self-esteem in children from one-parent families (Cox, 1975; Hetherington, 1972; Parish and Taylor, 1979; Rosenberg, 1965; Rouman, 1956; Tiller, 1958; Young and Parish, 1977) and to higher self-esteem in particular groups of children from one-parent families (Gordon, 1972; Hunt and Hunt, 1975, 1977). What is clear is that any relation there may be between divorce or living in a one-parent home and self-esteem or between self-esteem and achievement is moderated by a variety of other factors and that only selected aspects of the self-concept may be affected.

Finally, as we suggested earlier, the need for single parents to rely on their children for assistance with household and child-care tasks and routines of daily living may result in less time available for these children to attend to achievement-related tasks. Children who are expected to assist with preparation of meals, care for younger siblings, and perhaps even find part-time jobs to assist with financial management of the household may be unable to concentrate their efforts on school work. This, in turn, may result in lower grades and less positive evaluations by teachers and school personnel.

Sex Differences

The second major theme emerging from our review is that the intellectual and social development of males may be seen as more adversely affected by living in one-parent homes than that of females from similar family circumstances. The analysis of patterns of cognitive functioning revealed that one-parent males, but not females, scored lower on tests of quantitative aptitude and achievement compared with males in two-parent homes. One-parent females, on the other hand, but not males, scored higher on tests of verbal aptitude and achievement than did females in two-parent homes.

Numerous studies have suggested that the impact of marital discord and divorce on emotional and social adjustment are more pervasive and enduring for males than for females (Hess and Camara, 1979; Hetherington, Cox, and Cox, 1978a, 1979a, 1979c; Rutter, 1979b; Tuckman and Regan, 1966; Wallerstein, 1978). Males from divorced families, in contrast to females from divorced families and children from nuclear families, show a higher rate of behavior disorders and problems in interpersonal relations with parents, teachers, and peers. Why should males show more prevalent disorders in response to family disharmony and separation? When there is conflict in a family,

272 Children in One-Parent Households / Hetherington, Camara, and Featherman

males may be more directly exposed to it and may receive less support from parents, teachers, and peers in response to their expressions of distress than do females (Hetherington, Cox, and Cox, 1981). This may, in part, be because of sex-stereotyped notions that males should be able to control their feelings and be less needful of support than are females. In addition, the responses of males to marital discord and distress may be more overt and noxious than those of females. Finally, following divorce, most children are in mother-custody homes. The separation from the father may represent a more important loss for a male than for a female, both as a figure of identification and as a disciplinarian. A study by Santrock and Warshak (1979) has found that females in father-custody families exhibit some of the same difficulties in social behavior as do males in mother-headed, one parent families. This finding suggests that separation from the same-sex parent may be particularly difficult for children. However, under the present, most common custodial arrangement, males may be at higher risk for deleterious outcomes from family disruption and divorce than are females.

Conclusions

The factors that mediate intellectual and achievement outcomes in children from disrupted or divorced families involve a complex interaction of individual-difference, social, motivational, and cultural factors. Most children find divorce to be a stressful life transition, but the long-term effects of marital disruption on children may be modified by effective family functioning and by positive experiences of the child in extrafamilial settings such as the school, peer group, neighborhood, or workplace. The functioning of children and parents during and following divorce should be considered in relationship to the larger social context. Although much has been written about the stresses and support systems for divorced adults, little is known about the interrelation between stresses and support systems for children in one-parent families. This is an essential area of inquiry in understanding the cognitive, emotional, and social sequelae of divorce for children.

REFERENCES

Akeju, S. A. 1969. The reliability of General Certificate of Education Examination English composition papers in West Africa. *Journal of Educational Psychology*, 60, 231–243.

Albert, R. 1971. Cognitive development and parental loss among the gifted, the exceptionally gifted, and the creative. *Psychological Reports*, 29, 19–26.

Alpert, R. 1957. Anxiety in academic achievement situations: Its measurement and relation to aptitude. Doctoral dissertation, Stanford University.

Altus, W. D. 1958. The broken home and factors of adjustment. *Psychological Reports, 4,* 477.

Atkinson, B. R., and D. G. Ogston. 1974. The effect of father absence on male children in the home and school. *Journal of School Psychology, 12,* 213–221.

Bane, M. J. 1976. Marital disruption and the lives of children. *Journal of Social Issues, 32,* 103–117.

Barclay, A. G., and D. Cusumano. 1967. Father absence, cross-sex identity, and field-dependent behavior in male adolescents. *Child Development, 38,* 243–250.

Baumrind, D. 1971. Current patterns of parental authority. *Developmental Psychology Monograph, 4,* No. 4, Part 2.

Becker, S. 1974. Father absence and its relationship to creativity. *Graduate Research in Education and Related Disciplines, 7,* 32–52.

Bernstein, B. 1970. Education cannot compensate for society. *New Society, 387,* 344–347.

Bernstein, B. E. 1976. How father absence in the home affects the mathematic skills of fifth-graders. *Family Therapy, 3,* 47–59.

Birnbaum, L. 1966. A comparative study of the relation of broken homes to the social class and school success of secondary school boys. Doctoral dissertation, University of Southern California.

Blanchard, R. W., and H. B. Biller. 1971. Father availability and academic performance among third-grade boys. *Developmental Psychology, 4,* 301–305.

Bohannon, P. 1970. The six stations of divorce. In P. Bohannan (ed.), *Divorce and after.* Garden City, NY: Doubleday.

Bowerman, C. E., and D. P. Irish. 1962. Some relationships of stepchildren to their parents. *Marriage and Family Living, 24,* 113–131.

Brandwein, R. A., C. A. Brown, and E. M. Fox. 1974. Women and children last: The social situation of divorced mothers and their families. *Journal of Marriage and the Family, 36,* 498–514.

Briscoe, C. W., J. B. Smith, E. Robins, S. Marten, and F. Gaskin. 1973. Divorce and psychiatric disease. *Archives of General Psychiatry, 29,* 119–125.

Broman, S. H., P. L. Nichols, and W. A. Kennedy. 1975. *Preschool IQ: Prenatal and early developmental correlates.* New York: Wiley.

Brown, B. F. 1980. A study of the school needs of children from one-parent families. *Phi Delta Kappan,* April, 537–540.

Bumpass, L. L., and R. R. Rindfuss. 1978. Children's experience of marital disruption. Discussion paper for Institute of Research on Poverty, University of Wisconsin.

Burgess, R. L. 1978. Project Interact: A study of patterns of interaction in abusive, neglectful and control families. Final report. Washington, DC: National Center on Child Abuse and Neglect.

Camara, K. A. 1979. Children's construction of social knowledge: Concepts of family and the experience of parental divorce. Doctoral dissertation, Stanford University.

Camara, K. A., O. Baker, and C. Dayton. 1980. Impact of separation and divorce on youths and families. in P. M. Insel (ed.), *Experimental variables and the prevention of mental illness*. Lexington, MA: Heath.

Carlsmith, L. 1964. Effect of early father absence on scholastic aptitude. *Harvard Educational Review, 34*, 3–21.

Carlsmith, L. 1973. Some personality characteristics of boys separated from their fathers during World War II. *Ethos, 1*, 466–477.

Chapman, M. 1977. Father absence, stepfathers, and the cognitive performance of college students. *Child Development, 48*, 1155–1158.

Chess, S., A. Thomas, and H. O. Birch. 1968. Behavioral problems revisited. In S. Chess and H. Birch (eds.), *Annual progress in child psychiatry and child development*. New York: Brunner/Mazel.

Clarke, P. A. 1961. A study of the school behavior effects upon boys of father absence in the home. Doctoral dissertation, University of Maryland.

Coleman, J. S., E. Q. Campbell, C. J. Hobson, J. McPartland, A. M. Mood, F. D. Weinfeld, and R. L. York. 1966. *Equality of educational opportunity*. Washington, DC: U.S. Government Printing Office.

Coletta, N. D. 1978. Divorced mothers at two income levels: Stress, support and child-rearing practices. Unpublished doctoral thesis, Cornell University.

Collins, M. A. 1969. Achievement, intelligence, personality and selected school related variables in Negro children from intact and broken families attending parochial schools in central Harlem. Doctoral dissertation, Fordham University.

Coopersmith, S. 1967. *The antecedents of self-esteem*. San Francisco: W. H. Freeman and Company.

Cortes, C. F., and E. S. Fleming. 1968. The effects of father absence on the adjustment of culturally disadvantaged boys. *Journal of Special Education, 2*, 413–420.

Cox, M. 1975. The effects of father absence and working mothers on children. Doctoral dissertation, University of Virginia.

Crescimbeni, J. 1965. Broken homes do affect academic achievement. *Child and Family, 4*, 24–28.

Deutsch, M. 1960. *Minority group and class status as related to social and personality factors in scholastic achievement*. Monograph No. 2. Ithaca, NY: Society for Applied Anthropology.

Deutsch, M., and B. Brown. 1964. Social influences in Negro–white intelligence differences. *Journal of Social Issues, 20*, 24–35.

Domino, G. 1969. Maternal personality correlates of son's creativity. *Journal of Consulting and Clinical Psychology, 33*, 180.

Douglas, J. W. B., J. M. Ross, and H. R. Simpson. 1968. *All our future: A longitudinal study of secondary education*. London: Davies.

Dreyer, A. S., and M. B. Wells. 1966. Parental values, parental control, and creativity in young children. *Journal of Marriage and the Family, 28*, 83–88.

Duncan, B., and O. D. Duncan. 1969. Family stability and occupational success. *Social Problems, 16*, 273–285.

Dweck, C. In press. The development of achievement. in E. M. Hetherington (ed.), *Personality and social development.* Vol. 4. *Carmichael handbook of child psychology.* 4th ed. New York: Wiley.

Ebel, R. L. 1968. Standardized achievement tests: Uses and limitations. In W. L. Barnette (ed.), *Readings in psychological tests and measurements.* Homewood, IL: Dorsey.

Educational Testing Service. 1961. Judges disagree on the qualities that characterize good writing. *ETS Developments, 9.*

Edwards, H., and B. Thompson. 1971. Who are the fatherless? *New Society, 17*, 192–193.

Eisenman, R., and D. Foxman. 1970. Creativity: Reported family patterns and scoring methodology. *Psychological Reports, 26*, 615–621.

Eisenstadt, J. M. 1978. Parental loss and genius. *American Psychologist, 33*, 211–223.

Elder, G. H., Jr. 1974. *Children of the great depression.* Chicago: University of Chicago Press.

Essen, J. 1978. Living in one-parent families: Attainment at school. Unpublished manuscript, National Children's Bureau (London).

Evans, A., and J. A. Neel. 1980. A multivariate analysis of differences between measures of school behaviors of children from two-parent and one-parent family situations. Report to Institute for Development of Educational Activities, a division of Charles F. Kettering Foundation.

Featherman, D. L. 1980. Schooling and occupational careers: Constancy and change in worldly success. In O. G. Brim, Jr., and J. Kagen (eds.), *Constancy and change in human development.* Cambridge, MA: Harvard University Press.

Featherman, D. L., and R. M. Hauser. 1978. *Opportunity and change.* New York: Academic.

Feiring, C. 1976. The influence of the child and secondary parent on maternal behavior: Toward a social systems view of early infant–mother attachment. Doctoral dissertation, University of Pittsburgh.

Feldman, H., and M. Feldman. 1975. The effect of father absence on adolescents. *Family Perspectives, 10*, 3–16.

Felner, R., A. Stolberg, and E. L. Cowan. 1975. Crisis events and school mental health referral patterns of young children. *Journal of Consulting and Clinical Psychology, 43*, 305–310.

Ferri, E. 1976. *Growing up in a one-parent family: A long-term study of child development.* London: National Foundation for Educational Research.

Fowler, P. C., and H. C. Richards. 1978. Father absence, educational preparedness, and academic achievement: A test of the confluence model. *Journal of Educational Psychology, 70,* 595–601.

Fulton, J. A. 1978. Factors related to parental assessment of the effect of divorce on children: A research report. Paper presented at National Institute of Mental Health Conference on Divorce, Washington, DC.

Funkenstein, D. H. 1963. Mathematics, quantitative aptitudes and the masculine role. *Diseases of the Nervous System, 24,* 140–146.

Garmezy, N. 1975. The experimental study of children vulnerable to psychopathology. In A. Davids (ed.), *Child personality and psychopathology.* Vol. 2. New York: Wiley.

Gasser, R. D., and C. M. Taylor. 1976. Role adjustment of single parent fathers with dependent children. *Family Coordinator, 25,* 397–401.

George, V., and P. Wilding. 1972. *Motherless families.* London: Routledge-Kegan Paul.

Glass, G. V. 1978. Integrating findings: The meta-analysis of research. *Review of Research in Education, 5,* 351–379.

Glick, P. C. 1979. Who are the children in one-parent households? Paper presented at Wayne State University, Detroit.

Goldstein, H. S., and R. Peck. 1973. Maternal differentiation and father absence. *Archives of General Psychiatry, 29,* 370–373.

Goode, W. 1956. *After divorce.* Glencoe, IL: Free Press.

Gordon, C. 1972. Looking ahead: Self-conceptions, race and family as determinants of adolescent orientation to achievement. American Sociological Association Monograph Series, Washington, DC.

Graham, P., M. Rutter, and S. George. 1973. Temperamental characteristics as predictors of behavior disorders in children. *American Journal of Orthopsychiatry, 43,* 328–339.

Gregory, I. 1965. Anterospective data following childhood loss of a parent. Vol. 1. Delinquency and high school dropout. *Archives of General Psychiatry, 13,* 99–109.

Guttentag, M., and S. Salasin. 1979. *Families abandoned: Mental health in today's society.* New York: Academic.

Hampton, R. 1975. Marital disruption: Some social and economic consequences. In G. J. Duncan and J. N. Morgan (eds.), *Five thousand families: Patterns of economic progress.* Vol. 4. Ann Arbor, MI: Institute for Social Research.

Hardy, M. C. 1937. Aspects of home environment in relation to behavior at the elementary school age. *Journal of Juvenile Research, 21,* 206–225.

Hedges, L. V., and I. Olkin. 1980. Vote-counting methods in research synthesis. *Psychological Bulletin, 87,* 359–369.

Herzog, E., and C. E. Sudia. 1973. Children in fatherless families. In B. Caldwell, Jr., and H. Ricciuti (eds.), *Review of Child Development Research.* Vol. 3. Chicago: University of Chicago Press.

Herzog, J. D. 1974. Father absence and boys' school performance in Barbados. *Human Organization, 33,* 71–83.

Hess, R. D., and K. A. Camara. 1979. Post-divorce family relationships as mediating factors in the consequences of divorce for children. In T. E. Levitin (ed.), *Journal of Social Issues, 35,* 79–96.

Hess, R. D., V. C. Shipman, J. E. Brophy, and R. M. Bear. 1968. The cognitive environments of urban preschool children. Chicago: Graduate School of Education, University of Chicago.

Hess, R. D., V. C. Shipman, J. E. Brophy, R. M. Bear, and A. B. Adelberger. 1969. *The cognitive environments of urban preschool children: Follow-up phase.* Chicago: Graduate School of Education, University of Chicago. ERIC Document Reproduction Service No. ED 039 270.

Hetherington, E. M. 1972. Effects of paternal absence on personality development in adolescent daughters. *Developmental Psychology, 7,* 313–326.

Hetherington, E. M. 1981. Children and divorce. In R. Henderson (ed.), *Parent–child interaction: Theory, research, and prospect.* New York: Academic.

Hetherington, E. M., K. A. Camara, and D. L. Featherman, 1982. *Intellectual functioning and achievement of children in one-parent households.* Washington, DC: National Institute of Education.

Hetherington, E. M., M. Cox, and R. Cox. 1978a. The aftermath of divorce. In J. H. Stevens, Jr., and M. Matthews (eds.), *Mother–child, father–child relations.* Washington, DC: National Association for the Education of Young Children.

Hetherington, E. M., M. Cox, and R. Cox. 1978b. The development of children in mother-headed families. In H. Hoffman and D. Reiss (eds.), *The American family: Dying or developing.* New York: Plenum.

Hetherington, E. M., M. Cox, and R. Cox, 1979a. Family interaction and the social, emotional and cognitive development of children following divorce. In V. Vaughan and T. Brazelton (eds.), *The family: Setting priorities.* New York: Science and Medicine.

Hetherington, E. M., M. Cox, and R. Cox. 1979b. Play and social interaction in children following divorce. *Journal of Social Issues, 35,* 26–49.

Hetherington, E. M., M. Cox, and R. Cox. 1979c. Stress and coping in divorce: A focus on women. In J. Gullahorn (ed.), *Psychology and women in transition.* Washington, DC: Winston.

Hetherington, E. M., M. Cox, and R. Cox. 1981. Effects of divorce on parents and children. In M. E. Lamb (ed.), *Nontraditional families: Parenting and child development.* Hillsdale, NJ: Lawrence Erlbaum.

Hilker, D. L. 1976. The effects of increasing addition skill on self-concept in children. Unpublished doctoral dissertation, University of Maryland.

Hill, K. T. 1977. The relation of evaluative practices to test anxiety and achievement motivation. *Educator, 19,* 15–22.

Hodges, P. H., R. C. Wechsler, and C. Ballantine. 1978. Divorce and the preschool child: Cumulative stress. Paper presented at meeting of American Psychological Association, Toronto.

Hoffman, S. 1977. Marital instability and the economic status of women. *Demography*, 14, 67–77.

Hoffman, S., and J. Holmes. 1976. Husbands, wives, and divorce. In G. J. Duncan and J. N. Morgan (eds.), *Five thousand American families: Patterns of economic progress.* Vol. 4. Ann Arbor, MI: Institute for Social Research.

Holman, P. 1953. Some factors in the etiology of maladjustment in children. *Journal of Mental Science*, 99, 654–688.

Hunt, J. G., and L. L. Hunt. 1977. Race, daughters and father-loss: Does absence make the girl grow stronger? *Social Problems*, 25, 90–102.

Hunt, L. L., and J. G. Hunt. 1975. Race and the father–son connection: The conditional relevance of father absence for the orientations and identities of adolescent boys. *Social Problems*, 23, 35–52.

Hunt, M. 1966. *The world of the formerly married.* New York: McGraw-Hill.

Huston, A. C. In press. Sex-typing. In E. M. Hetherington (ed.), *Personality and social development.* Vol. 4. *Carmichael handbook of child psychology.* 4th ed. New York: Wiley.

Ilardi, L. R. 1966. Family disorganization and intelligence in Negro preschool children. Doctoral dissertation, University of Tennessee.

Jacobson, D. S. 1978a. Impact of marital separation/divorce on children: I. Parent–child separation and child adjustment. *Journal of Divorce*, 1, 341–360.

Jacobson, D. S. 1978b. The impact of marital separation/divorce on children: II. Interparental hostility and child adjustment. *Journal of Divorce*, 2, 3–19.

Jaffe, B. D. 1965. The relationship between two aspects of socioeconomic disadvantage and the school success of 8th-grade Negro students in a Detroit junior high school. Doctoral dissertation, Wayne State University.

Jencks, C., M. Smith, H. Acland, M. J. Bane, D. Cohen, H. Gintis, B. Heyns, and S. Michelson. 1972. *Inequality: A reassessment of the effect of family and schooling in America.* New York: Basic Books.

Jones, H. E. 1975. Father absence during childhood, maternal attitudes toward men, and the sex-role development of male college students. Doctoral dissertation, Michigan State University.

Kandel, D. B. 1971. Race, maternal authority, and adolescent aspiration. *American Journal of Sociology*, 76, 999–1020.

Keller, F. E. 1968. A comparative study of selected background factors related to achievement of mentally able fifth- and sixth-grade children. Doctoral dissertation, Michigan State University.

Kelly, F. J., J. North, and H. Zingle. 1965. The relation of broken homes to subsequent school behaviors. *Alberta Journal of Educational Research*, 11, 215–219.

Kelly, J. B. 1978. Children and parents in the midst of divorce: Major factors contributing to differential response. Paper presented at National Institute of Mental Health Conference on Divorce, Washington, DC.

Kelly, J. B., and J. Wallerstein. 1976. The effects of parental divorce: Experiences of the child in early latency. *American Journal of Orthopsychiatry, 46*, 20–32.

Kelly, J. B., and J. S. Wallerstein. 1979. Children of divorce. *National Elementary Principal, 59*, 51–58.

Kitano, H. H. L. 1963. The child-care center: A study of the interaction among one-parent children, parents, and school. *University of California Publications in Education, 12*, 293–344.

Kitson, G. C., and M. B. Sussman. 1976. The processes of marital separation and divorce: Male and female similarities and differences. Paper presented at meeting of American Sociological Association, New York.

Krantzler, M. 1973. *Creative divorce.* New York: Signet.

Kriesberg, L. 1970. *Mothers in poverty: A study of fatherless families.* Chicago: Aldine.

Lambert, L., and S. Hart. 1976. Who needs a father? *New Society, 37*, 80.

Landy, F., B. G. Rosenberg, and B. Sutton-Smith. 1969. The effect of limited father absence on cognitive development. *Child Development, 40*, 941–944.

Lane, D. M., and W. P. Dunlap. 1978. Estimating effect size: Bias resulting from the significance criterion in editorial decisions. *British Journal of Mathematical and Statistical Psychology, 31*, 107–112.

Layman, E. M. 1961. Discussion: Symposium: Father influence in the family. *Merrill–Palmer Quarterly, 7*, 107–113.

Leiderman, G. F. 1953. Effect of family experience on boys' peer relationships. Unpublished doctoral dissertaion, Harvard University.

Lessing, E. E., S. W. Zagorin, and D. Nelson. 1970. WISC subtest and IQ score correlates of father absence. *Journal of Genetic Psychology, 117*, 181–195.

Lindgren, H. C. 1980. *Educational psychology in the classroom.* New York: Oxford University Press.

McCord, J., W. McCord, and E. Thurber. 1962. Some effects of paternal absence on male children. *Journal of Abnormal and Social Psychology, 64*, 361–369.

McCord, W., J. McCord, and I. K. Zola. 1959. *Origins of crime.* New York: Columbia University Press.

McDermott, J. F. 1968. Parental divorce in early childhood. *American Journal of Psychiatry, 124*, 1424–1432.

McDermott, J. F. 1970. Divorce and its psychiatric sequence in children. *Archives of General Psychiatry, 23*, 421–427.

Mackie, J. B., D. N. Lloyd, and F. Rafferty. No date reported. The father's influence on the intellectual level of Black ghetto children. Unpublished manuscript, available from J. B. Mackie, Department of Psychiatry and Clinical Psychology Services, Redwood and Green Street, Baltimore, MD 21201. Cited in Shinn, 1978.

Mackler, B. 1969. The little Black school house: Success and failure in a ghetto school. Final report. Department of Urban Affairs, Hunter College of the City University of New York.

McNeal, R. E. 1973. A study comparing the relationship of broken homes to the school success of junior high school students. Doctoral dissertation, George Washington University.

Malmquist, E. 1958. Factors related to reading disabilities in the first grade of the elementary school. *Educational Research, 1,* 69–72.

Markham, L. R. 1976. Influences of handwriting quality on teacher evaluation of written work. *American Educational Research Journal, 13,* 277–283.

Maxwell, A. E. 1961. Discrepancies between the pattern of abilities for normal and neurotic children. *Journal of Mental Science, 107,* 300–307.

Mendes, H. A. 1976. Single fathers. *Family Coordinator, 25,* 439–440.

Mertz, R. E. 1976. The effect of father absence on the development of psychological differentiation in male black Carib students in Belize. Doctoral dissertation, University of Arizona.

Miller, B. A. 1961. Effects of father absence and mother evaluation of father on the socialization of adolescent boys. Doctoral dissertation, Columbia University.

Mitchell, D., and W. Wilson. 1967. Relationship of father absence to masculinity and popularity of delinquent boys. *Psychological Reports, 20,* 1173–1174.

Morrison, E. 1969. Underachievement among preadolescent boys considered in relation to passive aggression. *Journal of Educational Psychology, 60,* 168–173.

Moynihan, D. P. 1965. *The Negro family: The case for national action.* Washington, DC: Office of Policy, Planning and Research, U.S. Department of Labor.

Mueller, C. W., and T. L. Parcel. 1981. Measures of socioeconomic status: Alternatives and recommendations. *Child Development, 52,* 13–30.

Mueller, E. J. 1975. The effects of father absence on word analysis skills among Head Start children. Paper presented at meeting of American Educational Research Association, Washington, DC.

National Education Association. 1970. School marks and reporting to parents. *National Education Association Research Bulletin, 48,* 76–81.

Nelson, E. A., and E. E. Maccoby. 1966. The relationship between social development and differential abilities on the Scholastic Aptitude Test. *Merrill–Palmer Quarterly, 12,* 269–289.

Nichols, R. 1964. Parental attitudes of intelligent adolescents and creativity of their children. *Child Development, 33,* 1041.

Nielson, L. J. 1971. Impact of permanent father loss on the intellectual level, vocational interests, personal adjustment, and career plans of male war orphans. Doctoral dissertation, University of Utah.

Nye, F. I. 1957. Child adjustment in broken and in unhappy unbroken homes. *Marriage and Family Living, 19,* 356–360.

Orthner, D., T. Brown, and D. Ferguson. 1976. Single-parent fatherhood: An emerging lifestyle. *Family Coordinator, 25,* 429–437.

Oshman, H. P. 1975. Some effects of father absence upon the psychological development of male and female late adolescents: Theoretical and empirical considerations. Doctoral dissertation, University of Texas at Austin.

Parish, T. S., and J. C. Taylor. 1979. The impact of divorce and subsequent father absence on children's and adolescents' self-concepts. *Journal of Youth and Adolescence, 8,* 427–432.

Pearlin, L. I., and J. S. Johnson. 1977. Marital status, life strains, and depression. *American Sociological Review, 42,* 704–715.

Pedersen, F. A., B. T. Anderson, and R. L. Cain. 1977. An approach to understanding linkages between the parent–infant and spouse relationships. Paper presented at meeting of Society for Research in Child Development, New Orleans.

Pedersen, F. A., J. Rubenstein, and L. J. Yarrow. 1973. Father absence in infancy. Paper presented at meeting of Society for Research in Child Development, Philadelpha.

Pedersen, F. A., J. Rubenstein, and L. J. Yarrow. 1979. Infant development in father-absent families. *Journal of Genetic Psychology, 135,* 51–62.

Pemberton, D. A., and D. R. Benady. 1973. Consciously rejected children. *British Journal of Psychiatry, 123,* 575–578.

Phelps, D. W. 1969. Parental attitude toward family life and behavior of the mother in one-parent families. *School Health, 39,* 413–416.

Rees, A. H., and F. H. Palmer. 1970. Factors related to change in mental test performance. *Developmental Psychology Monograph, 3,* No. 2, Part 2.

Rosenberg, M. 1965. *Society and the adolescent self-image.* Princeton, NJ: Princeton University Press.

Rotter, J. B. 1966. Generalized expectancies for internal versus external control of reinforcement. *Psychological Monographs, 80,* 1–28.

Rouman, J. 1956. School children's problems as related to parental factors. *Journal of Educational Research, 50,* 105–112.

Rubin, R. H. 1974. Adult male absence and self-attitudes of black children. *Child Study Journal, 4,* 33–46.

Ruble, D. N., and A. K. Boggiano. 1980. Optimizing motivation in an achievement context. In B. Keogh (ed.), *Advances in special education.* Vol. 1. Greenwich, CT: Jai Press.

Rutter, M. 1971. Parent–child separation: Psychological effects on the children. *Journal of Child Psychology and Psychiatry, 12,* 233–260.

Rutter, M. 1979a. Maternal deprivation, 1972–1978: New findings, new concepts, new approaches. *Child Development, 50*, 283–305.

Rutter, M. 1979b. Protective factors in children's responses to stress and disadvantage. In M. W. Kent and J. E. Rolf (eds.), *Primary prevention of psychopathology*. Vol. 3. *Promoting social competence and coping in children*. Hanover, NH: University Press of New England.

Rutter, M., B. Maughan, P. Mortemore, J. Ouston, and A. Smith. 1979. *Fifteen thousand hours*. Cambridge, MA: Harvard University Press.

Santrock, J. W. 1972. Relation of type and onset of father absence to cognitive development. *Child Development, 43*, 455–469.

Santrock, J. W. 1975. Father absence, perceived maternal behavior, and moral development. *Child Development, 46*, 753–757.

Santrock, J. W., and R. L. Tracy. 1978. The effects of children's family structure status on the development of stereotypes by teachers. *Journal of Educational Psychology, 70*, 754–757.

Santrock, J. W., and R. A. Warshak. 1979. Father custody and social development in boys and girls. *Journal of Social Issues, 35*, 112–125.

Santrock, J. W., and P. Wohlford. 1970. Effects of father absence: Influence of the reason for and the onset of the absence. *Proceedings of the 78th Annual Convention of American Psychological Association, 5*, 265–266.

Schaefer, E. S. 1965. Children's reports of parental behavior. *Child Development, 36*, 413.

Schooler, C. 1972. Childhood family structure and adult characteristics. *Sociometry, 35*, 255–269.

Schlesinger, B., and R. Fordres. 1976. Motherless families: An increasing societal pattern. *Child Welfare, 35*, 553–558.

Sciara, F. J., and R. K. Jantz. 1975. Effects of father absence on the educational achievement of urban black children. *Child Study Journal, 5*, 45–55.

Scott, C. V. 1974. The effects of family structure on the academic status of fifth-grade students. Doctoral dissertation, University of Oklahoma.

Shelton, L. A. 1968. A comparative study of educational achievement in one-parent and in two-parent families. Doctoral dissertation, Univsity of South Dakota.

Shinn, M. 1978. Father absence and children's cognitive development. *Psychological Bulletin, 85*, 295–324.

Siegel, S. 1956. *Nonparametric statistics for the behavioral sciences*. New York: McGraw-Hill.

Siegman, A. W. 1966. Father absence during childhood and antisocial behavior. *Journal of Abnormal Psychology, 71*, 71–74.

Smart, L. S. 1977. An application of Erikson's theory to the recovery from divorce process. *Journal of Divorce, 9*, 67–79.

Smith, M. 1972. Model and methodology of the report. In F. Mosteller and D. Moynihan (eds.), *On equality of education*. New York: Random House.

Solari, R. L. 1976. Correlation of one-parent family and achievement scores of children in selected urban central city elementary schools. Doctoral dissertation, University of Michigan.

Solomon, D., J. G. Hirsch, D. R. Scheinfeld, and J. C. Jackson. 1972. Family characteristics and elementary school achievement in an urban ghetto. *Journal of Consulting and Clinical Psychology*, *39*, 462–466.

Spanier, G. B., and R. F. Castro. 1979. Adjustment to separation and divorce: An analysis of 50 case studies. *Journal of Divorce*, *2*, 241–253.

Spenner, K. I., and D. L. Featherman. 1978. Achievement ambitions. *Annual Review of Sociology*, *4*, 373–420.

Starch, D. 1927. *Educational psychology.* Rev. ed. New York: Macmillan.

Stetler, H. G. 1959. Comparative study of Negro and white dropouts in selected Connecticut high schools. Hartford: State of Connecticut Commission on Civil Rights.

Sutherland, H. E. G. 1930. The relationship between IQ and size of family in the case of fatherless children. *Journal of Genetic Psychology*, *38*, 161–170.

Sutton-Smith, B., B. G. Rosenberg, and F. Landy. 1968. Father absence effects in families of different sibling compositions. *Child Development*, *39*, 1213–1221.

Tessman, L. H. 1978. *Children of parting parents.* New York: Aronson.

Thomas, S. D. 1969. A study of environmental variables in the war orphan home and their effects on occupational interest patterns and college success. Doctoral dissertation, University of Southern Mississippi.

Thomes, M. M. 1968. Children with absent fathers. *Journal of Marriage and the Family*, *30*, 89–96.

Tiller, P. O. 1958. Father absence and personality development of children in sailor families. *Nordisk Psychologis Monograph Series*, *9*, 1–48.

Tuckman, J., and R. A. Regan. 1966. Intactness of the home and behavioral problems in children. *Journal of Child Psychology and Psychiatry*, *7*, 225–233.

Valin, E. 1961. La valeur des examens: Etude docimologique realisée au Liban. *Etudes et Documents d'Education*, No. 40. Paris: UNESCO.

Waller, W. W. 1967. *The old love and the new.* 2nd ed. Carbondale: Southern Illinois University Press.

Wallerstein, J. S. 1978. Children and parents 18 months after parental separation: Factors related to differential outcomes. Paper presented at National Institute of Mental Health Conference on Divorce, Washington, DC.

Wallerstein, J. S., and J. B. Kelly. 1974. The effects of parental divorce: The adolescent experience. In E. J. Anthony and C. Koupernick (eds.), *Children at psychiatric risk.* Vol. 3. New York: Wiley.

Wallerstein, J. S., and J. B. Kelly. 1975. The effects of parental divorce: Experiences of the preschool child. *Journal of the American Academy of Child Psychiatry*, *14*, 600–616.

Wallerstein, J. S., and J. B. Kelly. 1976. The effects of parental divorce: Experiences of the child in later latency. *American Journal of Orthopsychiatry, 46*, 256–269.

Wallerstein, J. S., and J. B. Kelly. 1980. *Surviving the break up: How children and parents cope with divorce.* New York: Basic Books.

Wasserman, H. L. 1972. A comparative study of school performance among boys from broken and intact black families. *Journal of Negro Education, 41*, 137–141.

Webb, J. B. 1970. A comparative study of the relation of broken homes to the school success of high school students. Doctoral dissertation, George Washington University.

Weiss, R. 1975. *Marital separation.* New York: Basic Books.

Weiss, R. 1978. Single-parent households as settings for growing up. Paper presented at National Institute of Mental Health Conference on Divorce, Washington, DC.

Weiss, R. 1979. Growing up a little faster: The experience of growing up in a single-parent household. *Journal of Social Issues, 35*, 97–111.

Weissman, M., and E. Paykel. 1972. Moving and depression in women. *Society, 9*, 24–28.

Weitz, H., and H. J. Wilkinson. 1957. The relationship between certain nonintellective factors and academic success in college. *Journal of Counselling Psychology, 4*, 54–60.

Westman, J. D., D. W. Cline, W. J. Swift, and D. A. Kramer. 1970. Role of child psychiatry in divorce. *Archives of General Psychiatry, 23*, 415–420.

Willerman, L., A. F. Naylor, and N. C. Myrianthopoulos. 1970. Intellectual development of children from interracial matings. *Science, 170*, 1329–1331.

Wilson, A. B. 1967. Educational consequences of segregation in a California community (Appendix C3). In U.S. Commission on Civil Rights, *Racial isolation in the public schools.* Washington, DC: U.S. Government Printing Office.

Winston, M. P., and T. Forsher. 1971. Nonsupport of legitimate children by affluent fathers as a cause of poverty and welfare dependencies. Rand Corporation.

Wiseman, R. S. 1975. Crisis theory and the process of divorce. *Social Casework. 56*, 205–212.

Witkin, H. A., R. B. Dyk, H. F. Paterson, D. R. Goodenough, and S. A. Karp. 1962. *Psychological differentiation.* New York: Wiley.

Young, E. R., and T. S. Parish. 1977. Impact of father absence during childhood on psychological adjustment of college females. *Sex Roles, 3*, 217–227.

Zill, N. 1978. Divorce, marital happiness, and the mental health of children. Paper presented at National Institute of Mental Health Conference on Divorce, Washington, DC.

5

Social Mobility Through Marriage and Career

Nancy E. Dunton

*New York State Council
on Children and Families*

David L. Featherman

University of Wisconsin

EDITOR'S OVERVIEW

In American society, people's social positions can be arranged in a hierarchy that reflects the prestige and rewards they are accorded. Critical ingredients in this stratification system, as sociologists have labeled it, are individuals' education, occupation, and income. The place that men and women achieve in this socioeconomic hierarchy has been shown to be related to their parents' status. Although people can, through their own efforts, rise above the station of their family of origin (or fall below it), it has repeatedly been shown that those who achieve high status relative to their peers are more likely to have been born into a family whose status was high among members of their generation. Conversely, those whose status is relatively low are more likely to have been born into a low-status family.

It has also been well documented that employed women tend to congregate in certain "female" occupations that are relatively ill-paying and accorded little prestige, despite the near parity of the sexes in those who graduate from high school and go on to college. Although greater numbers of women have been entering prestigious, male-dominated professions over the past decade, the gap between men's and women's vocational achievements remains large. Women, however, can attain status vicariously through the accomplishments of their husbands (as, indeed, can men through the attainments of their wives).

In this chapter, Nancy E. Dunton and David L. Featherman examine the relative chances men and women have for advancement in the social hierarchy through occupational activity and through marriage. In explaining the relative attainments of men and women, the authors stress the importance of the life-span sociological perspective and the usefulness of the notion of the "socioeconomic life cycle." This approach views achievement as a lifelong, intergenerational process: individuals' vocational attainments throughout their careers are related to their educational attainments in childhood and youth; both, in turn, are linked to their parents' education, income, and occupation. The socioeconomic life cycle thus defines a developmental process that reveals the linkages among the home, the school, and the economy. Simultaneously, the authors note, their life-span analysis is a study of individuals' social mobility—of changes within the stratification system from one generation to the next and of changes over the course of adult life.

In their assessment of men's and women's relative chances for advancement in the social hierarchy, the authors examine two large sets of data: one from a longitudinal study of 1957 high school graduates, and the second from a cross-sectional study of married couples. The authors base their study on the analysis of mobility tables—tables that cross-classify individuals so that the flow of individuals between certain "origins" and "destinations" is revealed. They present several different types of mobility tables. In one, the occupation of each individual's father (origins) is classified as to occupational category; the table displays, for each paternal category, the percentage of their sons and daughters whose current occupations (destinations) fall into each of the same set of occupational categories (outflow). Tables are also presented showing the percentage of individuals in each current occupational category (destinations) who came from each origin or paternal category (inflow). These inflow and outflow tables show *intergenerational* mobility—changes between the occupations of parents and their male and female children. Tables in which men and women are classified according to the category of their first job (origins) and the category of their current job (destinations) show *intragenerational* mobility—changes across individuals' life span.

The same tabular approach is used by the authors to study marital mobility. In these tables, classification involves occupational category of men's and of women's fathers and current occupational level of these men's and women's spouses. Thus, for example, a woman whose husband's occupation is lower in the stratification hierarchy than her father's can be said to exhibit downward marital mobility. Or a man married to a woman whose occupation is higher than his father's exhibits upward marital mobility.

The authors' analyses confirm that, for both men and women,

paternal occupational category and level are associated with the individuals' occupational achievements but also indicate that, overall, individuals exhibited upward intergenerational mobility. That is, at the point at which they entered the labor market, both sexes were higher in the stratification system than were their fathers. Over the course of their vocational careers, three-quarters of the men maintained their occupational position or moved up from it. The women's career histories were found to be quite different. They were far more likely than men to spend part of their lives out of the labor force—a factor that limited their upward mobility. The women also tended to enter female-dominated occupations, which limited their upward mobility still further. As a result, three-quarters of the women retained their original occupational position or moved down from it.

The authors' analyses of mobility through marriage reveal complex results. Overall, they indicate that, due to wives' intermittent participation in the work force and their restriction to gender-segregated occupations, men's opportunity for upward mobility through marriage is limited. For similar reasons, women's chances for upward social mobility are greater through marriage than through their own occupational efforts.

The authors conclude that, after continuity of participation in the labor force and gender-based occupational segregation are taken into account, men and women have similar opportunities for social advancement. One of the challenges presented by their finding is to determine the extent to which "employer tastes" and "employee tastes" contribute to these segregated occupational patterns. Other chapters in this volume (see, e.g., Chapter 2) suggest that the latter are partially responsible for women's preference for female-dominated professions and/or their avoidance of male-dominated ones and that employee tastes have a long developmental history.

For many Americans, one's income, occupation, and education often serve as important marks of achievement. We use these and similar indices in placing ourselves and others in a set of social roles that help identify who a person is, how he or she can be expected to behave, and how others should behave toward the person. Of course, these are only superficial personal characteristics, yet frequently they are the only type of information we have about casual acquaintances. Interestingly, these characteristics sometimes provide enough information to warrant judgments about the relative worth or social standing of persons.

For example, studies of jury deliberations consistently show that foremen tend to be selected from among persons having a professional job (versus a blue-collar one), a college education (versus high school), or a higher economic level. And when Americans are asked to rank their friends and neighbors with regard to their standing in the community, the rankings typically correspond with educational, occupational, and economic characteristics.

Such behaviors by juries and community residents are reflections of what sociologists identify as the *stratification system* in American society. This system includes the social positions, like jobs, and the social rewards or statuses that are accorded to the positions. These statuses include prestige, influence, deference, income, and other "rewards" that recognize the social value of the position and that create hierarchies of inequality across persons who occupy these positions.

According to this sociological perspective, an individual's achievement is indicated through the positions he or she occupies, and has occupied, in the stratification system. Achievement in this sociological sense is structured by the sequence of social positions— sometimes called roles—through which an individual passes from birth to death. Thus, achievement is a lifelong trajectory of role sequences and status attainments in the stratification system.

This research was supported by a grant from the Employment and Training Administration, U.S. Department of Labor (No. 91-55-78-08) and by a predoctoral fellowship from the National Institute of Mental Health (1 F31 MH07718-01). We gratefully acknowledge William Sewell and Robert Hauser for making available to us data collected under a grant from the National Institute of Mental Health (No. MH-06275). Partial support for Featherman was supplied by the Andrew Mellon Foundation while a Fellow at the Center for Advanced Study in the Behavioral Sciences, Stanford, California. Secretarial support was provided by Katy Knorowski.

An important feature of this view of achievement over the life span is that it is an outcome that reflects more than an individual's motivations, aspirations, or values to succeed or get ahead. For example, as social arrangements and institutions change from decade to decade, the sequences and sets of social roles that pattern life courses through the stratification system are altered. Consequently, an individual's opportunities for achievement also vary, motivation notwithstanding. (For an extended treatment of the relationship between continuity and change in achievement across the life course and changes in societal patterns of stratification, see Featherman, 1980.)

This chapter compares the achievements of American men and women through their careers in the economy. We stress the importance of the life-span sociological perspective in explaining the relative achievements of the sexes. In this connection, the notion of the "socioeconomic life cycle" (Duncan, Featherman, and Duncan, 1972) is useful. A representation of this life cycle is diagramed in Figure 5-1.

The socioeconomic life cycle calls attention to achievement as a lifelong, intergenerational process. That is, achievement in the economy through occupational careers is related to scholastic achievements in childhood and youth. In turn, attainments both in school (e.g., grades, degrees, length of attendance) and in the world of work (e.g., occupational advances, earnings) are linked to social background—i.e., to parental socioeconomic achievements through their schooling, occupations, and incomes. Thus, the socioeconomic life cycle calls attention to the dynamic course of achievement from birth to death. It defines a developmental process that mirrors the institutional linkages among home, school, and economy. These institutions provide the sociohistorical context—the macrosystem of the stratification system—that is part of an individual's environment (Bronfenbrenner, 1979). This life-span approach enables us to conclude that the role sequences through which men and women pass in their socioeconomic life cycles are at the core of sex differences in contemporaneous achievement. Simultaneously, our life-span analysis of occupational achievement is a study of social mobility— of movement within the stratification system from one generation to the next and within the career of an individual, from one job to the next. This larger interest in the social mobility patterns of men and women leads us also to consider mobility that occurs through marriage. The economic fortunes of a household are a function of the occupations and earnings of its several members. Similarly, the socioeconomic status and prestige others accord to a household reflect the achievements of its individual members (Alves and Rossi, 1978; Rossi, Sampson, and Bose, 1974). One's worldly achievements can also accumulate vicariously, through the attainments of one's spouse. In

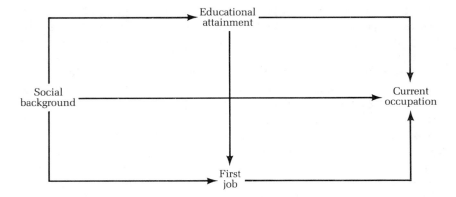

Figure 5-1
Schematic model of the socioeconomic life cycle.

this manner, marriage can serve as a supplementary or substitute channel of social mobility, particularly if the opportunities for achievement through one's own occupational career are limited.

REVIEW OF EXISTING RESEARCH

Sociologists who have studied the social mobility patterns of American men and women have often used the concept of the socioeconomic life cycle as the framework for a multivariate statistical analysis of the process of achievement. Commonly referred to as "status-attainment research" (Sewell, Haller, and Portes, 1969), these statistical models have attempted to explain the well-documented association between individuals' socioeconomic backgrounds (e.g., their parents' socioeconomic statuses) and such current achievements as their educational levels, occupational statuses, and earnings. Factors intervening in the relationship between socioeconomic origins and current achievements include early scholastic performance (e.g., grades and test scores), encouragement for postsecondary education from significant others (e.g., parents, teachers, peers), personal aspirations, and educational attainment as an indicator of qualification or certification for jobs. Differences in earnings among individuals are partially a function of these explanatory variables and of occupational status, number of years in the labor force, and full- or part-time work status. Status-attainment models provide a description of the intergenerational process of achievement. By making comparisons of status-attainment models obtained from data on men and women, sociologists attempt to describe how the sexes attain unequal socioeconomic positions.

Such comparisons have shown that men and women have nearly equal educational attainments—years of school completed. In the general population, males are less likely than females to complete high school, but, of those who graduate and go on to college, women traditionally have not taken advanced degrees as frequently as men. These differentials however, seem to be disappearing. Sewell and Shah (1968) and Alexander and Eckland (1974) have found only minor differences for young men and women in the sociological process whereby educational levels are achieved. Men's attainments (i.e., years completed) were more strongly related to academic performance (e.g., grades in courses) than were women's; whereas, for the latter, socio-economic background was more influential. Women's closer ties to family background indicate that they have less freedom to attain higher (or lower) educational levels than men. Interestingly, if women who achieve higher high school grades were able to convert those grades into additional years of higher education at the same rate as their male counterparts, they would ultimately complete more postsec-ondary education than do men (Carter, 1972).

At a midpoint in the socioeconomic life cycle, men hold jobs at slightly higher socioeconomic levels than do women. This contrasts with the first full-time jobs attained after schooling is completed, when women's average occupational status exceeds men's (Carter, 1972; Featherman and Hauser, 1976; McClendon, 1976; Treiman and Terrell, 1975). Women's work histories do not conform to conven-tional notions of "careers," since they typically remain in the same types of occupations at roughly the same socioeconomic levels across the life cycle. In contrast, men experience considerable upward career mobility from their first jobs (Sewell, Hauser, and Wolf, 1980). Addi-tionally, women continue to rely more on their educational attain-ments than on previous occupational experience for entry into suc-cessive jobs. Aside from these important gender differences in the occupation-based achievement process, the general pattern of attain-ment and mobility is similar for men and women.

Despite some similarity between the genders in the processes of educational and occupational achievement, the differences in their earnings are substantial (Featherman and Hauser, 1976; Suter and Miller, 1973). The conversion of educational attainments and occu-pational status into earnings is far more efficient for men than women, with the effect that a woman must stay in school longer and obtain a better job than her male counterpart in order to earn the same income. Women's full-time earnings have remained at about 60% of men's for the last 25 years. In 1977, for example, the median earnings of year-round, fully employed men was $14,626; for women, $8,618. This gap varies with occupation. Among computer specialists, for exam-ple, women earn 80% of the male median income for full-time, year-round employment; among salaried managers in manufacturing industries, however, women earn 54% of the male median (U.S. Department of Labor, 1979).

How might this discrepancy in the economic achievements of men and women be reconciled with the apparent similarity in the processes that account for their educational and occupational attainments? The answer is that the similarity in occupational attainment is partially misleading. The scales used to index occupational socioeconomic status (Duncan, 1961; Siegel, 1971) do not reveal the extensive segregation of women into different jobs from men. At any socioeconomic level on these scales, the jobs held by men permit them to earn substantially higher incomes and to exercise greater occupational authority and autonomy (McLaughlin, 1978; Wolf and Fligstein, 1979a). Also status-attainment models are applied only to those persons currently in the labor force and do not account for about half of all women who at any time are not employed or are looking for work. This omission has to do with the "selectivity" or "censoring" of the female labor supply: Women who do not find jobs compatible with their schooling and other talents may remain out of the labor force, potentially increasing the similarity of women's and men's occupational attainment processes. Fligstein and Wolf (1978), however, have shown such censoring to be a minor factor in the occupational attainment differences between men and women.

Given the possible importance of differential employment patterns of men and women as an explanation of their unequal earnings and socioeconomic achievements, it is important to understand the extent and basis of gender-segregated occupations. Gender segregation in employment patterns restricts the range of occupational achievement for women, who remain concentrated in semiprofessional, lower white-collar occupations (Grimm and Stearn, 1974). In 1979, 70% of all women would have had to change occupations for their proportion in each job to be equal to their proportion in the labor force as a whole (Williams, 1979). Furthermore, within broad occupational categories (e.g., white-collar), men have higher-status jobs than do women (Grimm and Stearn, 1974; Tyree and Treas, 1974). Although more women have paid employment now than ever before in this century, the growth of female-typed occupations has absorbed most of this increase so that the degree of gender segregation across occupations has not been reduced (Oppenheimer, 1970).

There are two hypotheses, but very little evidence, about the causes of gender-based occupational segregation. The first hypothesis is that of "employee tastes": Women enter a limited set of occupations because they find them attractive for their task content or working conditions. Bose (1973) has noted that women enter jobs that resemble their work at home. Female occupations are characterized by high rates of exit and reentry (Wolf and Fligstein, 1979b). Wolf and Rosenfeld (1978) have suggested that women attempting to coordinate familial and occupational roles try to avoid being penalized for intermittent labor-force activity by entering occupations that are not part of career lines and that have entry qualifications more closely related to formal training than to experience. This conclusion has been supported by Sewell, Hauser, and Wolf (1980).

The second hypothesis about the cause of occupational segregation is that of "employer tastes": Women enter those occupations that employers open to them. Several authors have suggested that, because employers believe women in general to be less qualified for particular occupations or less committed to the labor force, women are channeled into a special labor-market sector that is characterized by a lack of career lines and low levels of economic reward (Beck, Horan, and Tolbert, 1978; Hodson, 1978; Rosenfeld, 1979). Bergmann (1974) has stated that, because women are crowded into a few occupations, the female labor supply is inflated and their wages are lower. There has been no assessment of these alternative explanations of gender segregation in employment patterns.

Not all research on occupational achievements of the genders has used the status-attainment, multivariate-modeling approach. An alternative is the analysis of occupational mobility tables. A mobility table is a cross-classification that displays flows of individuals between "origin" occupations and "destination" occupations. It is conventional to list origin occupations in the rows of the table and destination occupations in the columns. Examples may be seen in Table 5-1, in which the rows show categories of parental occupation (origin) and the columns show categories of their sons' and daughters' current occupations (destination). The portion of the top, labeled "Outflow," shows the percent of individuals from each parental occupation category who fall in the destination or current-occupation category. The portion at the bottom, labeled "Inflow," shows the percent of individuals in each current-occupation category who came from each origin or parental occupation category. This type of table represents *intergenerational mobility*—changes between the occupations of parents and those of their children. Mobility tables can be prepared in which the rows represent individuals' first jobs and the columns represent their current occupations. This type of table summarizes individuals' careers, or *intragenerational mobility*, across the adult life span.

Based on this approach, studies using different samples and different levels of detail in the classification of occupations have found only limited gender differences in intergenerational mobility (Chase, 1975; DeJong, Brawer, and Robin, 1971; Hauser, Featherman, and Hogan, 1977; Rosenfeld, 1979; Stevens, 1977; Tyree and Treas, 1974). However, when Rosenfeld and Sørensen (1977) compared men's and women's intragenerational, or career, mobility, they found that women were less likely than men to be mobile from their early career jobs. That is, they were more likely than men to remain at the same occupational level. This finding corroborates the conclusion of Sewell, Hauser, and Wolf (1980), which was based on the status-attainment approach.

The same tabular approach to achievement has been used to study social mobility through marriage—*marital mobility*. The examples of marital mobility appear in Tables 5-4 and 5-5. Rows (origins) are categories of fathers' occupations; columns (destinations) are categories of spouses' occupations (i.e., wives' occupation, in the case of men's marital mobility; husbands' occupation, in the case of women's marital mobility). Outflow and inflow are computed as explained for Table 5-1.

A number of studies have compared marital mobility with mobility via employment in occupations. These comparisons have focused on the relative ease of achievement through two avenues of social mobility. In particular, some studies have compared men's intergenerational occupational mobility with women's marital mobility (where fathers' occupations are the origins and spouses' occupations are the destinations). For example, Glenn, Ross, and Tully (1974) have found that men's occupational mobility patterns were different for the various categories of origin; by contrast, women's marital mobility patterns were rather uniform regardless of their point of origination. Glenn et al. concluded that the social-class boundaries apparently affecting men's mobility through work did not affect the marital mobility of women. Chase (1975) has demonstrated that women experienced more mobility through marriage than men did through occupational mobility. He emphasized, however, that the differences between men's and women's mobility processes were small.

Tyree and Treas (1974) have also found small differences, relative to the contrast between women's and men's *occupational mobility*. Of course, women's occupational mobility tends to reflect the fact of gender segregation of occupations. This feature of the economy "forces" more women to be mobile from their fathers' occupations (as a point of reference for social origins) than is the case for men. This helps to account for the larger sex difference in the comparison of occupational mobility processes. By contrast, in comparing men's occupational mobility with women's marital mobility, the lesser influence of gender segregation of occupations in the marital mobility of women tends to render it less different from women's occupational mobility. Further, there is an artifactual similarity between men's occupational mobility and women's marital mobility. This arises for two reasons:

Men's and women's fathers hold very similar occupations. And the distribution of husbands' occupations that define the destinations of women in the marital mobility process is nearly identical to the destinations of men in the occupational mobility process, except that some occupations have fewer men who are married.

Because women have the option of not marrying if they cannot make "acceptable" matches, it has been argued that women may experience more upward social mobility through marriage than men do through occupational activity (Glenn, Ross, and Tully, 1974; Rubin, 1968). Contrary to earlier findings, Chase (1975) has reported that downward mobility through marriage is more prevalent for women. Tracing the mobility of women from their fathers' occupations at the time the women were in high school to the status of their husbands' first jobs, Chase has found more downward than upward movement. These findings are reconcilable, since the fathers would have had an opportunity to be mobile in their careers while the new husbands would be at the beginnings of theirs. This raises an important methodological point: Origin and destination occupations must be measured at equivalent points in the life cycle in order to avoid confounding career-mobility differentials with the amount of upward marital mobility.

Men also experience marital mobility, but the sociological literature on this subject is sparse. An unanalyzed issue is whether men defer marriage until they can contract a union that maximizes their achievement opportunities through this avenue. Chase (1975) has simply stated that men and women can experience both occupational and marital mobility. Wilensky (1966) has recognized that there are multiple ladders to social mobility and hypothesizes that intergenerational "occupational sliders" (the downwardly mobile) may try to compensate for their losses through upward marital mobility. Oppenheimer (1977) has suggested that women's occupations are taken into account in the prestige attributed by others to their husbands. There appears to be a tendency for employed spouses to have occupations at quite similar social levels, in terms of the prestige levels of their jobs. Women whose potential occupations are not very different from their husbands' may enter the labor force more frequently than women whose occupational prospects are either at a much higher prestige level or would be much lower than their husbands'.

A STUDY OF OCCUPATIONAL AND MARITAL MOBILITY

As our discussion makes apparent, much remains to be learned about social mobility through marriage and occupation. The increasing degree of women's labor-force participation makes the constant monitoring of their occupational mobility patterns desirable. Further, men's marital mobility opportunities have not been examined. The remainder of this chapter is devoted to such analyses. Our concern is twofold: determining the degree of equality of achievement between men and women in each of these mobility processes, and describing the relationship between occupational and marital mobility opportunities for each sex.

It is reasonable to expect patterns of opportunity for social mobility through marriage to differ from those through occupational activity in two ways. First, there should be more mobility through marriage than through occupational activity for both men and women. The mechanisms that result in individuals' retaining their occupational origins are probably stronger than those that result in individuals entering the occupations of their fathers-in-law. These mechanisms include, for example, specific vocational socialization, inheritance of family business, and job opportunities stemming from introductions to parental colleagues. Second, we would expect occupational and marital mobility patterns to differ because of gender-based occupational segregation, which limits women's opportunities for occupational mobility and therefore their husbands' opportunities for marital mobility.

The tendency of individuals to maximize their positions in the stratification hierarchy through marital and occupational activity may result in congruence between spouses' achievements. Blau and Duncan (1967) have found a positive association between the occupational achievements of spouses. Simkus (1978) has found that this congruence arises as a joint result of the association between socioeconomic background and occupational attainment and because men and women marry others who live near them in socioeconomically segregated neighborhoods or attend the same socioeconomically homogeneous schools. The congruence between spouses' occupations may limit individuals' social mobility opportunities.

As noted above, Oppenheimer (1977) has discussed the social norms that may produce congruence between spouses' occupations by limiting wives' labor-market activity. It is not suggested that men modify their labor-market activity to facilitate such congruence; however, they may opt to defer marriage until a congruent match can be made.

Aside from normative pressures toward status congruence, the amount of opportunity for achievement is limited by the degree of similarity between the two social mobility processes. There should be a positive association between occupational and marital mobility patterns, since both are a part of the same class or stratification system. If the opportunity structures presented through marriage and through occupational activity are similar, we may say that they are redundant or substitutable. That is, individuals encounter the same patterns of opportunity through both activities. A comparison of these two social mobility processes provides information about the degree of rigidity—the lack of opportunity—in the class structure of American society (Giddens, 1975).

Wilensky (1966), however, has suggested that there could be a reciprocal relationship between occupational and marital mobility processes. His "consolation prize" theory of social mobility suggests that failure in one type of mobility may be compensated for through another type. For example, if an individual's occupational attainments are less than his or her parents', then lifestyle expectations may not be met. Consequently, the individual may try to compensate for this loss through marriage. If these social mobility processes are complementary, or represent alternatives, the social-class system is more open—there is more opportunity—than if they are redundant.

Sample and Method

Our analysis of the occupational mobility patterns of men and women rests on a sample of 9000 persons who were interviewed as high school seniors in 1957 and again in 1975 when they were approximately 37 years old. The marital mobility analysis examines a national sample of 30,000 men and their wives. These latter data were collected in conjunction with the March 1973 Current Population Survey conducted by the Bureau of the Census. Occupational origins were measured by the occupation of the head of the household when the respondent was about 16 years old. This variable measures the socioeconomic environment of the home when individuals were developing their occupational aspirations and making decisions about continuing their educations. The head of the household was usually the individual's father. Own occupation and spouse's occupation were the current occupation, or the latest occupation held within a 5-year period if the individual was currently unemployed. By using current or latest occupation, we were able to assess the occupational mobility of more women and the marital mobility of more men, since at any time about half of all women were not in the labor force.

Our analysis also differs from published analyses in that the occupational classification contains 17 categories developed to make explicit the degree of gender segregation in the labor force. The major occupational groups used by the U.S. Census Bureau form the basis of this categorization, which has been further differentiated by the gender-segregated nature of occupations in specific categories. Although the classification of Hauser, Featherman, and Hogan (1977) also contained 17 categories, theirs had little specific gender differentiation.

The statistical technique used in our analysis of these data does not require the categories to be ordered. However, a socioeconomic hierarchy underlies the occupational classification. That is, individuals in categories at the "bottom" of this classification have less social prestige, less education, and lower earnings than do individuals in categories at the "top." For some analytical purposes, we have assigned these 17 categories to six occupational strata. The categories are divided into strata as follows:

1. The upper-nonmanual stratum contains salaried and self-employed professionals, salaried medical workers, teachers, managers, and nonretail sales workers.

2. The lower-nonmanual stratum contains proprietors, clerks, and retail sales workers.

3. The upper-manual stratum contains crafts workers.

4. The lower-manual stratum contains service workers, manufacturing and nonmanufacturing operatives, garment operatives, and laborers.

5. The farm stratum contains all farm workers.

6. The sixth stratum (seventeenth category) consists of all those individuals who have not been in the labor force within the preceding 5 years.

We have noted that a stratification system may be gauged in terms of its degree of opportunity for social advancement. However, not all movement away from occupational origins represents such opportunity. Some mobility occurs as a consequence of technological change. That is, the occupational positions available in a society are not identical at two points in time. Therefore, to judge adequately the openness of a stratification system, it is necessary to separate this "forced" mobility from the rest, sometimes called "free" mobility. This analysis differs from many previous studies in that its statistical method, log-linear analysis, separates more completely forced mobility from free mobility, thus more accurately representing the amount of opportunity available. This method is discussed in greater detail below.

RESULTS OF THE STUDY

Our analysis of occupational and marital mobility begins with a comparison of gross mobility patterns, without separating the two types of mobility. We then compare men's with women's chances for moving from their origins and their chances for moving upward. Finally, after taking forced mobility into account, we examine gender differences in patterns of free mobility. As each type of mobility measure is initially encountered, we present a rather detailed discussion of its interpretation. Subsequently, we emphasize the interpretation of statistical results rather than pursue a detailed examination of the mobility tables.

Occupational Mobility

The flow of individuals between occupational strata represents movement through the social hierarchy as a result of both free and forced occupational mobility. These mobility flows are presented in Table 5-1. The outflows, or row percentages, describe the current-occupation distributions for each of the origin strata (parental occupation). The inflows, or column percentages, consist of the origin distributions for each of the current-occupation strata. The rows of outflow totals represent men's and women's current-occupation distributions, and the columns of inflow totals are their origin distributions.

A comparison of the outflow and inflow totals indicates that, even though men and women have similar origins (parental occupations), their current-occupation distributions are very dissimilar. That so few women are in the craft occupations of the upper-manual stratum highlights the differential employment patterns of the genders. Approximately half of the women have been out of the labor force for at least 5 years, thereby limiting their access to the social rewards associated with occupational positions. For men, the absence of labor-market activity usually indicates temporary or unfortunate circumstances; for women, it is an ordinary part of the life-course organization as family formation balances with the need or desire to work.

Changes in the labor-market structure between individuals' origins and their current occupations can be assessed by comparing the outflow totals with the inflow totals for each gender. The processes of urbanization and industrial change are reflected by the fact that there are fewer men and women currently in farming occupations than had farming origins. Considerable upward mobility is implied by the greater numbers of individuals currently in nonmanual occupations. More men than women entered the upper-nonmanual stratum, whereas more women entered the lower-nonmanual stratum. Not unexpectedly, men were less mobile from their parental occupations than were women, who experienced not only forced mobility as a result of changes in labor-market structure over time but also forced mobility from their origins (usually father's occupation) because of gender-based occupational segregation.

As suggested by the totals, the body of the outflow percentages indicates that men and women from similar occupational origins enter different current occupations. The inflow percentages, however, show that, within any occupational stratum, individuals have similar occupational backgrounds. Thus, men and women are not differentially recruited into their current occupations on the basis of their family origins.

The mobility flows imply that, as groups, both men and women experienced upward intergenerational occupational mobility. Table 5-2 presents gender differences in the amount and direction of occupational mobility. These percentages were calculated from the disaggregated table involving all 17 occupational categories. Mobility is classified as upward or downward on the basis of the underlying socioeconomic hierarchy. The "Same" column presents the percentage of individuals who were occupationally immobile. Interstratum mobility indicates movement across at least one occupational stratum boundary, and intrastratum mobility includes only mobility that occurs within a stratum. For example, mobility from a craft origin to a current occupation of clerical worker would be classified as interstratum mobility (from upper manual to lower nonmanual), but moving from a retail sales origin to a current occupation of clerical worker would be counted as intrastratum mobility (from one lower-nonmanual occupation to another). These mobility percentages do not separate free mobility from forced mobility.

Men were more likely than women to remain in their occupational origins or to move up from them. They were three times more likely than women to experience intergenerational occupational immobility: 1 man in 6 remained in his occupational origin category compared with 1 woman in 17. Over 60% of all men moved up from their occupational origins; only 44% of women did so. In fact, when "Not in labor force" is included as the lowest-ranking category, women were slightly more likely to experience downward mobility than upward. The vast majority of all movement for both genders was interstratum, but a higher proportion of women's mobility was across stratum lines.

The percentage of individuals experiencing downward mobility is highly influenced by the number who are out of the labor force, since that category is at the bottom of the occupational hierarchy. Mobility experiences were more similar among individuals in the labor force than among the sample as a whole. Men and women in the labor force experienced nearly equal rates of upward mobility: about 60% move up. However, women in the labor force remained one-third as likely as men to be immobile and experienced twice the amount of downward mobility. Therefore, at a midpoint in the life cycle, women were less likely than men to retain their origin statuses and were more likely to be downwardly mobile, whether or not they were in the labor force.

Table 5-1

Outflow and inflow percentages for a six-stratum mobility table of movement from origin occupation to current occupation in 1975 for men and women who were 1957 Wisconsin high school seniors (N = 9107)

	Current occupation						
Origin occupation	Upper non-manual	Lower non-manual	Upper manual	Lower manual	Farm	Not in labor force	Total
				Outflow			
Men							
Upper non-manual	71.7	8.2	8.9	10.6	.7	.0	100.0
Lower non-manual	57.9	13.0	15.5	12.8	.6	.2	100.0
Upper manual	46.3	10.0	22.7	19.3	1.2	.5	100.0
Lower manual	41.3	11.2	18.8	27.8	.8	.1	100.0
Farm	28.1	8.2	21.4	23.6	18.5	.2	100.0
Not in labor force	34.7	14.9	20.8	29.7	.0	.0	100.0
Total	47.5	10.1	17.9	20.1	4.3	.2	100.0
Women							
Upper non-manual	35.7	23.4	.6	9.7	1.1	29.5	100.0
Lower non-manual	25.1	29.5	.9	14.3	.9	29.4	100.0
Upper manual	19.4	31.1	1.2	18.8	.9	28.5	100.0
Lower manual	15.9	31.7	1.5	22.5	1.4	27.0	100.0
Farm	16.9	29.0	1.3	21.4	6.7	24.7	100.0
Not in labor force	10.3	24.8	.0	33.3	2.6	29.1	100.0
Total	21.5	29.1	1.1	18.4	2.2	27.7	100.0

Note: See text for explanation of inflow/outflow computations.

Table 5-1 (continued)

Origin occupation	Upper non-manual	Lower non-manual	Upper manual	Lower manual	Farm	Not in labor force	Total
			Current occupation				
			Inflow				
Men							
Upper non-manual	29.2	15.7	9.6	10.2	3.2	.0	19.4
Lower non-manual	14.8	15.7	10.5	7.8	1.6	12.5	12.2
Upper manual	20.1	20.6	26.3	19.8	5.9	50.0	20.7
Lower manual	22.5	28.6	27.2	35.8	4.9	12.5	25.8
Farm	11.6	15.9	23.6	23.0	84.3	25.0	19.6
Not in labor force	1.7	3.5	2.7	3.5	.0	.0	2.3
Total	100.0	100.0	100.0	100.0	100.0	100.0	100.0
Women							
Upper non-manual	31.0	15.0	9.4	9.8	9.3	19.9	18.7
Lower non-manual	14.2	12.4	9.4	9.5	4.7	12.9	12.2
Upper manual	18.9	22.5	22.6	21.5	8.4	21.6	21.0
Lower manual	19.6	28.8	35.8	32.4	16.8	25.8	26.5
Farm	15.1	19.2	22.6	22.4	57.9	17.1	19.2
Not in labor force	1.2	2.1	.0	.8	.1	.7	2.4
Total	100.0	100.0	100.0	100.0	100.0	100.0	100.0

Table 5-2
Percentage mobile from a 17-by-17 mobility table from origin occupation to current occupation in 1975 for men and women who were 1957 Wisconsin high school seniors ($N = 9107$)

| | | Up | | Same | | Down | |
	Total	Inter-stratum	Intra-stratum		Total	Inter-stratum	Intra-stratum
			All individuals				
Men	62.2	55.4	6.8	17.4	20.4	13.6	6.8
Women	44.0	41.6	2.4	6.1	49.9	39.9	10.0
			In the labor force				
Men	61.4	50.8	10.6	17.8	20.8	15.0	5.8
Women	59.9	51.3	8.6	7.6	32.5	25.3	7.2

Note: See text for description of the strata.

Both the description of mobility flows and the discussion of the amount of mobility experienced by men and women have addressed the issue of gender equality in occupational achievements. However, since these measures are influenced by forced mobility resulting from technological change and from gender segregation in the labor market, we have not yet spoken solely to the issue of gender differences in opportunity for social advancement through occupational activity. To do so, we must eliminate the effects of technological change and gender segregation on individuals' mobility chances. These effects are removed from the observed mobility flows by a technique known as log-linear analysis. Through this technique, we can also develop models of the mobility association and outline differences in the free-mobility opportunities of men and women (Bishop, Feinberg, and Holland, 1975).

A Technical Note: Log-Linear Analysis Log-linear analysis is a statistical technique for comparing observed cell frequencies (particular origin/current-occupation combinations) in the mobility table with a set of expected frequencies. The expected cell frequencies are estimated as a function of a series of parameters derived from a model that describes the association in the table. These parameters are based on the odds of an individual being in a particular cell in the mobility table, relative to the odds of being in all other cells. The object of the analysis is to find the model, with the fewest parameters, that adequately explains the association. This is accomplished through an evaluation of the significance of the likelihood-ratio test statistic, G^2, which tests for departures of observed from expected cell frequencies. In this manner, log-linear analysis is similar to the more familiar chi-square statistic. In fact, for large samples, G^2 is distributed as chi-square. The interpretation of this test statistic is analogous to unexplained variance in regression analysis in that the G^2's indicate the degree of association in the mobility table that is not explained by the model. Those G^2's with probability levels (p) greater than .05 indicate models whose expected frequencies are not significantly different from the observed frequencies and thus provide a reasonably good fit to the data. Conversely, G^2's with probability levels less than .05 suggest that the model is significantly discrepant from the observed data and thus does not provide a good fit. By comparing G^2 statistics between alternative models, we test for improvement in the explanation of the association in the mobility table. Another method of assessing the fit of a model is through the index of dissimilarity, Δ. This statistic indicates the percentage of the individuals in the table who would have to change origin-destination cells for the expected cell frequencies to match the observed cell frequencies. Finally, the table can be divided into different mobility patterns, such as occupational immobility or interstratum mobility. The contribution of each of these patterns to the total mobility association is assessed through a comparison of log-linear models.

Intergenerational Gender Differences   The log-linear analysis of gender differences in intergenerational occupational mobility is presented in Table 5-3. A small constant (.01) has been added to each cell to facilitate the estimation of parameters. This fraction adds 5.78 cases to the total and accounts for the fractional sample sizes presented. The notation for the variables in the model descriptions are: origin occupation (F), current or last occupation (O), and gender (G).

Model A1 (FOG), representing the independent effects of the variables, postulates that there is no association between parental (origin) and current occupations or between gender and either origin or current occupation. These theoretical assumptions are known to be unlikely on the basis of previous research: Origin and current occupations are related, and the occupational distributions of men and women do differ. Thus, it is not surprising that the probability level associated with G^2 of this hypothetical model indicates that it does not provide a good description of the association in this mobility table. The only purpose in estimating Model A1 with its simplistic

Table 5-3
Analysis of gender-related differences in a 17-by-17 mobility table from origin occupation to current or last civilian occupation in 1975

	G^2	df	p	Δ
A. Full mobility matrix $(N = 9112.78)$				
Model A1: *FOG*	6388.93	544	.00	34.62
Model A2: *FG OG*	1658.96	512	.00	13.67
Model A3: *FO FG*	5047.57	272	.00	32.14
Model A4: *FO OG*	333.02	272	.01	4.70
Model A5: *FO FG OG*	314.92	256	.01	4.50
Model A2 vs. A5	1344.04	256	.00	9.17
Model A3 vs. A5	4732.65	16	.00	27.64
Model A4 vs. A5	18.10	16	.32	.20
B. In the labor force $(N = 7589.12)$				
Model B1: *FO FG OG*	283.74	225	.00	5.07
C. Movers $(N = 8073.44)$				
Model C1: *FO FG OG*	251.20	239	.29	4.23
D. Movers in the labor force $(N = 6583.80)$				
Model D1: *FO FG OG*	223.35	209	.24	4.82
	Hierarchical decomposition			
Model A5 vs. B1	31.18	31	.49	− .57
Model A5 vs. C1	63.72	17	.00	.27
Model A5 vs. D1	91.57	47	.00	− .32
Model B1 vs. D1	60.39	16	.00	.25
Model C1 vs. D1	21.85	30	>.5	2.29

Note: Symbols F, O, and G refer to the variables origin occupation, current occupation, and gender, respectively. See text for explanation of the models that specify relations among these variables.
Source: Wisconsin longitudinal study of the high school class of 1957. N = 9107.

assumptions is to establish a baseline or reference point, under the assumptions of statistical independence. Subsequent and more plausible models will attempt to account for the association left unexplained by the baseline model (G^2 = 6388.93 in Table 5-3, Panel A).

A two-letter term in the model description represents the interaction, or association, between two variables. For example, the mobility interaction, *FO*, is the association between occupational origin and current occupation. Models A2 through A4 include combinations of two two-way interactions, and Model A5 includes all three two-way interactions. We may assess the amount of association due to each two-way interaction (net of the effect of other interactions) by comparing a model containing only two of the two-way interactions with the model containing all three. The difference between their G^2's is the amount of association in the table due to the omitted interaction. The comparisons of models estimating the association due to each of the omitted interactions are presented at the bottom of Panel A in Table 5-3.

Model A2 (*FG OG*) postulates that gender segregation (or differences in current-occupation distributions) and gender differences in origin-occupation distributions account for the pattern of association found in the mobility table. This model also does not provide an adequate description of the association in the table; the probability of the G^2 indicates that the expected cell frequencies differ significantly from the observed. The delta column, containing the index of dissimilarity, indicates that the expected cell frequencies under Model A2 differ from the observed values by 13%. The comparison of Model A2 with Model A5, shown at the bottom of Panel A, demonstrates that the association between occupational origins and current occupation is a significant omission; it accounts for a significant part of the association in the table.

Model A3 (*FO FG*) posits gender differences in origin distributions and an association between occupational origins and current occupation. This model does not provide an adequate explanation of the association in the table, misclassifying almost one-third of the cases. The comparison of Model A3 with Model A5 indicates that the omitted interaction, gender differences in current occupation, accounts for two-thirds of the association in the table and is a significant omission from an adequate description of that association. The large size of this interaction is expected, since the occupational classification was constructed to emphasize the gender segregation in the occupational distributions.

Model A4 (*FO OG*) generates expected cell frequencies under the hypothesis that there are gender differences in the current-occupation distributions, but that the association between occupational origins and current occupations is the same for both sexes. This model misclassifies less than 5% of the cases and provides a marginally significant description of the association in the table. By comparing Model A4 with Model A5, we find that the omitted interaction, the association between gender and occupational origins, does not contribute significantly to the explanation of the mobility association. Therefore, there are only trivial differences in men's and women's occupational origins. This result coincides both with previous research and with the mobility flows examined above in Table 5-1.

Model A5 (FO FG OG) contains all possible two-way interactions, hypothesizing that the association in the table is due to gender differences in current- and origin-occupation distributions and to the association between origin and current occupations. It provides approximately the same quality of explanation of the association in the table as does Model A4. Because the interaction of gender and occupational origins did not add significantly to the explanation of the association, Model A4 provides the most parsimonious explanation of men's and women's mobility patterns—namely, that these patterns arise as a result of gender segregation in current occupations and because of an association between occupational origins and attainments.

The 5% of the association in the table unaccounted for by either Model A4 or Model A5 is due to the three-way interaction, FOG, which represents gender differences in free-mobility patterns. Although this small difference is marginally significant, the large sample gives our statistical tests the power to detect what may be substantively trivial differences.

The next section of this log-linear analysis partitions the mobility table into distinct types of mobility patterns, e.g., occupational immobility. This partitioning not only outlines the pattern of the mobility association but also may enable us to account for the small gender difference in free-mobility patterns. The association is partitioned by eliminating from the analysis selected portions of the table representing a mobility type. The comparison of all individuals to the subset that experienced a particular type of mobility indicates whether the omitted mobility pattern is a significant part of the total mobility association.

Individuals in the labor force may have a different relationship to their occupational origins from those who are occupationally inactive. As noted above, individuals currently in the labor force have different probabilities of upward mobility from those of all individuals, whether or not they are currently in the labor force. That women have higher rates of occupational inactivity than do men could be the source of the difference in occupational mobility patterns between the genders. The hierarchical decomposition in Table 5-3 that compares Model A5, the full matrix of all individuals, with Model B1, just those in the labor force, indicates that all individuals are not significantly different from those in the labor force. Consequently, differential rates of labor-force inactivity by men and women do not account for a significant portion of the mobility association, and they do not produce the small gender difference in mobility patterns.

Occupational immobility is a theoretically important component of the opportunity for advancement, and men and women differ in their gross rates of immobility. The comparison of the subsample of those who were mobile with all individuals, Model A5 versus Model C1, implies that occupational immobility is a significant part of the mobility association. Additionally, Model C1 provides a good explanation of the association in the table. Thus, men's and women's opportunities for social advancement through occupational mobility are very similar, differing only in that men are somewhat more likely to retain their occupational origins.

Components of Occupational Mobility   Intergenerational mobility to current occupation consists of two components that correspond to parts of the socioeconomic life cycle: mobility from parental origins to first job, or labor-market entry; and mobility from first job to current occupation, or the occupational career. An examination of these components leads to a better understanding of intergenerational mobility patterns and, thereby, of the structure of opportunities for occupational attainment. We are interested especially in the development of differences in men's and women's occupation distributions and in their rates of immobility.

The following discussion of mobility components concentrates on the conclusions to be drawn from a set of analyses that parallel those outlined in detail above. The illustrative character of the preceding section, which introduced the various mobility measures, is replaced by a focus on substantive issues. (Because of this focus, the analytical tables are not presented here; they are available to the interested reader upon request.)

The segregation of men and women into different occupations is apparent in the distributions of their first jobs and is constant over the course of the career. Early in the socioeconomic life cycle, over half of all women were in the lower-nonmanual stratum. By a midpoint in their careers, about half of all women became occupationally inactive—leaving the labor force in equal percentages from all first-job strata. Both men and women moved up from their occupational origins at labor-market entry, but, over the course of their careers, three-quarters of the men retained their first jobs or moved up from them, whereas three-quarters of the women retained the first jobs or moved down. In fact, half of the women in the labor force at a mid-point in their life cycles were still in the occupations they entered at the beginning of their careers. These figures reflect both forced and free mobility in the socioeconomic hierarchy. The tendency to retain one's occupational origin or first job is an important part of the struc-ture of free-mobility opportunities for both men and women, although there are small differences between the genders in rates of immobility both at labor-market entry and in career mobility.

Summary Comment   Were it not for gender segregation in the labor market, men and women would experience nearly identical patterns of occupational mobility. As women from every origin stratum com-bine family roles with careers, they are more likely than men to spend a part of their lives out of the paid labor force, limiting their access to the social-reward system. Gender segregation, resulting from either the employers' or employees' tastes, reduces the chances that women in the labor force experience the immobility and upward mobility that men enjoy. Gender-based occupational segregation and labor-market inactivity are important factors differentiating women's and men's labor-market experiences at all stages of the socioeconomic life cycle.

Marital Mobility

We examine now the structure of opportunity for achievement through a second channel of social mobility—through marital mobility, or movement through the social hierarchy from occupational origins to spouse's current occupation. By marrying, one may gain access to the social-reward structure via the reflected occupational attainments of one's spouse. We have chosen to discuss mobility to the spouse's current occupation, rather than occupation at marriage, in order to promote comparability in the career-mobility content of the measures of origin and spouse's occupations. Analyses not presented here in-dicate that the amount of upward mobility varies according to the measure of the spouse's occupation used, but the structure of free marital mobility opportunities does not. Men's and women's marital mobility flows, shown in Tables 5-4 and 5-5, may be compared use-fully with the occupational mobility flows presented in Table 5-1. The data examined in this analysis are from a 1973 national sample of men in the civilian labor force. Only those men who were in their first marriages, between the ages of 25 and 64, and married to women in the same age range were selected for analysis. Data were also avail-able for the wives of these men.

Table 5-4
Outflow and inflow percentages for a five-stratum marital mobility table for married women: movement from wife's origin occupation to husband's current occupation

Wife's origin occupation	Upper non-manual	Lower non-manual	Upper manual	Lower manual	Farm	Total
			Husband's occupation			
			Outflow			
Upper nonmanual	63.1	9.6	13.9	12.0	1.4	100.0
Lower nonmanual	47.6	13.1	18.2	18.7	2.5	100.0
Upper manual	35.8	11.5	26.3	24.8	1.5	100.0
Lower manual	25.9	10.7	26.9	34.2	2.3	100.0
Farm	22.0	9.2	23.7	32.4	12.7	100.0
Total	35.7	10.7	23.0	26.4	4.3	100.0
			Inflow			
Upper nonmanual	27.7	14.2	9.5	7.1	5.1	15.7
Lower nonmanual	16.2	14.9	9.6	8.6	6.9	12.2
Upper manual	22.1	23.7	25.2	20.7	8.1	22.0
Lower manual	20.3	28.1	32.7	36.3	14.6	27.9
Farm	13.7	19.1	22.9	27.3	65.3	22.2
Total	100.0	100.0	100.0	100.0	100.0	100.0

Source: "Occupational Changes in a Generation Survey," men aged 25–64 in March 1973 and their wives in the same age range. N = 15,061.

The marital mobility flows, which include both free and forced mobility, resemble the occupational flows in the growth of the non-manual strata and the decline of the farm sector. There are fewer husbands or wives currently in farming occupations and more in nonmanual occupations than there are individuals with those origins. Marital mobility flows mirror occupational mobility flows in that men's mobility opportunities are attenuated by the segregation of women (wives) into a restricted occupational range. The occupational attainments of men's spouses are less similar to the men's origins than the occupational attainments of women's spouses are to the women's origins. Approximately half of the men from each origin stratum are married to women who have been out of the labor force for more than 5 years and thus do not provide these men with reflected occupa-

Table 5-5

Outflow and inflow percentages for a six-stratum marital mobility table for
married men: movement from husband's origin occupation to wife's
current occupation

Husband's origin occupation	Wife's occupation						
	Upper non-manual	Lower non-manual	Upper manual	Lower manual	Farm	Not in labor force	Total
Outflow							
Upper nonmanual	21.0	21.1	.5	6.8	.4	50.2	100.0
Lower nonmanual	14.9	23.6	.5	10.2	.5	50.3	100.0
Upper manual	12.0	23.4	.7	14.8	.3	48.8	100.0
Lower manual	8.7	21.9	.8	18.7	.4	49.4	100.0
Farm	7.3	16.5	1.2	24.3	3.6	47.1	100.0
Total	11.5	20.9	.8	16.7	1.2	48.9	100.0
Inflow							
Upper nonmanual	25.8	14.2	8.7	5.7	4.1	14.4	14.0
Lower nonmanual	14.6	12.7	7.6	6.9	4.4	11.6	11.2
Upper manual	22.0	23.5	17.3	18.6	4.5	21.0	21.0
Lower manual	21.3	29.3	27.9	31.3	10.3	28.3	28.0
Farm	16.3	20.3	38.4	37.5	76.7	24.8	25.7
Total	100.0	100.0	100.0	100.0	100.0	100.0	100.0

Source: "Occupational Changes in a Generation Survey," men aged 25–64 in March 1973 and
their wives in the same age range. $N = 15,061$.

tional status or occupationally linked economic rewards. Women,
however, move into the upper-nonmanual and upper-manual strata
more frequently through marriage than they do through their own
occupational activity. Therefore, gender segregation restricts the range
of men's attainments through marriage and expands women's range
relative to their own occupational attainments.

Women are less likely to be socially mobile through marriage than
are men: 15% of women are immobile, whereas about 5% of men
remain in their origin category. Women who experience marital mobility
are twice as likely to move upward (60%) as downward. Men's marital
mobility rates are greatly affected by the number of wives out of
the labor force; about 60% of all men experienced downward mobility. However, among men whose wives were occupationally active,

70% had upward marital mobility. Therefore, individuals whose spouses are in the labor force are very likely to experience upward social mobility through marriage as a result of technological change, gender segregation in the labor market, and free opportunities for marital mobility.

In fact, the mobility that occurs as a consequence of the different current-occupation distributions of husbands and wives is a considerable part of the total amount of mobility. There is no difference in the free-mobility patterns of men and women. After taking forced mobility into account, mobility for either gender is no more likely to be upward than downward. Unlike occupational mobility patterns, the association between occupational origins and spouse's occupation is rather diffuse. Neither immobility nor labor-force inactivity contributes significantly to the pattern of marital mobility. As anticipated, it is easier to retain one's occupational origins—and the social status associated with it—through one's own occupational activity than through marriage.

Summary Comment   Men's and women's opportunities for achievement through marriage differ only as a consequence of gender segregation in the labor market, which restricts the occupational attainments of wives. As women coordinate family formation and occupational careers, intermittent labor-force activity limits their husbands' access to the social-reward system. Independent of these factors, there is no gender difference in opportunities for vicarious achievement through the occupational attainments of spouses. Contrasting with Chase's (1975) conclusion that women experience net downward marital mobility to the husband's first job, we find no evidence that individuals whose spouses are in the labor force experience a net status loss by a midpoint in the socioeconomic life cycle. Indeed, most of these individuals experienced upward marital mobility. Women's chances for upward social mobility are higher through marriage than they are through their own occupational activity. While there is no difference between the genders in free-mobility opportunities through marriage, these opportunities are not structured similarly to those that characterize occupational mobility. It is more likely that an individual can retain his or her origin status through occupational activity than through marriage.

Association Between Occupational and Marital Mobility

We are particularly interested in two issues concerning the association between occupational and marital mobility: first, the limits placed on occupational mobility by the level of a spouse's occupation (and the limits placed on marital mobility by level of one's own occupational attainment); and second, the degree of similarity in the structure of opportunities for social mobility through marital and occupational activity. Because the complex timing of occupational and marital decisions is not included in this analysis, we restrict the following discussion to noncausal statements about the association between these two mobility processes. We are able to make only inferences about the existence of normative limits or the use of marital and occupational activity as compensating social mobility mechanisms. However, we are able to speak directly to the issue of gender differences in opportunity provided by occupational and marital mobility processes. We examine these issues through an analysis of a sample of individuals in their first marriages who were Wisconsin high school seniors in 1957.

An association between the type of occupational mobility and the level of a spouse's occupation would indicate that the pattern of occupational mobility varied with the occupation of the spouse, implying limits on occupational mobility patterns. To examine this question, we have recoded the mobility association into five types: upward across stratum lines, upward within stratum lines, immobile, downward within stratum lines, and downward across stratum lines.

The log-linear analysis of gender differences in the relationship between type of occupational mobility and a spouse's occupational level provides support for an extension of Oppenheimer's (1977) thesis: Congruence between spouses' occupations provides a limit on an individual's occupational mobility opportunities. More concretely, there is a significant association between the type of occupational mobility and the level of a spouse's occupation. Individuals married to spouses in the nonmanual strata are more likely to experience upward occupational mobility than those married to spouses in manual and farm strata. This pattern of mobility would support the convergence of spouses' occupational levels. There is in this association a trivially significant gender difference produced by occupational inactivity; it accounts for only 1% of the association in the table.

An alternative analysis of mobility limits examines the association among occupational origins, own current occupation, and spouse's occupation. This analysis indicates that there is no interaction between occupational mobility and the level of a spouse's occupation once one takes into account patterns of occupational mobility, patterns of marital mobility, and the association between spouses' occupations. Therefore, the association between occupational mobility opportunities and the level of a spouse's occupation is brought about solely by the association between spouses' occupations.

A parallel analysis of the relationship between the type of marital mobility and the level of one's own current occupation indicates that upward marital mobility is more likely for individuals who are currently employed in the nonmanual strata than for individuals who are currently in manual and farm occupations. There is no interaction among occupational origin, spouse's occupation, and one's own current occupation once one takes into account the association among spouses' occupation, occupational mobility, and marital mobility. Thus, marital mobility opportunities differ according to the level of one's own occupational attainments as a result of the association between spouses' occupations.

Summary Comment   These analyses have led to the implication that occupational and marital mobility opportunities are related to and may be limited by the positive association between the spouses' occupational attainments. This association arises through the process of assortative mating (individuals tend to marry those with similar backgrounds whom they meet in socioeconomically segregated settings, e.g., school contexts) and because occupational attainments are positively related to socioeconomic background and educational attainment.

Alternative Mobility Pathways

The degree to which occupational and marital mobility processes provide alternative pathways to social mobility indicates the amount of opportunity for social advancement in a society. If social classes or occupational strata organize the opportunities for occupational mobility differently from those for marital mobility, then individuals will have multiple chances for retaining or improving upon their occupational origins through these two processes. For example, we have seen that it is more likely that individuals will retain their occupational origins through their own occupational activity than through marriage. If there are differences in the ease with which stratum lines are crossed, economically oriented individuals could distribute their energies between occupational and marital activities so as to maximize their social achievements. If the stratum lines are similar, individuals would have less opportunity, fewer behavioral alternatives, to recoup losses or improve upon contemporary attainments. An analysis of the relationship between the type of occupational mobility and the type of marital mobility and of the gender difference in that relationship follows.

There is evidence that individuals use occupational and marital mobility processes as alternative or complementary pathways to social advancement: A considerable fraction of the sample experienced downward mobility through one process and upward mobility through the other. However, there was more support for identical or overlapping mobility patterns, as indicated by a tendency toward congruence between the types of occupational and marital mobility experienced by the individual.

There was a trivial (1% of the association; table not shown), but statistically significant, gender difference in the association between social mobility processes. There was less overlap among men than women and among those in the labor force. Additionally, there was some indication that men move up more frequently through occupational activity than through marriage and that women move up more frequently through marriage than through occupational activity. These differences are probably related to gender-based occupational segregation and labor-market inactivity among women, although it was not possible to test that hypothesis.

Although some evidence suggests that individuals could use occupational and marital mobility as compensatory pathways to social mobility, there is greater support for the similarity of those opportunities. The ease with which individuals are mobile between strata varies little across processes, although the similarity is not absolute. The stratification system, under which both types of social mobility occur, presents only slightly less opportunity for social advancement, combined across mobility processes, for women and for those not in the labor force.

SUMMARY AND DISCUSSION

This chapter has examined the degree of gender-based inequality in two avenues of socioeconomic achievement: occupational mobility and marital mobility. The free-mobility patterns of these processes indicate that men and women have roughly equal opportunity for social advancement. However, occupational segregation by gender attenuates the range of occupations held by women and results in different mobility experiences for men and women. As a result, women's occupational and men's marital mobility patterns are modified so that these individuals experience less immobility and more inter-stratum mobility than they would otherwise. Similarly, the fact that, at any time, about half of all married women are out of the labor force, as they emphasize different adult roles, limits the access that these women (and vicariously, their spouses) have to social rewards.

To a certain extent, individuals may use occupational and marital mobility processes as alternative methods for gaining social status. There is, however, a large degree of redundancy in the opportunity structures presented by these social mobility processes. This redundancy means that an individual has approximately equal chances for upward mobility through marital or occupational activities and that one process can be used only to a limited extent to compensate for a status loss through the other. There is very little difference between the genders in the degree to which these processes represent alternatives for status acquisition.

Our findings underscore the importance of a life-course approach to the study of men's and women's achievements in economic roles and their social mobility through occupational careers and marriage. It is the episodic (rather than continuous) labor-force participation of women, their temporary withdrawal from paid employment as they undertake unpaid roles as homemakers and child-care providers, that militates against achievements that compare equally to men's. But aside from these dissimilar role trajectories that differentiate the life courses of men and women, the structural segregation of women into a restricted range of occupations further limits their relative achievements.

In closing, we note the absence of statistically large and substantively significant gender interactions in mobility patterns and achievement, once the impact of gender-segregated occupational opportunities is taken into account. That is, men and women would achieve equally were it not for sociological features of the economy (e.g., discrimination). By implication, it is not the ways that females are reared—their values, attitudes, aspirations, or motivations in connection with career and marriage—or their biology that governs their mobility chances and socioeconomic achievements vis-à-vis their brothers and husbands. While these factors are associated with the distinctive features of female life cycles, they are less important overall as a basis for the different achievements of the sexes than the (unspecified in our data) set of factors that limits entry of a woman into any and all occupations for which she is qualified.

REFERENCES

Alexander, K., and B. Eckland. 1974. Sex differences in the educational attainment process. *American Sociological Review, 39*, 668–682.

Alves, W. M., and P. H. Rossi. 1978. Who should get what? Fairness judgments of the distribution of earnings. *American Journal of Sociology, 84*, 541–564.

Beck, E. M., P. M. Horan, and C. M. Tolbert II. 1978. Stratification in a dual economy: A sectoral model for earnings determination. *American Sociological Review, 43*, 704–720.

Bergmann, B. R. 1974. Occupational segregation, wages and profits when employers discriminate by race or sex. *Eastern Economic Journal, 1*, 103–110.

Bishop, Y. M., S. E. Feinberg, and P. M. Holland. 1975. *Discrete multivariable analysis: Theory and practice*. Cambridge, MA: MIT Press.

Blau, P. M., and O. D. Duncan. 1967. *The American occupational structure*. New York: Wiley.

Bose, C. E. 1973. Jobs and gender: Sex and occupational prestige. Unpublished doctoral dissertation, Center for Metropolitan Planning and Research, Johns Hopkins University.

Bronfenbrenner, U. 1979. *The ecology of human development: Experiment by nature and design*. Cambridge, MA: Harvard University Press.

Carter, N. D. 1972. The effects of sex and marital status on a social-psychological model of occupational status attainment. Unpublished master's thesis, University of Wisconsin.

Chase, I. D. 1975. A comparison of men's and women's intergenerational mobility in the United States. *American Sociological Review, 40*, 483–505.

DeJong, P. Y., M. J. Brawer, and S. S. Robin. 1971. Patterns of female intergenerational occupational mobility: A comparison with male patterns of intergenerational occupational mobility. *American Sociological Review, 36*, 1033–1041.

Duncan, O. D. 1961. A socioeconomic index for all occupations. In A. J. Reiss, Jr. (ed.), *Occupations and social status*. New York: Free Press.

Duncan, O. D., D. L. Featherman, and B. Duncan. 1972. *Socioeconomic background and achievement*. New York: Seminar.

Featherman, D. L. 1980. Schooling and occupational careers: Constancy and change in worldly success. In O. G. Brim, Jr., and J. Kagan (eds.), *Constancy and change in human development*. Cambridge, MA: Harvard University Press.

Featherman, D. L., and R. M. Hauser. 1976. Sexual inequalities and socioeconomic achievement in the U.S., 1962–1973. *American Sociological Review, 41*, 462–483.

Fligstein, N. D., and W. C. Wolf. 1978. Sex similarities in occupational status attainment: Are the results due to the restriction of the sample to employed women? *Social Science Research, 7*, 197–212.

Giddens, A. 1975. *The class structure of the advanced societies*. New York: Harper and Row.

Glenn, N. K., A. A. Ross, and J. C. Tully. 1974. Patterns of intergenerational mobility of females through marriage. *American Sociological Review, 39*, 683–699.

Grimm, J., and R. Stearn. 1974. Sex roles and internal labor market structure: The female semi-professions. *Social Problems, 21,* 690–705.

Hauser, R. M., D. L. Featherman, and D. P. Hogan. 1977. Sex in the structure of occupational mobility in the United States, 1962. In R. M. Hauser and D. L. Featherman (eds.), *The process of stratification.* New York: Academic.

Hodson, R. 1978. Labor in the monopoly, competitive and status sectors of production. *Politics and Society, 8,* 429–480.

McClendon, M. J. 1976. Sex and occupational status. *American Sociological Review, 41,* 52–64.

McLaughlin, S. 1978. Occupational sex identification and the assessment of male and female earnings inequality. *American Sociological Review, 43,* 909–921.

Oppenheimer, V. K. 1970. *The female labor force in the United States: Demographic and economic factors governing its growth and changing composition.* Population Monograph Series, No. 5.

Oppenheimer, V. K. 1977. The sociology of women's economic role in the family. *American Sociological Review, 42,* 387–406.

Reiss, A. J., Jr. (ed.) 1961. *Occupations and social status.* New York: Free Press.

Rosenfeld, R. A. 1979. Race and sex differences in career dynamics. Paper presented at meeting of American Sociological Association, Boston.

Rosenfeld, R. A., and A. Sørensen. 1977. Sex differences in patterns of career mobility. Institute for Research on Poverty, Discussion Paper No. 392–77. Madison: University of Wisconsin.

Rossi, P. H., W. A. Sampson, and C. E. Bose. 1974. Measuring household social standing. *Social Science Research, 3,* 169–190.

Rubin, Z. 1968. Do American women marry up? *American Sociological Review, 33,* 750–760.

Sewell, W. H., A. O. Haller, and A. Portes. 1969. The educational and early occupational attainment process. *American Sociological Review, 34,* 82–92.

Sewell, W. H., R. M. Hauser, and W. Wolf. 1980. Sex, schooling and occupational careers. *American Journal of Sociology, 86,* 551–583.

Sewell, W. H., and V. P. Shah. 1968. Parents' education and children's educational aspirations and achievements. *American Sociological Review, 33,* 191–209.

Siegel, P. M. 1971. Prestige in the American occupational structure. Unpublished doctoral dissertation, University of Chicago.

Simkus, A. 1978. Residential segregation by occupation and race. *American Sociological Review, 43,* 81–92.

Stevens, G. 1977. Women's intergenerational occupational mobility: A new perspective. Unpublished master's thesis, Carleton University, Ottawa.

Suter, L., and H. Miller. 1973. Income differences between men and career women. *American Journal of Sociology, 78,* 962–974.

Treiman, D. J., and K. Terrell. 1975. Sex and the process of status attainment: A comparison of working women and men. *American Sociological Review*, 40, 174–220.

Tyree, A., and J. Treas. 1974. The occupational and marital mobility of women. *American Sociological Review*, 39, 293–302.

U.S. Department of Labor. 1979. *The earnings gap between men and women*. Ray Marshall, Secretary. Women's Bureau, A. Herman, Director. Washington, DC: U.S. Government Printing Office.

Wilensky, H. 1966. Measures and effects of social mobility. In N. J. Smelzer and S. M. Lipset (eds.), *Social structure and mobility in economic development*. Chicago: Aldine.

Williams, G. 1979. The changing U.S. labor force and occupational differentiation by sex. *Demography*, 16, 73–87.

Wolf, W. C., and N. D. Fligstein. 1979a. Sex and authority in the work place. *American Sociological Review*, 44, 235–255.

Wolf, W. C., and N. D. Fligstein. 1979b. Sexual stratification: Differences in power in the work setting. *Social Forces*, 58, 94–107.

Wolf, W. C., and R. A. Rosenfeld. 1978. Sex structure of occupation and job mobility. *Social Forces*, 56, 823–844.

6

The Academic Performance of Afro-American Children

A. Wade Boykin

Howard University

322

EDITOR'S OVERVIEW

As a group, Afro-Americans tend to complete fewer years of formal schooling than White Americans and to score below their White counterparts on standardized tests and other measures of academic achievement. The sources of these discrepancies are a matter of continuing controversy. Although some investigators contend that they reflect, in part, an innate difference between the two racial groups in certain cognitive capacities, and others have completely ruled out this contention, the majority view among behavioral scientists appears to be that the evidence is not definitive enough to permit any conclusions to be drawn about the role of genetic factors (Loehlin, Lindzey, and Spuhler, 1975).

In any event, there is agreement that the life experiences of Afro-Americans are critical determinants of their lower educational and vocational attainments. But even here there is controversy. One influential point of view has been that factors associated with the depressed socioeconomic circumstances of many Black families have resulted in the failure of many Black youngsters to acquire the necessary cognitive skills to do well in school or the appropriate attitudes and supportive behaviors that facilitate school performance.

In this chapter, A. Wade Boykin takes issue with this deficit theory and the rationale of intervention programs designed solely to improve the performance of Black students by remediating their purported deficiencies. Although these programs and the theory that inspired them may be well-intentioned, Boykin contends, they reveal ethnocentrism on the part of individuals who have embraced a Euro-American world view and interpret all peoples through their own cultural lens. He proposes, instead, that there is an intact Afro-American culture whose origins may be found in Africa, a culture that has its own integrated system of beliefs, values, and behavioral styles. This system conflicts in crucial ways with the dominant Euro-American tradition, thus presenting the Afro-American with the challenge of trying to reconcile the demands of two incompatible cultures. Further compounding their dilemma, Black Americans must find ways of coping with racial discrimination and economic oppression.

The clash between cultures, Boykin persuades us, is particularly acute for Black children from working-class backgrounds. These children enter school with their own characteristic repertoire of behavioral styles, to be faced with teachers whose values and expectations are typically those of the White middle class and whose educational practices are designed around the middle-class "mainstream" child. Efforts to make the child behave "properly," all too often unsuccessful, replace teaching the child academic skills. Predictably, the frequent result is mutual misunderstanding, mistrust, and a contest of wills in which everyone loses—the teacher, the child, and, ultimately, society at large.

It is only blindness to cultural differences, the author argues, that insists that the child must be remolded to fit the schools rather than the reverse. From his analysis of Black cultural styles, he has developed a number of concrete suggestions about the ways in which classroom practices and curricular materials might be modified to better serve the needs of Afro-American children. Included among his prescriptions is the necessity of greater understanding and acceptance of Black cultural reality on the part of school personnel, researchers, and policy makers. The mirror that the author has held up to "mainstream" readers of the prevailing values in our society, as well as his portrait of Afro-American culture, should contribute to the development of this cultural sensitivity.

$\boxed{\text{T}}$ he evidence documenting the failure of Afro-Americans to achieve academically at the same level as their Euro-American counterparts is overwhelming in its quantity and consistency. In the classic Coleman report (Coleman, Campbell, Hobson, McPartland, Mood, Weinfeld, and York, 1966), for example, Black children in a nationwide sample scored on the average 1 standard deviation below White children on several different standardized achievement tests. These differences were demonstrated across all school grades and in all regions of the country. In a more recent national survey, Hare (1979) reported poorer achievement-test performance among Black fifth- and tenth-graders, even with socioeconomic class, sex, and region held constant. Intensive investigations conducted in specific localities reveal the same picture (e.g., Ashbury, 1978; Hare, 1980; Ogbu, 1977; Smith, 1979).

Low academic achievement is manifested in other ways than test performance. The school-dropout rate is alarmingly high among Afro-American youths. Tucker, Jackson, and Jennings (1979), for example, cite evidence showing that, by age 17, the dropout rate among inner-city Black youths is more than three times the rate for Whites. Similar findings are reported by Norton (1971).

The question of the factors that bring about the failure of Afro-Americans to achieve academically at the same level as the White majority has generated a considerable amount of research and has prompted often passionate debates. The various solutions of the problem that have been proposed have led to social intervention programs of enormous proportions and wide-ranging socioeconomic implications.

Despite the attention that has been given to the plight of Afro-American youths over the past two decades, opinion remains divided about how to account for their academic difficulties and how best to alleviate them. The most popular type of explanation, which might be labeled the person-centered or victim-blame (Ryan, 1971) approach, presumes that performance deficiencies are to be found in the individual and the inadequacy of his or her prior life experiences; once the appropriate repairs are made, the individual should fit better into the traditional educational system. Other observers, representing a cultural-difference approach, argue that the educational process has been insensitive to the cultural skills and styles of Afro-Americans; consequently, educational practices should be altered to accommodate these attributes. Still others view the educational process as part and parcel of an overarching social system that is designed to preserve the status quo and, as a consequence, oppresses and exploits the underprivileged. It follows that, unless radical structural transformation of the social order takes place, there is no hope of altering the academic and vocational achievements of such groups.

In this chapter, it will be argued that the traditional person-centered, victim-blame approach has little to offer because it is misdirected and noncomprehensive, being particularly remiss in ignoring the nature of the Afro-American psychological experience (Boykin, 1977a, 1979). The other two approaches—the cultural-difference and social-structural perspectives—have been gathering an increasing number of supporters in recent years. These views, however, have not been without their detractors. The cultural-difference model has been faulted for being too simplistic and for failing to incorporate the larger societal picture into its explanatory framework. The social-structural model has been criticized for being unduly pessimistic and for ignoring the dynamics of the educational process. Despite their shortcomings, these latter two perspectives retain considerable explanatory power. The intent of this chapter is to fuse these two complementary approaches in an attempt to provide a framework for reinterpreting the performance deficits of Afro-Americans and for suggesting the ways in which educational practices might be redirected.

A brief review of the three approaches outlined above and the major criticisms directed at each will be presented before a synthesis is attempted. The discussion proceeds on the basis of certain simplifying assumptions. First, I assume that race and class are not explanatory variables per se; rather, each serves as shorthand notation for a complex of social processes with diverse origins. Second, no attempt will be made to disentangle race from class since, in American society, they are inevitably confounded (Silverstein and Krate, 1975). Thus, when reference is made to Black and White people, the intent is to signify two groups who have generally had divergent socioecological and cultural experiences. My responsibility will be to characterize these experiences while avoiding the complication of discerning what is due to race and what is due to class. Third, my focus will be almost exclusively on Afro-Americans in the United States. Although some observations may be applicable to other peoples of African descent or to members of other ethnic and racial minorities in this country, the experience of each group is to some extent unique.

TRADITIONAL APPROACH

The traditional approach posits that Afro-American youth suffer from deficiencies that result in their poor performance. Beginning in the 1960s under the banner of cultural deprivation or disadvantage, a profusion of specific explanations appeared that were consistent with this traditional perspective. These explanations fell into three discernible subclasses. One group of investigators proposed that Afro-Americans exhibit cognitive deficits such as inadequate language skills of the type required for academic success, inability to think in abstract terms, or poor perceptual discrimination skills (e.g., Ausubel, 1966; Bereiter and Engelmann, 1966; Deutsch, 1965; Marans and Lourie, 1967).

Others have suggested deficits in personality due to "emotional scars" brought about by discrimination and poor living conditions: mistrust of authority, self-depreciation, lack of impulse control, a lessened sense of personal control over the environment, defensiveness, inwardly turned reactions to stress, unwillingness to follow adult-generated rules—to cite only the most prominent (Ausubel and Ausubel, 1963; Battle and Rotter, 1963; Davidson and Greenberg, 1967; Pavenstedt, 1967; Silverstein and Krate, 1975). Motivational deficits have also been proposed. Minuchin (1971), for example, has suggested that, in an academic context, Black children have dampened intellectual curiosity, and other investigators have proposed that Black children have failed to develop an adequate degree of intrinsic or achievement motivation (e.g., Hunt, 1968; Katz, 1973; McClelland, 1961).

The causes of these purported deficiencies are typically believed to be rooted in the inadequate socialization experiences of Black children. Black parents are said not to provide an appropriate intellectual atmosphere in the home or the kinds of toys, books, and so forth that promote intellectual growth (e.g., Ausubel, 1966; Deutsch, 1963; Marans and Lourie, 1967; Trotman, 1977). There is said to be a greater emphasis on obedience to arbitrarily designated rules, reliance on physical forms of discipline, and less parental warmth in the home (Hess, 1970; Radin and Kamii, 1965; Silverstein and Krate, 1975).

All of these characteristics are assumed to be exacerbated by or otherwise linked to a purported lack of structural integrity in the Black family, particularly in homes lacking a male head of household (Ausubel and Ausubel, 1963; Moynihan, 1965; Rainwater, 1966; Schultz, 1969). Outside the home, Black children are said regularly to fall prey to the influence of inappropriate role models and to become increasingly cynical and alienated by their abject life circumstances (Proshansky and Newton, 1973; Silverstein and Krate, 1975).

All in all, the picture that emerges is of Black children growing up in a web of social pathology and inadequacy that leaves them ill-equipped to meet academic demands. As Rollins, McCandless, Thompson, and Brassell (1974) have described it, school failure comes early to the inner-city Black child and lays down a foundation for future failure and lack of interest in the classroom.

In recent years, this general line of argument has been shown to be vulnerable to criticism on a number of fronts. Evidence supporting claims of deficiencies in Black children and their families is often weak, as are the data supporting the presumed relationships between academic performance and the characteristics of Black students. For example, W. C. Banks' (1976, 1979) examination of the empirical literature indicates that no evidence exists to support the contention that Blacks are lower than Whites in achievement motivation or in self-esteem or that these constructs can be used to explain the divergent achievements of Blacks and Whites. The contention that Afro-Americans are linguistically deficient is challenged by the work of Labov (1970, 1972) and others (e.g., Smitherman, 1977; Stewart, 1970).

The notion that the Black family is epitomized by pathology, weakness, and disorganization has also been effectively countered by several scholars (Allen, 1978; Billingsley, 1968; Blackwell, 1975; Hill, 1972). More particularly, the evidence refutes the contention that children reared in single-parent homes (which, at least in the past, were found more frequently among Blacks than among Whites) exhibit marked differences in academic achievement from children reared in two-parent homes (see Chapter 5, this volume, for a review of these data).

Although the argument that Black parents provide inadequate socialization experiences for their children cannot be sustained, the possibility that they do a less effective job in rearing their children to be like the White middle-class ideal demanded in the classroom remains a viable position.

If Black children do not exhibit many of the deficiencies attributed to them, it is not surprising that school busing programs and so-called compensatory education programs, such as Head Start, which were designed to remedy these deficiencies, have failed to have the beneficial effects that were expected of them (Bradley and Bradley, 1977; Epps, 1980; Ogbu, 1978; Stephan, 1978; Zigler, Abelson, and Seitz, 1973).

The seeming failure of compensatory programs prompted many social scientists to conclude that the extent of deprivation and the depth of social inadequacy of Black children were far greater than they had anticipated and called for earlier and more drastic forms of intervention (e.g., Seltzer, 1973). In programs inspired by such conclusions, parents were trained in "appropriate" parenting skills or, in some cases, infants or toddlers were taken away from the home for specified daily periods in order to experience more "intellectually stimulating" interactions with adults. Some of these programs did have positive effects on cognitive measures (e.g., Project Home Start, Scott, 1973; the Milwaukee Project, Strickland, 1973). However, it can be argued that the ecological interventions represented by such programs are socially unethical, attempting to alter the very social fabric of a people and serving to undermine their humanity (Gay, 1975). Yet such programs were implemented, with the apparently sincere conviction that no meaningful, coherent social system governed the lives of Black people and no damage would be done by intervening in what was no more than a "culture of poverty."

Those who have imposed deficit explanations on the psychological functioning of Black children have gone to great lengths to portray what is lacking, deficient, and inferior. In doing so, they can be faulted for failing to consider the adaptiveness and integrity of Afro-American culture (Boykin, 1979). It is largely because of the dehumanizing and degrading implications of this perspective that it has been called into question (J. Banks, 1976; Baratz and Baratz, 1970; Billingsley, 1968; Gay, 1975; Lightfoot, 1976).

These person-centered explanations further imply that it is the victim who must change and who must be blamed for not changing (Ryan, 1971; Caplan and Nelson, 1973). This scheme is rejected by many because it fails to implicate in any meaningful way the wider institutional context. People don't have social problems; social orders do. Exclusive concentration on the victim rather than on that which is doing the victimizing will produce woefully insufficient intervention programs if the goal is to eliminate the disparity between Black and White youth.

CULTURAL-DIFFERENCE APPROACH

The cultural-difference view has posited that the academic difficulties of Afro-Americans result not from social and cultural deficiencies but from a cultural conflict between the values, behavior patterns, and performance styles demanded in their home and immediate ecological environments and those required in academic settings (Baratz and Baratz, 1970; Gay and Abrahams, 1972; Hale, 1980; Inkeles, 1966; Stewart, 1970; Williams, 1974). At first glance, some versions of a cultural-deficiency position do not appear to be inconsistent with the cultural-difference approach. Hess (1970), for example, has suggested that Black children, particularly those from impoverished backgrounds, acquire a systematic set of attitudes and patterns of learning that grows out of their proximal socialization experiences and helps them to survive in their immediate environments. He further acknowledges that the socialization such children receive arises from a social and cultural matrix that has the family at its hub. However, he goes on to propose that these learning styles and attitudes maladaptively serve the Afro-American child in his encounters with the schools. A similar position has been taken by Whiteman and Deutsch (1968) and Radin and Kamii (1965), among others. The clear implication of this position is that success would not be possible unless Black children were somehow resocialized to eliminate their maladaptive and inappropriate behavioral and attitudinal orientations.

The cultural-difference view can be contrasted with this latter position in several important and interlocking ways. First, the cultural-difference approach proposes that Black peoples' attitudes and behaviors are shaped less by the ravages of poverty and racism per se, leading to coping strategies that would be pathological in "normal" contexts, but more by the intrinsic character of an intact cultural experience transmitted through generations of Black people and linked to their ancestral African heritage. The Black experience should thus be viewed as representing a "fully adequate system of behavior" (Baratz and Baratz, 1970) that is just as sophisticated, coherent, and complex as that of any other culturally identifiable group. Thus, the argument goes, the onus of responsibility must fall on the school for the failure of Black children. Black children are not deviant, but different. Black children are not ignorant; schools are ignorant of these children's cultural needs. Black children's behavior patterns are not symptomatic of psychological weakness, but of psychological strength (Baratz and Baratz, 1970; Hilliard, 1974; Miller, 1973). In failing to take Black culture into consideration in designing pedagogic formats, schools are doing Black children a moral disservice. Black children can and will learn if they are taught in culturally appropriate ways.

Adherents of the cultural-difference perspective have argued compellingly against traditional notions of psychological deficit. However, this point of view has also attracted its share of critics. Its major limitation at present is its lack of elaboration. Yet to be specified are the stylistic manifestations attendant on the Black cultural experience, the philosophical principles or system of values that provides the structure for organizing the child's psychological repertoire into a coherent and intelligible matrix, and the ways in which standard school curricula and teaching practices interfere with Black children's academic and task performance. Indeed, relatively little systematic documentation or corroborative empirical evidence has been gathered to support the contention that the needs and styles of Black children are at odds with standard educational practices, and proposals about how to accommodate such styles in the schools have not been developed. The cultural perspective remains a plausible approach whose promise has yet to be fully realized.

SOCIAL-STRUCTURAL APPROACH

A particularly lucid summary of the social-structural position has been offered by Persell (1977). She argues that previous explanations of Blacks' academic performance have been insufficient for at least two essential reasons. First, too much emphasis has been placed on locating the causal influences in individuals per se—be these influences construed as strengths or weaknesses—when the more proper emphasis is on the social contexts impinging upon these individuals. Furthermore, person-centered explanations have essentially overlooked the fact that cognitive achievement is not the only outcome of formal schooling and may not even be the most important outcome. Education is inextricably linked to economic and political forces in the wider society. Persell argues that analysis must start with and concentrate on the character of the system of social and economic stratification in this society and how this system maintains and reproduces itself over time. She states that this perpetuation occurs principally through the existence of a shared belief system in the dominant group, a package of commonly held ideologies. These ideologies extend into the educational system, this system serving in turn to perpetuate and legitimate the "structure of dominance" in American society. Since schools by and large serve the interests of the prevailing ruling order, schools consequently serve to preserve the economic, political, and social status quo and to keep Afro-Americans in their historical position at the bottom of the socioeconomic hierarchy.

Thus, if we wish to understand the poor academic performance of a group low in the structure of dominance, a macrolevel analysis is called for, in which an attempt is made to understand the influence of the ruling order's ideologies in determining educational practices and structures. Teachers, administrators, and researchers are successful participants in society and are likely to have internalized the prevailing ideologies. These ideologies, Persell notes, in turn influence how children are taught, what is expected of them, and what they learn. Thus, teachers and other personnel react toward children based on the attributes presumably associated with their socioeconomic status, sex, or race. If they believe, for example, that lower-class children are unintelligent or unteachable, they will treat them as such and be likely to elicit the behaviors that confirm their convictions. These teacher-expectancy effects can be expected to influence children's images of themselves, so the process becomes self-sustaining.

The adverse effects of teacher expectancies on the academic performance of lower-status children are only a part of the social-structuralist arguments. Advocates of this position (e.g., Bowles and Gintis, 1973, 1976; Carnoy, 1974; Jencks, Smith, Acland, Bane, Cohen, Gintis, Heyns, and Michelson, 1972; Persell, 1977) contend that schools are set up to reproduce the structures and demands of the workplace and to prepare people for their places in the occupational hierarchy. Thus, as Bowles and Gintis (1973, 1976) have argued, we should expect to find different patterns of socialization in schools populated by youths from different social levels, employed as a means of preparing children for and channeling them into their assigned positions in the social and economic strata. Specifically, schooling is organized for lower-class children to foster obedience to rules, docility, and subordination and to teach them to expect negative sanctions for disobedience to prepare them for the kinds of sanctions they will receive in their vocational lives. Schools serving children from middle- and upper-class backgrounds foster initiative, internalization of organizational goals, self-reliance, assertiveness, and responsiveness to such positive incentives as increased status and salary. Schools simultaneously promote the meritocratic ideal that life success is bestowed on individuals who are talented and who work hard. Their task is thus to convince individuals from the lower strata of the legitimacy of inequality and that their failures are their personal responsibility. As Carnoy (1974) has put it, "formal schooling is an important component of the capitalist system primarily as an allocator of social roles and only secondarily as a transmitter of cognitive knowledge" (p. 344).

A variant of the social-structural stance has been provided by Ogbu (1977, 1978), who argues for the preeminence of race as opposed to class stratification in determining the life outcomes of Afro-Americans. Racial stratification operates principally through the imposition of vocational barriers that have historically denied Black people access to higher-status occupations. Ogbu further proposes that Black children become aware of this racial caste system early in life and realize that school achievement will not pay off in the attainment of desirable jobs. Rather than passively acquiescing to being molded by the educational system, they are apt not to put forth the effort and instead channel their energies into nonmainstream activities in order to achieve success. If they do attempt to succeed in the educational arena, they choose to adopt personal styles of behavior quite different from those of White middle-class children. In trying to negotiate their way through school, Black children are more apt to utilize deference, compliance, and subservience—"skills" picked up initially from their parents—as opposed to learning to be competitive, industrious, and persistent in school-related activities (Ogbu, 1977). For the same reasons, Black parents have come to prepare their children for the lower rungs on the social-economic ladder and thus do not give them adequate encouragement at home for the development of cognitive, motivational, and language skills necessary for adequate academic performance. These factors make it easier for schools to carry out their designated function within the caste system.

The social-structural view provides a highly cogent descriptive analysis of the factors leading to the academic failures of Black children, but is devoid of a viable prescriptive component. The absence of suggestions of concrete strategies for teaching these children seems attributable to the essentially pessimistic stance taken by these theorists. Unless the structure of society is radically transformed, it is tacitly or explicitly assumed, attempts to design more effective schools are bound to fail. Some (e.g., Jencks et al., 1972) have gone so far as to argue that schooling and cognitive outcomes are so irrelevant to occupational success that formal education is an unnecessary exercise for Black children.

These views, I contend, are unduly extreme. Although for Blacks (as for women—see Chapter 5, this volume), education does not "pay off" at the same rate as for Whites, the claim that it has no payoff in contemporary society is not supportable. It would be unfortunate if educators, researchers, and social planners resigned themselves to the status quo or discontinued their efforts to find more effective ways of promoting cognitive skills and improving academic performance in Black children, waiting for society as a whole to reform itself.

As an explanation of the academic problem of Afro-American youth, the social-structuralist position leaves much to be desired. Teacher expectancies are often evoked as the vehicle by which the schools discourage children's academic achievement. Although such an explanation cannot be dismissed out of hand, its credibility is strained when it is recognized that empirical support for the phenomenon is not particularly robust. Several recent studies have failed to substantiate the initial claims of Rosenthal and Jacobsen (1968) for the unilateral impact of teacher expectancies on children's performance or have revealed that the putative effects are not pronounced (Flemming and Anttonen, 1971; Rubovits and Maehr, 1973).

It should also be noted that no convincing evidence can be found to support the claim that Black parents devalue achievement strivings in their children or fail to have high aspirations for them. In fact, Black parents have been demonstrated to have a strong orientation toward achievement in general and educational achievement in particular (e.g., Hill, 1972; Moos and Moos, 1976, Rodman and Voydonoff, 1978). In general, it appears that many of the values and socialization goals of even lower-class Black families are not particularly different from those of American society at large (e.g., Billingsley, 1969; Lewis, 1970; Kamii and Radin, 1967). It has also been repeatedly demonstrated that, at all grade levels, Black children have aspirations and hopes for educational and vocational achievement at least as high as those of their White counterparts (e.g., Debord, Griffin, and Clark, 1977; Massey, Scott, and Dornbusch, 1975; Picou, 1973; Pouissant and Atkinson, 1970; Simmons, 1979a). (Black children's expectations that they will realize their aspirations, however, are somewhat lower; e.g., Phillips, 1972.) These and other sources of evidence suggest that neither Black children nor their parents reject mainstream goals or the instrumental value of an education. If teachers—those agents of the schools who have the most direct influence on children—have indeed been conveying different messages to their pupils, the children have not been their passive recipients.

SUMMARY OF APPROACHES

In summary, each of the major approaches outlined above suffers from too-exclusive an emphasis on one aspect of the Black experience, has been insufficiently elaborated, or fails to consider how the academic performance of Black children might be improved. Traditional approaches have been useful in describing some of the patterns of performance found among Black groups, but have confused description with explanation. If Black children do not do as well as Whites on a test of arithmetic, for example, it has been assumed, without convincing documentation, that they must therefore lack arithmetic skills. In addition to the traditionalists' failure to provide illuminating analyses of the performances they have described, they have proposed solutions that essentially involve no more than repairing the deficient child and his or her family—an example of the approach that Ryan (1971) has labeled "blaming the victim." The cultural-difference view, while recognizing the integrity of Afro-American culture and the significance of the Black psychological experience, has not provided adequate analyses of how Black people's cultural repertoire works to impede academic performance nor how it can be used to facilitate performance. The social-structuralists present a full-bodied, descriptive account of the societal forces with which the Black children must contend—forces that can obviously hinder the children's successful passage through the educational system and their acquisition of cognitive skills. However, the social-structuralists tend to underestimate the strengths and the adaptability of Black culture and are unduly pessimistic about the capacity of the schools to develop teaching methods that will be better adapted to the styles of Black children. Long-term solutions to the range of difficulties encountered by Afro-Americans in American society may well require the structural changes called for by these theorists, but the Black community is ill-served if the possibility of alleviating some of these difficulties in the short term is dismissed out of hand.

A perspective is sorely needed that fuses and extends the explanatory strengths of the cultural-difference and social-structural positions. This syntheis would give equal emphasis to institutional variables and to the individual in the context of his or her milieu. It would seek to describe in some detail the character of the Black social-cultural frame of reference, illuminating its strengths but not ignoring its maladaptive features. It would place the primary responsibility on institutions to accommodate to the needs and requirements of children, rather than the reverse. The blending of the cultural-difference and social-structural positions should lead to a model that, as applied to the academic arena, is prescriptive as well as descriptive, suggesting changes in educational practice.

In the following pages, the development of such a scheme is undertaken. Of immediate concern would seem to be an understanding of the prevailing cultural context for academic performance that the Black child currently confronts. What, for example, is the "standard middle-class format" of the classroom (Rollins, McCandless, Thompson, and Brassell, 1974)? What are the essential ingredients of the prevailing cultural ideology in mainstream American society, and how is the academic setting informed by them? What are the features of the Afro-American culture that are at odds with the mainstream ideology, and how might classroom practices be modified?

TOWARD A CULTURAL APPROACH

Euro-American Ethos

In the process of organizing reality and developing a basis for civilization, every society must confront a universal set of concerns. The way a group orients itself toward this set of concerns forms the basis for the belief system and world view on which their culture is predicated. Du Bois (1972) has argued that there are three broad issues on which every society or group must take a position: (1) a view of the universe, (2) man's relation to it, and (3) man's relation to other men.

Du Bois holds that the White American middle-class resolution of these concerns is primarily rooted in the Protestant ethic and eighteenth-century rationalism, and to these I would add British empiricism (Boykin, 1979). She argues that the dominant beliefs among Euro-Americans are that (1) the universe is mechanistically constructed, (2) human beings are its masters, (3) people are equal, and (4) people are perfectible. Her position is congruent with the views of several other analysts of American society (e.g., Elison, 1973; Gergen, 1978; Israel, 1979; Kluckhohn and Strodtbeck, 1961; Rossides, 1978; Sampson, 1977, 1978; Weber, 1958).

That the universe is conceived on a mechanistic basis has several implications. The natural order, being "machinelike," is necessarily an impersonal one. Moreover, all natural phenomena, including humans, are best understood on a mechanistic-materialistic basis. That human beings are construed as the masters of the general system of things also has several implications. Since humans have a preeminent status, they can justifiably conceive of themselves as functionally separate from the universe. They achieve their roles as conquerors and masters through their unique ability to exercise their rational and empirical powers. As Dixon (1976) has said, "Man essentially does battle with an external impersonal system. Since any force of nature does not have his interest at heart, man should and can subordinate nature to his own goals" (p. 58).

Although humans are perceived as superior to and separate from the rest of the universe, this view is somewhat tempered by the premise that they are equally endowed with imperfect incarnations. Thus, they are all entitled to equal treatment, equal judgment, and equal depictions. However, it is within man's capacity to perfect himself. It follows that not all people are at the same point in the perfecting process. Thus, individuals can rightfully be placed along a perfectibility continuum, and interpersonal relations are largely dictated by the linear-hierarchical position of people along this continuum (Kluckhohn and Strodtbeck, 1961).

The manner in which these beliefs have been interpreted forms the basis for the core values of Euro-American culture. Among the most salient are (1) effort optimism, (2) material well-being, (3) possessive individualism, (4) egalitarian-based conformity, (5) the democratization of equality, and (6) a person-to-object orientation (Dixon, 1976; Du Bois, 1972; Israel, 1979; Sampson, 1978).

Du Bois (1972) describes effort optimism as, first, the belief that work is a positive good for its own sake. Through such a work ethic, man strives not only to obtain mastery over a mechanistically conceived universe, but also to achieve his own perfectibility. Effort optimism, then, literally means effort viewed optimistically.

The accumulation of material possessions and the production of material entities, achieved through hard work, serve as benchmarks in man's conquest of nature and further serve to signal his state of perfectibility. Upward mobility and material prosperity can be used interchangeably and as indices of an individual's level of mastery and perfectibility (Du Bois, 1972; Kluckhohn and Strodtbeck, 1961). At the level of society as a whole, material prosperity is seen as synonymous with progress. Thus, Euro-Americans seem to value and to practice what Israel (1979) has called "possessive individualism." One's individual identity is bound up with what one acquires, possesses, or earns. One's individualism is linked to the accumulation and ownership of private property, be it in the form of material goods, monetary wealth, status, power, intellect, or even other people. Individuals can thus be properly distinguished on the basis of their possessions, which become their moral duty to work hard to achieve. The linkage between material well-being and self-worth leads to an emphasis on comparison, differentiation, and competition. Through various sorts of comparisons, individuals can adequately gauge the relative success of their process of self-actualization and can use others' attainments as standards that they strive to surpass.

It would be a mistake to view individualism per se, as some have done, as a value unique to Euro-Americans. All groups or societies must negotiate a balance between individual identity and group identity: to view the individual as a singular entity but simultaneously as merged into group. In this society, the balance is tipped toward the individual. Thus, individual responsibility takes precedent over any other form (Furby, 1979; Sampson, 1978).

At the same time, a premium is placed on conformity. According to Du Bois (1972), conformity links the premises of perfectibility and equality with the core value of effort optimism. Whereas people are expected to aspire toward self-realization, it is recognized that they are unable to master their environment completely alone; some degree of cooperation and coordination of effort is needed. If societal institutions are to be maximally effective, individuals must work in synchrony (not unlike the parts of a machine) according to a common set of rules. Individuals, it would seem, retain their individuality, at the same time accepting being cut from the same mold, through gaining the competitive edge over other individuals or groups. The goal is not who can be the most idiosyncratic, but who can apply the formula most successfully, who can be the first with the most. It is important to stress that these contentions do not imply that Euro-Americans are all alike, but that likeness is valued (Du Bois, 1972).

As was noted above, to function properly, societies must balance the rights and needs of individuals against those of the group. Individualism without group norms and codes would lead to anarchy. Group norms and codes that deny individual freedom of expression result in an oppressive, policelike society. Rugged (possessive) individualism socially cemented to egalitarian conformity achieves this balance quite well within the Euro-American cultural purview.

Another important value can be called the "democratization of equality" (Sampson, 1978). In earlier centuries it was held that certain groups, such as the clergy or feudal lords, had privileged access to truth. As Sampson points out, "bourgeois liberalism" denied that such privileged access should exist and, in its place, sought to make access to truth universal. A premium was also placed on finding general laws that would be applicable to everyone equally. This democratic approach requires several assumptions about how truth is acquired. For one, it is crucial to stress the cognitive over the affective. This orientation was reinforced by the Puritan ethic, which valued rational instruction and was suspicious of emotion. Further, understanding is enhanced when knowledge is essentially depersonalized. Truth is tantamount to objective facts and is inherent in the natural order or the mechanical, impersonal universe. Moreover, as Gay (1978) has stated, for Euro-Americans, understanding is largely an analytical process achieved through the reduction of object, idea, or problem to its core elements.

This emphasis on reason and detachment intrudes into all the major institutions in this society—economics, politics, religion, law, science, even social relationships (Sampson, 1978). Objectification of social relationships personifies what Dixon (1976), among others, has labeled a "person-to-object orientation." Such an orientation is also implied in Max Weber's (1958) notion of "rationalization," which has often been cited as the backbone of the form of bureaucratic organization so widely utilized in American institutions. As Sampson observes,

"To rationalize a human activity is to abstract it and to impersonalize it; rationalization eliminates the personal and the unique from organizational practice" (p. 778). One outcome of this depersonalization, as Bowles and Gintis (1973) point out, is to make the thrust of institutions and social relationships within them toward uniformity, objectivity, and efficiency.

In the search for universal laws and principles, cultural considerations are deemphasized (Gergen, 1978; Persell, 1977; Sampson, 1977). Groups whose values and behaviors are different from those of the White middle class are likely to be regarded as deficient and imperfect, either because they lack the capacity to meet these standards (the conservative doctrine) or because (according to the liberal doctrine) they have not yet had the opportunity to embrace White middle-class beliefs and patterns of behavior and thus to achieve "equality," i.e., the desired similarity. Given the emphasis on individualism, the responsibility for melding into the dominant culture is bestowed on the deviant individual or group (Sampson, 1977).

Built into this Euro-American cultural ethos is an insensitivity to the fact that its values and rules are culturally bound and culturally determined. Although insistence on uniformity may work well for culturally homogeneous groups, this cultural imperialism has potentially deleterious implications for divergent groups that, for whatever reason, are unwilling or unprepared to acculturate. It seems important at this juncture to issue a disclaimer of sorts. Not all Euro-Americans embrace these views. There is also reason to believe that these ideals are not as strong or pervasive at present as they were in previous eras (Albee, 1977; Bell, 1976). Further, if one probes deep enough into this matrix of beliefs and values, inherent contradictions can be found (Bowles and Gintis, 1973; Du Bois, 1972).

Yet these considerations, for our present purposes, help to illuminate certain patterns of behaviors and attitudes that are common in American society. Even if given individuals do not fully embrace the ideals, they are still apt to be more prepared to accept such conceptions as the appropriate metaphors, definitions, and idealized forms of behavior for the society in which they live. Moreover, the power brokers in the society, although surely few in number, are more likely to embrace and live out these conceptions and to work to perpetuate them (Sampson, 1977). Indeed, they are likely to have gained their power precisely because of their abilities to manifest the cultural ideals in question.

Moreover, many intellectuals have assimilated these values (Furby, 1979; Israel, 1979). Acceptance of the value of individual achievement—success in school or on the job—is a premise that, for example, provides the raison d'être for this volume.

The Euro-American ethos is also reflected in scientific theories. In psychology, healthy, well-adjusted, successful individuals have been postulated to be characterized by a high level of achievement motivation (McClelland, Atkinson, Clark, and Lowell, 1953; Murray, 1938) and by the tendency to perceive that their own actions control consequences—a theme to be found in Rotter's (1966) theory of internal versus external locus of control, Seligman's (1975) concept of learned helplessness, and Weiner's (1979) internal versus external attributional tendencies. The focus on the individual can be seen further in such constructs as Witkin's (Witkin, Dyk, Fatterson, Goodenough, and Karp, 1962) field independence, R. White's (1959) "effectance motivation," and Deci's (1975) "intrinsic motivation." These psychological properties are implied to be human beings' natural heritage, though often dimmed or corrupted by life circumstances. In humanistic psychology, concerns such as "becoming" (Allport, 1955) and "self-actualization" (Maslow, 1954) are prominent. The values that these theories presume and the nature of the constructs they propose can be fairly said to be rooted in the Puritan ethic. That this model may be satisfactory for describing individuals who share this ethic and for predicting their behavior cannot be denied. The assumption that they are models of universal applicability and thus acultural in nature may be seen as an example of ethnocentrism.

Educational administrators, teachers, and school boards typically come from the cultural mainstream, and thus are likely to exhibit this same cultural chauvinism and to create an atmosphere within the schools that is largely dictated by the cultural ideals of the dominant group. As Silverstein and Krate (1975) have put it:

> from the vast array of human attributes, every culture selects for cultivation those few that meet the requirements of successful functioning within the system. Children who possess these characteristics, which adults expect will lead to success in high status occupations, are likely to receive favored treatment in the schools, thus ensuring the frequent confirmation of initial expectations. American schools operate to socialize and sort out those children who are best able to adopt the behavior requirements of employees within a corporate-capitalistic technocratic political economy. Among these behavioral characteristics are strong impulse controls, and the subordination of emotions to rational-conceptual thinking, the willingness to channel attention and energy into somewhat autonomous efforts to achieve high levels of performance, in a dispassionate manner, on tasks unrelated to one's own personal motives and desires, cooperativeness and willingness to accept directions from those in authority (pp. 205–206).

Gay (1975) has listed other characteristics particularly treasured in the academic settings. These include being individualistic and competitive in performing work tasks; being serious at the expense of gaiety and physical movement; compartmentalizing cognitive, emotional, and physical activities; emphasizing written formats over oral ones; valuing structure, planning, and mental discipline over spontaneity and emotional reactions; and adopting a task orientation rather than a person orientation. She states, "All of these school values have built into them behavioral expectations that are considered 'appropriate' or 'right' for students if learning is to take place" (p. 31).

If this general line of argument has merit, then it might be expected that academically successful Black children are more likely to conform to the prevailing cultural norms than are their less successful peers. The data suggest that this is indeed the case. For example, Riley and Denmark (1974) report that among working-class Black children, field independence (Witkin et al., 1962) is strongly related to measures of verbal ability and general intelligence. Others have found that successful working-class Black students, in comparison to the less successful, are more internal in locus of control, have stronger impulse controls, and exhibit more highly directed individual achievement strivings (Buck and Austrin, 1971; Mackler, 1970; Davidson and Greenberg, 1967). Silverstein and Krate (1975) report that, in their observational study of the schooling process in central Harlem, the most academically successful group of children were those whom the authors labeled "mainstreamers." This designation was deemed appropriate because such children, more than any other group, most closely approximated middle-class White children in their behavioral styles, demeanors, self-presentations, interactional patterns, and implicit values. Seegmiller and King (1975) found that, for Black infants as young as 22 months of age, performance on the Bayley mental scales is linked to "object responsiveness" more than to "social responsiveness." Shade (1978, 1981) has summarized the findings from several projects that tend to conform to the pattern of results described above.

Data such as these could be used to justify the claim that Black children must accommodate their values and behavior to those of the White middle class if they are equal the academic and cognitive achievements of Whites. However, all that can safely be concluded from the evidence is that children who conform to what is expected of them perform better than those whose values and behavioral styles are at odds with these expectations. No evidence can be found to demonstrate that learning and academic performance are necessarily superior when they take place in the middle-class cultural context. Further, to the extent that there exists among Afro-Americans an integrated social-cultural frame of reference, the demand that Blacks accommodate themselves to the schools rather than the reverse represents cultural imperialism. In any event, Black children who are "mainstreamers" seem to be the exception rather than the rule.

Appreciation of the prevailing Afro-American cultural ethos may lead to a better understanding of the sources of the academic problems of many Black youngsters, which, in turn, should lead to insights into how educational practice might be modified to serve their needs.

Black Cultural Reality: African Perspective

To understand the Afro-American cultural ethos, it has been argued, requires insight into its African roots. Yet ultimately, Afro-Americans are, as Nobles (1976) says, of "African root but American fruit." Given

Afro-Americans' physical and temporal separation from the African continent and the culture of their African ancestors, neither the Euro-American nor the African perspective is wholly descriptive of the Afro-American social-cultural frame of reference. In understanding Afro-Americans on their own terms, I propose to adopt an "Afrographic" approach—one that begins with the African experience, but acknowledges the intrusion of the Euro-American culture.

It would be erroneous to posit a monolithic African philosophy or cultural reality. However, examination of the literature reveals many lines of convergence across the works of social historians (Gutman, 1976; Levine, 1977), anthropologists (Herskovitz, 1958; Thompson, 1966; Young, 1970, 1974), educators (J. Banks, 1976; Gay, 1975; Hale, 1980; Morgan, 1980; Smitherman, 1977; Wilson, 1972), indigenous African philosophers (Abraham, 1962; Mbiti, 1970; Senghor, 1962; Wiredu, 1980), and among those whose work falls under the rubric of Black psychology (Akbar, 1976; Brown, 1978; Jackson, 1976; J. Jones, 1979; Nobles, 1976; J. White, 1980; J. White, Parham, and Parham, 1980). A distillation of the writings of these scholars reveals many recurring themes, particularly among West African peoples, the ancestors of most contemporary Afro-Americans.

The earlier discussion of Euro-American culture, it will be recalled, revolved about the resolution of three issues: (1) how the universe is viewed, (2) humankind's relation to the cosmos, and (3) how people relate to each other. The African world view stands in contrast to that adopted by Euro-Americans. The African (particularly the West African) belief system holds that the universe is essentially a vitalistic life force; human beings are harmoniously conjoined with the cosmos; there is an interconnection among all people that produces oneness, yet everyone is unique (e.g., Abraham, 1962; Akbar, 1976; Dixon, 1976; Mbiti, 1970; Nobles, 1976, 1980; Nyang, 1980).

To elaborate somewhat, the view that the universe is a vitalistic life force implies that its essence is organic, living, and spiritual. Spiritual forces are part and parcel of all entities, animate or inanimate, material or nonmaterial. Man-made objects are imbued with the life force in that they represent the manifestation of man's life force and as such are extensions of it. God and inanimate objects are the two anchor points in a hierarchical arrangement in nature, defined in terms of the degree of possession of life force.

Given the flow of cosmic energy throughout the system of things, human beings are inextricably bound up in it. Since man is united with nature, he cannot extricate himself from it because it would be tantamount to extricating himself from himself (Boykin, 1977a). Humans, however, have a fairly lofty status because they embody a greater spiritual life force than do inanimate objects or other living things (Mbiti, 1970).

The same conception of interdependence that exists among all facets of the hierarchical natural order exists at any given level as well. Thus, all people are interconnected. Yet each entity, human and nonhuman, is unique, manifesting its combination of the corporal and spiritual in its own characteristic way. Within the confines of their interconnectedness, people thus have the freedom to be themselves.

This belief system has eventuated in a core set of values, the most discernible and important of which are (1) a rhythmic-music-movement orientation, (2) an emphasis on affect, (3) communalism, (4) expressive individualism, (5) a social time perspective, (6) orality, and (7) a person-to-person orientation.

Belief in the vitalistic quality of the natural order has led African culture literally and figuratively to dance to the ontological beat of the rhythmic flow of the universe. The drum beat is a central vehicle through which rich and varied rhythmic interpretations can be expressed. Drums are used to communicate. They convey information about and insight into the natural order and man's niche within it (Wiredu, 1980). To play music is to dance and to dance percussively. To listen to music is to move to its beat (Thompson, 1966). African culture is thus a rhythmic, percussive one that fuses movement and music into a spiritual medium through which man gets in step with the rhythm of his existence.

The combination of a personal orientation toward the universe and the transcending importance of the interconnectedness among all things implies that the character of the natural order cannot be understood unemotionally (Brown, 1978; Dixon, 1976). Objects and events are understood in terms of their affective and emotional significance, and to understand is in large measure to become personally involved with the phenomenon to be understood (Brown, 1978; Senghor, 1962). Affective bonds are transcendant ones through which entities manifest their spirituality. Thus, in large measure, feelings are a prime means of affirming one's existence. Feelings also cement an intrapsychic unity of existence, such that thoughts, feelings, and actions are inseparable. To think is to feel; to feel is to do (Brown, 1978; Dixon, 1976).

The essence of African communalism lies in the construction of the group as a living microcosm of the universal order. Society does not exist to protect and preserve individual rights, but rather individuals exist in order to serve the collective. "Personhood" is not something with which one is automatically born, but achieves by becoming a social entity through the shedding of egocentric dispositions associated with early childhood. As Oguah (1979) maintains, only when one's society prospers can it be said that an individual prospers. If one seeks one's own good apart from or at odds with the community's good, one is necessarily seeking one's own destruction. Consequently, mutual aid is viewed as a moral code.

The social interrelatedness that is communalism also implies the cultivation of human contacts and the exchanging and sharing of goods and property (Maurier, 1979). In essence, possessions belong to the community at large rather than to individuals. All in all, communalism serves as an appropriate and effective means for manifesting the oneness of being.

At the same time, individualism is valued. The way Africans characteristically resolve the individual versus group dilemma is by blending communalism with expressive individualism. One achieves individual identity through exercising one's duties to the collective in one's own characteristic manner. One achieves individuality by bringing one's own style or personal interpretation to one's duties and responsibilities. People are expected and encouraged to put their own personal touch to their endeavors, to walk their own walk and talk their own talk as the feeling moves them to do so. Expressive individualism also implies naturalness and spontaneity. The individualistic mode of self-expression makes for an essentially artistic approach to life (J. Jones, 1979). One's creative self-interpretation becomes one's hallmark and signals one's uniqueness as a human being.

Transcending importance is attached to the spoken word (Jahn, 1961; Levine, 1977; Smitherman, 1977). The medium of the spoken word makes communication more alive, gives it a rich emotional texture, and allows for rhythmic, percussive expression (Thompson, 1966). The spoken word is even said to take on magical powers (Jahn, 1961). When used in a call-and-response fashion, it becomes a communalistic medium and a vehicle for affective bonding. Relatedly, verbal facility is admired. Praise is to be bestowed on the teller of folk tales, the reciter of proverbs.

Traditional African societies also have a social orientation toward time (Nobles, 1980; Nyang, 1980; Wilson, 1972). As Nyang (1980) asserts, reality is construed as a social phenomenon; it follows that the units of time are governed more by the "mental and spiritual processes of man and his community" than by objective reality. As Wilson (1972) states, time is used "for the enhancement of intragroup relations." Time is what is done (King, 1976). Thus, we see an event orientation toward time in which time passes across a social space, not a material one. What "time" does an event start? When people get there. What "time" does the event end? When people feel like leaving. Moreover, time does not simply move unidirectionally from the past to the future. Instead, time pulsates throughout social space.

It is recurring, cyclical, personal, and phenomenal (Nobles, 1976, 1980). This does not imply that Africans have no demarcations for time in the objective sense. Instead, as Pennington (1976) notes, time becomes real only when it is experienced. The length of a given month, for example, can be varied as a function of the relevant activities contained within. Time is thus elastic, so that in essence Africans can produce as much as they wish.

One final value can be noted, one that is actually derived from all others. As Dixon (1976) notes, personal relationships are of paramount importance. Although this point has clearly been implied in the previous discussions, it seems important to set the issue apart as a distinct value orientation. One significant implication of this orientation is that leadership and authority are invested in the person rather than the office. Ad hominem arguments are not considered to be inappropriate. Subjective, personal, and passionate interpretations of others' actions are not out of the ordinary.

Afro-American Culture

It would be inappropriate to conclude that these traditional world views and values have been transferred wholesale into the life experiences of contemporary Afro-Americans, completely intact, unmitigated, and untransformed. Yet it would seem highly unlikely as well to infer that no meaningful cultural correspondences exist. I will argue that nine interrelated, yet distinct dimensions can be discerned that grew out of the belief system and orientation of traditional African society and that manifest themselves in contemporary Afro-American culture. These nine realms or dimensions are spirituality, harmony, movement, verve, affect, communalism, expressive individualism, orality, and social time perspective.

1. *Spirituality*. Spirituality entails approaching life as though its primary essence were vitalistic rather than mechanistic. It means conducting oneself in a manner consistent with the possibility that the nonobservable and nonmaterial have governing powers in the everyday affairs of people. Permeating all sectors of one's life space is the conviction that greater powers than man are continuously at play. One strives to remain in touch with the greater spiritual essences (Brown, 1978; J. Jones, 1979; Levine, 1977).

2. *Harmony*. Rather than seeing oneself as distinct from one's environmental surroundings, one sees oneself as, and in turn acts as though one were, inextricably linked to one's surroundings. Rather than striving to partition one's life space into discrete elements, the aim is to blend them together into some kind of organic, harmonious

whole. The conviction is that what will happen will happen, mainly because it is supposed to or because it is best that it does. Rather than attempting to maximize one's effort or attain excellence with regard to a single dimension or a relatively narrow range of expertise, one strives to be versatile. (Boykin, 1977a; Dixon, 1976; Nobles, 1976; among others, have argued that such a stylistic orientation is characteristic of Afro-Americans.)

3. *Movement.* Movement is actually a shorthand designation for the interwoven mosaic of movement, music, dance, percussiveness, and rhythm, personified by the musical beat. Music and dancing are ways of engaging life itself and are life-sustaining media, vital to one's psychological health. Also implied is a rhythmic orientation toward life: a complex and multidimensional recurrent pattern that typifies one's personal conduct and self-presentation (Akbar, 1976; Boykin, 1978; Guttentag, 1972; J. Jones, 1979; Morgan, 1980).

4. *Verve.* This dimension is essentially extracted from the psychological residue of the movement dimension. It connotes a disdain for the routinized, the dull, and the bland, regardless of what ends are served. It implies a propensity for the energetic, the intense, the stimulating, and the lively. It connotes a tendency to attend to several concerns at once and to shift focus among them rather than to focus on a single concern or a series of concerns in a rigidly sequential fashion (Boykin, 1977a, 1978, 1979; Gay and Abrahams, 1973; Young, 1970, 1974).

5. *Affect.* Affect implies integration of feelings with thoughts and actions, such that it would be difficult to engage in an activity if one's feelings toward the activity ran counter to such engagement. Also implied is the importance of emotional expressiveness, the affective value of information, and a particular sensitivity to emotional cues given off by others (Brown, 1978; Silverstein and Krate, 1975; J. White, 1980).

6. *Communalism.* Communalism denotes awareness of the interdependence of people. One's orientation is social rather than being directed toward objects. One acts in accordance with the notion that duty to one's social group is more important than individual privileges and rights. Sharing is promoted because it signifies the affirmation of social interconnectedness; self-centeredness and individual greed are disdained (Foster, 1971; Hale, 1980; Nobles, 1976; Wilson, 1972).

7. *Expressive individualism.* Expressive individualism refers to the cultivation of a unique or distinctive personality or essence and putting one's own personal brand on an activity, a concern with style more than with being correct or efficient. It implies genuineness and

346 The Academic Performance of Afro-American Children / Boykin

sincerity of self-expression, an emphasis on spontaneity rather than on systematic planning. It is what is being manifested when we witness the gorilla dunk in basketball, or the end-zone touchdown spike/dance in football. It is the expressive essence of the jazz artist or the soul singer. It implies approaching life as though it were an artistic endeavor (Dixon, 1976; J. Jones, 1979; Young, 1974).

8. *Orality.* Orality refers to the special importance attached to knowledge gained and passed on through word of mouth and the cultivation of oral virtuosity. It implies a special sensitivity to aural modes of communication and a reliance on oral expression to carry meanings and feelings. Words cannot always be interpreted literally, but must be understood in terms of the interpersonal context in which they are uttered. There is a reliance on the call-and-response mode of communication; to be quiet and wait one's turn to speak often implies a lack of interest in what the other is saying. Speaking is construed as a performance and not merely as a vehicle for interacting or communicating information (J. Jones, 1979; Levine, 1977; Smitherman, 1977).

9. *Social time perspective.* Commitment to time as a social phenomenon implies construing time primarily in terms of the significant events to be engaged in and not to be rigidly bound to clocks and calendars. It also connotes that behavior is bound to social traditions and customs of the past that serve as guideposts and beacons for future endeavors. Nobles (1980), Pennington (1976), and Green (1972) have spoken to these tendencies among Afro-Americans.

Comparison of the core features of the traditional African cultural ethos with those of the Euro-American indicates that, in a number of significant ways, the beliefs, values, and folkways of the two frames of reference are *noncommensurable*. The African perspective emphasizes spiritualism in the universe, whereas the Euro-American perspective emphasizes materialism. The former emphasizes harmonic unity with nature and other people, whereas the latter stresses mastery over nature and prizes individualism. The African values feelings, expressiveness, and spontaneity; the Euro-American values control of impulses, self-discipline, and dispassionate reason. In one, the individual's duty is to the group, and possessions belong to the group; in the other, the rights of the individual are paramount, and the notion of private property is sacred.

These sketches of the African and Euro-American traditions are too boldly drawn to do justice not only to their richness and complexity, but also to the variations among subcultures and individuals. Be that as it may, they are sufficient to indicate profound ways in which the two cultures differ in their world views and values. This bifurcation presents a special challenge to the Afro-American who is a product of the two cultural traditions. Even the task of discerning the structure and textural qualities of Afro-American culture and how that culture integrates its several heritages is an imposing one. A conceptual framework for such an integration is presented in the following section.

TRIPLE QUANDARY FOR AFRO-AMERICANS

The process by which youths are acculturated, it is widely agreed, involves teaching them the conventional beliefs, values, and patterns of behavior prescribed by their society. Typically, information about these values and expected behaviors is passed on in unambiguous form from a variety of sources such that children readily internalize them and come to guide their own behaviors along expected paths. In this way, if the socialization process is successful, individuals learn to take their place in the social order, permitting that order to reproduce itself in successive generations.

But what, for Afro-Americans, are these "conventional" beliefs, values, and behaviors? What is the social order into which the Black youth is being inducted? It can be argued that the contours and textures of the Afro-American psychological experience are products of the interplay among three realms: the mainstream experience, the minority experience, and the Black cultural experience (Cole, 1970; J. Jones, 1979).

Undeniably, the behaviors, beliefs, and values of Afro-Americans have been shaped through contact with mainstream American society. As Young (1974) has stated: "Participation in standard American culture is characteristic of [Blacks] of all social classes, rural and urban. [Blacks] participate in work systems, judicial systems, in consumption systems, in bureaucratic organizations both as clients and employees. They share values transmitted by general American institutions and by the mass media" (p. 406). However, the imposition of the dictates of mainstream society is less likely to be successful or fully realized in the case of Afro-Americans because of the conflicting influences of the minority and Black cultural experiences. Such a set of circumstances is likely to lead to socialized duality, stylistic flexibility, rejection or cynicism about mainstream conventions, or unevenness in the extent to which mainstream imperatives are internalized or acted upon.

The minority experience comprises that set of social forces impinging on Afro-Americans that result from economic, political, and social oppression due to their race. Participation in the minority experience results in the development of a particular set of coping styles, adaptive reactions, social outlooks, defensive postures, and compensatory reactions that allow individuals to adjust to the burdens imposed by their racial membership. Although these burdens are to a certain extent shared by other oppressed groups, the particular repertoires of behaviors developed by Afro-Americans are shaped both by Black culture and by the unique history of Black people in this country.

In spite of the elusiveness of the Black cultural experience, participation in it is arguably a major determinant of the behavior patterns of Afro-Americans. The actual character of the Afro-American cultural ethos will be entertained shortly. Suffice it to say for now that it would be a mistake to posit that Afro-Americans are White people painted Black, save only that they have been denied full access to the bounties of America by racial discrimination and have adapted defensively to that exclusion. There is an intrinsic base from which Afro-Americans order, interpret, and negotiate social reality that is functionally linked to a distinctive patterning of behavior.

It is crucial to realize that success in each of these three realms of social negotiation requires essentially three distinctly different, apparently nonoverlapping repertoires of behavior. It is not difficult to conclude that being truly effective in any one realm is likely to militate against the same level of effectiveness in the others, since the demands in each domain often operate at cross purposes.

Given the lack of support in wider American society for traditional African beliefs and values, the exigencies of having to cope with minority status within a Euro-American social order, and the historical discontinuities between present-day Afro-Americans and their traditional African past, the fully elaborated character of the Afro-American cultural ethos does not exhibit a straightforward correspondence to the traditional African scheme. Yet I argue that the core character of the Afro-American cultural ethos can largely be understood in terms of *Black cultural styles*. (A similar position has been taken by Young, 1974.)

By cultural style, I refer to motifs, patterns of behavior, and predilections—tendencies and thoughts that tend to distinguish a given group of people from others and are the result of cultural conditioning. As I have argued elsewhere (Boykin, 1977a), a style is not fixed or immutable. However, since it is essentially habitual, it is altered only when one makes a continued conscious effort to change it or, on occasion, when environmental support for it ceases to exist. It is crucial to distinguish between *elaborated* and *tacit* cultural styles. Elaborated cultural styles are those that are inculcated through the explicit guidance of a set of beliefs and values. They typically result from the top-to-bottom elaboration of a homogeneous cultural ethos. Tacit cultural styles, on the other hand, typically arise out of socialization experiences within the family and the immediate community and have a less direct or implicit relationship with beliefs and values. Tacit cultural styles can conceivably eventuate in explicit links to beliefs and values, but ordinarily do not. A third type of cultural style can be identified as *mimetic* or imitative. Clearly, some cultural styles result from superficial imitation and arise more or less fortuitously, without being embedded in a larger system of values and styles.

In a monocultural framework, a quite direct hierarchical relationship exists between world views, beliefs and values, and behavioral and cultural styles. In the case of Afro-Americans, the repertoire of African-based behavioral motifs has not grown as directly out of the corresponding African beliefs and values. These motifs are manifested in spite of the embeddedness of Afro-Americans in a Euro-American social reality and typically reflect at best only a tacit understanding of the values and beliefs from which they originally developed. Some African values and beliefs may have been explicitly preserved in diluted form but, on the whole, the Black cultural styles of Afro-Americans are not as coherently related to the traditional African cultural ethos as in the case of the Euro-American ethos.

The explicit beliefs and values of most Afro-Americans are primarily shaped by the dominant or overarching society to which they have a distal relationship, whereas their habitual patterns of actions, behavioral motifs, and feelings are primarily shaped by their proximal experiences within their families and immediate community. This bifurcation occurs because stylistic patterns are likely to be molded earlier in the socialization process than are beliefs and values, the latter requiring greater maturation and awareness on the part of the developing child before they can be adopted. These beliefs and values are apt to develop about the time the child begins to be aware of and have experiences with the larger society's social institutions, as represented by school personnel, peers from outside the Black community, the media, and so forth.

Most Afro-Americans are taught the ideals and values of the larger society both inside and outside the home. However, in their role as socialization agents and value transmitters, Afro-American parents may grasp this value system less securely, have less facility with it, and fewer resources to realize it than Euro-American parents. Although there are surely differences from home to home and from one neighborhood to another, the degree to which Black children acquire Euro-American cultural ideals and the corresponding stylistic manifestations is less than in the case of their White counterparts (Staples, 1976).

As was described above, the behavioral motifs and styles acquired by Afro-Americans during their formative years are largely determined by a cultural conditioning process whose premises are typically unarticulated. This conditioning results from the confluence of a number of sources. First, there are perhaps inherent proclivities on the part of Black children to be receptive to such conditioning (Clark, McGee, Nobles, and Akbar, 1975; Morgan, 1980; Wober, 1975). More certainly, children model themselves after siblings and adults in the home. Finally, children are subject to direct molding attempts on the part of older peers or others who have come to see such styles as enjoyable, appropriate, or "cool." Thus, such cultural styles can become firmly entrenched at an early age without the guidance of any overarching set of values and beliefs.

These behavioral styles are likely to be retained, despite their incompatibility with the styles that flow from Euro-American value systems. The reasons are not hard to discern. Black cultural styles form a sort of coherent, internally consistent behavioral grammar. The styles are thus mutually reinforcing. They are habitual, familiar, and comfortable. And finally, they are acquired and practiced in relative isolation from the mainstream of society. All these factors conspire to make the Black cultural styles resistant to change, despite their lack of coordination with the values of the larger society that Black children are also being taught.

The issue of social isolation again calls attention to the role of racial and economic oppression. The difficulties inherent in attempts to negotiate culturally between two noncommensurable systems are exacerbated by such factors as restricted opportunities and decreased expectations for success in the institutions of the overarching society. Parents and other socialization agents in Black communities find themselves in a dilemma. They may understand and accept the goals or end products of the Euro-American socialization process, such as becoming vocationally successful. But they likewise understand that the realities of racism will make such success difficult to achieve. This leads to ambivalence and confusion about what values and aspirations to instill in their children (Comer, 1974). Further, the devices they teach their children that permit them to get along and avoid trouble in an oppressive society may be incompatible with the realization of mainstream goals.

Afro-Americans, then, are faced with a triple quandary. They are likely to be incompletely socialized in the Euro-American cultural ethos. They typically develop a stylistic repertoire that arises out of their African heritage but is at odds with mainstream ideology. And finally, they are victimized by racial and economic oppression.

The psychological experience of any given Afro-American can largely be understood in terms of:

1. The extent to which the individual has incorporated Euro-American goals and values.

2. The particular domains in which these goals and values have been adopted.

3. The extent to which Black socialization goals have been overtly embraced.

4. The pattern of responses the individual has developed to cope with racial discrimination in all of its manifestations.

5. The extent of Black cultural conditioning, particularly during the early years, prior to entering school.

Thus, the Afro-American psychological experience can properly be characterized as complex, rich, and diverse, and, simultaneously, as intelligible, coherent, and integrated.

The triple-quandary framework helps us apprehend the complexity of the bicultural character of the Afro-American psychological experience. This experience, in short, can be seen as a mixture of motifs, styles, and patterns of behavior historically linked to and typically tacitly informed by the traditional African cultural ethos, with stated goals, aspirations, and beliefs of the Euro-American cultural ethos not fully actualized in the corresponding motifs, styles, and patterns of behavior. This particular brand of biculturalism helps to explain the relative social isolation of Black people in this country. The diversity of this bicultural expression should be understood in terms of the distribution of passive resignation to, tacit or overt endorsement of, and inadequate approximation of traditional African versus Euro-American world views, values, and behavioral styles. Certain values may be rejected because they contradict unstated (Black) world views or beliefs. The intent of a given value, to which an individual claims to subscribe, may be violated because of an attempt to actualize the value through stylistic expressions that extrapolate to a noncomplementary value. Certain beliefs and behavioral styles may be present, without the corresponding values. Values and/or styles may be present without the corresponding beliefs. In all, the various possibilities outlined represent important variations on a uniquely Afro-American cultural theme. The way these various forms of expression are negotiated across Afro-Americans and even within the same individuals exemplifies the various forms of what might appropriately be labeled the *Afro-American cultural ethos*.

An important corollary of the triple-quandary framework is the notion of the expanding sphere of socialization influence. During the early years of children's lives in which their initial repertoires of styles are becoming established, the primary source of influence is the home and its immediately surrounding environment. As children's spheres enlarge to include awareness of and exposure to mainstream institutions outside the home, they correspondingly become susceptible to the values and then to the beliefs promulgated by the representatives of these institutions. For most Euro-American children, these values and beliefs are congruent with those espoused by their parents and with the styles they have previously learned. For most Black children, as I have emphasized, there is a discordance, so that they begin to receive mixed socialization messages.

The fact that children learn a set of cultural styles during their formative years does not preclude the possibility that they will be able to acquire additional styles in later years. The issue of stylistic flexibility becomes important to consider at this point. In general, as children mature, they become more flexible in their stylistic expressions, more adept at employing the style that is appropriate in a given situation (Davis, 1971; Simmons, 1979b). The young child, however, is relatively inflexible and unresponsive to situational demands. Until greater stylistic flexibility obtains and there is greater awareness of the adaptive value of stylistic flexibility and switching, it is not unreasonable to believe that Afro-American children resist the imposition of styles that are unfamiliar or contrary to their behavioral grammar. When such children are instructed to act in ways that violate their tacit beliefs and values, it can be expected that many will resist. Although young children may not yet be able to articulate what they value or believe, they surely can discern what feels inappropriate in this regard. The scenario just depicted, I suggest, is highly likely to obtain in the course of the Black child's initial encounter with formal schooling. Unless some kind of stylistic rapprochement is worked out early on, stylistic inflexibility can become entrenched, even if the child does not actively attempt to achieve it, essentially as a protective device or a defensive mechanism (McDermott, 1974). Stylistic inflexibility can also arise if the developing child's proximal and distal socialization experiences render him or her oblivious to alternative stylistic orientations. Such lack of stylistic adaptiveness typifies most middle-class Euro-American children.

EDUCATIONAL IMPLICATIONS OF THE TRIPLE QUANDARY

There are at least four interrelated but separable perspectives from which to view the child's encounter with school. The interaction can be examined in terms of what the child does or does not do, what the child can or cannot do, what the child will or will not do, and what the child should or should not do.

The question of what a child does or does not do essentially refers to academic performance. It is what Black children do not do that defines the problem to which this chapter is centrally addressed. The issue of what the child cannot do is essentially one of competence. In its strong form, this issue addresses limitations in ability or essentially irreversible influences that constrain what a child could be expected to achieve. In its weak form, it bespeaks of what a child cannot presently do but, given appropriate conditions, might be able to do in the future. The question of what a child will do concerns the child's motivational orientation, motives, strengths, and the nature of the events that, for the child, constitute rewards and punishments. What a child will do typically reflects what feels comfortable and familiar or enables the child to reach some desired goal. The question of what a child should or should not do essentially reflects values and beliefs—as they are defined by the child or by those who endeavor to teach the child.

The fact that Black children do not do as well in negotiating the academic ladder as their White peers does not necessarily imply that they cannot do well. Whether the causal factors are attributed to nature or to nurture, there is no convincing evidence to support the hypothesis that Black children cannot do as well as others. It is assumed here that the potential to learn and to perform well is not at issue in attempting to account for Afro-Americans' performance. It is thus necessary to look beyond, to the questions of will and should, that is, to questions of motivation and beliefs and values.

By the time Black children enter school, they already have a well-developed set of Black cultural styles and, in some form, a modicum of the values and beliefs consistent with these styles. Children bring these qualities to the classroom and interpret the meaning of what goes on there from their own frame of reference (Gay, 1978). Black children are likely to find that their characteristic attitudes and ways of behaving do not fit what their teachers expect of them. They therefore find it difficult to put their stylistic repertoires in the service of learning. Typically, they feel stifled, with a consequent decrease of interest and enjoyment in school. The probability is also high that tasks to be performed are construed differently by the teacher and the child. The task the teacher perceives the child as doing could conceivably be quite different from what the child perceives himself or herself as doing.

Findings reported by Guttentag (1972) are highly pertinent to these contentions. In a study of 3- and 4-year-old working-class Black children and working-class and middle-class White children, Guttentag systematically observed the patterns of activity exhibited by these children in a variety of free-play settings. Black children displayed a more varied and more active movement style than either group of their White counterparts. The White children in both groups were more prone to engage in essentially stationary activities, such as sitting, squatting, and lying down. The Black children were more apt to engage in running, kicking, and jumping. About 7% of the activity of the Black children was devoted to dancing, and none in the White children. About 2% of the Black children's activity was unique to the observers, so that they could not be classified by the system the investigator had devised. Consider that these are pre-school children. When they enter school, they almost certainly will be expected to conform to traditional classroom decorum—sitting quietly in their seats, listening or working on assigned tasks. Black children can be expected to have a difficult time suppressing their movement style. Children are also expected to be silent while the teacher or others are talking and to raise their hands and be acknowl-edged by the teacher before they speak. Yet speaking out sponta-neously when one has something to say and speaking along with others are part of both the oral style and the expressive individualism brought to the school setting by Afro-American children.

The problems created by the demands on Black children that they adopt different and uncomfortable stylistic behaviors in the class-room are further compounded when, as typically occurs, children are faced with academic tasks that are both unfamiliar and presented in contexts that are alien to their life experiences. Several commen-tators have argued that, under these circumstances, Black children have a more difficult time applying their preexisting competencies to classroom materials than do mainstream White children already familiar with them (Franklin and Fulani, 1979; Hall, Reder, and Cole, 1979; Simmons, 1979b). Failure to do well can itself discourage inter-est. When the content of the curriculum ignores the child's experien-tial reality, the child's interest and motivation are still further depressed (W. C. Banks, McQuater, and Hubbard, 1979).

These same considerations can be examined from the standpoint of the teacher, who, typically, is steeped in Euro-American values and attitudes and is unaware of the Afro-American cultural ethos. Teachers thus view their pupils through the Euro-American lens. Children who move about rather than sitting quietly or who speak out of turn are perceived as being disruptive and impolite. When children attempt to cooperate on an academic assignment—an expression of communalism, if you will—the teacher may interpret cooperativeness as cheating (Gay and Abrahams, 1973). When chil-dren exhibit behaviors that are highly stylized and that call attention to themselves, the teacher perceives these behaviors not as a mani-festation of expressive individualism to be admired, but as "showing off"—an undesirable behavior that should be discouraged. Still fur-ther, teachers are likely to construe the characteristic behaviors of Black children as representing failures of socialization in their homes and communities—the results of neglect, indifference, or overindulgence. Rather than being regarded as having been socialized differently, Black children are perceived as unsocialized.

Typically, teachers also assume that learning can proceed effectively only in an atmosphere in which children behave "properly," i.e., correspond to the middle-class ideal, and with teaching methods that have proved successful with middle-class children. It follows that if Black children do not come to school with the proper behavioral repertoires, the teachers' first duty is to train them to become good classroom citizens. Unless or until the children become socialized, the teacher is apt to reason, the education of these children cannot effectively proceed. The children, however, are likely to feel inhibited and be puzzled by efforts to remold their behaviors and to become increasingly recalcitrant and alienated. The more difficulty teachers experience in exacting this training, the more concerned they become with the children's classroom deportment at the expense of training in cognitive skills. A vicious circle is likely to be set up, with teacher and students becoming antagonists and more classroom time being devoted to getting unruly students to behave than to teaching.

The ethnocentricity of teachers and other school personnel (which they share with the larger community) frequently leads them to conclude that Black children's failure to be responsive to the procedures used so effectively with White middle-class children and to perform as well academically as the latter is due to their lack of ability. They don't perform well because they can't. Teachers may thus come to expect failure, rather than success, on the part of their students and, disheartened by the expectation, minimize their teaching efforts.

There is considerable evidence to support the contention that the chief concern of schools "serving" Afro-American children is control, discipline, and conformity. For example, Radin and Kamii (1965) matter-of-factly state about Afro-Americans: "This subculture is known to produce children who are extremely difficult to educate" (p. 138). In a survey of the teachers of fifth-graders, Leacock (1969) reports that teachers of White middle-class children tend to emphasize independence and self-reliance, and teachers of Black lower-income children tend to emphasize discipline and obedience. Data obtained by Stein (1971) suggest that these differences begin early; kindergarten teachers of Black children listed socialization goals as being more important than educational goals, whereas teachers of White middle-class children said the reverse.

Illuminating data were also reported by Rollins, McCandless, Thompson, and Brassell (1974). Rules of conduct agreed upon by elementary school teachers of Black children were (1) stay in your seat, (2) work hard, (3) pay attention, (4) raise your hand to speak. The major purpose of the Rollins et al. (1974) study, however, was not to determine teachers' views of proper classroom behavior, but whether such behavior could be promoted in inner-city Black children by the introduction of response-contingent positive incentives (token reinforcers) into the classroom. They advocated, in their words, a setting in which "appropriate behavior is rewarded, inappropriate behavior is ignored and almost no aversive incentives are used" (p. 168). "Appropriate" behavior, it goes without saying, meant conformity to the rules of conduct, specified by teachers, listed above. It also should be obvious that these "appropriate" behaviors have Euro-American cultural overtones or are construed as desirable in the absence of considerations for the (culturally) supportive contexts that might foster them. The results of an experimental program led the investigators to an optimistic conclusion that makes clear the assumption that behavior control is necessary for acceptable school performance: "The results of the study are promising. The authors believe a clear demonstration has been made that most, if not all, inner city teachers can learn to use a positive contingency management procedure to insure behavior control, accelerated academic achievement, and probably as a function of the latter, substantial IQ gain" (p. 177).

Further support for the linkage that school personnel and educational researchers have assumed between control and achievement in Black youths is provided in the work of Kerckhoff and Campbell (1977). These investigators found that, for Black adolescent boys, socioeconomic background was virtually unrelated to academic performance. More importantly, they found that disciplinary problems in junior high were particularly strong predictors of high school performance for these Black youths, but were far less predictive for Whites. Alker and Wohl (1972) have reported that academically successful Black students are apt to perceive that achievement is just as appropriately sought through conformity to prescribed norms as through independent-minded individual strivings. On the other hand, academically successful White suburban youths tend to perceive that independence is more important than conformity.

Despite the optimistic conclusions of Rollins et al. (1974), it seems unlikely that any method aimed at remolding Afro-American children into the image of the ideal White middle-class child will be successful. No one can fault the greater use of positive rewards of all sorts—including teacher praise and encouragement—instead of reliance on negative sanctions. But attempts to modify behavior that is not directly relevant to the acquisition of cognitive skills is misguided, being based on two erroneous premises: first, that the cultural styles exhibited by Black children reflect an absence of socialization, as opposed to positive socialization in behaviors arising from a different (albeit unarticulated) value system than that espoused by Euro-Americans; and second, that middle-class behaviors within the classroom are pedagogically necessary.

The issue of the cognitive skills that Afro-American children bring to the academic setting must also be addressed. It would be a mistake to assume that the academically relevant skills of the average Black child entering school are on a par with those possessed by the average White child. Due to the trifocal character of their socialization experiences, Black children do not come to school as well-versed or as well-practiced in the particular cognitive skills demanded by the school curriculum as are children whose socialization experiences are singular in focus (Boykin, 1978).

This lack of initial parity should not be seen as a deterrent to successful educational attainment. What are schools for? Surely they ought not be designed to penalize those with a modest initial disadvantage in skill. What Black children have not brought with them is no indication of their ability (or inability) to learn. However, for the kinds of reasons already described, all too often what Black children do not initially do is taken as an indication of what they are unable to do, or of how little they can be expected to do until they are properly "socialized." Some form of remediation may be necessary. However, attempts at remediation that ignore cultural and contextual factors supportive of skill attainment are likely to be—and indeed have been found to be—relatively ineffective.

In summary, the clash between the cultures of the Black child and the teacher creates a snowball effect in which misperception, mutual suspicion and antagonism, and conflicting goals compound. Failure breeds failure—and the expectation of failure—on the part of student and teacher alike. These failures lead to debilitating mutual self-protective strategies and defensive reactions (McDermott, 1974; Ogbu, 1978; Silverstein and Krate, 1975). Thus, the slight difference in the initial preparation of Afro-American children in comparison with their White peers evolves into a gap that widens year after year. For too many Black youngsters, it ends in functional illiteracy, in cynicism and hostility, and in increased alienation from school, even as they become increasingly convinced of the value of material affluence and the importance of status as goals in life.

In the process, Black children may react to attempts to disparage their cultural styles by hanging onto them and becoming stylistically inflexible. Rather than developing the adaptive capacity to utilize the appropriate style for the appropriate setting or to utilize a conventionally inappropriate one in an adaptively creative fashion, Afro-

American children may cling tenaciously to their Black cultural styles and seek supportive contexts for their expression, typically outside of school or the academic context. Their unilateral clinging to Black cultural styles is likely to continue into adulthood and, especially combined with inadequate education, contribute to the limiting of vocational opportunities. Those who retain these styles can also be expected to model them for their children, even while paying homage to wider societal beliefs and values.

In the present day and age, it seems unlikely that many teachers and school officials consciously sabotage Black children's academic achievement or actively attempt to keep them in their place within the traditional status hierarchy. Yet the attempt to impose upon these children values and styles that conflict with their Afro-American cultural ethos, according to the analysis offered here, has deleterious personal and educational consequences. Whether wittingly or unwittingly, the schools come to serve as agents of the social-structural status quo. In effect, the *unsuccessful* efforts to mold Afro-American children into good classroom citizens, intended to further their academic attainments, turn out to be highly *successful* in preparing these children to occupy, as adults, low-status positions in society's hierarchy. Perpetuation of the low socioeconomic status of Black Americans cannot be blamed solely on the school system, but some of the responsibility must be attributed to the nature of the schooling to which they are exposed.

STRATEGIES FOR CURRICULAR CHANGE

Presentation of concrete proposals for curricular changes is well beyond the scope of this chapter. Instead, four general strategies will be sketched that follow from the analyses offered on the preceding pages.

Responsiveness to Black Cultural Styles

First and foremost, academic procedures should be modified to be more compatible with Black cultural styles, particularly in the early school grades. Such alterations could take many forms. Movement (particularly rhythmic movement) might be meaningfully incorporated into the learning process. Greater emphasis might be placed on social relatedness and on group, as opposed to individual, responsibility for intellectual tasks. The orality of Black children might be encouraged, rather than suppressed, to heighten interest and active participation in academic tasks. Not all styles are necessarily amenable to all academic tasks, and not all manifestations of a given style

are appropriate to a given context. Thus, both flexibility and inge-
nuity may often be required in designing effective procedures for
teaching Black children.

Sensitivity to Black cultural styles may be particularly important
during the child's critical early years in school. A corollary of this
proposition is that, over time, attempts should be made to introduce,
in appropriate contexts, behavioral patterns associated with the
mainstream American society. There is adaptive significance in preparing Black children to be culturally bistylistic and to learn to discriminate when one mode of expression might be more effective than
the other.

The relevant research, while not plentiful, provides support for
the contention that modifications of educational practices to be more
congruent with Afro-American styles have beneficial outcomes.
Treadwell (1975), for example, found that group academic counseling
had a more positive effect on the academic achievement of Black
college freshmen than did individual counseling—an effect that may
have been mediated by the greater communalistic and interpersonal
orientation of Black students. Similarly, Slavin (1977) found that, in
comparison with controls, seventh-grade Black students' academic
performance was dramatically increased when they worked in cooperative learning teams. Only minimal improvement was obtained
among a comparable sample of White students. Then too, in a review
and critique of the literature (Boykin, 1977b) on the standardized
testing of minority-group children, I noted a number of studies indicating that Black students' test performance can be significantly
enhanced when administration is done in an interpersonally supportive context, in comparison to more interpersonally neutral contexts. This affective facilitation is typically not observed with White
samples. In a field study, Piestrup (1973) observed that the teachers
who were most effective in teaching reading to first-grade working-
class Black children were those who employed what she called a
"Black Artful style." This style is characterized by lively gesticula-
tions and rhythmic, protracted, verbal intonational interplay between
the teacher and the students. These teachers were also more apt to
use Black dialect in their transactions with students and more likely
to encourage its selective use by students. Interestingly enough, Piestrup (1973) found that students who learned to read under this reg-
imen were the least likely to persist in the use of Black dialect in the
reading process when it was not called for. This finding lends credence to the notion that stylistic inflexibility can result when such
styles are dishonored by the teachers.

The work of Rohwer and Harris (1975) is also relevant. They
found that, for fourth-grade working-class Black children, a com-

bined media presentation of oral plus print information enhanced the prose learning of inter- and intrasentence relations. Such combinations were of no benefit to a sample of White children from higher socioeconomic backgrounds. In my own research, I have found that Black third-graders perform markedly better on a set of four different types of tasks when the tasks are presented in a variable sequential format (which accommodates more verve), as opposed to a blocked or relatively nonvariable order (Boykin, 1982; Boykin and DeBritto, 1981). This effect is not as pronounced for White children or for Black middle-class children.

Work of the kind cited above simultaneously demonstrates that adapting teaching methods and task contexts to take advantage of Black cultural styles leads to improvement in the performance of Black students and that the Black–White disparity in performance can be reduced when children are taught in a manner congruent with their cultural styles.

Use of Culturally Relevant Material

The acquisition of academic skills should be facilitated by embedding tasks in a context that is experientially familiar or culturally compatible. Examples of research supporting this suggestion can also be found. In a study of the use of a clustering strategy in free recall (a technique that is both more sophisticated and more effective than rote memorization), Franklin and Fulani (1979) found that Black adolescents and White adolescents were more likely to use clustering when the words to be remembered were pertinent to the social experiences of their own group. C. Jones (1979) reported that marked success in teaching reading to Black children was achieved when the children were allowed to construct their own personal reading texts based on their own everyday experiences. The work of Rychlak (1975) and his associates (Rychlak, Hewitt, and Hewitt, 1973) is also pertinent. Black students and working-class students performed better on material that they liked than on material they disliked, suggesting their responsiveness to their affective assessment of the material to be mastered. The effect was less pronounced for White and middle-class students. These studies suggest the desirability of using both familiar task contexts and materials that are congruent with the child's cultural frame of reference.

Teacher Responsiveness

Realization of the strategies outlined above depend on the capacity of researchers, teachers, and educational planners to understand the nature of the Black psychological experience and its attendant values and styles, so that they may design more effective teaching materials and procedures. In order to implement these programs, teachers and other school personnel must also understand and have respect for a tradition that in most instances is not their own. These goals might appear to be simple to achieve, but in reality are not. Information about Afro-Americans (and other ethnic groups whose values and world views differ from those of Euro-Americans) could be introduced into the curricula of schools of education or in-service teacher-training programs. But changing ingrained attitudes (not only in classroom teachers, but in those who must be persuaded to offer such training programs) is another matter.

Good-hearted intentions, while necessary, are not sufficient. Teachers and others must learn not only to acknowledge the existence of Black cultural reality but also to recognize that this cultural reality has integrity and that the behavioral grammar of Black children is informed by this reality. Ideally, they would learn that the values and cultural styles of Afro-Americans are not to be devalued in relation to the Euro-American ethos. If teachers have no appreciation of Black culture, if they have no respect for it, it would be unrealistic to expect them to alter their teaching methods successfully, let alone their attitudes toward their Black pupils, particularly those from working-class homes. The conviction that one's own values and ways of doing are superior, I have admitted, is not easy to overcome. However, if teachers and other school personnel were made to see the pedagogical effectiveness of molding educational practices to fit the child, perhaps changed attitudes may follow.

Acceptance of Child

The fourth mode of facilitation involves a blending of procedural and attitudinal concerns. It seems imperative to acknowledge that, because of the multifocal nature of their psychological experience, Black children as a group enter school at a lower level of skill development than do their White peers. But it should also be recognized that rate of learning, especially in the early years, has been overemphasized (Ginsburg, 1972). I would argue, as does Nicholls (1979), that teachers of Black children should place increased emphasis on instilling the will to learn in the formal school setting and on inspiring intrinsic interest in academic tasks and task persistence. If children are optimally motivated, they will make academic progress. If children are task-involved and task-persistent, then through sheer practice alone, if nothing else, they will attain educationally. Increased task involvement is likely to follow from infusing teaching practices and learning content with cultural relevance and from having culturally sensitive and supportive teachers.

CONCLUSION

Many of the analyses and remedies offered in this chapter are predicated on the desirability of facilitating the performance of Afro-American children on academic tasks that embody traditional criteria for success. The alternative schooling processes envisioned here would not require different cognitive demands per se, but only different methods for fulfilling them. However, the possibility should not be ruled out that there is an inherent contradiction in this approach or, at least, that it may be of limited utility. Meaningful preservation of Black cultural life styles, or of cultural pluralism in general, may also require and imply different cognitive processes, different ways of knowing, different criteria for success, different intellectual skills, and different competencies from those in the Euro-American tradition. This, of course, remains to be seen. Long-term cognitive consequences that are potentially desirable, however, may naturally evolve out of the kinds of changes in the educational system that have been proposed here.

REFERENCES

Abraham, W. 1962. *The mind of Africa.* Chicago: University of Chicago Press.

Akbar, N. 1976. Rhythmic patterns in African personality. In L. King, V. Dixon, and W. Nobles (eds.), *African philosophy: Assumptions and paradigms for research on Black persons.* Los Angeles: Fanon Center.

Albee, G. 1977. The Protestant ethic, sex, and psychotherapy. *American Psychologist, 32,* 150–161.

Alker, H., and J. Wohl. 1972. Personality and achievement in a suburban and an inner city school. *Journal of Social Issues, 28,* 115–130.

Allen, W. 1978. The search for applicable theories of Black family life. *Journal of Marriage and Family, 40,* 117–129.

Allport, G. 1955. *Becoming.* New Haven: Yale University Press.

Ashbury, C. 1978. Cognitive factors related to discrepant arithmetic achievement of White and Black first graders. *Journal of Negro Education, 47,* 337–342.

Ausubel, D. 1966. The effect of cultural deprivation on learning patterns. In S. Webster (ed.), *The disadvantaged learner.* San Francisco: Chandler.

Ausubel, D., and P. Ausubel. 1963. Ego-development among segregated Negro children. In A. Passow (ed.), *Education in depressed areas.* New York: Teachers College Press.

Banks, J. 1976. Crucial issues in the education of Afro-American children. *Journal of Afro-American Issues, 4,* 392–407.

Banks, W. C. 1976. White preference in Blacks: A paradigm in search of a phenomenon. *Psychological Bulletin, 83,* 1179–1186.

Banks, W. C. 1979. Achievement in Blacks: A case study in cultural diversity in motivation. In E. Gordon (ed.), *Human diversity and pedagogy.* Washington, DC: National Institute of Education.

Banks, W. C., G. McQuater, and J. Hubbard. 1979. Toward a reconceptualization of the social-cognitive bases of achievement orientations in Blacks. In A. W. Boykin, A. J. Franklin, and J. F. Yates (eds.), *Research directions of Black psychologists.* New York: Russell Sage.

Baratz, S., and J. Baratz. 1970. Early childhood intervention: The social science base of institutional racism. *Harvard Educational Review, 40,* 29–50.

Battle, E., and J. Rotter. 1963. Children's feelings of personal control as related to social class and ethnic group. *Journal of Personality, 31,* 482–490.

Bell, D. 1976. *The cultural contradictions of capitalism.* New York: Basic Books.

Bereiter, C., and S. Engelmann. 1966. *Teaching disadvantaged children in the preschool.* Englewood Cliffs, NJ: Prentice-Hall.

Billingsley, A. 1968. *Black families in White America.* Englewood Cliffs, NJ: Prentice-Hall.

Billingsley, A. 1969. Family functioning in the low-income Black community. *Social Casework, 50,* 563–572.

Blackwell, J. 1975. *The Black community: Diversity and unity.* New York: Dodd Mead.

Bowles, S., and H. Gintis. 1973. I.Q. in the U.S. class structure. *Social Policy, 3,* 65–96.

Bowles, S., and H. Gintis. 1976. *Schooling in capitalist America.* New York: Basic Books.

Boykin, A. W. 1977a. Experimental psychology from a Black perspective: Issues and examples. *Journal of Black Psychology, 3,* 29–49.

Boykin, A. W. 1977b. On the role of the context in the standardized test performance of minority group children. *Cornell Journal of Social Relations, 12,* 109–124.

Boykin, A. W. 1978. Psychological/behavioral verve in academic/task performance: Pretheoretical considerations. *Journal of Negro Education, 47,* 343–354.

Boykin, A. W. 1979. Black psychology and the research process: Keeping the baby but throwing out the bath water. In A. W. Boykin, A. J. Franklin, and J. F. Yates (eds.), *Research directions of Black psychologists.* New York: Russell Sage.

Boykin, A. W. 1982. Task variability and the performance of Black and White schoolchildren: Vervistic explorations. *Journal of Black Studies, 12,* 469–485.

Boykin, A. W., and A. DeBritto. 1981. Ethnicity and class as separate factors in the "variability effect." Unpublished manuscript, Howard University.

Bradley, L., and G. Bradley. 1977. The academic achievement of Black students in desegregated schools: A critical review. *Review of Educational Research, 47,* 399–449.

Brown, I. 1978. Psychology of the Black experience: A cultural integrity viewpoint. Unpublished manuscript, Stanford University.

Buck, M., and H. Austrin. 1971. Factors related to school achievement in an economically disadvantaged group. *Child Development, 42,* 1813–1826.

Caplan, N., and S. Nelson. 1973. On being useful: The nature and consequences of psychological research on social problems. *American Psychologist, 28,* 199–211.

Carnoy, M. 1974. *Education as cultural imperialism.* New York: McKay.

(Clark) X. C., D. McGee, W. Nobles, and N. Akbar. 1975. Voodoo or I.Q.: An introduction to African psychology. *Journal of Black Psychology, 1,* 1–15.

Cole, J. 1970. Culture: Negro, Black and Nigger. *Black Scholar, 1,* 40–43.

Coleman, J. S., E. Q. Campbell, C. J. Hobson, J. McPartland, A. M. Mood, F. D. Weinfeld, and R. L. York. 1966. *Equality of educational opportunity.* Washington, DC: U.S. Government Printing Office.

Comer, J. 1974. Black children in a racist society. *Current, 162,* 53–56.

Davis, A. 1971. Cognitive style: Methodological and developmental considerations. *Child Development, 42,* 1447–1459.

Davidson, H., and J. Greenberg. 1967. *School achievers from a deprived background.* New York: Associated Educational Services.

Deci, E. 1975. *Intrinsic motivation.* New York: Plenum.

Debord, L., L. Griffin, and M. Clark. 1977. Race and sex influences in the schooling process of rural and small town youth. *Sociology of Education, 50,* 85–102.

Deutsch, M. 1963. The disadvantaged child and the learning process: Some social psychological and developmental considerations. In A. Passow (ed.), *Education in depressed areas.* New York: Teachers College Press.

Deutsch, M. 1965. The role of social class in language development and cognition. *American Journal of Orthopsychiatry, 35,* 78–88.

Dixon, V. 1976. World views and research methodology. In L. King, V. Dixon, and W. Nobles (eds.), *African philosophy: Assumptions and paradigms for research on Black persons.* Los Angeles: Fanon Center.

Du Bois, C. 1972. The dominant value profile of American culture. In R. Shinn (ed.), *Culture and school.* San Francisco: Intext.

Elison, R. 1973. An American dilemma: A review. In J. Ladner (ed.), *The death of White sociology.* New York: Random House.

Epps, E. 1980. The impact of school desegregation on aspirations, self-concepts and other aspects of personality. In R. Jones (ed.), *Black psychology,* 2nd ed. New York: Harper and Row.

Flemming, E., and R. Anttonen. 1971. Teacher expectancy as related to the academic and personal growth of primary age children. *Monographs of the Society for Research in Child Development, 36* (Serial No. 145).

Foster, B. 1971. Toward a definition of Black referents. In V. Dixon and B. Foster (eds.), *Beyond Black or White: An alternate America.* Boston: Little, Brown.

Franklin, A. J., and L. Fulani. 1979. Cultural content of materials and ethnic group performance in categorized recall. In A. W. Boykin, A. J. Franklin, and J. F. Yates (eds.), *Research directions of Black psychologists.* New York: Russell Sage.

Furby, L. 1979. Individualistic bias in studies of locus of control. In A. Buss (ed.), *Psychology in social context.* New York: Irvington.

Gay, G. 1975. Cultural differences important in education of Black children. *Momentum, 2,* 30–33.

Gay, G. 1978. Viewing the pluralistic classroom as a cultural microcosm. *Educational Research Quarterly, 2,* 45–59.

Gay, G., and R. Abrahams. 1972. Black culture in the classroom. In R. Abrahams and R. Troike (eds.), *Language and cultural diversity in American education.* Englewood Cliffs, NJ: Prentice-Hall.

Gay, G., and R. Abrahams. 1973. Does the pot melt, boil, or brew? Black children and White assessment procedures. *Journal of School Psychology, 11,* 330–340.

Gergen, K. 1978. Toward generative theory. *Journal of Personality and Social Psychology, 36,* 1344–1360.

Ginsburg, H. 1972. *The myth of the deprived child.* Englewood Cliffs, NJ: Prentice-Hall.

Green, H. 1972. Temporal attitudes in four Negro subcultures. In J. Fraser, F. Haber, and G. Muller (eds.), *The study of time.* New York: Springer-Verlag.

Gutman, H. 1976. *The Black family in slavery and freedom, 1750–1925.* New York: Pantheon.

Guttentag, M. 1972. Negro–White differences in children's movement. *Perceptual and Motor Skills, 35,* 435–436.

Hale, J. 1980. Demythicizing the education of Black children. In R. Jones (ed.), *Black psychology,* 2nd ed. New York: Harper and Row.

Hall, W., S. Reder, and M. Cole. 1979. Story recall in young Black and White children: Effects of racial group membership, race of experimenter, and dialect. In A. W. Boykin, A. J. Franklin, and J. F. Yates (eds.), *Research directions of Black psychologists.* New York: Russell Sage.

Hare, B. 1979. School desegregation variations in self-perception and achievement: An analysis of three national samples by race, socioeconomic background, sex, and region. Paper presented at meeting of American Educational Research Association, San Francisco.

Hare, B. 1980. Self-perception and academic achievement variations in a desegregated setting. *American Journal of Psychiatry, 137,* 683–689.

Herskovitz, M. 1958. *The myth of the Negro past.* Boston: Beacon.

Hess, R. 1970. The transmission of cognitive strategies in poor families: The socialization of apathy and underachievement. In V. Allen (ed.), *Psychological factors in poverty.* Chicago: Markham.

Hill, R. 1972. *The strengths of Black families.* New York: Emerson Hall.

Hilliard, A. 1974. The intellectual strengths of Black children and adolescents: A challenge to pseudoscience. *Journal of Non-White Concerns, 2,* 178–190.

Hunt, J. McV. 1968. The psychological basis for preschool cultural enrichment programs. In M. Deutsch, A. Jensen, and I. Katz (eds.), *Social class, race and psychological development.* New York: Holt, Rinehart and Winston.

Inkeles, A. 1966. Social structure and the socialization of competence. *Harvard Educational Review,* Reprint Series, *36,* 265–283.

Israel, J. 1979. From level of aspiration to dissonance. In A. Buss (ed.), *Psychology in social context.* New York: Irvington.

Jackson, G. 1976. The African genesis of the Black perspective in helping. *Professional Psychology, 7,* 292–308.

Jahn, J. 1961. *Muntu: An outline of the new African culture.* New York: Grove.

Jencks, C., M. S. Smith, H. Acland, M. J. Bane, D. K. Cohen, H. Gintis, B. Heyns, and S. Michelson, 1972. *Inequality: A re-assessment of the effect of family and schooling in America.* New York: Basic Books.

Jones, C. 1979. Ebonics and reading. *Journal of Black Studies, 9,* 423–448.

Jones, J. 1979. Conceptual and strategic issues in the relationship of Black psychology to American social science. In A. W. Boykin, A. J. Franklin, and J. F. Yates (eds.), *Research directions of Black psychologists.* New York: Russell Sage.

Kamii, C., and N. Radin. 1967. Class differences in the socialization practices of Negro mothers. *Journal of Marriage and the Family, 29,* 302–310.

Katz, I. 1973. Alternatives to a personality deficit interpretation of Negro underachievement. In P. Watson (ed.), *Psychology and race.* Chicago: Aldine.

Kerckhoff, A., and R. Campbell. 1977. Black–White differences in the educational attainment process. *Sociology of Education, 50,* 15–27.

King, J. 1976. African survivals in the Black American family: Key factors in stability. *Journal of Afro-American Issues, 4,* 153–167.

Kluckhohn, F., and F. Strodtbeck. 1961. *Variations in value orientations.* Evanston, IL: Row, Peterson.

Labov, W. 1970. The logic of nonstandard English. In F. Williams (ed.), *Language and poverty.* Chicago: Markham.

Labov, W. 1972. *Language in the inner-city.* Philadelphia: University of Pennsylvania Press.

Leacock, E. 1969. *Teaching and learning in city schools: A comparative study.* New York: Basic Books.

Levine, L. 1977. *Black culture and Black consciousness.* New York: Oxford University Press.

Lewis, H. 1970. Child rearing practices among low income families in the District of Columbia. In M. Goldschmid (ed.), *Black Americans and White racism.* New York: Holt, Rinehart and Winston.

Lightfoot, S. 1976. Socialization and education of young Black girls in school. *Teachers College Record, 78,* 239–262.

Loehlin, J. C., G. Lindzey, and J. N. Spuhler. 1975. *Race differences in intelligence.* San Francisco: W. H. Freeman and Company.

McClelland, D. C. 1961. *The achieving society.* New York: Van Nostrand.

McClelland, D. C., J. W. Atkinson, R. A. Clark, and E. L. Lowell. 1953. *The achievement motive.* New York: Appleton-Century-Crofts.

McDermott, R. 1974. Achieving school failure: An anthropological approach to illiteracy and social stratification. In G. Spindler (ed.), *Education and cultural process.* New York: Holt, Rinehart and Winston.

Mackler, B. 1970. Blacks who are academically successful. *Urban Education, 7,* 210–237.

Marans, A., and R. Lourie. 1967. Hypotheses regarding the effects of child-rearing patterns on the disadvantaged child. In J. Hellmuth (ed.), *Disadvantaged child.* Vol. 1. New York: Brunner/Mazel.

Maslow, A. 1954. *Motivation and personality.* New York: Harper.

Massey, G., M. Scott, and C. Dornbusch. 1975. Racism without racists: Institutional racism in urban schools. *Black Scholar, 7,* 10–19.

Maurier, H. 1979. Do we have an African philosophy? In R. Wright (ed.), *African philosophy: An introduction,* 2nd ed. Washington, DC: University Press of America.

Mbiti, J. S. 1970. *African religions and philosophy.* Garden City, NY: Anchor Books.

Miller, L. 1973. Strengths of the Black child. *The Instructor, 82,* 20–21.

Minuchin, P. 1971. Correlates of curiosity and exploratory behavior in preschool disadvantaged children. *Child Development, 42,* 939–950.

Moos, R., and B. Moos. 1976. A typology of family social environments. *Family Process, 15,* 357–371.

Morgan, H. 1980. How schools fail Black children. *Social Policy, 11,* 49–54.

Moynihan, D. 1965. *The Negro family.* Washington, DC: Office of Policy Planning and Research, U.S. Department of Labor.

Murray, H. A. 1938. *Explorations in personality.* New York: Oxford University Press.

Nicholls, J. 1979. Quality and equality in intellectual development: The role of motivation in education. *American Psychologist, 34,* 1071–1084.

Nobles, W. 1976. *A formulative and empirical study of Black families.* Final Report, #90–C–255, Office of Child Development, Department of Health, Education and Welfare.

Nobles, W. 1980. African philosophy: Foundations for Black psychology. In R. Jones (ed.), *Black psychology*, 2nd ed. New York: Harper and Row.

Norton, J. 1971. School dropouts. In V. Ficker and H. Graves (eds.), *Social science and urban crisis.* New York: Macmillan.

Nyang, S. 1980. Reflections on traditional African cosmology. *New Directions: The Howard University Magazine, 7,* 28–32.

Ogbu, J. 1977. Racial stratification and education: The case of Stockton, Calif. *IRCD Bulletin, 12,* 1–27.

Ogbu, J. 1978. *Minority education and caste: The American system in cross-cultural perspective.* New York: Academic.

Oguah, B. 1979. African and western philosophy: A comparative study. In R. Wright (ed.), *African philosophy: An introduction*, 2nd ed. Washington, DC: University Press of America.

Pavendstedt, E. (ed.). 1967. *The drifters: Children of disorganized lower class families.* Boston: Little, Brown.

Pennington, D. 1976. The temporal element in the perceived lack of aspiration in Black youth. *Journal of Afro-American Issues, 4,* 215–234.

Persell, C. 1977. *Education and inequality: A theoretical and empirical synthesis.* New York: Free Press.

Phillips, B. 1972. School-related aspirations of children with different sociocultural backgrounds. *Journal of Negro Education, 41,* 48–52.

Picou, J. 1973. Black–White variations in a model of the occupational aspirational process. *Journal of Negro Education, 42,* 117–122.

Piestrup, A. 1973. Black dialect interference and accommodation of reading instruction in first grade. Monograph No. 4, Language Behavior Research Laboratory, University of California, Berkeley.

Pouissant, A., and C. Atkinson. 1970. Negro youth and psychological motivation. In A. C. Orstein (ed.), *Educating the disadvantaged.* New York: AMS Press.

Proshansky, H., and P. Newton. 1973. Color: The nature and meaning of Negro self-identity. In P. Watson (ed.), *Psychology and race.* Chicago: Aldine.

Radin, N., and C. Kamii. 1965. The child-rearing attitudes of disadvantaged Negro mothers and some educational implications. *Journal of Negro Education, 34,* 138–146.

Rainwater, L. 1966. Crucible of identity: The Negro lower-class family. *Daedalus, 95,* 172–217.

Riley, R., and F. Denmark. 1974. Field independence and measures of intelligence: Some reconsiderations. *Social Behavior and Personality, 2,* 25–29.

Rodman, H., and P. Voydonoff. 1978. Social class and parents' range of aspirations for their children. *Social Problems, 25,* 333–344.

Rohwer, W., and W. Harris. 1975. Media effects on prose learning in two populations of children. *Journal of Educational Psychology, 67,* 651–657.

Rollins, H., B. McCandless, M. Thompson, and W. Brassell. 1974. Project success environment: An extended application of contingency management in inner-city schools. *Journal of Educational Psychology, 66,* 167–178.

Rosenthal, R., and L. Jacobson. 1968. *Pygmalion in the classroom: Teacher expectation and pupils' intellectual performance.* New York: Holt, Rinehart and Winston.

Rossides, D. 1978. *The history and nature of sociological theory.* Boston: Houghton Mifflin.

Rotter, J. B. 1966. Generalized expectancies for internal versus external control of reinforcement. *Psychological Monographs, 80,* 1–28.

Rubovits, P., and M. Maehr. 1973. Pygmalion Black and White. *Journal of Personality and Social Psychology, 25,* 210–218.

Ryan, W. 1971. *Blaming the victim.* New York: Vintage Books.

Rychlak, J. 1975. Affective assessment, intelligence, social class, and racial learning style. *Journal of Personality and Social Psychology, 32,* 989–995.

Rychlak, J., C. Hewitt, and J. Hewitt. 1973. Affective evaluation, word quality and the verbal learning styles of Black versus White junior college females. *Journal of Personality and Social Psychology, 27,* 248–255.

Sampson, E. 1977. Psychology and the American ideal. *Journal of Personality and Social Psychology, 35,* 767–782.

Sampson, E. 1978. Scientific paradigms and social values: Wanted—a scientific revolution. *Journal of Personality and Social Psychology, 36,* 1332–1343.

Schultz, D. 1969. *Coming up Black: Patterns of ghetto socialization.* Englewood Cliffs, NJ: Prentice-Hall.

Scott, R. 1973. Home start: Family centered preschool enrichment for Black and White children. *Psychology in the Schools, 10,* 140–146.

Seegmiller, B., and W. King. 1975. Relations between characteristics of infants, their mother's behaviors and performance on the Bayley Mental and Motor Scales. *Journal of Psychology, 90,* 99–111.

Seligman, M. E. P. 1975. *Helplessness: On depression, development, and death.* San Francisco: W. H. Freeman and Company.

Seltzer, R. 1973. The disadvantaged child and cognitive development in the early years. *Merrill–Palmer Quarterly, 19,* 241–252.

Senghor, L. 1962. What is Negritude? *Negro Digest, 7,* 3–6.

Shade, B. 1978. Social-psychological characteristics of achieving Black children. *Negro Educational Review, 29,* 80–86.

Shade, B. 1981. Afro-American cognitive style: A variable in school success? Unpublished manuscript, University of Wisconsin.

Silverstein, B., and R. Krate. 1975. *Children of the dark ghetto.* New York: Praeger.

Simmons, W. 1979a. The relationship between academic status and future expectations among low-income Blacks. *Journal of Black Psychology, 6,* 7–16.

Simmons, W. 1979b. The role of cultural salience in ethnic and social class differences in cognitive performance. In W. Cross and A. Harrison (eds.), *The fourth conference on empirical research in Black psychology.* Washington, DC: National Institute of Mental Health.

Slavin, R. 1977. Student team learning techniques: Narrowing the achievement gap. Report of Center for Racial Organization of Schools, Johns Hopkins University.

Smith, R. 1979. Race/class differences in the susceptibility to helplessness. In W. Cross and A. Harrison (eds.), *The fourth conference on empirical research in Black psychology.* Washington, DC: National Institute of Mental Health.

Smitherman, G. 1977. *Talkin' and testifyin': The language of Black America.* Boston: Houghton Mifflin.

Staples, R. 1976. *Introduction to Black sociology.* New York: McGraw-Hill.

Stein, A. 1971. Strategies for failure. *Harvard Educational Review, 41,* 158–204.

Stephan, W. 1978. School desegregation: An evaluation of predictions made in *Brown* vs. *Board of Education. Psychological Bulletin, 85,* 217–238.

Stewart, W. 1970. Toward a history of American Negro dialect. In F. Williams (ed.), *Language and poverty.* Chicago: Markham.

Strickland, S. 1973. Can slum children learn? In C. Senna (ed.), *The fallacy of I.Q.* New York: Third World Press.

Thompson, R. 1966. Dance and culture: An aesthetic of the cool. *African Forum, 2,* 85–102.

Treadwell, V. 1975. Group and individual counseling: Effects on college grades. *Journal of Non-White Concerns, 5,* 73–82.

Trotman, F. 1977. Race, I.Q., and the middle class. *Journal of Educational Psychology, 69,* 266–273.

Tucker, M., J. Jackson, and R. Jennings. 1979. Occupational expectations and dropout propensity in urban Black high school students. In A. W. Boykin, A. J. Franklin, and J. F. Yates (eds.), *Research directions of Black psychologists.* New York: Russell Sage.

Weber, M. 1958. *The Protestant ethic and the spirit of capitalism.* New York: Scribner.

Weiner, B. 1979. A theory of motivation for some classroom experiences. *Journal of Educational Psychology, 71,* 3–25.

White, J. 1980. Toward a Black psychology. In R. Jones (ed.), *Black psychology,* 2nd ed. New York: Harper and Row.

White, J., W. Parham, and T. Parham. 1980. Black psychology: The Afro-American tradition as a unifying force for traditional psychology. In R. Jones (ed.), Black Psychology, 2nd ed. New York: Harper and Row.

White, R. 1959. Motivation reconsidered: The concept of competence. Psychological Review, 66, 297–333.

Whiteman, M., and M. Deutsch. 1968. Social disadvantage as related to intellective and language development. In M. Deutsch, A. Jensen, and I. Katz (eds.), Social class, race, and psychological development. New York: Holt, Rinehart and Winston.

Williams, R. 1974. Cognitive and survival learning of the Black Child. In J. Chunn (ed.), The survival of Black children and youth. Washington, DC: Nuclassics and Science.

Wilson, T. 1972. Notes toward a process of Afro-American education. Harvard Educational Review, 42, 374–389.

Wiredu, K. 1980. Philosophy and an African culture. Cambridge, England: Cambridge University Press.

Witkin, H. A., R. B. Dyk, H. F. Faterson, D. R. Goodenough, and S. A. Karp. 1962. Psychological differentiation. New York: Wiley.

Wober, M. 1975. Psychology in Africa. London: International African Institute.

Young, V. 1970. Family and childhood in a southern Negro community. American Anthropologist, 72, 269–288.

Young, V. 1974. A Black American socialization pattern. American Ethnologist, 1, 405–413.

Zigler, E., W. Abelson, and V. Seitz. 1973. Motivational factors in the performance of economically disadvantaged children on the Peabody Picture Vocabulary Test. Child Development, 44, 294–303.

Index